The Mighty Eighth at War

The Mighty Eighth at War

USAAF Eighth Air Force Bombers versus the Luftwaffe 1943–1945

Martin W. Bowman

Pen & Sword
AVIATION

First published in 2010 and reprinted in this format in 2014 by
PEN & SWORD AVIATION
An imprint of
Pen & Sword Books Ltd
47 Church Street
Barnsley, South Yorkshire
S70 2AS

ISBN 978 1 47382 277 1

A CIP catalogue record for this book is
available from the British Library

Typeset in 10/12pt Palatino by
Concept, Huddersfield

Printed and bound in England
By CPI Group (UK) Ltd, Croydon, CR0 4YY

Pen & Sword Books Ltd incorporates the Imprints of Aviation, Atlas,
Family History, Fiction, Maritime, Military, Discovery, Politics, History,
Archaeology, Select, Wharncliffe Local History, Wharncliffe True Crime,
Military Classics, Wharncliffe Transport, Leo Cooper, The Praetorian Press,
Remember When, Seaforth Publishing and Frontline Publishing

For a complete list of Pen & Sword titles please contact
PEN & SWORD BOOKS LIMITED
47 Church Street, Barnsley, South Yorkshire, S70 2AS, England
E-mail: enquiries@pen-and-sword.co.uk
Website: www.pen-and-sword.co.uk

Contents

PROLOGUE

The Forts Fly High

by Bruce Sanders

In the summer of 1941 the Berlin correspondent of the Italian newspaper *La Stampa* began giving his readers pep stories. One of them was to the effect that a Nazi fighter pilot had alone brought down no less than nine Flying Fortresses out of a squadron of twelve in one single engagement. Actually, for the day he mentioned the Air Ministry stated the weather was so bad that not a single British bomber was operating.

But that is by the way.

A year later the absurdity of the claim was manifest to the whole world. For in the summer of 1942 the American Army Air Corps, based in Britain, began active co-operation with the RAF in attacking the strongpoints of the European mainland. The Flying Fortresses of the Americans flew high, by daylight, and their crews indulged in high-altitude precision bombing. Armed with .5-inch machine guns, they were able to trounce soundly any fighter opposition that came up to deny them right of way. In proportion to the numbers of aircraft employed and in view of the fact that the Fortresses were flying on offensive operations, it was the fighter defence that was defeated.

At first, the Forts flew with fighter protection, as when they roared over Rouen on the afternoon of 17 August and bombed the marshalling-yards, with their commander-in-chief, Brigadier-General Ira C Eaker, leading in an aircraft named *Yankee Doodle*.

It was a highly successful debut. Air Marshal Sir Arthur Harris, on behalf of Bomber Command, sent General Eaker the following message of congratulation:

> Congratulations from all ranks of Bomber Command on the highly successful completion of the first all-American raid by the big fellows on German-occupied territory in Europe. Yankee Doodle certainly went to town and can stick yet another well-deserved feather in his cap.

Bomber Command was no longer alone on the offensive. The four-engined bombers of the American Air Force had joined in the invasion of German-held skies. The Americans systematically went to work, testing out their aircraft and teaching their bomber crews the art of modern war. For two months the Forts flew into Europe and strafed military targets in the hinterland. At the end of that time the Office of War Information in Washington issued a considered statement to the American public on the performance of the Fortresses and other American warplanes. It was a frank statement and it held many criticisms of some existing types of United States aircraft. But of the heavy Boeing B-17s it had this to say:

> The actual employment of the B-17 (the Flying Fortress) over Europe has exceeded even the fondest expectations of its American proponents. It has shown the B-17 capable of high-altitude day bombing of such precision that it astounded Allied observers. The public is already familiar with some of the B-17's feats, such as the recent flight over occupied Europe wherein gunners in a flight of B-17s engaged forty German fighters. Ten Focke-Wulfs were knocked down and eight more claimed as probables. All the B-17s returned to their British bases, although one had been hit by six cannon-shells and over two hundred machine-gun bullets. In the October 10th raid over France – the largest and most damaging raid ever staged over Europe – 115 Flying Fortresses and Liberators, B-24s, accompanied by Allied fighters, proved their ability to fight their way through to the target and back again against large and fierce opposition by the Nazi's newest and best Messerschmitts and Focke-Wulfs. We lost only four of our bombers, while over a hundred enemy planes were destroyed or damaged.

Possibly the Berlin correspondent of *La Stampa* rubbed his eyes when he read the announcement.

Two months later, in December, the Fortresses were probing deeper into Europe under the daylight skies of winter. The crews had learned much. The pilots of the Messerschmitts and Focke-Wulfs were still learning. On the afternoon of Sunday the 20th the Forts flew to Romilly-sur-Seine and attacked the German air depot there. They roared high over Paris, with Focke-Wulfs streaming after them and circling on their flanks, seeking for an opening through which to dart with cannon spurting. But again the Nazi fighter pilots came off second best. The American bombers kept close ranks and the Focke-Wulfs were given little chance to demonstrate their killer propensities.

One of the Forts flying on that occasion was captained by Captain Allen Martini. His aircraft was already famous in its squadron as *Dry Martini* and his crew were known as the 'Cocktail Kids'. They had been together as a combat crew for several months when they went on the 'pranging' job to Romilly, and sitting hunched up over his cannon in the Fort's tail was a bright-eyed Filipino, Staff Sergeant Henry Mitchell. Mitchell was a man with a long score to settle with the Axis. His father was a major on the staff of General MacArthur during the Pacific battles but it was believed that his wife and child were prisoners in the hands of the Japanese. Henry himself was on a merchantman when the 'Wild Eagles' of Tokyo descended on Pearl Harbor. He enlisted for service in the American Army Air Force as soon as he got ashore.

That afternoon he showed the race-prejudiced Aryans of the Luftwaffe that the colour of a man's skin has little to do with his ability to shoot straight. His straight shooting was largely responsible for the safe return of the *Dry Martini.*

The Cocktail Kids and their Fortress comrades played the old year out to the tuneful rattle of their .5-inch guns. On 30 December the Forts flew high over Lorient and gave the submarine pens a heavy strafing. On that occasion the Flying Fortress *Boom Town* got badly shot up but returned to Britain's friendly shores covered in glory.

Boom Town winged over the pens on schedule and the bombardier let go the bomb load. Over the intercom the crew heard him shout excitedly, 'Bull's eye!' While the words were still in their ears flak tore into the Fort's hull and German fighters swooped down to attack.

The bombardier died at his post. The navigator, Lieutenant W M Smith, of Ashland, Wisconsin, was wounded in the arm. A shell splinter passed out through his flight jacket, knocking him off his seat. As he lay prone, stunned for the moment, bullets from the fighters tore through the space where he had been sitting a moment before. Then an exploding shell ripped the base out of the ball-turret. Sergeant Green, the ball-turret gunner, had his oxygen mask destroyed and his cases of spare ammunition were jammed so tightly against his side that he thought his leg had been torn off. Blinded by spurting oil and cordite fumes, he stayed there, perched over space, covering his target area with his gun. In the tail-turret Sergeant Krucher, of Long Island, was badly hit, but he remained sighting his gun as a Focke-Wulf swooped to finish off the mauled Fortress. Krucher waited until the Fw 190 was closing up in his sights and then gave it a long burst. His bullets ripped off half of one of the German's wings and the fighter went spiralling down. Staff Sergeant Stroud, of Kansas, manning the right waist gun, covered another Fw 190 that attacked from the front. Stroud coolly waited until he could see the German pilot's helmeted head in the Focke-Wulf's glasshouse.

'He came in at twelve o'clock,' Stroud said afterwards, explaining the angle at which he saw the German in his gun-sight. 'As he banked and started in on our tail I let him have it. It looked as if part of the fuselage came off and he fell off toward the sea.'

Boom Town's pilot, Captain Clyde D Walker, of Tulsa, Oklahoma, headed out to sea as the enemy fighters came on in pairs, attacking furiously. The first blast of fire had broken the driving shaft of one engine and another had been hit on the top cylinder, so that it had only emergency power left to struggle with as the pilot opened the throttle.

'The prop would run away when I advanced it a bit,' was how Walker explained the predicament in which he found himself. Oil pressure was dropping and a shell splinter had made a large dent in a blade of a third engine. There was also a gaping hole in the nose of the aircraft and the bomb-doors had been badly shot up. The de-icing system had been punctured, the radio equipment badly damaged, and the control cable knocked off the elevator. 'They missed the pilot and co-pilot,' Walker explained. 'That's all. And the co-pilot had a piece of flak in his parachute.'

But he did not give the order to bale out. If he could get *Boom Town* back across the Channel he was going to, despite wintry weather conditions and the worst the Nazi airmen could do.

Walker pushed his aircraft into a cloud bank and cleverly manoeuvred to evade another onslaught from the whirling Focke-Wulfs. Another Fort came close, to cover the staggering aircraft, but when Walker came out of the cloud formation he was alone and *Boom Town* was dropping at the rate of 2,000 feet a minute.

The crew were at their posts, facing looming disaster, ready to fight off any further attack that might mature, for they knew the Focke-Wulfs' liking for lame ducks. All, that is, except the bombardier and Sergeant Krucher, who had been relieved by Stroud.

'I had to get rough with Krucher,' Walker afterwards reported, 'to make him lie down. Stroud cut open his electric suit to give him first aid and when he put on the iodine Krucher didn't even let out a whimper.'

Just afterwards they sighted land.

'We were all looking for England,' Walker admitted. 'We were looking for land so hard that when we saw some a little off to the right we started in. We thought it was England and started looking at the roads to see which side the cars were running on. We saw one bicycle. Green called on the intercom, "That don't look like England to me!" Then all of a sudden we saw the sub pens we'd bombed before and we knew it was Brest.'

The Fort was now down to some 600 feet and still losing height. The Americans were over the harbour before the merchant ships there could get up their balloon barrage. Walker headed out to sea again, keeping the aircraft in the sky with great difficulty. The airscrew of his number two engine was still running away with itself and threatening to wreck the aircraft. The sea suddenly flashed up to engulf them. Desperately Walker hauled on the controls. The Fort bounced like a ball on the waves, rising 100 feet in the air. He gave the order to prepare for a crash-landing on the sea and the crew began throwing overboard everything they could spare. Ammunition, oxygen bottles, masks, parachutes and any loose equipment. As the last drums of ammunition went out through the hatch a couple of German fighters were sighted overhead.

Those Focke-Wulf pilots were themselves out of ammunition or they had taken enough punishment from the Flying Forts for one day: they did not attack. The lame duck bounced on out of their reach and finally clambered up into the English sky, to make a safe landing and await the prospect of another lucky New Year.

In the last half of 1942 the Forts went twenty-five times to bomb German-held Europe.

They started the New Year in fine fettle and within a few days the *Dry Martini* was in the news again. The 'Cocktail Kids' took their bomber to Lille, with Major T H Taylor at the controls in place of the regular pilot, who was ill. The bombardier got his bombs away over the target, which was the Fives-Lille steel and locomotive works, but as the bomber continued on over the target an avenging Focke-Wulf came racing in to attack, weaving from side to side like a pugilist, all guns blazing. One of its cannon shells tore through the cockpit and burst beside Major Taylor, killing him instantly.

The controls ran slack, the *Dry Martini*'s nose dipped and the aircraft began a sickening dive earthwards.

The co-pilot, wounded and dazed, lay beside Taylor. It looked as though nothing could save the high-spirited Cocktail Kids from total destruction. The commander of the flight, Brigadier-General H S Hansell, watching the episode from his station in the leading Fort, thought the *Dry Martini* was done for.

But B-17s were built to take punishment as well as administer it. The *Dry Martini*'s engines were still functioning and the crew continued blazing back at the German fighters following it down in its apparent death dive.

The co-pilot, Second Lieutenant J B Boyle, who came from Teaneck, in New Jersey, suddenly came to and in a split second realized the desperate nature of the aircraft's plight. He hauled Taylor's body from in front of the controls and took the dead man's place. The *Dry Martini* flattened out and began climbing again to regain the formation of Fortresses. The Fw 190s that had followed the American bomber down sheered off. The *Dry Martini* was in a sorry state, but under Boyle's careful handling got back to base.

General Hansell had some words of praise to offer.

'I was profoundly impressed', he said, 'with Lieutenant Boyle's skill and courage in flying a B-17 in good defensive formation at high altitude when he had been painfully wounded around the face and shot through the leg. Flying a B-17 in formation requires a great deal of physical effort at any time. I am still amazed that Lieutenant Boyle, despite the difficult conditions, could exert enough stamina to land his plane safely at its base. He and his crew deserve the highest credit.'

Not long afterwards the Forts took off for their first assault on the German mainland. This attack was an outstanding success and marked the beginning of a new onslaught on the Reich's war potential. The episode brought words of congratulation once more from Sir Arthur Harris, who sent the following warm message to Brigadier-General Newton Longfellow, Commanding General of the Eighth Bomber Command of the United States Army Air Corps:

> Greetings and congratulations from Bomber Command to all who took part to-day in the first US raid on Germany. This well-planned and gallantly executed operation opens a campaign the Germans have long dreaded. To them it is yet another ominous sentence in the writing on the wall, the full import of which they cannot fail to grasp. To Bomber Command it is concrete and most welcome proof that we shall no longer be alone in carrying the war to German soil. Let us press past this milestone on the road to victory, assured that between us we can and will bust Germany wide open

That was on 27 January. The next day General Longfellow replied. In his message to Sir Arthur Harris he said:

> The entire personnel of the Eighth Bomber Command join me in an expression of thanks for your cordial message of greeting and congratulation upon the occasion of the first US raid on Germany. Our effort would have been impossible without the splendid co-operation and help, which has constantly been extended to us by the RAF since our arrival in this theater. Our first raid was only the beginning. Men of the Eighth Bomber Command are eager to lend a hand to British Bomber Command in the business of bombing Germany.

In February the Forts went raiding again into Germany. They made another particularly daring raid on Wilhelmshaven. On this occasion the *New York Times* correspondent, Robert P Post, went with them to get a first-hand account of the attack. He did not return.

A month later the Forts staged their memorable and daring raid on Vegesack. The night before the raid was scheduled a well-known RAF bomber pilot, Wing Commander N J Baird-Smith, was visiting an American Eighth Air Force bomber station. He chanced to remark that he had made forty-nine bombing raids in RAF aircraft and at once received an invitation 'to make it a golden wedding in a Flying Fortress.' He accepted the offer gratefully.

When he came back from Vegesack he had this to say:

> As soon as we approached the enemy coast the fighters came up to have a look. They hung about, apparently waiting for an aircraft to stray out of the fold and I felt that they disliked the idea of coming near the American guns. In spite of pretty heavy flak our pilot got on to his target all right and made a good bombing run – straight and level. It was evident that the bombs of the preceding aircraft had found their mark, for the whole target was already obscured by thick smoke. You can judge a good deal about the crew of a bomber by its efficiency on the return journey. By this time they had been flying for quite a considerable time and with the obvious strain such close formation flying imposes they became tired. I can say, however, that the formation returned as they had set out – closely packed and ready to do battle with anybody. The fighters were on the lookout for the lone aircraft homeward bound, possibly shot up by flak or disabled by fighters, thus being unable to keep with the main formations. There were plenty of fighters and they attacked until we were a considerable distance from the enemy coast. But these attacks became less and less aggressive as they saw the German coast receding; until just before they left us they were milling round in the hope that a Fortress would straggle. Our particular formation had all the answers ready. One more aggressive Ju 88, which came in too close was met by an intense volume of fire and blew up and I saw a Fw 190 spinning out of control on its way down towards the sea. The meticulous planning of this operation, combined with the efficiency of the crews and leaders in carrying out this no mean task, seems to me to be the keynote to the successful bombing of Vegesack with such a small loss of aircraft to the USAAF.

On that raid Lieutenant Jack Mathis, a young Texan, died as he sent his bombs whistling over the U-boat yards. As his formation approached the main target he was bent over his bombsight. Flak was flying up in a heavy curtain of exploding steel. Mathis' aircraft, *Duchess*, was leading its particular group and upon the young Texan's aim much of the success of the following bombardiers depended. *Duchess* drew close to the target and Mathis pinpointed the spot where his bomb load would land. At that instant flak burst beneath him. His right arm was almost torn from his body. His right side was peppered with steel fragments. The force of the exploding shell threw him back fully nine feet, to the lower hatch.

He did not lose consciousness. In great agony he crawled back to the bombsight, using his left hand to lever his mortally wounded body. He sighted, reached for the 'toggles off' switch and down went the *Duchess*'s load of bombs.

Over the intercom his crewmates heard him begin the customary 'Bombs away.'

'Bombs ...' he murmured faintly.

They heard no more. One of them went down to him. He was dead, his left hand outstretched to the bomb-bay door switch. As he died he had closed the doors.

His was the eagerness to which General Longfellow referred. The attack on Vegesack brought congratulations from Mr Churchill, who sent the following message to Lieutenant-General Frank M Andrews, Commanding General, European Theater of Operations, US Army, and to Major-General Eaker, Commanding General, US Army Eighth Air Force:

'All my compliments to you and your officers and men on your brilliant exploit of yesterday, the effectiveness of which the photographs already reveal.'

Lieutenant-General Andrews replied: 'The officers and men of the United States Forces in the British Isles appreciate and are deeply grateful for the interest and congratulations expressed in your message last night.'

Major-General Eaker's acknowledgment was:

> The message received last night from you congratulating our air forces on the Vegesack raid was promptly transmitted to the combat crews, as I am sure you would want. It will give them a great lift to have this message from you. It has been of tremendous importance and value to our air forces in this theater to know of your keen interest in their work. They join with me in realizing the paramount importance to us of your militant leadership. Again thanking you for your message and assuring you that we will repeat these efforts many times and on an ever-increasing scale.

The Vegesack raid was made on Thursday, 18 March. Four days later the Forts went without fighter escort to raid Wilhelmshaven in daylight for the third time. Six days passed and the Flying Fortress offensive swung to Rouen. Three days after that attack it was Rotterdam's turn. On this day, 31 March, Captain Clyde D Walker, who brought *Boom Town* back from Lorient, was piloting *Boom Town Junior*. The *Junior* made its bombing run with one engine dead and another giving only a third of its normal power. But the bombs went down accurately on the target and Walker brought his aircraft and crew back to Britain.

Five days later the *Junior* was being eased through a fine-meshed net of flak by Walker as he made his bombing run over Antwerp. The Erla Aero Engine Works was the target. Staff Sergeant Krucher was again handling the tail guns and he had one eye on the enemy fighters and one on the

Spitfires covering this probe into the outer shell of the German defence network.

'The group ahead of us got the worst attacks,' Krucher reported when he arrived back. 'At various times over the intercom I heard reports of Fortresses in trouble. I saw an Fw blow up after being hit by one of us – I don't know which. I was glad to see the Spit cover coming.'

Only the day before, on 4 April, *Dry Martini*, with the Cocktail Kids doing their stuff, had gone with other Fortresses to the Renault works on the outskirts of Paris and created an American Army Air Force record. Against a furious onslaught from the Focke-Wulf pack the *Dry Martini*'s gunners had chalked up a score of ten definite kills. The Nazis were so stunned by the performance that their English-language broadcaster at Friesland went to the microphone and referred to Captain Martini as 'an outstanding example of American boastfulness'. The commentator went on to say that the Cocktail Kids' bombs fell, not on the Renault works, but on a school. However, the Kids had seen the evidence of their own camera.

'That broadcast was good for my morale,' one of them laughed.

Not that the morale of the Forts' crews needed any stimulants. It was at its peak when a fortnight later a concentrated daylight attack was made on the Focke-Wulf plant at Bremen. The Forts cut through the fighter opposition like a hot knife through butter. The target was smothered with bombs and more than half of the factory buildings were destroyed or very heavily damaged.

This was the occasion when Second Lieutenant L C Sugg and Captain Pervis E Youree got back to base after the order to prepare to ditch had been given. The Fort's bombs went down on the Focke-Wulf plant and Youree turned to meet a Focke-Wulf 190's headlong attack. Sugg was the co-pilot. His rudder pedals were shot away by German fire, four hydraulic lines were knocked out and the control cables to three of the aircraft's four engines were cut. Two of the engines failed.

Youree could do nothing but leave the high-flying formation. As the Forts crossed the coast he went down almost to wave-top height. 'So low that we left a wake in the water,' were the words of one of the crew. But try as he would he found control of the aircraft impossible. Reluctantly he gave the order to prepare to ditch. Before the aircraft could be abandoned, however, Sugg crawled under the catwalk, fumbled with the severed wires and cables and found which cables controlled the engines. He stayed there and attended the engines by pulling on the cables.

But the intercom system had been shot up. When he wanted to communicate with Youree he had to leave the broken cables. This meant risking the aircraft. So Sugg devised a way out of the difficulty by tying the broken cables to a ring on some parachute harness and then stretching the harness to the cockpit. When he wanted to deliver a message he handed the parachute strap to Youree, who flew the Fort with his left hand and controlled the engines with his right.

It was a nightmare piece of flying, but the ingenious device saved the aircraft – and the crew.

On 13 May the Forts put on their biggest show up to that time, when they flew, escorted, to bomb the aircraft works and repair shops at Meaulte. General Hansell went with them.

'The Allied fighter support was splendid,' he commented afterwards. 'It is my opinion that together we did a good job.' Colonel Stanley T Wray, of Birmingham, Alabama, the commander of one of the most famous groups of Fortresses, known affectionately as 'Wray's Ragged Irregulars,' took his four-engined high-fliers through the hoops and over the hurdles at Meaulte. He too was impressed by the supporting fighter squadrons.

'Some Fws,' he said, 'came in six at a time from God knows where. But our cover was beautiful. I saw nine or ten Spits going up at one time to take out three Fws.'

The next day the record was broken by a still larger force of American bombers going out from Britain. This time in a four-pronged attack spread out over Europe, with the Forts concentrating on the U-boat base and the marshalling yards at Kid and the General Motors plant at Antwerp.

Three days later the high-flying bombers swung round towards Bordeaux and after a day's rest turned back to Kiel and added Flensburg to their visiting-list. Over Kiel that day the Fortress in which Edward Lewis, one of British Paramount News' cameramen, was travelling as a passenger, was shot down.

Another day's rest and then the Forts were raiding in daylight again over Wilhelmshaven. Emden was added to the day's calls.

The offensive was stepping up. The Americans were by this time well into their bombing stride. Major-General Follett Bradley, Inspector-General of the US Army Air Forces, went as an observer on the Wilhelmshaven raid. He journeyed in the Flying Fortress *Wham Bam* and when he returned he gave out this considered statement:

> My impression is that the mission was extremely well planned. The methodical, painstaking seriousness with which this crowd of splendid young airmen go about their job convinced me, more than ever, that when adequate forces are available to hit Germany in six or eight places at once, the war will be brought to a speedy conclusion. I've never seen finer fighting spirit nor higher morale than is exemplified by the Eighth Air Force in this theater.

The Fort crews were getting really tough, too, in their handling of the enemy. Seventy-four German planes were destroyed that day by

American gunners, for the loss of twelve US machines. That figure was a new record, the previous highest total being sixty-seven enemy aircraft destroyed during the May 14th raid over Kiel and other targets in occupied territory.

This raid also saw the *Dry Martini*'s record of ten enemy fighters destroyed by a single bomber beaten by the crew of a Fort piloted by Lieutenant R H Smith, from Lamesa, in the Lone Star State. Smith and his crew, however, could not make it back to England. On the return journey their badly shot-up aircraft was unable to keep aloft and they had to ditch it. The Americans spent thirty hours in their dinghies, concealed in thick mist, before being rescued by a British ship.

May was the Americans' record month. That month the Forts destroyed 355 enemy fighter aircraft, more than twice the previous highest monthly total. In addition 70 per cent more bombs, by weight, were dropped than in any previous month.

On the debit side for the monthly account was a loss of seventy-two bombers.

La Stampa failed to report these figures. Perhaps because it had other things to mention – such as the arrival of new squadrons of high-flying Forts over Italy from bases in North Africa. Or perhaps it had lost all interest in the Forts. Or even forgotten them.

Fascist memories are notoriously short.

CHAPTER 1

Mission 115

From the beginning, mission No. 115 was in doubt. A persistent low overcast had hung over the English bases for three days. Over the Continent the target areas were also blanketed by varying degrees of cloud coverage that had led to the enforced rest period granted the combat crews. The weather had permitted the maintenance crews to change many battle-damaged engines and patch up thousands of bullet- and flak-damaged bombers that had returned from the furious fights over north Germany and Poland. The night sky of 13 October showed no change, in fact there seemed to be some deterioration, as a damp mist fell silently from the dark windless sky. Nevertheless, those who might fly on the morrow must be prepared and at the bases the bars closed early.

Colonel Budd J Peaslee

During the afternoon of 13 October 1943 Brigadier General Frederick L Anderson, Commanding General, Eighth Bomber Command, and his senior staff officers gathered in the War Room at Daws Hill Lodge at High Wycombe on the green flanks of the rolling Buckinghamshire Chilterns for the daily Operations Conference. Prior to military use, 'Pinetree', as the headquarters was code-named, had been a girls' school. Some of the bedrooms still displayed a prim little card that said, 'Ring twice for mistress.' It was here on 22 February 1942 that Eighth Bomber Command was formerly activated. Now, inside the large square room with a high ceiling buried beneath 30ft of reinforced concrete the decision was taken to attack the ball bearing plant at Schweinfurt for the second time in three months. On 17 August the Eighth Air Force had sacrificed 600 aircrew, 60 Fortresses and many injured men in a simultaneous attack on the ball bearing factories at Schweinfurt and aircraft plants at Regensburg. General Fred Anderson, who at that time was commanding the 4th Wing at Elveden Hall near Thetford, had said, 'Congratulations on the completion of an epoch in aerial warfare. I am sure the 4th Bombardment Wing has continued to make history. The Hun now has no place to hide.' Unforunately the words had a hollow ring and the Luftwaffe was as strong as ever. On 1 October 1943 British Intelligence sources had estimated that despite RAF–USAAF 'round-the-clock' bombing of aircraft factories and component plants, the Luftwaffe had a first line strength of 1,525 single- and twin-engined fighters for the defence of the western approaches to Germany. American sources put the figure at around 1,100 operational fighters. In reality, the Luftwaffe could call upon 1,646 single- and twin-engined fighters for the defence of the Reich, 400 more than before the issue of the Pointblank directive. Only about a third of this force was ready for immediate use, however, the remainder being reserves or temporarily unserviceable. The Allies' figures confirmed their worst fears. Once again the intention was to deliver a single, decisive blow against the German aircraft industry and stem the flow of fighters to the Luftwaffe.

Anderson and his senior staff officers were told that good weather was expected for the morrow. At once a warning order was sent out to all three Bomb Division headquarters with details of a mission, No. 115, to Schweinfurt. The orders were then transmitted over teletype machines to the various combat wing headquarters. Anderson hoped to launch 420 Fortresses and Liberators in a three-pronged attack on the city of Schweinfurt. The plan called for the 1st and 3rd Bomb Divisions to cross Holland 30 miles apart while the third task force, composed of sixty Liberators of the 2nd Bomb Division, would fly to the south on a parallel course. The 923-mile trip would last just over seven hours and meant that the B-17s of the 1st Division, which were not equipped with 'Tokyo tanks', would have to be fitted with an additional fuel tank in the bomb bay. However, this meant a reduction in the amount of bombs they could carry. A P-47 Thunderbolt group would escort each division while a third fighter group would provide withdrawal support from 60 miles inland to half way across the Channel. Two squadrons of RAF Spitfire IXs were to provide cover for the stragglers five minutes after the main force had left the withdrawal area and other RAF squadrons would be on standby for action if required. Despite these precautions, 370 miles of the route would be flown without fighter support. The plans then had been laid, but the success of the mission was in the lap of the gods. It needed fine weather and, above all, the fighters had to be on schedule.

During the early evening of 13 October and the early hours of 14 October, all the necessary information for the raid was teletyped to all Fortress and Liberator groups in eastern England. At 23.15 hours Brigadier General Robert B Williams, the commanding officer of the 1st Bombardment Division, received a message sent by General Anderson. It said:

> To all leaders and combat crews. To be read at briefing. This air operation today is the most important air operation yet conducted in

> this war. The target must be destroyed. It is of vital importance to the enemy. Your friends and comrades that have been lost and that will be lost today are depending on you. Their sacrifice must not be in vain. Good luck. Good shooting and good bombing. [Signed] Anderson.

The 96th Bomb Group would lead the 3rd Division, with Colonel Archie Old, CO, 45th Wing, in the lead ship, while the 92nd Bomb Group, at the head of the 40th Combat Wing, would lead the 1st Division with twenty-one Fortresses. Its commander would be Colonel Budd J Peaslee, deputy commander to Colonel Howard 'Slim' Turner of the 40th Combat Wing and formerly CO of the 384th Bomb Group. Budd Peaslee's pilot on the mission would be Captain James K McLaughlin of the 92nd Bomb Group. He recalls:

> I shall never forget the many target briefings that Ed O'Grady, my bombardier, Harry Hughes, my navigator and I went through preparing for this famous raid. We had led our squadron [the 326th] on the first Schweinfurt raid on 17 August and, along with the others, did a pretty good job of missing the target too. We had all been apprehensive of the second raid because we'd been flying missions since we'd arrived in England in August 1942. And we had first-hand experience of how the Luftwaffe would punish us; particularly when we failed to knock out a target for the first time and attempted to go back.

Among the first of the 91st Bomb Group personnel to hear the news at Bassingbourn was David Williams, who in September had been promoted to captain and appointed group navigator. Like McLaughlin, Williams had also been on the first Schweinfurt raid:

> I vividly recall the operations order when it came over the teletype in Group Operations during the wee hours of the morning of 14 October, as I had to do the navigational mission planning while the rest of the combat crews were still asleep. Thus we had already overcome the initial shock which we were to see on the faces of the crews somewhat later when the curtains were dramatically pulled back to reveal the scheduled second deep penetration to Schweinfurt.

At Kimbolton Captain Edward Millson, or 'Togglin' Ed' as he was known in the 379th Bomb Group, was his Group's lead bombardier. He recalled: 'I was awakened at 03.30 to go to Base Operations, where I found navigator Captain Joe Wall hard at work on the flight plan and a map on the wall. A long line snaked its way across the map into the heart of Germany to Schweinfurt. That old feeling of excitement grew inside me.' At Polebrook 1st Lieutenant Jim Bradley, a lead bombardier in the 351st Bomb Group, really wanted to 'get' Schweinfurt since his original crew, without Walter Stockman and himself, went down on the first mission on 17 August. 'When the order came during the night of 13 October I had already studied all approaches to the target and was confident that I knew it like my hometown. On the way to my barracks a couple of crewmen asked me where we were going on the 14th. I told them it was a real milk run.'

In a hut at Rougham near Bury St. Edmunds, Staff Sergeant Leo Rand, a replacement gunner who had arrived early that month and was awaiting his first mission on the morrow was one of several who played Black Jack through the night. He won all the money in the pot and one of the losers said jokingly, 'I hope you get shot down tomorrow.'

Crews slept in their beds piled high with blankets, uniforms and anything else they could lay their hands on to keep out the freezing east wind, dreading the knock at the door which told them the mission was on. Colonel Peaslee continues:

> The footsteps came in the early black hours of 14 October, as inevitably as the approaching day. The footsteps came to hundreds of crewmen over the English countryside and the doors rattled as they were yanked open and the darkness was ripped by the dazzling brightness of light bulbs. The voices of the runners were harsh, with a barely discernible note of compassion, as they sung out, 'Crew 37 hit the deck, briefing at 05.00.' Black Thursday had begun.

The same scene was being replayed at all the bases in the east of England. At Thurleigh, Staff Sergeant James E Harris, a tail gunner in the 367th Bomb Squadron, 306th Bomb Group recalled:

> It was a cold, dreary, damp, typical English morning when the CQ (charge of quarters) came into our Nissen hut to waken the crews for a mission. We had heard the sounds of big engines being run up and pre-flighted on the hard stands around the perimeter of the airfield. As it was raining quite hard, I figured that the mission would be scrubbed. I was not feeling up to par so I remained in my warm sack while the others left for the mess hall. The CQ soon returned and told me to get to the briefing. I lost no time getting dressed and riding my bicycle on the shortest route to the flight line and the briefing.[1]

The sky was still dark and windless and a heavy mist clung to the buildings and surrounding countryside as thousands of men cycled or trudged their way to the mess halls for unappetizing breakfasts of powdered eggs, toast and hot coffee. At Chelveston Sergeant William C Frierson, a spare ball turret gunner on 2nd Lieutenant Robert W Holt's crew in *The Uncouth Bastard* peered in the direction of the airfield and saw nothing. Even the runways were obscured. He was sure that the mission would be called off.[2]

Soon the crews were on their way again to the briefing halls to hear about the part they would play in the forthcoming mission. Colonel Budd J Peaslee describes the briefing at Podington:

> The briefing room filled rapidly as 210 crewmen and perhaps 25 briefing officers and key specialists, including flight surgeons, chaplains and unit commanders, completed the gathering. The senior officers, including the 92nd commander, Colonel William Reid of Augusta, Georgia, occupied the more comfortable seats near the stage in the front of the room. Ranged toward the rear on rows of hard chairs and benches were the crews... all these were present as the doors were closed and guarded against intrusion and prying eyes. A dignified middle-aged major opened the briefing. In civil life he had been a teacher in a small southern community. He had himself learned a thousand things never dreamed of when he volunteered to serve his country. Now he was an intelligence specialist and a good one. He opened the briefing in a calm and scholarly voice.
>
> 'Gentlemen, may I have your attention? This morning we have quite a show.' So saying, he drew back the curtains that had covered a large-scale map of Europe and the British Isles. In the hushed room all leaned forward intently to study the map with its heavy black yarn marking the routes over Britain, the Channel and across the occupied countries to a point deep in Germany. 'It's Schweinfurt again,' said the major. For a moment there was dead silence as the major's words struck home with full impact on the minds of the men. Then a buzz of intelligible comment filled the room, punctuated by whistles, curses, moans and just plain vocal explosions. Above all came one remembered phrase that stood out in the tumult of vocal sound.
>
> 'Son-of-a-bitch and this is my twenty-fifth mission!'
>
> Eyes turned towards the speaker and there were expressions of sympathy and condolence until a baby-faced pilot spoke. 'What the hell are you crying about? This is my first!'

Bill Rose recalls: 'When the briefing officer said, "Gentlemen, your target for today is Schweinfurt," everyone groaned. The ball bearing plants would be heavily defended. We knew our third mission would be one hell of a fight.'

For the next half-hour the major and his aides spoke on the plan for the mission. Then it was the air commander's turn to say a few words to the crews he was to lead. Colonel Reid introduced Budd Peaslee to the expectant crews. Peaslee spared no punches. He told them straight out they were in for a fight. Their responsibility was to the group, not to the stragglers and there was no room for useless heroics. He tried to think of something humorous to dispel the tension, which had suddenly gripped the men, but he could think of nothing funny about the situation. Finally, he said, 'If our bombing is good and we hit this ball-bearing city well, we are bound to scatter a lot of balls around on the streets of Schweinfurt. Tonight I expect the Germans will all feel like they are walking around on roller skates.'

'It was a weak effort,' wrote Peaslee, 'but they all laughed loudly, too loudly and the tension was reduced.'

The news that Schweinfurt was their target brought mixed reactions from men. At fog-shrouded and rain soaked bases throughout East Anglia, crews were weary from days of bitter combat and fitful sleep. There were few men on the bases who doubted it was an excursion into Hell despite some officers' platitudes that it was going to be a milk-run. At most briefing rooms the pulling of the curtain covering the wall map shocked the aircrews into silence. At Ridgewell the shock was probably felt the greatest. Crews were briefed at 07.00 hours and the mention of the word 'Schweinfurt' brought back bitter memories of the 17 August raid when the 381st had lost eleven B-17s, the highest loss of all the groups. A medical detachment log earlier that month had concluded that the 'mental attitude on morale of the crews is the lowest that has been yet observed.' The Intelligence Officer (S-2) therefore decided that it would perhaps be best not to mention that the entire Luftwaffe fighter force of 1,100 aircraft was based within 65 miles of the bombers' route. As the Medical Officer went around to the crews to check equipment and pass out sandwiches and coffee he noticed that the crews were 'scared and it was obvious that many doubted that they would return.'[3]

Crewmen who had flown only a few missions noticed that even the veteran crews appeared to be in a state of shock. At Chelveston as the curtain was jerked back and they all saw what the target was there was instant whistling, nervous laughter and wise-cracking. Solemnly, one captain performed a ceremony that was reserved for tough targets: he took out a roll of toilet paper, tore off ten squares for each man and passed them out. Lieutenant Edwin L 'Ted' Smith, co-pilot in Lieutenant Douglas L Murdock's crew in *Sizzle*[4], which would be No. 6 in the low squadron, recalls: 'When we saw the tapes stretching that deep into Germany we all had misgivings. The gunners knew we were in for a fight and so they lugged extra ammo boxes out to our aircraft.'[5]

Eight men at the briefing had a special reason for wanting to complete the mission. Lieutenant Frederick E Helmick was the bombardier on *Rigor*

Mortis flown by 1st Lieutenant Frederick B 'Barney' Farrell. Staff Sergeant Herman E Molen was flying with 2nd Lieutenant Gerald B Eakle's crew as toggelier (bombardier). Staff Sergeant Thomas E Therrien was right waist gunner on Flight Officer Verl D Fisher's crew. All of these men were flying their 25th and final mission of their tour. So too were Lieutenant Raymond P Bullock and Carl J Brunswick, his engineer/top turret gunner, left waist gunner Harold E Coyne and tail gunner Alden B Curtis, all aboard *Sundown Sal* (a brand new B-17G, which was named but never painted) in the 365th Squadron.

Lieutenant Alden C Kincaid, a pilot who had flown twenty-one missions and before that had flown Wellingtons on RAF night bombing operations, discovered that he would be the aircraft commander for Lieutenant Norman W Smith's crew. Smith, who hailed from Hawaii where his parents owned a pineapple plantation and had witnessed the Japanese bombing of Pearl Harbor on 7 December 1941, would move over to the co-pilot's seat.[6]

At the end of the briefing Lieutenant Joseph Pellegrini, lead bombardier in the B-17 flown by 2nd Lieutenant Joseph W Kane, with Major Charles G Y Normand the Command Pilot, had a question for the CO, Lieutenant Colonel Donald K Fargo. As the target was so important could he take the sixteen B-17s of the group over the target again if clouds obscured the aiming point? Fargo said, 'Yes Pellegrini – you can go around a second time and a third and a fourth today. This is one target you must hit.'[7] Pellegrini, one of fourteen children born to Italian parents, from South Philadelphia, was one of the few that did not have 'butterflies' in his stomach.

Forrest J Eherenman, the navigator in Lieutenant Corson's crew and who had arrived at Kimbolton on 17 August in time to watch the bedraggled survivors return from Schweinfurt, had not forgotten the word 'Schweinfurt'. 'On 14 October,' he recalls, 'we heard that name again. Our crew in *Gay Caballeros* would be Tail End Charlie at the end of the low squadron. This would be our tenth mission.'

Elmer Bendiner, a navigator who had flown the 17 August raid, recalled:[8]

> Sitting on the wooden benches in the briefing room at Kimbolton at four that morning, we took the news that we were going back to Schweinfurt with only a few groans to indicate that we were alive to the problem. The neophytes among us were more boisterous. Actually in the group of eighteen crews slated to represent the 379th on that mission, only four had been in the Schweinfurt battle two months earlier when we were told we were going to write history and win the war. The spiel was more solemn this time. The message had not changed, but now the sacrifices of August recurred to mind like an insistent, muffled drumbeat beneath the text.

General Anderson sent us a personal message calling on us – not very tactfully, I fancied – to remember the blood and sacrifice of our comrades who had died on the same errand in August. We were to finish their job. Such high-toned dramatics usually read better than they play. For men like ourselves, the remnants of *Tondelayo*'s crew,[9] the message from beyond the grave sounded particularly inappropriate. It was barely arguable that those who had died some seven weeks earlier at Schweinfurt or *en route* had a right to cry, like Hamlet's lugubrious father, 'Remember me.' But we – Bohn [E Fawkes Jnr, the pilot], Bob [Hejny, bombardier], Larry, Duke and I – had flown with those nagging ghosts. We had gone through the fire with them and by luck had survived. Now they were using their exalted position to drive us into doing it all over again. It was easy for them to talk; they were safely dead and out of it all...

After the call to vengeance the briefing turned to the economic, political, social and psychological significance of ball bearings. The twice-told tale was intoned like a chant. This was again the day when the German machine was to be castrated.

Mo Preston would not say that our job was to be less difficult or less costly than it had been in August. He was an honest man. He would not fly with us that day and so wore his pinks, as if it were a holiday. Little Rip Rohr was in his flying suit, energetically waving his pointer like a sword. This would be his day.

At the briefing at Thurleigh Staff Sergeant James E Harris, who had been on the first Schweinfurt, recalls that when the route map was uncovered and they saw that the 'damned red line led to Schweinfurt, you could have heard a pin drop.' George Roberts, radio operator in W S Kirk's crew recalls:

Our Group commander Colonel Robinson told the assembled crews that we would be bombing the most important target to date: the ball and roller bearing factories at Schweinfurt. The name had no meaning to me. The red string on the map told us we in for a long flight over heavily defended territory. The weather over England would remain marginal, but would be clear over the continent. We could expect serious fighter opposition, moderate to intense flak and a long cold ride. With this dire information we completed our pre-flight work and assembled for final instructions. Lieutenant Kirk said that this mission would be as rough as the one to Bremen and an hour longer. We had from three to fifteen missions behind us. Kirk cautioned everyone to stay alert, conserve ammunition and guns by firing short bursts and be brief on the intercom.

Having flown the first Schweinfurt raid on 17 August James E Harris believed that:

> Most secretly thought that this would be a one way trip. Schweinfurt again, deep into Germany, with a short-range escort. Was this trip necessary? Of course, we knew that it was. 'Theirs is not to reason why, theirs was but to do and die.' Oh, so true. W N Thomas, our regular pilot, was hospitalized and grounded and also Joe Lukens, our regular bombardier was riding with a 'green' crew.[10] A combat crew that had trained together always had second thoughts whenever there was a replacement. A good crew could be compared to the precision of a fine watch or a good ball team, whose members know their plays and anticipate each other's moves and act accordingly; no mistakes. It was especially hard for a crew to accept a replacement pilot.[11] There were no reflections against the person, but our feelings were justified in situations like this.[12]

At Molesworth Lieutenant Robert Hullar, pilot of *Luscious Lady* in the 427th Bomb Squadron, and his 24-year-old co pilot Wilbur Klint, learned that they would be in the second flight. Both men had flown the first Schweinfurt and from that experience they knew that Mission 115 was destined to be 'a shakey do' as Klint called it. 'The first Schweinfurt had been our second mission. This was Mission No. 11 for our crew.' Colonel Stevens opened the briefing. 'Today's mission, if successful, can shorten the war by six months.' Briefing officers spoke of routes where the flak was minimal and of areas where fighters were not expected. They referred to the friendly fighter cover in glowing terms. But the majority of crews were not fooled, as 2nd Lieutenant Roy G Davidson, one of the pilots in the 333rd Bomb Squadron at Bury St. Edmunds (Rougham), recalls:

> When the covers were drawn on the route map, it showed that the fighter escort only went a short way with us to the target. We would have a long way from France onwards without fighter cover and on the way back too. We knew that we were in for a pretty rough time but we had no idea just how rough it was going to be. We had not been on the first Schweinfurt raid and didn't realize how bad Schweinfurt was. Despite this I really looked forward to the mission because I thought the accomplishment would be great. It never crossed the minds of the crew that we would not complete our twenty-five missions. A telegram was read out telling us that this was one of the most important missions of the war. When we had knocked out the ball-bearing plants the war would come to a halt. We felt we were really going to contribute a lot toward winning the war.[13] I was flying in the low squadron as last man – the most

vulnerable spot in the entire formation.[14] But we felt safe because even though we were the last plane in a string of over 200 bombers, there were going to be a whole lot of Liberators following right behind us. This would really put us right in the middle of the whole string, which seemed to be a pretty good spot to be in.[15]

Staff Sergeant Leo Rand noticed that some of the veteran crews appeared to be in shock. The former steelworker from Youngstown, Ohio did not scare easily and Rand put it down to the fact that these men were tired and were probably overreacting. Then someone near him mumbled, 'This is gonna be a tough day,' and others agreed.

Phillip R Taylor, a waist gunner in the 91st Bomb Group at Bassingbourn recalls: 'After the briefing my crew went back to our quarters and put on wool uniforms (ODs). Knowing what our target was, we expected to either end up in Heaven or a prisoner of war camp and we wanted to be properly dressed.' At Molesworth Robert Voltz looked at the low clouds and wagered a £1 note with radio operator Sergeant Warren L Harvie that they would not leave the ground. However, the green flare was fired to signal 'start engines' and a second flare was shot to start to taxi. They had three 1,000lb bombs plus an auxiliary fuel tank in the bomb bay. The auxiliary tank would be used for assembly and later jettisoned in the Channel. At Thurleigh, Jim Harris and the rest of Richard Butler's crew and George Roberts and the others in Lieutenant W S Kirk's crew donned their flying gear and checked out their parachutes, oxygen masks, escape kits and the codes for the day. Then they boarded the trucks that took them to their hardstands. Kirk's crew had been assigned *Cavalier* and Butler, 42-30175.

At Snetterton Heath, Eugene Sebeck, the engineer in 2nd Lieutenant Silas S Nettles' crew in the 96th Bomb Group had been called at 04.30 but he had reasons to be happy. The night before he and two others on the crew had been the last shooters on the skeet range and they decided to try a little hunting in the fields near the base. Within an hour they had rabbits and pheasants aplenty and they took them to the Red Cross Club where a lovely English lady had said she would fix them up in exchange for one rabbit. That evening they had a feast fit for a king, which was quite a change from the usual menu of Spam and such like. On returning to his Nissen hut Sebeck had found a letter on his bunk that looked good. He had applied for Aviation Cadet training in July and this was a notification that he had been accepted and would be called when an opening existed. He showed the letter to his pilot who read it and said, 'Well Sebeck, you won't be with us too much longer.' How right he was. Sebeck put the letter in the pocket of his leather A2 that he always hung in the tail section of the plane. To make matters more tense, after the briefing Silas Nettles and his crew were sent by truck the 25 miles to Bury St. Edmunds to get a plane from the 94th Bomb Group. There they were given 42-23453 for this, their second mission. Their first had been to Bremen on 8 October when they had flown a new B-17 called *V Packet* (which was given to 2nd Lieutenant John J Scarborough's crew who shared their hut, to fly on the Schweinfurt mission). Nettles' crew had returned, somehow, with over 100 holes and one feathered engine. Jerry V Lefors, the co-pilot, recalls:

> I had told the Crew Chief that all the engines would have to be replaced because we had flown for about 45 minutes on full RPM and maximum manifold pressure. (The rule was that an engine should be replaced if run under such conditions for 'several' minutes.) The Maintenance Chief laughed and said that they would fire them up and if they ran, 'the plane goes up again.' There were few extra engines available. After the Bremen mission we felt like veterans because 'no mission could be rougher than that.' We scrounged the next day for armor plate and discussed carrying more ammunition. We were a green crew but united in our determination to complete our missions.[16]

At Thorpe Abbotts the 100th Bomb Group was still licking its wounds after the severe maulings of 8 October, when seven crews were lost, and 10 October, when twelve out of thirteen crews failed to return. Despite these extremely serious losses and an unsuccessful appeal by Colonel 'Chick' Harding, the CO, the 'Bloody Hundredth' was still expected to make some contribution to the tonnage of bombs to be dropped on Schweinfurt. Lieutenant Robert L 'Bob' Hughes, pilot of *Nine Little Yanks and a Jerk* says: 'The call came for the Hundredth to mount a maximum effort but there were only eight crews available. Some of the key positions, therefore, had to be taken by personnel from other groups.'

The day before the mission Lieutenant William D Allen, a bombardier in the 384th Bomb Group, was relaxing in the Officers Club at Grafton Underwood when a captain approached him accompanied by the 'biggest, toughest MP' he had ever seen. Allen was ordered to report to Operations where he was informed that he would be a fill-in lead bombardier in the 100th Bomb Group.[17]

Robert Hughes continues:

> The eight crews were broken down into flights. Four aircraft would be led by 'Cowboy' Roane, flying with the 390th Bomb Group, with four being led by myself flying with the 95th Bomb Group.[18] The mess hall seemed virtually empty as we had our usual breakfast of dried eggs, Spam, coffee, toast and good old orange marmalade with vast amounts of good American butter to go on that wonderful dark English bread.

For many it was to be their last breakfast on English soil. There was little hope for any man holding low rank who wished to take leave that was owing to them either. It was a maximum effort and everyone was needed. At Framlingham, home of the 390th Bomb Group, Lieutenant Richard H Perry had hoped to receive a short period of leave in London after his crash four days before:

> The squadron CO, Joe Gemmill, felt differently. His view was that the best way to get the 'butterflies out of our stomachs' was to participate in another mission immediately. We did fly the Schweinfurt mission, which was no 'milk-run' and I think in our case his approach worked fine. Later, when I became operations officer, I used this approach on many other crews that had rough missions.

As H-Hour approached the tension on the bases mounted. The weather in England was very bad but at 09.00 hours an American-crewed Mosquito in the 25th Bomb Group, 35,000ft over the Continent, radioed back the news to Eighth Air Force headquarters that all of central Germany was in the clear. An hour later the Fortresses began taking off. The weathermen had predicted overcast to only 2,000ft, but the bombers were still flying around in cloud at heights of 6,000ft and above, forcing the lead aircraft to circle for two hours. Flares were fired in a vain attempt to pull the formations together.[19]

Colonel Peaslee, the mission leader, and his pilot Captain McLaughlin, sat waiting in the lead Fortress of the 92nd Bomb Group on the runway at Podington. Green flares shot skywards from the control tower and the lead bomber moved to its take-off position. The time was 10.12 hours. James McLaughlin released the brakes and throttled out towards the fading runway lights in the distance. Colonel Peaslee, sitting in the right-hand seat, listened intently as McLaughlin announced over intercom that he was taking off on instruments. He directed Peaslee to watch the runway and if the B-17 should start to wander to one side or the other he was to overpower him on the rudder control and bring it back to safety on the runway. The lead bomber gathered speed and at 100mph, in the last 100 feet of runway, it was airborne. Peaslee released the locks and pulled the 'gear up' lever. They were followed by a further twenty bombers, and crews peered into the overcast for recognition points on the ground. In the dimness of the approaching day there was only a brief glimpse of the dark shadows of the woodland on either side of the runway clear zone, but this was almost instantly blotted out as the bombers entered the overcast.

The same procedure was happening at Thurleigh. George Roberts recalls that 'shortly before start engine time at 09.00 word came of a one-hour weather delay. It remained foggy with a 200 feet cloud ceiling.' 1st Lieutenant Harold K McCaleb doubted that the raid would go ahead:

> Crews had been briefed at 04.00 on the morning of 12 October for Schweinfurt. With rain and fog covering England, the mission was canceled before the B-17 engines were started. Crews were again briefed for Schweinfurt on Wednesday and again, because of weather, the mission was canceled. Now the end of the runway was not visible through the fog and rain. Most crews expected word that the mission had been canceled again.

George Roberts continues:

> Promptly at 10.00 the green flare was fired from the control tower and the engines came to life. We moved in line down the taxiway. Pilots did engine run-ups before moving onto the main runway. Under full throttle we began the dash down the concrete strip. Very near the end of the runway we felt the heavy plane leave the ground and ascend into the low hanging clouds. We would not break out of the overcast for another thirty minutes.

Aboard Butler's Fortress the engines were started. Kenneth McCaleb recalls: 'Unbelievably the command for take off was given for the bomb- and gasoline-loaded bombers to climb through the overcast with pilots wondering how they were going to land when the cancelation order was given.'

Jim Harris continues:

> All secure, Butler waited for the signals to start engines and taxi to take-off position. It was a tense, anxious moment waiting for the flare, which signaled takeoff. I presumed that everybody involved, especially the flight crews, hoped for the word to scrub the mission. No such luck, so we proceeded to take off in the rain. It took quite a while to climb through the overcast. As we broke through the clouds, B-17s were popping up all around us. We were concerned about the instrument takeoff because we knew that the pilots, as good as they might be, had not had the opportunity to gain experience in instrument flying. Due to the weather, many groups failed to reach their predetermined assembly points. Many fighter groups could not take off in time to be of much help.

The Forts emerged from the overcast at several thousand feet, assembled in formation and approached the enemy coast of Europe as the clouds disappeared. Kenneth McCaleb observed that it was an 'October Indian Summer day'. George Roberts noted:

> Our assembly and climb appeared normal, though other groups were having difficulty getting organized. We were in the high group of the 40th Combat Wing. Colonel Peaslee was leading the high group with the 92nd Bomb Group and the rest of the First Division. The 305th Group from Chelveston was flying the low element of the Wing. I listened on the radio for a possible recall, but all I heard was the steady call sign '7MT' and the regular time check.[20]

At Molesworth, William C Heller, who would soon take command of the 360th Bomb Squadron, taxied out for takeoff in heavy rain, which limited visibility. 'Since we could not see the end of the runway, takeoff and climb were on instrument conditions from the start of the roll until break out in the bright sunshine at 7,000ft.' At Kimbolton, after an exhaustive check Colonel 'Rip' Rohr took *Rag'n Red* off at 10.30 into what 'Togglin' Ed' Millson, lead bombardier for the 379th Bomb Group, called 'a sky already dotted with other Fortress formations.' Twenty minutes later Lieutenant Corson took *Gay Caballeros* off and headed for the Tail End Charlie slot at the end of the low squadron. Forrest J Eherenman, his navigator, recalls: 'In an hour and a half we got assembled over the departure point (Splasher 6). A few minutes later we were committed to go to the target no matter what lay in wait over Germany.'[21]

Peaslee and McLaughlin had meanwhile levelled out at 8,000ft and they began craning their necks to spot other aircraft. McLaughlin recalls: 'After we were airborne and formed up, the first warning of what the day would be like came when we discovered that some of the groups and wings had not joined up in their proper sequences. The mission thus began in confusion because some group leaders could not find their wings.'

The 92nd Bomb Group had cruised to the splasher beacon over Thurleigh and formed as a group, but at the second splasher, where the 40th Combat Wing was to assemble, the 305th Bomb Group failed to rendezvous.[22] Peaslee therefore decided to continue with just the 306th Bomb Group to the third assembly area at Daventry in the Midlands and fly on at 20,000ft to the English coast. Standing orders dictated that no air commander could send out a two-group combat wing: the risk of total annihilation of such a small defensive force was too great. However, Peaslee did not want to abort while he still had some options open to him. The 40th Combat Wing orbited according to procedure and at 12.20 hours led the 1st Division assembly line over the coast above Orford Ness. George Roberts in the 306th Bomb Group recalls: 'We fired test rounds over the Channel and noted a few P-47 Thunderbolts as we crossed the French Coast. These "Little Friends" did not remain with us long.'

Further south, the 45th Combat Wing, with the 96th Bomb Group in the van, led the 3rd Division over the Naze and headed for the Belgian coast. With five other crews, Silas Nettles in the borrowed 94th ship rendezvoused with the 96th Bomb Group and they flew Tail End Charlie. By 12.30 they were crossing the Channel at 23,000ft. Jerry Lefors says: 'Flying Tail End Charlie was quite a job. We all knew what happened to stragglers so we tried to maintain a tight formation.' Eugene Sebeck, the engineer, had his hands full. After take off he had never seen cloud conditions as bad and he thought that they might run into another plane at any minute. They had finally got above the overcast and were on their way but he had to maintain a watchful eye on the No. 1 engine, which kept losing and then gaining about 100 RPM. Fuel consumption was high. Nettles requested his navigator, Robert O'Hearn to calculate the rate of fuel use. They had barely enough to make it back if all went well. 'Knowing we might have to bale out if we ran out of gas,' says Jerry Lefors, 'the crew elected to continue on.' The crew test-fired their guns over the Channel and everything seemed OK. A short time later Sebeck swung his turret around towards the tail and watched their P-47 fighters leave after they had reached the limit of their fuel. Very soon he heard the message in interphone: 'Enemy fighters coming.' Things now started to get rough and to add to their troubles the No. 1 engine 'ran away' after attempts to feather the prop failed. The only thing to do, says Sebeck, 'was to cut power and fuel or it would tear itself apart. The windmilling prop dragged our airspeed down by 20 or more mph.' Although the lead plane was flying at a steady speed the slight variation in airspeed of the ships near the leader would parlay back through the formation. 'We were going from full RPMs to cutting back to near stall-out. This amounted to a lot of physical labor to handle the controls. We had learned we would flip onto our side and lose a thousand feet quickly by getting into wake turbulence created by the ships ahead.'[23]

Behind the 45th Wing came the 4th Combat Wing, consisting of the 94th and 385th Bomb Groups, followed by the 13th Combat Wing made up of the 95th, 100th and 390th Bomb Groups. Fifteen of the 164 aircraft in the 1st Division and eighteen aircraft of the 160 aircraft in the 3rd Division either turned back with mechanical problems or became lost in the cloudy conditions. The long and complicated assembly was also responsible for diminishing the Fortresses' vital fuel reserves, especially those carrying bombs externally to make up for space taken up by the bomb bay fuel tanks. Many of these crews were forced to dump their wing-mounted bombs in the Channel or abort the mission. The 94th Bomb Group, part of the 4th Combat Wing, had difficulty in forming. Major Charles Birdsall led the twenty-four B-17s of the 94th off from Rougham and soon disappeared into cloud at only 2,000ft. Crews cursed the weather forecasters who had predicted cloud at 6,500ft. Birdsall managed to get his B-17s into the correct slot in the wing formation and they headed for the coast. Soon there was an opportunity for gunners to test-fire their .50 calibre machine-guns. In the waist section aboard

Davidson's B-17, Claude Page and Arthur Howell fired off a few rounds. Page had asked Davidson to keep the $600 he had won at a crap game. He was afraid to go to bed with all this money. Page had promised himself 'I'll send it home tomorrow.'

The 3rd Bomb Division crossed the coast of Belgium near Knocke at 12.55 hours and proceeded on a converging course with the 1st Bomb Division towards Aachen. The escorting P-47 Thunderbolts departed and the Fortresses carried on alone to Schweinfurt. 'Gus' Mencow, navigator of *Betty Boop, the Pistol Packing Mama,* in the 570th Bomb Squadron, 390th Bomb Group, piloted by Lieutenant Jim 'Rally' Geary, recalls:

> We were leading the high squadron, with Bob Brown's crew of the 571st flying group lead. As our fighter escort left us everyone sensed that we were in for a tough mission. The German fighter attacks came sporadically, mostly in waves and it soon developed into a running battle extending for hundreds of miles across the skies of Europe. Although we were having it tough, it seemed that the 1st Bomb Division was really getting the brunt of the attacks in their formations well ahead of us.

Aborts had now reduced the 40th Combat Wing from fifty-three B-17s to forty-two, one third of a complete wing formation. Standing orders in the Eighth prohibited bomber commanders from penetrating enemy defences with less than a complete wing formation. In this situation the wing would have to abort. However, Peaslee reasoned that the loss of forty-two bombers would deprive the division of much needed fire-power and, most importantly, additional bombs. He called for a report from the tail gunner, a regular lieutenant co-pilot for the lead crew, who was acting as the eyes of the air commander by taking over the tail gun position. The lieutenant reported that the 1st Division was in excellent position and at full strength except for the missing 305th Bomb Group. Peaslee decided to continue to the target moving the 92nd and 306th formations into the high slot just above and to the left of the 91st. In effect this would give the 1st Wing five groups. Peaslee retained air command but would relinquish the lead to Lieutenant Colonel Theodore Milton, CO of the 91st, flying at the head of the 1st Combat Wing in the *Bad Egg*, piloted by Captain Harry Lay (subsequently killed on a second tour in fighters). The air commander broke radio silence long enough to advise Milton of the plan, at the same time advising the new leader that the 40th Combat Wing would join his formation in close support, thus grouping nearly 100 bombers in a mutually protective mass. Milton must have had mixed feelings because he had only taken off with eleven B-17s, now reduced to just seven because of aborts. Having the 305th along must have provided some relief. The news that the 91st was to take over the lead prompted Captain David Williams, the lead navigator flying with Milton, to think back to that fateful day on 17 August when the 91st had led the first Schweinfurt raid:

> Mission 115 was my twenty-third combat mission and the second time that I would have the dubious honour of being in the very first B-17 over the target. It was an eerie feeling once more to be the vanguard, striking out across the Channel toward a target, which had dealt us so many devastating losses just a few months before. All the more so this time since four of our group had already aborted and we were setting course with just seven aircraft comprising the 91st effort. I kept thinking of the ten we had lost in August and somehow could not seem to reconcile the mathematics, which were going through my mind. The navigational chore ahead left little time for such speculation.

Bringing up the rear of the 1st Division bomber stream was the 41st Combat Wing, the third and final wing. In the lead was the 379th Bomb Group led by Lieutenant Colonel Louis W 'Rip' Rohr in *Rag'n Red*. The 303rd was in the high spot and the 384th low, in 'Purple Heart Corner', led by Major George W Harris who had flown the first Schweinfurt mission, flying with Captain Philip Algar in *Windy City Avenger*. At mid-Channel the lieutenant tail gunner aboard Peaslee's ship reported, 'Fighters at 7 o'clock climbing. They look like P-47s.' The delay in forming up over England had put the Fortresses ten minutes behind schedule and the forty-four P-47s of the 353rd Fighter Group, which were on schedule, had met the bombers in mid-Channel. The 1st Bomb Division crossed the mouth of the Scheldt at 12.25 hours, the same time as the 3rd Division was leaving the coast of England. Old's force was only five minutes behind schedule, having avoided the bad weather problems that had dogged the 1st Division assembly. Aborts had reduced the numbers of Fortresses too.

In the 379th Bomb Group, *Ensign Mary* – named by the engineering officer who was dating a Navy nurse – took the place of an abort at the French coast. Staff Sergeant Sam Mehaffey, the ball turret gunner, recalls, 'A flak barrage hit the group over France. The navigator called on interphone: "The bombardier's hit, he's hit!" The pilot asked "How bad?" "Pretty bad" was the reply. (The bombardier had lost an arm). The pilot signaled to drop out and made a 180° turn.' Mehaffey swung his turret to the 6 o'clock position to watch the formation go on and he saw their replacement become a black puff of smoke where they had been. It must have been a direct hit in the bomb bay. His friend Francis S Chard, from Minnesota, was on the unlucky ship that was blown out of the sky.[24]

Up front in the 379th formation Captain Edwin Millson, the lead bombardier riding up front in *Rag'n Red*, recalls:

> At 12.26 the tail gunner reported the high and low formations in position as the English Coast slipped by below us. Overhead, waves of P-47 escort fighters appeared. Below was the icy Channel and ahead lay the long route yet to be covered. Light inaccurate flak to our right as we passed over the enemy coast indicated that Joe had us on course. The crew, alert and watchful, called out the presence of friendly fighters and we felt good with them around. Shortly after entering enemy territory near Aachen they had to leave us. Their departure spelled trouble. We observed enemy 'Bandits' climbing. Little black dots grew into formations of Me 109 and Fw 190 fighters, which began sweeping attacks on our formations. They came in fast from 11–11.30 o'clock direction, rolling as they fired then split 'essed' out of range. The interphone crackled: 'Fighters at one o'clock!' 'I smoked the Hell out of that one.' 'Fort down – six 'chutes!'

Luscious Lady in the 303rd Bomb Group crossed the enemy coast at 12.59 hours, flying at 24,000ft. Wilbur Klint recalls:

> From that minute until we left enemy territory at 16.42 we were under almost constant attack by every type of plane the Krauts could coax up at our altitude. As on our first Schweinfurt raid, we encountered all the usual single and twin-engine fighters plus obsolete fighters and medium bombers. Intelligence had informed us that we would be within range of 1,100 fighters. (Though subsequent reports estimated that only about half that number attacked, it seemed that 1,100 struck our group alone.) We were tucked away in the No. 6 position of the lead squadron of the lead group. While this offered a definite advantage for protection from fighters, we were hemmed in on all sides by other B-17s. Everyone was using violent evasive action, which was an added hazard. With the Forts packed in a tight defensive formation, both Bob and I were at the controls almost all the time, trying to get the most evasive action possible without ramming one of our own planes.'[25]

At 13.05 hours forty-eight P-47s of the 56th Fighter Group rendezvoused with the 3rd Division. Of the 164 B-17s assigned to the 1st only 149 remained after mechanical failures resulted in fifteen aborts and the 3rd was reduced from 160 B-17s to 142 for the same reason. Over Walcheren Island more than twenty Me 109s and Fw 190s, zooming in from over 34,000ft, attacked the 1st Division. The Thunderbolt pilots stood their ground and met the attacks at around 31,000ft – a height at which the Thunderbolt had the advantage over the enemy fighters. At 13.30 hours, at a point between Aachen and Duren, the 353rd Fighter Group, at the limit of their range, was forced to break off and return to England. They had done their job well, beating off a succession of attacks and claiming ten fighters shot down and another five damaged or destroyed for the loss of one P-47 in combat and another which crashed in England on the return leg.[26] As the 1st Division continued its southeasterly course, away from the heavily defended towns of Antwerp and Aachen, and as soon as the Thunderbolts had departed, the Luftwaffe sailed into the attack. Some 300 to 400 enemy fighters ripped through the unprotected Fortress formations amid fierce return fire from the gunners.[27] Some of the enemy fighters were specially equipped to fire rockets and cannon shells into the wings and fuselages of the B-17s to blast and scatter the tightly packed formations and make many of them easy prey for the fighters.

Captain McLaughlin recalls:

> The first big jolt came when my co-pilot riding in the tail called out. 'A large formation approaching at 5 o'clock,' which we believed to be the 40th Combat Wing and which thereafter proved to be a large gaggle of twin-engined Messerschmitts passing us on the starboard side, positioning themselves for head-on passes and firing large rockets into the midst of our formations. With no fighter protection we soon became easy targets for the German rockets and as our damaged wingman fell behind we could see the Fw 190s finishing them off with relative ease.

Crews had guessed before take-off that the Luftwaffe would be up in force, and after the 'Little Friends' had departed the next fighters the 306th Bomb Group crews saw were Germans at 3 o'clock. The lead ship piloted by Captain Charles Schoolfield and Captain Charles Flannagan was one of many that carried an extra 12,000 rounds of ammunition. Three B-17s in the 306th Group had already turned back with mechanical problems, the last leaving at 13.20 hours just as the Luftwaffe were beginning their attack. The fifteen remaining B-17s fought off the persistent attacks with as much firepower as they could muster. George Roberts aboard *Cavalier* recalls:

> The intense battle began with the Me 109s flying right between the Squadrons, ignoring the fire from the bombers. It was the most daring attack I had seen to date. The Germans were determined to stop the formations at any cost. The *Cavalier* was being raked with enemy fire. Quite suddenly, the plane shuddered from an explosion in the waist section. Sergeant Eugene Kelly called to say that a 20mm shell had hit his partner Sergeant Robert Webber. I went back and noted Webber was bleeding from the upper right leg and the pelvic area. We moved him to the ledge near the ball turret. Kelly injected morphine, applied a sulfa pad and covered him with a blanket. As I was returning to my gun, an explosion in the radio room ruined my transmitter. At the same time my oxygen supply dropped to zero.

> I plugged into an emergency tank, which I turned on about once per minute. This fifteen minute supply was to last me for two hours.
>
> Ball turret gunner Robert Hill called on the interphone that he was out of ammunition and needed his guns reloaded. Kelly told him that he also was out of ammo in the waist and a little too busy to come to his aid. I told Hill that there was no spare ammo and no way that I could help him reload. He replied: 'Load me up or I'm coming out of this tin can.' I said to stay in, move his guns around and pretend to be firing to discourage fighter attacks. His return words were, 'Like Hell, these guys are checked out and they are going to press the attack without fear of fire!' Lieutenant Kirk gave Hill permission to leave the ball and take over the waist gun left by the injured Webber. An ammo check revealed that all gun positions were nearly out of bullets. Kirk told us to conserve our ammo and fire only short bursts and as the fighter got close he would take evasive action when the fighter, coming from the rear, had lined up on us. Sergeant Cecil Poff in the tail and I in the radio room called each time we saw tracers coming from lined up fighters with the advice to: 'Kick it Sir.' This manouevre probably did more than anything to save us. I noted several planes with smoking engines and/or feathered propellers. As we approached the bomb run I saw seven 'chutes at 9 o'clock low and a B-17 in a slow spin.[28]

At 14.00 hours 1st Lieutenant Douglas H White in the 367th Squadron was the first to be shot out of formation by the German rocket-firing fighters, after taking hits in the horizontal stabilizer. White's Fortress, a new B-17G, went down and exploded. Only the radio operator survived. 1st Lieutenant Willard H Lockyear's B-17 was hit at about the same time by rockets, and three engines were set on fire. The radio room also erupted in flames and 2nd Lieutenant Paul N Welton, the navigator, and 1st Lieutenant Albert J Nagy, the bombardier, were killed in the nose of the aircraft. The stricken aircraft finally fell at Neuweld. The rest of the crew managed to bale out but the ball turret gunner later died in hospital from internal injuries.

The fight reached a crescendo and *Queen Jeannie* flown by 2nd Lieutenant Robert 'Bob' McCallum was shot down.[29] 1st Lieutenant Vernon K Cole's B-17 in the 423rd Squadron also went down, hit by a rocket-firing Ju 88, which set the bomb bay on fire.[30] The 306th gunners fought back. At 14.10 hours Staff Sergeant William L Threatt Jnr, a waist gunner in 1st Lieutenant Virgil H Jeffries' B-17, lead ship in the first element in the 423rd Squadron, shot down a Fw 190 and damaged another. Technical Sergeant James S Porter, the top turret gunner, aimed at a gaggle of four Ju 88s and scored hits on one of the attackers just as it fired off two rockets. The Ju 88's right engine appeared to leave its mounting and the fighter spun away out of control. Porter himself was hit in the leg by a machine-gun bullet but he stuck to his task and hit another fighter, which burst into flames. Henry C Cordery, co-pilot, recalls:

> We were under constant attack. I don't know how long the first attacks lasted but there was a lull. I left my position to get more ammo from the radio room. Passing through the waist I found the right waist gunner, Michele, severely wounded. His leg was off. The left waist gunner was also wounded. I called Lieutenant Moon, the bombardier. He came back and we both administered first aid. I took the protective covering off the needle of the morphine only to discover it was frozen. I must have had at least five uncovered and I put them all in my mouth to thaw them. I had considerable difficulty getting them out, as my hands were numb from the cold. Then I returned to my position and just about in time, as the attacks started again.

At 14.15 hours a combination of flak and fighters shot down 1st Lieutenant John D Jackson's B-17[31] over Friesburg. In the 369th Squadron, *The Wicked WAAC*[32] flown by 1st Lieutenant George C Bettinger and *Piccadilly Commando* piloted by 1st Lieutenant Gustav S Holmstrom had also been lost.[33] In the 367th Squadron, 1st Lieutenant Richard Butler's B-17 was also in trouble, as Jim Harris, the tail gunner recalls:[34]

> We had seen our Squadron and our Group picked off one by one. Problems began as we crossed the French Coast when flak practically tore off the right stabilizer. The tail section was vibrating badly. A few miles into France our rival crew in the 369th Squadron aborted for reasons unknown to us. Our navigator reported after an oxygen check that we had only enough oxygen to reach the target. We had just reasons to abort, but it would have taken more nerve to turn back than to continue on. This was a maximum effort mission, so we kept going. We had a few P-47 escorts, which had to turn back due to limited fuel. The German fighters hit us as soon as our escort left. I had never seen so many enemy fighters and planes of various types. The single engine Fw 190s and Me 109s rolled through the bomb groups, twin engined planes beyond our range lobbed rockets at us, as bombers dropped aerial bombs from above into our formations. When we saw the fighters flying through their own flak, it was evident that they were going all out to stop us. The intercom was bedlam with crewmembers calling out fighter attacks. It got so bad that it didn't do any good to call them out. Our plane was shot up pretty bad, with three engines on fire. We were forced to bale out near the target.[35]

For a little over three hours, from 13.33 to 16.47 hours, exceptionally large numbers of enemy fighters attacked the 1st Division. The worst of these took place between Aachen and the Frankfurt area, and the out-of-position 305th Bomb Group suffered worst of all. Three B-17s in the Chelveston outfit had already turned back, one with a broken exhaust stack, one with an oxygen leak and a third that had lost its way during forming up. Fifteen remained but any semblance to a group formation was non-existent and it was every squadron for itself![36] When the attacks began the high squadron was at 22,000ft and the low was at 21,400 feet. Far ahead of these two units was Major Charles G Y Normand's four-ship lead squadron at 21,700 feet. At first it was the low squadron that bore the brunt of the attacks, where none came in for rougher treatment than *Sizzle* and Lieutenant Douglas L Murdock's crew in the 'tail-end Charlie' slot in the Purple Heart Corner. Three Fw 190s led by Major Johannes Seifert, CO of II./JG 26, came in from the tail firing their 20mm cannons and hit *Sizzle* hard in the first pass. Ted Smith, co-pilot recalls:

> An explosion occurred between the No. 1 and 2 engines, stunning both Murdock and me. On coming to, we recovered control of the plane but realized both engines were out and that we were way out of formation. We also realized it was impossible to get back to the formation or to the deck in time to save the crew as six or eight Fw 190s and Me 109s were chewing us up at close range. I ordered the crew out, flipped the auto-flight control on and baled out. Murdock was to follow but I never saw him again. The toggelier and the navigator[37] had already left when I checked their positions on the way past. Bill Menzies was the only crewmember I ever saw again.[38]

Seven minutes after the fighting commenced the 305th began to come apart. In just five minutes (from 13.40 until 13.45) four of the group's B-17s crashed west of the German border. Three went down in Holland and one in Belgium.

2nd Lieutenant Dennis J McDarby[39] had been playing 'catch up' since the mid morning group assembly over England. Once again he was out of his No. 3 position behind the low squadron, with the low squadron still trailing Major Normand. McDarby was still struggling to recover from Normand's earlier, rapid acceleration that had left the high and low squadrons behind and far too spread out. The McDarby crew had become a straggler and was a target for German fighters. The top turret gunner, Technical Sergeant Arthur E Linrud recalls:[40]

> From my position in the upper gun turret, I could see enemy planes in varying numbers high above us, climbing to altitude to attack our bomber formations and all around us. Shortly, it became a matter of picking out one, getting it in the gun sight and squeezing off several

bursts from the twin .50 caliber machine guns until it swept past, above or below, then repeating the action when another wave of fighters came in. Unless a plane blew up or smoked badly while in his sights, the gunner could not know if he damaged or shot one down. There wasn't time to look to check the results. One thing was for sure: an enemy caught in the gunner's sight was greeted with a hailstorm of bullets and red streamers of tracers as it came within range.[41] The attack continued unabated. Fw 190s and Me 109s came diving at high speed, cannon and guns flashing along the leading edge of their wings. Occasionally, one dove through our formation, barely missing a bomber. Previously, the enemy was cautious, today was different. This was a reckless and fierce last encounter for many airmen on both sides.

As we moved deeper into enemy country, our bombers were damaged at an increasing rate. Unable to keep up, the damaged B-17s fell behind, then turned back, hoping to be lucky enough to make it to the Channel where Air Sea Rescue might get them out of the cold water. Going back with a damaged bomber meant probable attacks and a tense fight until one or the other went down. The more fortunate crewmembers were able to parachute to earth. Smoke poured from a bomber behind us and to our right. The next time I looked, it had pulled away from the formation and was in a dive, on fire and out of control. As I turned my turret to fire I could see that no part of the formation was escaping attack.

Our plane shook violently from the impact and explosion of a cannon shell, or rocket, that smashed into the rear of the No. 2 engine. It ripped a hole in the leading edge and left a smoking mass of ruin, just a few feet from my turret and the Pilot's position.

Fortunately, McDarby was not injured and quickly got the plane under control. However, we were unable to stay in the formation. As we dropped down and fell back, McDarby checked the crewmembers, who were OK and reported that there was no way we could make it to the target with our bomb load. We would dump the bombs and go to low level and attempt to fight our way back to cloud cover to escape the fighters who were pressing the attack now that we were without the protection of the formation. As we descended, bullets hitting the fuselage had the sound of hailstones on a tin roof. The smoke from the No. 2 engine turned into flames. Fanned by the slipstream, they reached the fuel tanks. Soon a huge ball of fire trailed past our tail section. A call on the interphone got me out of the turret. Lieutenant Donald Breeden, the co-pilot, motioned me to the cockpit. McDarby said, 'Remove the escape hatch cover. We'll never get this fire out now.' I snapped my parachute pack in place, climbed down, grabbed the emergency hatch release and gave the door a kick with my foot. It disappeared. As if by magic a hole cut

> out into the sky appeared. I was climbing back up to the cabin, when McDarby touched my head and said, 'Bale out, I've already given the order. The wing is going to break off. We're coming too.'
>
> I went back and sat with my feet hanging out the door. Glancing into the nose section, I saw navigator Lieutenant William Martin and bombardier Lieutenant Harvey Manley getting ready to follow me. With a quick departing wave, I gripped the 'D' ring and tumbled out into space. Onrushing air alerted me to give a firm pull on the 'D' ring. There was a sudden slap in my face from the chest parachute pack as it passed upward, then a jolt as the 'chute filled with air. Being suspended in the quietness was a contrast to the clatter and vibration of machine guns, tension of battle and the roar of engines. How quickly it had changed! The roar of a German plane passing overhead, too close for comfort, quickly brought me to reality. Several 'chutes were visible in the sky. Our plane, below and to one side, was falling out of control. The burning wing had broken off. The ground moved up to meet me. What before seemed like small dots were German civilians and soldiers moving to intercept landing airmen. I came down in a small field, landing on my feet but falling to the ground from the impact. After getting to my feet I heard that statement that would become familiar: 'For you the war is over,' spoken by a soldier with a pistol pointed at me.[42]

Next to go down was 2nd Lieutenant Gerald B Eakle's B-17. Staff Sergeant Herman E Molen, the toggelier, was cut on the neck by a piece of flying plexiglas and the navigator received wounds in both legs from shell fragments. An intercom check indicated that the waist area of the plane was 'like a sieve'. Alone and unable to keep up with the remainder of the 364th Squadron, Eakle did a diving 180° turn and headed for home, but they never made it. Further fighter attacks wrecked the aircraft and Eakle gave the order to bale out. He and eight of the crew survived. Lieutenant Charles W Willis Jnr and five of his crew baled out over Holland four miles west of the German border after their B-17 was hit repeatedly by single and twin engined fighters firing shells and rockets into the formation. As the B-17s entered Germany *The Uncouth Bastard* flown by 2nd Lieutenant Robert W Holt was shot down and he and five crew were killed. Only Bill Frierson and three other gunners got out alive.

Lazy Baby flown by 2nd Lieutenant Edward W Dienhart was knocked out of formation. The throttle controls for No. 1 and 2 engines were shot away. No. 3 engine was dead and a huge hole in the right wing fuel tank trailed a stream of gas that could ignite at any moment. A shell burst against the B-17's plexiglas nose. It badly wounded bombardier Carl Johnson and navigator Lieutenant Donald F Rowley, 'a sunny optimistic golden boy from California ... an athletic Los Angeles native with arms like oak branches who could do ten pushups at a clip [and who] never smoked, drank or swore ...' The navigator, whose arms were nearly blown off in the explosion, plotted the B-17 crew's route to Switzerland even as he slowly bled to death. Another explosion had broken radioman Hurley 'Smitty' Smith's left arm and riddled him with shrapnel. Staff Sergeant Bernie Segal, tail gunner, was anxious about the idea of baling out over Germany as he was Jewish. Incredibly, *Lazy Baby* made it to neutral territory and when Ed Dienhart belly-landed the badly ravaged B-17 in a sloping potato field at Reinach-Aesch, Donald Rowley ribbed his pilot that it was the best landing he had ever made. The young navigator, who the crew used to tease for being such a Boy Scout but who they all secretly admired him for it just the same, died from his wounds that same evening. He was buried four days later in Basle's Hornli cemetery.[43]

Approaching the Rhine the B-17 flown by Flight Officer Verl D Fisher, the *Mary T* flown by 2nd Lieutenant Robert S Lang, *Lallah-V III*[44] piloted by 2nd Lieutenant Ellsworth H Kenyon, and 2nd Lieutenant Robert T Skerry's B-17, were shot down.[45] Four men were killed aboard Fisher's B-17. One of them was Thomas Therrien, who before trying to exit the doomed plane helped the wounded radio operator and the other waist gunner out. Just as Therrien prepared to jump through the waist window a 20mm shell exploded next to him and killed him.

Luftgaukommando VI awarded the downing of Skerry's B-17 to six German flak units who had reported no fighters in the area. JG 26 *'Schlageter'* however, awarded the B-17 to Oberfeldwebel Willi Roth of 5./JG 26. When Skerry gave the order to bale out, he had run out of options. The B-17 had two engines shut down and feathered, one of which was on fire, most of the tail surfaces were gone and there was a large hole in the radio room. The Fortress was being shot to pieces from both ends and flak was bursting all around the front of the ship while fighters were attacking from the rear. When it hit the ground the B-17 was 29 miles behind Normand's lead squadron.[46] By the time the 305th Bomb Group could see the city of Schweinfurt, 12 miles in the distance, it had lost ten aircraft including all five in the low squadron and parts of the high and lead squadrons. Only five B-17s remained and a Fortress from another group joined them.[47]

The 92nd was also badly hit as Captain McLaughlin recalls: 'Under the pressure of continued heavy attacks our ranks were soon greatly decimated. After three hours, as we closed our formation for the target run, my group looked more like a squadron. We had but twelve airplanes left out of the twenty-one we took off with.'

Bill Rose captained one of the 92nd crews that reached the target:

The Germans rose to meet us in full force. It was indescribable. This was the first time I had any thoughts that we were in for a fight. Fighters were everywhere. Rather than calling out when one was spotted, the gunners just shot. Everyone had his own target. I called Keith Kent my waist gunner to get the fighter on his side. He replied, 'Don't bother me, my gun's jammed. I'll get him in a minute.' He was so calm I thought we were back in gunnery school. I will always remember our tail gunner, Wally Eilers, reporting that we were going to get some protection from the rear by a group of Forts. We thought we weren't going to have the attacks on the tail like we had been getting on our last two missions. When they got close, he saw they were German multi-engine planes. Then, all of a sudden, 'Oh my God!' They fired a salvo of rockets into our formation. I was fortunate in that one went right past my window. The rocket landed right in the wing of the element leader right by a gas tank. I watched it burn and it wasn't long before the entire wing was on fire. The pilot dropped back and the stricken crew baled out. Eventually, the B-17 blew up. It was a terrible sight to see. I slid into his position and was the lone plane in the second element. The attacks continued. Our ball turret gunner pleaded for someone to help him get out. His guns were broken and the turret jammed. All he could see were planes going down out of control and in flames. He was trapped. No one could be spared from his guns. When he became emotional I told him, 'Get off the interphone, we will get to you as soon as possible.'

Phillip R Taylor in the 91st Bomb Group did not know what squadron his B-17 finally joined, but they ended up as a lead ship:

We had our wing plane shot away three times. One scene remains as clear now as the day it happened. From the left waist position I watched one of the wing ships get hit and immediately start to burn. The pilot slipped the ship out of formation and held it steady so the crew could bale out. Within seconds she was really burning. The co-pilot looked up and saw me watching. He made no attempt to leave the ship or save himself. Instead, he waved at me. I waved back until she blew up a couple hundred yards out. There were only a couple of 'chutes out, one of which got tangled in the tail. That co-pilot, knowing he was about to die, did one of the coolest gestures I have ever seen.[48]

The 3rd Division encountered some fighter opposition, but it was not as intense as that experienced by the 1st Division. Only two Fortresses were shot down before the Thunderbolt escort withdrew. Bob Hughes, flying in the 100th Bomb Group formation, recalls:

We were a little south of our course and about four minutes late. We could hear chatter on the radio from units and their escorts ahead

> of us, who seemed to be drawing enemy fighters. We seemed to be getting much less action than the 95th and 390th Bomb Groups in our wing.

It was still an unnerving experience as Jerry Lefors recalls:

> As co-pilot without a gun to fire, you sit and watch. Three enemy fighters coming through our formation firing and being fired upon as they rolled upside down and peeled off below us fascinated me. About one out of three aircraft doing this maneuver went down in smoke. The intercom was busy at the beginning of the attacks: 'Fighters 1 o'clock high . . . .' As the attacks gained in intensity – they were coming from all directions – the gunners were quieter, but I'm sure they weren't bored!

The 3rd Division had proceeded on a converging course with the 1st Division towards Aachen. At 14.10 hours the 1st Division, now flying an almost parallel course to the 3rd Division, arrived at a point 25 miles north of Frankfurt where it was to change course and head south-south-east for the River Main. This was designed to deceive the German defences into thinking that Augsburg or Munich was their destination. About 10 miles south of the River Main, the 1st Division turned sharply onto a northeasterly heading for Schweinfurt.

By the time it entered the target area, the 1st Division had lost thirty-six bombers shot down and twenty turned back, but the 3rd Division had come off surprisingly lightly, losing only two bombers to fighter attacks. This left a total of 224 Fortresses to win through to the target itself. Collectively, this seems a reasonable force but most of the groups in the 1st Division had been torn to shreds by the intense fighter attacks and some were barely skeleton formations. Of the thirty-seven Fortresses in the 40th Combat Wing that had crossed the Channel, only sixteen remained – and worse losses were to follow. Crewmembers recall the dozens of great red flashes in the flak columns as they turned on the IP (Initial Point). Many called out that the enemy was using red flak, not realizing that they were in fact witnessing the explosions of many B-17s in the groups ahead. The enemy pilots showed complete disregard for the tremendous flak barrage over the target and made almost suicidal attacks on the bombers. For the moment the lead bombardier aboard the *Bad Egg* had to try and ignore the attacks as he set up the Automatic Flight Control Equipment (AFCE) that linked the aircraft's controls to the bombsight. The *Bad Egg* led the 91st over the city and at 14.39 hours they began unloading their deadly cargoes on the streets, houses and factories of Schweinfurt. Budd Peaslee described it as 'a city about to die'.

Notes

1. *In My Book You're All Heroes* by Robert E O'Hearn. Privately Published 1984.
2. *Wrong Place! Wrong Time! The 305th Bomb Group and the 2nd Schweinfurt Raid October 14 1943*. George C Kuhl. Schiffer 1993.
3. USAF Historical Research Agency, *History of the 381st Bombardment Group*, Maxwell AFB, Montgomery, Alabama.
4. 42-29952 in the 366th Bomb Squadron.
5. *Sizzle* was the last B-17 off the ground at Chelveston.
6. *Wrong Place! Wrong Time! The 305th Bomb Group and the 2nd Schweinfurt Raid October 14 1943*. George C Kuhl. Schiffer 1993.
7. *First of the Many* by Captain John R 'Tex' McCrary and David E Scherman. 1944.
8. *The Fall of the Fortresses* by Elmer Bendiner. Souvenir Press 1980.
9. 2nd Lieutenant Bohn E Fawkes' crew were given a brand new B-17G for the mission, which no one else wanted because the chin turret caused drag. The crew had been flying *Duffy's Tavern* on recent missions since losing *Tondelayo* on the mission to Stuttgart on 6 September when they were forced to ditch in the Channel.
10. 1st Lieutenant Joseph W Lukens was flying with Lieutenant William C Bisson and crew.
11. 1st Lieutenant Richard Butler was Thomas' replacement.
12. *In My Book You're All Heroes* by Robert E O'Hearn. Privately Published 1984.
13. Roy Davidson's engineer, Fred Krueger, declined the B-17 assigned to the crew (this ship, 42-3453, was flown on the first Schweinfurt raid by Lieutenant Silas Nettles' crew in the 96th Bomb Group and a windmilling engine contributed to their demise near the IP) and Davidson was allocated *Wolf Pack* instead. Nettles' crew meanwhile, flew the mission in the 100th Bomb Group formation.
14. The 333rd Bomb Squadron was used at Rougham as a fill-in squadron. This meant that crews were usually given the tail-end positions.
15. Unfortunately for Davidson and the mission as a whole, unpredictable weather would intervene before take-off and effectively end the Liberators' participation in the mission.
16. *In My Book You're All Heroes* by Robert E O'Hearn. Privately Published 1984.
17. William 'Bill' Allen flew 103 missions including some on a second tour in the 350th Bomb Squadron, 100th Bomb Group.
18. These two groups would fly in the 13th Wing, the last wing in the 3rd Division task force.
19. The 60 Liberators in the 2nd Air Division took-off from their airfields in Norfolk and Suffolk but only 24 arrived at the rendezvous point. The remaining 25 managed to link up with 53 P-47s of the 352nd Fighter Group but such a small force would have been decimated by the Luftwaffe and the flak guns, so both fighters and bombers aborted after circling for half-an-hour. The B-24s and their P-47 escort were redirected on a diversionary sweep over the North Sea as far as the Friesian Islands to aid the Fortress formations.
20. *In My Book You're All Heroes* by Robert E O'Hearn. Privately Published 1984.
21. *In My Book You're All Heroes* by Robert E O'Hearn. Privately Published 1984.

22. Seventeen B-17s in the 305th Bomb Group led by Major Charles G Y Normand had taken off from Chelveston six minutes late and, after completing assembly, had been unable to find either the 92nd or 306th Groups. Normand led his group first to Daventry and then to Spalding without sighting the rest of the 40th Wing. He tried in vain to contact Peaslee by radio, but about 30 miles short of the enemy coast the 305th caught sight of the 351st and 91st Bomb Groups of the 1st Combat Wing. Normand's B-17s filled the still vacant low group spot provided by the absence of the 381st Bomb Group, which had taken longer to assemble than anticipated due to a 10,000ft overcast which hung over Ridgewell. Eventually, Major George Shacklady's 16 aircraft finally caught up with the 1st Combat wing over the Channel and moved in next to the 351st Bomb Group in the high position.
23. *In My Book You're All Heroes* by Robert E O'Hearn. Privately Published 1984.
24. Though Sam Mehaffey did not get to Schweinfurt, he had his share of the excitement and fright. In the following months, he flew many more missions with several crews in just about every position in the formations, from tail-end-Charlies to lead crews and finished a tour of 32 missions on 23 July 1944.
25. *In My Book You're All Heroes* by Robert E O'Hearn. Privately Published 1984.
26. This, the only US fighter lost on the mission was shot down by Addi Glunz of 5th *Staffel* JG 26 near Budel at 14.00 hours. See *The JG 26 War Diary Vol. 2* by Donald Caldwell. Grub Street, London. 1998.
27. Bf 110s of the *Zerstörergruppen* and Fw 190A-5/R6s and Bf 109Gs of JG 1, JG 3, JG 26 and JG 27 carried two underwing *Wurfgranaten* W Gr. 210mm rocket tubes for the unguided W Gr. 21 *Dodel* missile. II./JG 26 were the first to test these in battle but they were too cumbersome for single-engined fighter aircraft and it was decided to equip the *Zerstörer*, or heavy twin-engined fighter units, with the rocket devices instead. Fw 190s and Bf 109Gs carried a streamlined and jettisonable underbelly *Rüstsatz R3* or auxiliary 66-gallon (300 litre) drop tank for long-range missions.
28. *In My Book You're All Heroes* by Robert E O'Hearn. Privately Published 1984.
29. McCallum and his co-pilot, 2nd Lieutenant Homer D Fitzer, who was flying his first mission, and three others were KIA. Five men were taken prisoner.
30. The radio operator and ball turret gunner were both killed by rocket fragments. One of the waist gunners failed to bale out and Cole, who elected to remain in the aircraft to allow the others to bale out, was blown out in the subsequent explosion and his body was found later, hanging in his parachute from a tree.
31. 42-30710 in the 423rd Bomb Squadron. Jackson went down with his aircraft and Bernard Bernstein, navigator, was killed as he baled out. Two gunners were also KIA. The rest of the crew landed safely.
32. 42-30199. 1 Evaded, 1 KIA, 8 PoW.
33. *Piccadilly Commando* had lost its No. 4 engine in one of the first attacks, but it had been feathered successfully and Holmstrom managed to maintain formation. Just past Frankfurt a large hole appeared in the left wing and fuel began streaming out. The pilot asked Flight Officer Philip D Anderson, his navigator, for a heading to Switzerland, but just as Holmstrom pulled out of formation a German fighter followed and opened fire. *Piccadilly Commando* went into a climb and Holmstrom ordered the crew to bale out. Anderson and 1st Lieutenant Jack A Kelly, the bombardier, went out through the nose hatch and were never found. Holmstrom and five of the crew survived.

34. *In My Book You're All Heroes* by Robert E O'Hearn. Privately Published 1984.
35. The B-17 had been hit on the bomb run between Würzburg and Schweinfurt; three engines were hit and one was on fire when Butler pushed the bale-out alarm button. All the crew baled out safely before the aircraft exploded and were captured. Jim Harris concludes: 'I was picked up by a farmer and was soon joined by our navigator, Ken McCaleb who had landed near me. We were taken to a military post of some sort. Later that night we were transported to a fighter base where we were kept for a few days. Many of us at the fighter base were wounded, some seriously. I had a minor shrapnel wound in my shoulder and had injured my back when my 'chute opened. We were given no medical treatment. As a point of interest, I had learned to respect the German fighter pilot for his skill and courage. However, while confined at the fighter base I learned that our regular bombardier, Joe Lukens [who flew with 1st Lieutenant William C Bisson], was strafed and killed in his 'chute. I also learned that others had been hanged and shot by civilians. German pilots came to the room where we were held. The younger pilots were very arrogant and boastful. The older pilots were altogether different. They apologized for the actions of their younger cohorts when we complained.'

    In the lead ship, one of Schoolfield's waist gunners, Technical Sergeant Robert J Conley, was seriously wounded in the left hand by an exploding 20mm cannon shell. Staff Sergeant Bert Perlmutter, the other waist gunner, applied a tourniquet and Conley returned to his guns, shooting down a Fw 190 at 150 yards. Conley passed out and after recovering returned to man his guns again. He later received the DFC for his action.
36. While leading his lone group across the North Sea, Major Normand had attempted several long turns to try to join the wing following. He finally elected to speed up and try to join the wing in front, which he thought was the 40th but which turned out to be the 1st Wing. Normand slowed to this wing's speed and took over the vacant low group position left by the absent 381st Bomb Group, which when it did arrive, took a high position on the right of the 351st Bomb Group. The 305th's epitaph is contained in the 1st CBW history which recorded, 'Fortunately for us, the 305th, which was unable to find its own gang, came along with us and flew low box on our incomplete wing formation. This they did at their own expense ...'
37. Staff Sergeant John E Miller and Lieutenant John C Manahan, respectively.
38. *Sizzle* was much lower than the other bombers and had come under attack from three Fw 190s led by Major Johannes Seifert of the 3rd *Staffel* JG 26. They came in from the tail and Staff Sergeant William B Menzies, the 17-year old tail gunner, claimed a hit on one of them (Unteroffizier Horst Richter of 3rd *Staffel* in Fw 190A-4 5807 'Yellow 9' was KIA), as they went by. As *Sizzle* passed over the northern outskirts of Maastricht, Seifert broke off the engagement as *Sizzle* rolled over on its left wing and began to spin. At 13.40 it crashed near Limmel, a small Dutch village north of Maastricht and several miles east of the Belgian border. Shortly after the crash, the bomb load exploded. Murdock, if not already dead as a result of enemy gunfire, died in the crash. Smith, Menzies and Sergeant John W Lloyd, ball turret gunner, all landed safely. They were captured within 15 minutes of each other in the vicinity of Maastricht. Technical Sergeant Thelma B Wiggins, radio operator, had been wounded in the right heel by shell fragments just prior to baling out through

the waist exit. He landed right beside a canal nearly 16 miles southwest of his crewmates at Tongeren, well inside the Belgian border. He now went into hiding with some newfound friends. Sergeant Lester J Levy, right waist gunner, hit the ground. He was captured immediately and spent several weeks in the hospital. Later that day, Technical Sergeant Russell Kiggens, engineer and waist gunner, and Staff Sergeant Tony E Dienes were found dead in the wreckage. Kiggens was last seen stepping down from the top turret and seemed fine but for some reason he never made it out of the B-17. The severely wounded and unconscious Dienes was last seen lying on the floor by the left waist and had no chance to jump. John C Manahan's parachute failed to open and he fell on the dike of a canal. He was discovered lying with his unopened 'chute later that day by two civilian workers. It was rumoured that after baling out John E Miller joined the Dutch Underground and was active with them until his death on 26 March 1945.

39. Flying 42-3436 in the 364th Bomb Squadron.
40. *In My Book You're All Heroes* by Robert E O'Hearn. Privately Published 1984.
41. One of the attackers, 23-year-old Feldwebel Helmut F Brinkmann of 7./JG 1 flying a Bf 109 was shot down by fire from several of McDarby's gunners. The 109 went into a steep dive and crashed near Haanrade, Holland. The pilot's remains were never found. *Wrong Place! Wrong Time! The 305th Bomb Group and the 2nd Schweinfurt Raid October 14 1943*. George C Kuhl. Schiffer 1993.
42. McDarby's Fortress went down and crashed at Maastricht. Linrud, tail gunner Dominic Lepore, ball turret gunner Ben Roberts, radio operator Hosea Crawford and McDarby survived and were captured. Five others were KIA.
43. *Legacy of Lazy Baby* by Jean-Pierre Wilhelm, *Reader's Digest*, October 1993. Jean-Pierre Wilhelm and his friends were among those who arrived at the crash scene only minutes after the crash. '[We were] tingling with excitement at the prospect of seeing our heroes up close. But when I dropped my bike and ran to where a small crowd of locals had gathered what I saw was horrifying. My heroes were there all right but the "invulnerable" Flying Fortress was nothing more than a smoking shrapnel-riddled wreck splattered with gore and reeking of aviation fuel. The crew's uniforms were stained with blood; their faces lined with tension. They looked suspiciously like ordinary human beings.' Donald Rowley's young widow Jerrie would later receive her husband's Silver Star.
44. 42-30242.
45. Kenyon's radio operator was killed and the other nine survived to become PoW. Later that evening as the four officers of the Kenyon crew sat in their adjacent prison cells, they were visited by a 21 or 22-year-old German officer who claimed to be the Fw 190 pilot who shot them down. He offered to take them to dinner but the Americans declined.
46. B-17 42-30814 crashed about 220 yards short of the village of Adendorf, about 40 miles east of the Belgian border and about 8 miles southwest of Bonn 1 KIA. Eight men, including Skerry, were taken prisoner.
47. See *Wrong Place! Wrong Time! The 305th Bomb Group and the 2nd Schweinfurt Raid October 14 1943*. George C Kuhl. Schiffer 1993.
48. Phil Taylor and his crew survived and finished their 25 missions. On his second tour he completed 15 more missions as a bombardier.

CHAPTER 2

Black Thursday

Looking back now I have to admire the courage of Harry Hughes as I listened to him on the aircraft interphone coolly directing Edward O'Grady to the target amidst the constant rock and roll of the exploding flak shells and fighter attacks. We had to calm down one of our leaders whose anxiety overcame him and he began to interrupt the interphone conversation during the bomb run by muttering to himself and damning the Germans!

Captain James K McLaughlin, 92nd Bomb Group

For *Flakhelpers* like 16-year old Gerald Bellosa, whose family home was destroyed by a bomb, 14 October was a horrendous experience similar to that of the 17th of August. 'It was the day we received our baptism of fire,' says Bellosa:

> The 14th of October was a beautiful fall day with sunshine and blue skies. Then, suddenly, a plane-position announcement: 'Several hundred enemy aircraft heading from Maastricht at a speed of 450km, southeasterly course.' And then the following further report: 'Schweinfurt in danger again!' At 2:07 pm the alarm bells started ringing a second time. That means: Be ready for action! We dashed to the guns and the fire-control equipment. In the rush many of us had forgotten to put on our ear protectors: one had even forgotten his helmet. Our emplacement in Euerbach was not completely finished at that time. Our gun carriages were in the open fields and protective mounds had not been built up yet. Soon the contrails of the first large bomber unit of the Americans appeared in the sky. Their target was obvious: the city of Schweinfurt. Our fire control equipment registered the formation immediately. The major battery at Ettleben opened fire at 2:35 pm; shortly afterwards all the other batteries around Schweinfurt did the same.
>
> Our first volley was a relief from the tremendous tension we were under. Every time we fired we opened our mouths to reduce the

effect of the report. Every three seconds the alarm bell rang. That means: volley fire from all guns! The loading gunners did heavy physical labour at the large gun barrels, which were pointing sharply upwards. At 2:38 pm the first bombs fell on the industrial section of the town. Wave after wave of Flying Fortresses dropped their deadly burdens. The bomber units were easy to recognize in the clear autumn sky. The town, too, was clearly visible from above. A smoke screen was not used because it would have risen under these weather conditions and would have made focusing accurately on a target more difficult. In spite of heavy anti-aircraft artillery fire and the constant attacks by German interceptors, the bombers flew a well-disciplined and accurate mission. The enemy aircraft were densely surrounded by the air-bursts of anti-aircraft shells. Trails of smoke joined the contrails of the hit bombers, which then had to go their own ways. We continued to fire at top speed. At 2:56 pm the last wave of bombers appeared and soon afterwards the flak ceased firing.

Large dark, in some places blood-red, clouds of smoke and dust hung over the city. Often only afterwards were we stricken with fear. We 16-year-olds had to overcome it each in his own way.

Every one of us does his duty! The attack and resistance had not left us any time to think things over. Only afterwards did we realize that a single hit in our completely unprotected emplacement would have been a devastating disaster.

The 91st was to claim the best overall bombing results for the 1st Division. However, the 351st Bomb Group was the most accurate, with Captain H D Wallace, squadron bombardier in part of the group formation, placing all his bombs within 1,000ft of the MPI (Mean Point of Impact). The composite group led by Major John R Blaylock, whose lead bombardier was 1st Lieutenant Jim Bradley, also did a commendable job on hitting the ball-bearing factories at the target. After the mission, the crew would be ordered to report to the Eighth Air Force Headquarters to receive a commendation for a job well done. Jim Bradley recalls:[1]

We had great fighter protection to Aachen, Germany. When our Spits and P-47s left, the German Air Force was ready with a fighting welcome. The group to our rear was wiped out by the time we started the bomb run at Würzburg. When one German unit left, another took its place. I was a voluntary non-shooter, explaining to the crew that my hands were like those of a fine concert pianist and I could not get my bombing fingers tight from the recoil of the fifty caliber guns. Actually, I had grazed a couple of B-17s on a prior mission. For the good of the Eighth Air Force, I decided that I was too lousy in my

> shooting to risk the lives of the other crews. Major Blayloc perfect pilot, cool and poised. I had trained with him a nu times over the Irish Sea just to give me practice in turning a g wing. Another group tried to cut in front of us on the bomb run, but we won in a game of 'Chicken' with them and didn't change course. I always took from five to seven minutes to set up the course and rate to drop the bombs. At the last second, the lights didn't come on, so I had to salvo six bombs and the bomb-bay gas tank. The cross hairs never moved after the bombsight clicked and the bombs were dropped. On the final run Paul Post lost an eye and the other waist gunner lost a leg. As we turned away from the target and headed back to England I went to the waist of the ship and closed the two side gun ports and tried to comfort the wounded. I feel badly that I wasn't a better medic who possibly could have saved Paul's eye. I couldn't tell him what was wrong with his eye, since there was no blood. The gunner's wound was in the upper groin area, so it was necessary to wrap it in telephone cable to stop the blood.[2]

Minutes from the IP Lieutenant Victor C Maxwell's B-17 became the eleventh Fortress to be lost from the 305th Bomb Group formation when it came under heavy fighter attack and spun out of formation on fire. Maxwell and six of the crew died trapped in the bomber and only three gunners got out. 2nd Lieutenant Alden C Kincaid on Major Normand's right wing had been wounded in the right arm by machine-gun fire and Lieutenant Norman W Smith lay slumped in his seat. He had been dead for almost an hour. Four minutes into the bomb run Kincaid's plane took a number of direct hits from 20mm cannon fire and two engines were put out of action. Kincaid ordered everyone out and he and six of his crew made it. *Sundown Sal* flown by Ray Bullock was hit during the same attack that downed Kincaid's aircraft and a 20mm cannon shell lodged in the fuel cell of the left wing and set it on fire. Bullock still had six minutes to fly before reaching the target and *Sundown Sal* could blow up at any minute, but he told his crew that they could bale out if they liked but he was going to complete the bomb run before leaving. All his crew agreed to stick with him until after bombs away. Bullock's burning B-17 and Barney Farrell's *Rigor Mortis* remained in formation with the lead ship flown by 2nd Lieutenant Joseph W Kane. Lieutenant Joe Pellegrini could see the target in his bombsight and knew he could hit it but Normand did not think they could hold it on the run. Pellegrini, who had already set the cross hairs of the bombsight on the aiming point, begged Normand, 'Major, please let me continue this run. Visibility is perfect; we can't miss!' But Normand decided to follow the 91st Bomb Group and ordered Pellegrini to bomb with them. Unfortunately the eighteen 1,000lb bombs dropped from the three B-17s in the 305th Bomb Group fell in a civilian neighborhood. Immediately after 'Bombs away' *Sundown Sal* became the unlucky thirteenth and final victim in the 305th Bomb Group formation when it was abandoned by Bullock's crew who all baled out successfully. Joe Kane's and Barney Farrell's B-17 turned away from the target and followed the lead group home.[3]

Then it was the turn of the 40th Combat Wing. McLaughlin and his bombardier, Edward T O'Grady, conferred over the interphone and as the bomber rolled out on a heading towards Schweinfurt they hooked up to the AFCE. Ahead of them was the daunting sight of the 1st Wing almost blotted from sight by the concentrated flak barrage. Flying in the No. 5 slot in the 92nd Bomb Group formation directly beneath Peaslee and McLaughlin was Bill Rose:

> I had positioned my plane directly under our squadron leader to give us protection from the top and both sides. I looked straight up when the bomb bay doors opened and I could see right into the bomb bay. If his bombs fell out prematurely they would fall on us so I told Mike [Erro A Michelson, bombardier] to let me know one minute before 'bombs away' so I could cut the throttles and drop back. The bombs fell right in front of the nose of our plane. When all his bombs had gone and he had closed his bomb bay doors, I tucked back in as we headed for home. In my position the German pilots had a real hard time getting at us. The only way they could get to us was to come underneath. I think this was how we were able to survive; protected in every direction apart from underneath. We came home, the four of us, one right underneath another and one out on each side. The German attacks were less intense on our return over France. We ran out of ammunition. Our oxygen system was knocked out and we stayed in formation by using our 'bale out' bottles of oxygen.

The 306th Bomb Group formation followed the 92nd Bomb Group. The fighters had left by now and, ahead and low, George Roberts aboard *Cavalier* saw:

> Several white puffs of flak which became darker and more accurate as we approached the target. The barrage did not seem as heavy as that over Bremen, but I could feel the concussion and hear the 'Woof' and the peppering of the fuselage. When the bombardier called 'Bombs away,' I checked the bomb bays to see that all bombs were out. The bomb-bay doors did not close, so Lieutenant William Pleasant the bombardier spent several minutes correcting the malfunction. Very few B-17s were left in our formation. I thought the fighters could easily finish us off. Luckily, we had only 13 minutes of new attacks, which were not as intense as before. Evidently, the German fighters had gone to attack the incoming bombers.

The 306th dropped its 1,000lb bombs. Sixteen of them exploded within a 1,920-foot circle. About twenty minutes after the target flak scored direct hits on two engines of 1st Lieutenant William C Bisson's B-17 in the 367th Bomb Squadron while enemy fighters riddled the rear of the Fortress. Only the co-pilot and four of the crew in the rear of the aircraft baled out of the doomed B-17. *En route* to the target a Ju 88 firing rockets had knocked out the No. 3 engine of the Fortress flown by 1st Lieutenant Ralph T Peters. The Fortress, which was also riddled with hundreds of flak fragments and 20mm bullet holes managed to stay in formation until after bombs away, but when the 306th Bomb Group went into a climb from the 22,500ft bombing altitude, Peters was unable to stay with them. At 15.20 hours with the No. 3 engine propeller running away Peters gave the order to bale out. 1st Lieutenant James V Vaughter, the bombardier, recalls:[4]

> The plane exploded shortly after the last man jumped. It was normal operating procedure for the bombardier to jettison the escape hatch and tumble out headfirst. The other crewmembers thought I was afraid to bale out, as I was so long at the escape hatch door. Actually, the door was jammed and I was working to get it loose. Our wing commander ordered the pilots to climb 4,000ft in an attempt to avoid some flak and reduce enemy fighter abilities at the higher altitude. The climb put sufficient extra stress on our damaged engines to cause the runaway prop. We were at 24,000ft when I tumbled out of the escape hatch. We had been briefed to free-fall when at high altitude for many reasons. This did not register with me, as I pulled the ripcord at the count of three. When German fighters were flying so close that I could see their faces quite clearly, I was wishing that I had been smarter. Crew members using chest 'chutes in lieu of seat 'chutes were able to wear only the 'chute harness and hook the 'chute to the harness to bale out. This gave us more comfort and mobility, but also the dire possibility of not having a chance to hook on our 'chutes. I cannot remember hooking on my chest pack. I cried as I was floating down in the bright sunshine that October day some 20 miles southwest of Schweinfurt. Tears came because I immediately thought about my mother, how she would worry, cry and pray about her baby boy. Crying was also the result of being frightened over the realization that I was helpless, was going to become a prisoner, was not going to make it back to Thurleigh and because I was so mad that the enemy had gotten the best of us. To this day, I don't consider myself a good loser; at times not even a good winner.[5]

As the 303rd Bomb Group turned and began the bomb run. Wilbur Klint in *Luscious Lady* saw three B-17s from the wing ahead 'completely disintegrate and fall earthward in flaming shreds. Not a chance that anyone got out of those bombers. This was our introduction to the recently developed German rocket launcher. The bomb run looked perfect. We were briefed to expect fifty-six heavy anti aircraft guns defending the target but they gave us little trouble compared to the hordes of fighters we met on the way in and who picked us up again before we were even out of the flak zone.'

Technical Sergeant Leroy Mace, ball turret gunner in *Knock-Out Dropper* flown by Lieutenant John Manning, who was leading the low squadron in the 303rd Bomb Group formation, was glad that when they finally reached the target it was covered in a large amount of flak. Mace, who was on his tenth mission, believed that as long as they were in the flak, the fighters would leave them alone. But he was surprised when they flew right through the flak to get at them:

> It was a good clear day for bombing. I watched our bombs hit the target; it was one of our best jobs ever. Then we were hit by a 20mm cannon shell that exploded and tore a terrific hole in the middle of our stabilizer. It knocked us out of formation. We dropped about 400ft and found ourselves all alone. We had never seen so many fighters! Lieutenant Manning was fighting to keep the nose of the ship down and told us to stand by to bale out, but to stand by our guns. I took off my electric heated clothing and stayed in the ball turret. One could see ships of all kinds going down. We expected to be knocked out at any time. There were 20mm shells passing all around us; we never can tell how they missed. There was a time when my guns, the tail guns and one upper turret gun were out. We finally got them all working again. Several planes that I shot at blew up. I think every gunner in the crew shot down at least two, but we did not claim them. The pilot called and said, 'Well, this looks like it!' He told us to stand by as we had an engine with a windmilling prop. We were waiting for the final word to bale out, but with God's help, we did not have to. I never left the ball. You never know what one goes through at times like this. Finally, the fighters left and we breathed a big sigh of relief. The sky was filled with parachutes, like flowers in the spring. I had never seen so many fighters in my life.

By the time Bill Heller's B-17 approached the target they were in trouble. His Fortress was carrying bomb-bay tanks with extra fuel, which proved to be a mixed blessing:

> After this extra fuel was used we found that due to a malfunction, we could not drop the tanks, even after a half hour of freezing activity by engineer Huston and bombardier DeSousa in the bomb bay at 25,000ft altitude. The crew realized that we would have to carry this additional hazard. An empty fuel tank, even on an automobile, can

be a virtual bomb if hit by a red-hot bullet or shell. The crew did not relish this prospect of sudden death, but with typical dedication and courage, wanted to put the bombs on this target of special importance.

As the formation proceeded into Germany, fighter attacks began that would continue in intensity for hours. The formation waded through literally clouds of flak. Fighters continued to harass the bombers. It became apparent that when two engines began losing power, we were unable to stay in formation. We could not continue under the present conditions of a heavy bomb load plus the extra gas tanks. The only chance of survival was to stay with the formation. I ordered the bombardier to salvo the tanks and bombs. We were then able to rejoin the formation. We flew over the target with open bomb-bay doors so as not to attract any more fighters than necessary. The bombs from the formation fell with good accuracy.

Fighters and Forts were going down everywhere. The sky seemed full of 'chutes, some burning and some peacefully floating in the sky. I saw a Fort up ahead start to smoke; the next instant a sheet of flame. Then nothing! I saw a Fortress fly upside down in a very slow roll and then dive for terra firma. Ten 'chutes popped out from it on their start of a journey to a PoW camp. The flight continued with our crew calling out fighter attacks to be followed by that comforting shudder of the fifty caliber guns firing. The fighters included twin engine and single engine planes.

Sometimes I wonder how we stayed in formation. My tail gunner Staff Sergeant Tony Laurinitis would yell through the interphone, 'Fighters coming in at 6 o'clock.' At the same time George Payne was yelling, 'Fighter coming in at 4 o'clock.' Then his guns would blaze. When gunners gave this information to the pilot, he flipped the Fortress in all attitudes to screw up the enemy's aim. Just as sure as I'd slip or dive the ship within the formation, shells would burst in clusters all about us, usually in the same spot where we were a second before. Wonderful co-operation between gunners and pilots. No wonder I loved them. It was a great moment when Tony yelled: 'I got him! There he goes!' Payne and Huston confirmed the kill as they saw the Me 110 go down and two 'chutes eject from it. We got two more that day; another Me 210 and a Fw 190. 'chutes were seen popping from both fighters.

Our left waist gunner Leo Lanier, Jnr called on the interphone to say that the left horizontal stabilizer was badly shot up. Tail gunner Laurinitis added that the fabric was gone from the top of the flipper. There was a hole in the leading edge of the wing. Inches from my head, the windshield glass was shot out. I didn't notice the damage until sweat and the condensation from my oxygen mask started to freeze. The ball turret was inoperative, which the Germans noticed

> and gave their full attention. Ball turret gunner Staff Sergeant Shultz found himself a sitting duck in a shooting gallery. I was used to doing evasive action on cue from the gunners, but was somewhat mystified by co-pilot Coppom's signals. I truly wondered, but seriously obeyed his motions. Any question in my mind was answered when just after following his motion to skid left, a great cluster of 20mm shells burst right where we had been; between Lieutenant Jokerts' Fort and mine. Jack Coppom was trained as a fighter pilot before being assigned as a B-17 co-pilot. Looking right into the sights of the fighters, he instinctively knew when they would fire. The technique worked every time.[6]

The 40th Combat Wing turned away from the target and headed in the direction of the 1st Combat Wing, now making for the French border. The withdrawal route, well away from the line of penetration, was devised by General Anderson to limit casualties and took the bombers south of Paris and then north towards England. In the 306th Bomb Group formation Henry C Cordery, the co-pilot in Lieutenant Jeffries' B-17 recalls:

> We came off the target and re-grouped. I looked around at the group and there wasn't much of us left. In my squadron we started with six ships in two three-ship elements and being in the lead ship I saw all five of them go down. Out of eighteen aircraft we had six left. I remember someone, I believe it was Lieutenant Jeffries, saying, 'That's the government's half, now for ours.'[7]

Captain McLaughlin spoke into his oxygen mask to his tired crew and Colonel Peaslee sitting beside him: 'We've flown this far for Uncle Sam, from here we fly for the US – us.'

The third and final wing, the 41st, comprising the 379th and 384th Bomb Groups, added its bombs to the conflagration. Near the target Howard Stumpf, the radio operator-gunner aboard *Tallywhacker* in the 384th Bomb Group, flown by Robert L Robinson, counted thirty-five fighters flying parallel to them off their left wing. 'We flew tail end, high squadron of the low group. After abortions and shoot downs we became the only plane left in the 544th Squadron.' Ball gunner Stanley Mozarka adds: 'We shot our way in and we shot our way out.'

'Togglin' Ed' Millson in the 379th lead ship recalls:

> We wove our way through spotty opposition near Koblenz and Frankfurt. Joe Wall was successful in evading flak areas. We reached the initial point (IP) of the bomb run. I took control of the aircraft from Colonel Rohr. One glance took in the points we had spent weeks studying. Up ahead lay the target – Schweinfurt. Flak was

uncomfortably close. One burst blotted my view for a long second. Rattle like hail on the roof announced another close call. I had the target lined up in the Norden bombsight. Smoke from hits on the other two factories was beginning to roll over our aiming point. As another burst rattled against *Rag'n Red* I called 'Bombs away. Doors closing. Let's get to Hell out of here!' As we turned off the target a formation of fifteen Fw 190s ripped out of the sun in a vicious attack. Before anyone could open his mouth I heard the sharp crack of a bursting 20mm shell in back of me. I whirled around expecting to find Joe badly injured. Instead, I found him laughing and pointing at my chest 'chute, ripped and torn by the exploding shell. I was left without a 'chute, but it saved both of us from serious injury. The group lost three B-17s on that pass, one of which was rammed by an attacker. I think Jerry had every plane they owned in the sky. I saw three Forts in the wing ahead explode from rocket hits. The Germans were attacking from all directions around the clock. We saw several obsolete type aircraft, one of which was a Dornier 217. Forts from our group glided out of formation with feathered props or telltale damage. Frequently, the dark 'chutes of the German crews would be mingled with the white ones of the Americans.

At around 14.50 the crew of the *Gay Caballeros* in the Tail End Charlie slot in the 379th Bomb Group formation started the bomb run through thick flak. Forrest J Eherenman, navigator, who shot down one Me 109 and possibly damaged another recalls that 'fighter attacks were too many to count.' In his log he wrote: 'Thousands of fighters attacking in squadrons.'

Later, I estimated that the number of enemy fighters at any one time to be around forty. In a single sweep our Group lost three B-17s, one of which was rammed by a German fighter. For two and half hours I was too busy to make any more entries in my navigator's log. I ran out of ammunition again and again. I called for some more from the waist positions who didn't seem to be getting as many attacks as the frontal positions. In six hours of hell our oxygen was gone, our ammo was gone, our control cables gone and we had large holes in the left wing, waist and stabilizer and the flaps were shot away and the hydraulic system was out. Fortunately, we were able to stay with the formation, flying on three engines.

As the 41st Wing turned off the target in came the 3rd Bomb Division, flying six minutes behind, to take its turn. First over the target was the 96th Bomb Group at the head of the 45th Combat Wing. Amazingly the Fortress piloted by Silas Nettles and Jerry Lefors was still holding formation despite the loss of their No. 1 engine. Jerry Lefors says:

As we neared the Initial Point of the bomb run we could see the familiar pattern of flak: a tri-dimensional checkerboard of deadly puffs of smoke. Through this we would reach the target. We were on the bomb run when the left inboard engine was hit. Nettles hit the feathering button and the prop slowed to a near stop but the system failed and the run away prop revved the engine up to about 3,300 RPM. On bombardier Ed Jones' request, the crew elected to hang on and try to drop our bombs, since we had come this far. We dropped the bombs as the Group was making its turn to the right. We cut the turn short to try to catch up. Our screaming runaway prop was slowing us down to about 143mph. I was nervously pushing against the knobs for every ounce of power from the three struggling engines. Cutting the corner still didn't catch our formation. Nettles and I communicated through sign language that we would join the next one. It's near certain doom to be alone with a crippled B-17. The Germans like the easy ones. We were being sprayed with bullets. We dove, hoping the prop would come off and give us that extra few mph we needed. The runaway prop was just as determined to hang on as we were. We joined the following group as they caught up to us. This Group was moving too fast for us, so we joined the last Group in the formation. Nettles tucked in level with the leader. This was our last hope, the last Group in Germany that day. There was a great expression of relief on the intercom. Someone said, 'Looks like I'll keep my date tonight.'

Then we heard on the command channel: 'Group Leader, we're stalling out back here, can you speed up the formation?' Nettles broke in and said they would lose us if they went faster. For a short time we seemed to be holding our own, then the Group left us behind at about five miles per hour. Nettles and I were both perspiring freely, trying to keep the big bird flying. I had an odd feeling as the last group pulled away from us. I looked behind at the empty sky. We were certainly 'Tail End Charlie' now! The sight of black smoke pouring from the left outboard engine startled me. I thought, 'Oh God, I hope it's just oil smoke.' I strained to see if it was on fire, then noticed that Nettles was looking at the right wing. Our heads swung to opposite sides and we knew we had two engines burning.

Time was running out, as Eugene Sebeck recalls:

We had been getting heavy flak and fighter attacks. All guns were busy. Without full power we were losing altitude and dropping back. As we passed our IP for the bomb run, thick black smoke poured out of No. 1 engine. We were ordered to stand by to bale out. Not being able to wear my 'chute in the top turret, I had to step down to get it. My separate oxygen supply had been acting up so I hooked one side of my 'chute and hooked in to the main oxygen supply. When I got back into the turret I remember thinking, 'Boy I can see a lot better with that new oxygen,' then I realized that while I was out of the turret it had been hit, but good! The gunsight, which would have been only a couple of inches from my face, was pulverized. Gears and pieces of the case were everywhere. Thinking that the turret was worthless, I got back out of the turret and was looking out the window near the cockpit when the pilots saw me. I heard those famous last words: 'Sebeck, get the hell back in that turret.' I got back in the turret. Then things *really* got rough. Our No. 4 engine was smoking and fighters were everywhere. Four Fw 190s hit at once with the whole crew trying to keep them away. Three broke off the attack, but one was determined. He came in from 6 o'clock. I laid the .50s on him and let loose. It was like he ran into a stone wall and dropped like a rock. I can still hear the radio operator, Pat Putnam screaming in the intercom, 'Sebeck got him!'

We were now in real bad shape. We had dropped our bombs on the target and were trying to get home. Our hopes were shattered when the No. 4 engine burst into flames, with the wing melting under the heat. Nettles said, 'Let's get outa here' and rang the bale-out bell. I went to the bomb bay and tripped the doors, then opened the door to the radio room to see all the crew in the back leaving. I left through the bomb bay.

Lefors again:

Nettles slapped my left arm and said, 'Let's get outa this thing Lefors.' I nodded. There was no doubt! Nettles had previously given the order to prepare to bale out. Now the final order: a bell signal and 'Bale Out!' According to our emergency plan I was to check that O'Hearn and Jones had heard the bale-out bell. The pitch of excitement had reached a peak. I'm sure we were all scared. I crawled down to the nose, my oxygen mask disconnected but still on my face. I looked at O'Hearn and pointed at the door, he nodded. I crawled and climbed back to the cockpit. We had our parachute harnesses on, but the chest pack 'chutes were behind our seats. I snapped on my chest pack and then I realized that I had not fastened my leg straps and panicked. There was no time to lose: Either engine could blow up the plane any second and the sound of German bullets penetrating the already riddled bomber added to the urgency of the moment. I struggled, reached over my chest pack, unbuckled my left leg strap from the side of the harness and with much strain, brought it between my legs and finally got it snapped.

> Meanwhile Nettles had set the automatic pilot, checked the rear of the plane and went to the bomb bay. While I struggled to get my straps fastened I think I signaled for him to go ahead. Just as I got the snaps together, I saw Nettles drop feet first out of the bomb bay. His parachute harness hooked on the bomb rack. I thought that as soon as I got my leg straps snapped I would get him loose. However, he shook himself free. As I stepped on the catwalk in the open bomb bay I knew that I was alone. Bullets were still tearing into the ship. A 500lb bomb remained in the nearby rack. I looked at the peaceful landscape four miles below and stepped into thin air. The loud blast of air at around 140mph (the forward speed of the ship) surprised me. I was tumbling, trying not to pull the ripcord too soon. Finally, I found the ripcord handle with my left hand: I had snapped my chest 'chute on upside down in the excitement of the moment! There was a sudden jolt as the 'chute opened – then silence except for the whisper of the air passing through the silken canopy above. I watched our B-17 flying unmanned, until with a puff of smoke, the right wing blew off. I counted the other nine 'chutes floating earthward.[8]

The 96th Bomb Group's target was obscured by smoke from the preceding bomb runs, but crews had not flown this far to be thwarted by smoke from their own bombs and released them anyway. In the 94th Bomb Group formation waist gunner Leo Rand was standing ankle deep in spent shell casings after two hours of combat and thinking that all the good things that were supposed to happen, according to the morning's briefing, had not come about. He cursed to himself; 'All this briefing propaganda had to be a load of crap.' A few miles from Würzburg an attacking Bf 109 was met by a burst from Leo's .50 calibre gun. The only effect he noticed was that the fighter's engine stopped. While he was concentrating on putting more lead into the attacker, the 109 pilot baled out into his line of fire and the .50 calibre slugs cut the unlucky German in two, leaving the indelible and gruesome sight of the upper part of a body hanging from a parachute. Rand became convinced that he had committed an unpardonable slaughter. He thought that if he lived through this mission, disgrace and probably a court martial would be his lot.

The second group in the wing was the 388th with sixteen aircraft. The lead bombardier was unable to identify either the Kugelfischer ball-bearing works or the marshalling yards located to the south, so he set his sight on the bridge over the River Main and released his bombs slightly to the right of the ball-bearing plant. The bombs cascaded down into the southern half of Schweinfurt and the western end of the marshalling yards.

The 13th Combat Wing was the last wing in the 3rd Division to cross Schweinfurt. 'Gus' Mencow in the 390th formation recalls:

> As we neared the Initial Point the target came in to view and we started to peel off by groups to begin the bomb run. The sky over Schweinfurt was an awesome sight, with the black bursts of flak and here and there a ball of fire where a B-17 was hit. 'Mac' McCarthy, bombardier, looked back at me and from the look in his eyes over the oxygen mask I knew he was experiencing the same feeling of apprehension that I had. Suddenly, the look changed dramatically in his eyes and a twinkle appeared. I knew he was grinning under his mask. He reached for the microphone switch and said, 'Bombardier to pilot – Hey Geary, is there any way you can back up this crate? I think that would be our best way out of here!'
>
> 'Will you shut up, McCarthy and get ready to drop your bombs,' said Geary.
>
> I could tell from the sound of his voice he was having difficulty to keep from laughing! God bless Mac. I knew then that if anything was going to happen over Schweinfurt at least we would all die in a happy mood.

Joey Poulin, the 19-year-old French-Canadian ball turret gunner on *The Eight Ball* in the 390th Bomb Group, flown by Bill Cabral and Dick Perry, had a lucky escape when a piece of flak ripped off his turret door. Only his slender lifebelt prevented him from falling 25,000ft without a parachute (like almost all ball turret gunners, Poulin could not wear one in the close confines of his turret). Many gunners might have scrambled back into the belly of the aircraft, but if any Luftwaffe fighters spotted that the ball turret was out of action it would have been an open invitation to attack. Poulin chose to stick it out, praying all the time that the lifebelt would hold. Close on the heels of the 390th Bomb Group were the 95th and 100th Bomb Groups, their crews eager to release their bombs and head for home as quickly as possible. Lieutenant Bob Hughes, pilot of *Nine Little Yanks and a Jerk* in the latter group recalls:

> We saw gas and oil fires dotting the countryside, attesting to the furiousness of the defence and the determination of the bomber crews to place their bombs squarely on the target and not be denied. From time to time, we had seen flak from a distance but as we neared the target area it took on a more personal feeling. Periodically, we could see the red hearts of the bursts of 'Big Stuff'. We could now see the target area. Lieutenant Richard F Elliott our bombardier and I had attended a special briefing on the target even though we were scheduled to drop on the lead bombardier's release. This intense target study before take-off paid off handsomely because it allowed

us to distinguish the target under the most unfavorable conditions. We had also been briefed about the smudgepots marking a dummy target area. Elliott and I recognized them for the dummies they were. They were smoking like the whole town was on fire.

Suddenly, our attention was diverted. The leader of the 95th was struck by flak just as we approached the IP for the final turn to the target. He descended rapidly from formation. Flak was intense and my co-pilot Lieutenant Donald S Davis, yelled 'Move Bob!' I had felt the 'whump' from the burst, which had lifted our wingman's plane and was sending it directly into us. Lieutenant Howard Keel temporarily lost control of the craft. The Good Lord kicked left rudder, down stick, left aileron, then back-stick and rolled out of a well-executed diving split 'S'. It allowed Keel to pass through the space, which we had occupied to execute a co-coordinated recovery. It also placed our ship on a direct course to the primary target. Dick Elliott picked up the target immediately and called 'Skipper, target dead ahead, set up and follow PDI!'

Nine Little Yanks and A Jerk was by now completely alone so Hughes questioned Elliott. 'Dick, I do not have the right to commit a man to this course of action against his will. It would have to be a 100 per cent volunteer.' Dick called for a vote starting with the lowest ranking man. One by one all agreed and I said 'Gentlemen, we go!'

We considered we had the element of surprise on our side and that we could maintain an appearance of a crippled aircraft by not opening our doors until just before 'bombs away'. We reinformed the crew that we were flying in a heavily defended area and the best information had it that the German planes would not penetrate the area. We also doubted that the flak guns would fire upon the one ship but would allow us to leave the area and become fighter bait. It was our best guess that they did not want to draw attention to the steam-plant and allied ball-bearing shops by firing on one ship. If we couldn't find it, they were not going to disclose it. Dick Elliott opened the doors just long enough to release the bombs. We already had our strike camera running. It was on intervolometer but our bombsight was not. Dick, knowing that he had the rate killed and the course was beautiful, set the selector switch on 'Salvo'. Bombs were away at 14.54 hours. All fell in the MPI. The roar on the intercom was 'PICKLE BARREL!'

Nine Little Yanks and a Jerk had just opened up the north segment of the target area and there were more bombs to follow. Our aircraft was strike photo aircraft for the 100th Bomb Group and we had picked up the 95th Bomb Group, which was still struggling, trying to get into formation. My wingmen joined me and we asked the new

> leader if we could be of assistance in re-forming the group, explaining that we had an experienced formation controller, Sergeant Robert L McKimmy, one of the finest formation critics in the business, riding the tail guns. The offer was graciously accepted. He lined them up for us in a hurry because we were running out of the defended area and in a very short time the 95th was formed and the 100th flight took its proper position in the high squadron. We rejoined the 390th Bomb Group and we were once again the 13th Combat Wing.

The 45th Combat Wing of the 3rd Division crossed Schweinfurt and dropped its bombs. The 4th Wing was the second wing to cross Schweinfurt and they headed for the VKF plant. Roy Davidson recalls:

> My position in the group formation as 'Tail end Charlie' really put us in the center of the whole shooting match. We went into the target amid very heavy flak and fighter attacks. The fighters continued to attack us right through to the target area. They even flew through their own flak with no let up at all. But we were able to fight them off all the way to the target and out. Carl F 'Hoot' Gibson, ball turret gunner, shot down a Bf 109 and the boys were really excited about this. But pretty soon the fighters came in thick and fast and everyone was getting to do a lot of shooting. By the time the fight was over I think most of the gunners aboard were out of ammunition. Fred Krueger, in the top turret, ran out and never did get to reload.

It was after the target that the 3rd Bomb Division met its stiffest opposition. Davidson recalls:

> We had gone into the target, dropped our bombs and had started back out, when the fighters made passes through the middle of the formation. They continued to attack the last group (385th) until they ran out of fuel and were forced to seek land. Maybe the fighters would make one pass at one group and then keep zigzagging through the formation until they got to the last group where they would continue attacking. We outfought the fighters but Richard Mungenast, the tail gunner, shouted that a Bf 110 behind us out of range was firing something at us and it was leaving a black stream of smoke. We didn't know what it was at the time but we discovered later that it was a rocket. We had never been told of the existence of such a device. The first shot burst way behind us. The Bf 110 pulled up closer and fired another one. It still burst short. Mungenast cried out, 'Here comes another black stream of smoke!' Right after that the missile exploded right under our plane. It felt as if we were on an elevator; it lifted us up and did all kinds of damage. The plane felt as it if was trying to turn a loop. Chochester and I had to apply full

> forward pressure with both hands and our knees on the wheels to keep the plane straight and level. Right after the explosion there was an awful lot of excitement on board. All the men in the back of the plane were wounded and screams of, 'I'm hit, I'm hit!' filled the intercom. I presume the explosion had also knocked off or damaged the flaps. The cable must have been broken because I could not adjust the trim tabs.[9]
>
> It wasn't long before we had a Bf 109 off each wing about 50 yards out. We had no ammunition left and anyway, three men had baled out and Mungenast was wounded. The only guns we had left were in the nose. The 109s were so close we could distinguish the pilots' facial features. I figured they were talking to each other to decide who would finish us off. They took it in turns to shoot at us, turning in directly from 3 o'clock. Whenever I saw his wings light up with cannon fire I took evasive action and turned towards him, like I was trying to ram him. Somehow or other, neither fighter succeeded in hitting us. I'll never know how in the world they missed us at such short range. We really gave it violent evasive action during each of their two or three passes and the maneuvering worked.

Eventually, Davidson's third engine cut out and he was forced to make a wheels-up landing in a cow pasture near the village of La Chappele-sur-Orbais. Guns protruding from the ball turret caused the B-17 to crack in the centre and bent the middle and tail sections upwards.[10]

The city of Schweinfurt had soaked up over 483 tons of high explosives and incendiaries. The 3rd Division had dropped the most bombs on target and the 390th was the most successful. Despite the lead ship experiencing difficulty, all fifteen aircraft placed 50 per cent of their bombs within 1,000ft of the MPI. The Fortresses turned off the target and flew an almost complete 180° circle around Schweinfurt. A group of Fw 190s headed for the 1st Division formation and singled out the trailing 41st Combat Wing. The leading 379th Bomb Group lost three B-17s in the first pass and another bomber also hurtled to earth after a collision with one of the fighters, which also went down. Both divisions headed for their respective rally points and began forming into combat wings again for the return over Germany and France. The surviving B-17s headed for the coast. 'Togglin' Ed' Millson in the 379th lead ship recalls:

> Along the route home we could see smoking or flaming wreckage of bombers that had gone down during the aerial battle. After an eternity of bucking strong winds, which the German fighters utilized for head on attacks, friendly fighters appeared, swept in and dispersed our attackers. As the friendlies circled around us, one of the gunners was heard to utter, 'Thank God,' voicing the sentiments of

> the entire formation. Soon, Joe announced that we had reached the cloud covered 'Tight Little Island' – England.

At 16.40 hours the 1st Division crossed the Channel coast and was followed, just five minutes later, by the 3rd Division. Approaching the French coast the two surviving aircraft in the 305th Bomb Group sighted the 92nd and 306th Bomb Groups for the first time on the mission. Luckily, the two B-17s had met little fighter opposition on the way home for they had used almost all their ammunition before the target.

Incredibly, *Knock-Out Dropper* in the 303rd Bomb Group had made it this far, as Leroy Mace recalls:

> How glad we were to see England! The pilot said, 'Well men, we made it!' He called me and said I could get out of the turret, but to put on my parachute and stand by. I was glad to get out of that turret. Manning said it looked like we would have to leave the ship, as he didn't expect it to stay in the air long. He asked us how it looked in the back. We told him we thought it would hold but we could not be sure, it was a mess; the pilot said that anyone who wanted to could jump out. All the crew from the tail to the nose of the ship told him that if he stuck with it, we would too. If he was man enough to bring it in. we were men enough to stay with him. He waited a minute and said: 'OK. If that's the way it is, get ready for a crash landing. We are going in!' He made a perfect three-point landing. The ground crews were watching us, afraid we were going to crash. They said that in a few more minutes the whole stabilizer would have fallen off. There were a large number of holes all over the ship, but no one was hurt.

Robert Voltz was another in the 'Hells Angels' Group who was 'especially thankful to our Lord for being able to set foot on the good earth of England again.' Bill Bergeron, first pilot with Colonel Kyle, leading the 41st Combat Wing on his second trip to Schweinfurt, touched down at Molesworth after having to make three circles in order to give priority to the many badly damaged ships, several with wounded aboard. Bergeron recalled that 'It looked like the Fourth of July fireworks so many flares were being shot of by the landing aircraft in distress.' Lieutenant Robert Hullar and Wilbur Klint managed to get their badly damaged Fortress back, as Klint recalls. 'Our *Luscious Lady* suffered a broken wing spar, a shattered top-turret and a wide assortment of holes, which sent her off to the repair depot for a major overhaul. The *Lady* had to be patched up before she was flown to the depot. Many planes that made it back were out of commission for a week.'[11]

The Fortresses' return to England was hampered by the same soupy weather that had dogged their departure. Captain McLaughlin recalls:

This really topped it all off. Low ceilings and poor visibility loomed as an almost insurmountable problem because most of our remaining twelve aircraft were damaged and at least two had wounded on board who needed immediate attention.[12] Harry Hughes directed me to the landing end of our home runway at Podington, using for the first time an inter-setting *Gee* box line as an instrument approach system. With our wounded wingman – who as I recall was Lieutenant 'Smoke' McKennon – we tracked into a descending approach to the runway and when we had it in sight by prearrangement we pulled up and let him land. Then we led the other two remaining aircraft around and back to the final approach and landing... a long, tough, soul-searching day I'll not soon forget.

George Roberts, the radio operator aboard *Cavalier*, recalls:

Clouds covered the Channel. Lieutenant Kirk, opting to return over the clouds, found the break he needed over England and circled the *Cavalier* to below the ceiling. I fired a flare as we approached the runway to signal the medics for the injured Webber. In bad weather, with a damaged plane in descending darkness, Kirk and Flight Officer Clyde Cosper made a good landing. Medics met us at the hardstand. Only five out of the eighteen planes of our group had reached the target. We were the only one from our 367th 'Clay Pigeon' Squadron. We had over 300 holes in the *Cavalier*, one of them large enough to fall through. Sergeant Webber, in serious condition, was taken to a regional hospital. It was his second Purple Heart in four raids. This was his last mission. One hundred of our friends did not return to Thurleigh. It was indeed a Black Thursday for those who had given their all on this 14th of October.[13]

Bill Rose recalls:

On the order to 'Land any place you can,' our squadron dispersed over the Channel. Out of the eighteen planes in the 92nd Bomb Group which flew the mission, only four landed at our own base. Nine others landed at fields throughout England. One crash-landed and one burned after ground looping. Six were missing in action. When we spotted outer perimeter lights, I racked the plane around and tried to get in. The tower said that there was another B-17 on the same lights trying to land. We never saw one another and the tower could only hear us. I managed to land on the third try. There was a jeep at the end of the runway with a guide who stood in the rear to direct me to a parking spot. He didn't realize how fast I was coming. I saw his eyes get as big as saucers. He started beating the driver like a jockey hitting a racehorse to get in front while traveling backwards,

> ahead of us. I turned right at the end of the runway without ground looping, shut off the engines and turned into a parking stand off the taxiway. At debriefing, we learned that we were at Bovingdon, from where we had left the Combat Crew Replacement Centre only three weeks before. Our de-briefing officer had survived the first Schweinfurt mission in August so he understood what we reported. We were served supper. Though we had not eaten since early that morning, none of us had an appetite. While we were picking at our food another crew came in. They had been in the traffic pattern with us, but had gone back up, headed for the Channel, turned on the autopilot and baled out.[14]

The *Gay Caballeros* in the 379th Bomb Group had managed to stay with the formation, flying on three engines, but it lost another engine before reaching the English coast and began to lose altitude rapidly. Forrest Eherenman recalls:

> Lieutenant Corson made an emergency landing at a RAF base at Biggin Hill with much wiggling and ending up in a ground loop. Nobody was hurt and needless to say, the crew was thankful to be on the ground. We were overnight guests of the Royal Air Force. The RAF lived a bit better than American crews. Our plane never flew again. It was stripped and left to deteriorate in the English weather. Eleven out of seventeen 379th crews did not return to Kimbolton from the mission. Strike photos showed we had done a fine job on the target. We'd have other rough missions, including one to Berlin, but none like the October trip to Schweinfurt. Looking back, my 273 hours of combat seems like three hours of watching a movie. Your mind blots out things that are unpleasant and lets you remember more pleasant times.

The 388th Bomb Group did not lose a single plane on the Schweinfurt raid. Lieutenant Dan Sullivan put *Susie Sagtits* down at Biggin Hill, having lost all hydraulic fluid from a flak hit, and with no brakes he still managed to avoid the Spitfires parked all around. The plane, whose name even by Eighth Air Force standards was more than a little risqué, was showing red on all fuel tanks and had been through a lot, as Richard Donner explains:

> After bomb release we lost an engine and started to drop out of formation. Dan Sullivan took a poll as to whether we should go to Switzerland or try to get to France where the girls are prettier. France it was! Problems arose with enemy fighters after leaving the Group. After damaging two Fw 190s our tail gunner was hit. We were able to hold altitude at 5,000ft but the 'Abbeville Kids' were distracting us.

> Sullivan went down to some low clouds. The next poll was whether we should try to get across the Channel. We got in sight of the chalk cliffs and then unbelievably, the solid cloud cover over England opened up. Beneath was an airstrip. We had lost the hydraulic system along the way, so we cranked down the wheels.

Susie Sagtits made six or eight ground loops with no damage. The crew were able to get repairs and fly back to Knettishall after three days.

Bill Heller in the 303rd also put down at a RAF base as he recalls:

> With England a solid overcast ahead and not enough fuel to make an instrument let down, it was imperative that we leave the formation and try to find a hole through which we could descend. Twenty minutes before the fuel would have been exhausted a small hole appeared and we were able to spiral down at a rate of descent that frosted the instrument panel. We found a small RAF field just outside of London. The RAF recognized the emergency and immediately gave us a clear runway. A doctor and a chaplain met us as we taxied up to the line. We needed neither, thank God, but the thought that they were prepared for us again boosted our admiration for that organization. Three women mechanics (WAAF) repaired the battle damage temporarily and gave us enough fuel from their meager stores to get us back to our base at Molesworth. Our RAF hosts served us tea and dinner and provided beds for us. Before going to bed the gunners cleaned and oiled their guns. By 21.00, after a good day's work, I went to bed with a word of thanks to Our Lord for our preservation.[15]

In all, the 1st Division had lost forty-five Fortresses on the raid. At Chelveston the ground staff and crews left behind were devastated to learn that theirs had been the highest loss of the day. Of the eighteen B-17s that had taken off that morning, only Kane's and Barney Farrell's *Rigor Mortis* had returned to base. There was not even the consolation that some crews might have put down at other bases. Aboard Farrell's ship Max Guber the navigator was removed unconscious from the plane and it appeared at first that he had lost both eyes after being hit in the face and chest by an exploding shell. Guber owed his life to bombardier Fred Helmick, who though badly wounded in his shoulder and back had kept his oxygen supply going. While tending to the navigator Helmick noticed that his own flying boots were filling with blood. He was slowly bleeding to death but somehow he survived the almost three and a half-hour flight back. Not only that but he also navigated for his pilot too. Helmick needed fifty-six stitches to close the wounds. After hospitalization he was returned Stateside having completed his twenty-fifth mission.

Second highest loss in the division went to the 306th Bomb Group with ten. John E Corcoran was the 19-year-old ball turret gunner in William Tackmier's crew in the 367th 'Clay Pigeons' Squadron:

> When we landed I think we were the first aircraft back. Our pilot, from Taft, California, was 6ft 3in and 215lbs; age about 26 and a great guy. We were surrounded by 'brass' in jeeps. Major George Bucky and Major Ken Reechen asked where the others were. We told them that as far as we knew we were all that was left. I could see tears streaming down Bucky's face. He had sent us out and he had lost many friends. I have no idea how far we got into Germany but we did not reach the target. We were badly shot up and came home on the deck harassed by fighters and people shooting at us from the ground. I have no knowledge of where we bombed. With over eight hours' flight time we got credit for the mission. We had led the high Group to Schweinfurt in August when, due to our position in the formation, we'd had rather an easier time of it. The guys behind us were pounded. On 14 October we were so far behind that we had no chance and the Germans had plenty of time to jump on us.

The 92nd Bomb Group had lost six, and a seventh was written off in a crash landing at Aldermaston. The 379th and 384th Bomb Groups had each lost six B-17s in combat and three crews from the latter group had to abandon their aircraft over England, making nine in all.[16] *Windy City Avenger* was the only 384th Bomb Group B-17 to land back at Grafton Underwood; *Tallywhacker* and five others landed at other airfields. The 303rd Bomb Group lost two aircraft, including one which crash-landed after the crew had baled out near Riseley. The 91st, 351st and 381st Bomb Groups each lost one B-17.

Stella in the 384th Bomb Group made it back to Grafton Underwood early after being forced to abort as Staff Sergeant Don Gorham, the ball turret gunner, recalls:

> Not far out the lead ship developed trouble and aborted. As we were the only other lead crew in the squadron and flying the No. 4 slot, we took over the squadron lead. As we crossed the enemy coast No. 2 engine gave out, but we continued on. We were having difficulty keeping up with the formation on three engines. 150 miles further into enemy territory No. 3 engine gave out, forcing us to leave the formation. Perhaps it would have been better to continue, as we were now alone and open to enemy attacks. We lowered our wheels as a signal we were leaving formation and peeled off to our right. To abort so far inland was no picnic. Five minutes after we left a pair of determined Fw 190s attacked us. The tail gunner called out the attack and Jake put *Stella* into a steep dive for evasive action. We

dropped about 6,000ft a minute and it was tough on our ears going down. The fighters still came in and opened up with 20mm cannon from 800 yards but missed. I guess we were hitting 250mph in the dive, really too much for a B-17 with a bomb load. However it was an emergency and Jake began to rock the ship. Both Compton and I had good shots, though they at first seemed out of range. The fighters stayed till we hit the coast where we finally sighted Spitfire escort fighters. We fired green flares signaling for protection. We salvoed the bombs in the Channel, as we couldn't climb with them aboard.[17]

Captain David Williams in the 91st concludes:

Our crew in the *Bad Egg* was extremely fortunate on this trip for I do not recall any casualties and very little, if any, battle damage to the aircraft. Nonetheless, we had a grandstand view of the entire frightening battle, which once more was characterized by vicious frontal fighter attacks. They appeared to be concentrating their efforts on the low group rather than the lead group of aircraft. In any event we expended many thousands of rounds of .50 caliber ammo against the attacking fighters on their way to the less fortunate Fortresses of our wing.

Fortunately, the overcast had disappeared at the southern German border and the weather was absolutely clear for the remainder of the route to the target and withdrawal until just east of Paris. This provided us with an opportunity for precise navigation and excellent bombing but also provided a field day for the German fighters and anti-aircraft gunners. It was a long day, eight hours of logged air combat, 4 per cent of complete a tour and one fifth of an Air Medal. We lost one aircraft from the 91st and we made it back. It was also good for some combat grog, but not quite yet for the lead crew-members. Our day was not finished. We had to replot the mission track and write a report on the day's effort. All in all it was a very tiring day for those who had to plan it, brief it, fly it and report it. At least there was the satisfaction of having flown the mission as briefed.[18]

One by one the B-17s in the 379th Bomb Group landed back at Kimbolton and at other bases. Lieutenant Bohn Fawkes' B-17 made it back but the pilot was not happy that Rip Rohr 'had left his troops to flounder in the muck of an October fog.'[19]

'Togglin' Ed' Millson concludes:

At 18.40 *Rag'n Red*'s wheels hit the runway. We had been in the air over eight hours. I knew our losses had been heavy but I felt the results of the bombing would help make the mission worthwhile.

After de-briefing I rushed over to the photo lab where Captain Ted Rohr, our Group photo interpreter, was examining the wet prints. He answered the unasked question: 'You hit it. Brother you plastered it!' The Group that preceded us also had excellent results. This somewhat alleviated our losses.

Richard Simmons landed with two badly wounded waist gunners. James Foster, the right waist gunner, who was on his thirteenth mission, had looked at his watch as they were over the target and consoled himself with the thought that the mission was half over. Ten minutes later two formations of Bf 109s attacked the 379th. Foster saw the lead B-17 in the element to his left go down and then he saw the right wing ship and the last ship in the formation go down. The last thing he remembered of the battle was seeing a very bright yellow spinner on a Bf 109 and then 'all hell broke loose.' He was badly injured. Left waist gunner Ron Britten saved his life by holding an oxygen mask to his face. Britten was also injured and he and Foster suffered severe frostbite before their journey ended when the ship staggered back to Kimbolton and landed. Jim Foster suffered numerous injuries including a fractured skull, and his left eye was gone, his right eye was badly damaged and his right hand was broken. The medics were amazed that he still had some vision in his right eye when they took the bandages off.

Despite the 'melange of planes in trouble – ours and theirs – parachutes, flak and fighters-fighters-fighters,' Arvid Dahl landed *Dangerous Dan* at Kimbolton with just one hole in the left stabilizer:

It was put there by my left waist gunner. There was so much to shoot at that he got carried away. To make a more difficult shot for the fighters who had us in their sights we would pull hard back on the control yoke, then back down. We got quite adept at 'jumpit' without losing our place in formation. The extra rounds we stole sure came in handy too! My crew usually fitted out a practice 'blue pickle' bomb and printed nasty sayings on it. We filled it from the product of the nearest outhouse. We rigged it with a fuse and small amount of explosive. In retrospect the Germans probably thanked us for the gift of fertilizer. It was our little special contribution to Schweinfurt. I wonder where it hit?

Walter Bzibziak's B-17 in the 524th Bomb Squadron made it back as William F Barrett, co pilot recalls:

I remember vividly that for some reason the 303rd Group did not maintain its low group position, but moved into a double high group position to our left which may account for its low loss record that day. This left us somewhat unprotected from below. Most

> attacks were four abreast from head on. During one such attack my navigator or top turret gunner made a direct hit on the cockpit of a Fw 190. The 190 then collided with the left wing of Lieutenant Zack's B-17 and both airplanes went down. Zack's crew and mine were roommates.[20] We suffered minor damage to our airplane: that is fourteen holes. We lost all radio communications and were running low on fuel. I recorded 8 hours and 20 minutes' flight time that day. When we arrived back in England there were only three planes in our group: Bill Hawkins', on his twenty-fifth raid, the first 379th Bomb Group crew to complete twenty-five missions; Colonel Rohr and our crew. It was solid undercast and with low fuel and no radio, we were sweating a landing place. Finally, a hole opened in the clouds and an airfield was visible. Colonel Rohr gave us a hand signal for peel-off and we followed the other two planes through this opening. We landed immediately, with out the conventional wing-waggle past the tower and the green biscuit-gun light. We found that we were at Little Staughton, a repair depot ten miles from our base at Kimbolton. Colonel Rohr and Bill Hawkins, knowing where they were, went on to land at Kimbolton. After calling our base, we were unceremoniously delivered home in the back of a GI truck about four hours later.[21]

The 3rd Division had lost fifteen aircraft. The 96th had lost seven including *Dottie J III* flown by 2nd Lieutenant Raymond F Bye, which made a wheels-up landing in France,[22] but the losses could have been higher. *Dry Run IV*, Lieutenant Bill Burdick's B-17 was attacked by four Bf 109s and the Fortress slid out of formation. One of the fighters dived from ahead and showed no sign of veering off. Burdick thought that the pilot was dead and tried to avoid a collision but the fighter tore through the vertical stabilizer. At the same time another three fighters closed in. Burdick recalled:

> Our navigator shot down one at about 200 yards and the waist gunner got another which exploded off to our right. The plane that struck our rudder went into a dive. The fourth 109 beat it for home. After this attack the Fortress went into a spin and plunged from 23,000ft to about 5,000ft. Two engines were out and things looked very glum indeed. With the automatic pilot we pulled out at 1,800ft. Over occupied territory this is too close for comfort. We did make it back to England and landed at Hornchurch.

In the 413th Bomb Squadron, *Paper Doll* piloted by Lieutenant Robert H Bolick, had come through the hell over Germany unscathed and the crew, who were on their seventh mission, were feeling relieved that the worst was over, when 20 miles from the French coast, their luck ran out. Flak suddenly exploded around them, hitting the right wing. Bolick went into violent evasive action; it was only a matter of seconds before a direct hit could be expected. The manouevres and the flak put them out of the formation. Suddenly they were alone, the formation far in the distance. Two fighters came out of the sun firing shells and rockets, while a third attacked from below, making a row of holes in the belly of the plane. When a rocket exploded against the right side of the cockpit canopy shrapnel showered the pilots and the ship was out of control. A moment later a 20mm shell missed the co-pilot Fred Downs and almost blew Bolick to pieces. He had bad wounds in his face, neck and legs. More cannon shells exploded in the bomb bay, the rudder, and the No. 1 engine. *Paper Doll* skidded to the left and dropped a wing and was going down. With the interphone system out, H Miles McFann, the navigator, climbed up to the cockpit to check the situation and found a gory sight. Bolick was slumped over the wheel. Badly wounded, he sat up and levelled off the B-17 from her dive, then went down again, unable to move. Downs said, 'See what you can do for Bolick.' Downs needed help himself. He was hit in the right arm, right side, right leg and multiple bleeding wounds in his face. McFann had some pilot training in light aircraft before the war and had flown the B-17 in a straight and level attitude on a couple of occasions, but now he was to learn more very quickly. Downs kept passing out and recovering briefly. The crew removed Bolick to the nose and McFann climbed into the pilot's seat. He knew he was in real trouble. By now he didn't know his exact location. Downs would come to and try to give Miles advice on flying the Fortress. McFann got the radio operator to transmit 'Mayday'. This brought a pair of RAF Spitfires, which led them to an airfield with a long runway. Downs came to and with his badly ripped arm, put his hands on the controls to help McFann. He'd shake his head as a signal to retard the throttle and nod as a signal for more power. Two thirds of the runway was used and they still hadn't settled. When he saw Downs trying to pull the wheel, McFann jerked it back into his stomach, kicked right rudder and got it straightened out. It veered slightly but stopped safely. Robert Bolick died before they landed but the crew went on to finish twenty-five missions.[23]

Leo Rand's Fortress touched down at Rougham and at debriefing his mind was occupied by the macabre experience of cleaving the German fighter pilot in two. At the first opportunity he sought out the Interrogation Colonel and blurted out that he had killed a man in a parachute. He was asked, 'You didn't do it on purpose did you?' Rand replied that he had not. The colonel put his arm around the distraught ex-steelworker's shoulders and said not to worry.

The 94th lost six Fortresses and the 95th and 390th each lost one B-17. Gus Mencow, lead navigator, 520th Bomb Squadron, 390th Bomb Group recalled later:

> We got fifteen planes over Schweinfurt. One was lost to a combination of flak and fighters. Other groups did not fare so well. The flak was extremely thick but fortunately the Luftwaffe concentrated on other groups. When we got back to base and learned of the high losses it turned out to be a sad day. The week was just too much for all of us and Schweinfurt put the finishing touch. We felt convinced that getting through the war was impossible but somehow we carried on.

The 100th, 385th and 388th Bomb Groups suffered no loss although few aircraft if any escaped scot-free. Of the bombers, which returned to England, 142 in both divisions were blackened and charred by fighter attacks and holed by flak.

Sixty Fortresses and 600 men were missing.[24] A further five B-17s had crashed in England as a result of their battle-damaged condition and twelve more were destroyed in crash landings or so badly damaged that they had to be written-off. Of the returning bombers, 121 required repairs, and another five fatal casualties and forty-three wounded crewmen were removed from the aircraft. The losses were softened by Press proclamations that 104 enemy fighters had been shot down. The actual figure was something like thiry-five but both the Press and the planners alike were carried away on a tidal wave of optimism. Even the British Chief of the Air Staff, Air Marshal Sir Charles Portal, said, 'The Schweinfurt raid may well go down in history as one of the decisive air actions of the war and it may prove to have saved countless lives by depriving the enemy of a great part of his means of resistance.' Later, Brigadier-General Orvil A Anderson, Chairman of the Combined Operational Planning Committee, publicly stated that, 'The entire works are now inactive. It may be possible for the Germans eventually to restore 25 per cent of normal capacity, but even that will require some time.'[25] Four days after the raid General 'Hap' Arnold confidently told gathered pressmen, 'Now we have got Schweinfurt!'[26]

Four days after the raid Arnold told the press:

> Regardless of our losses, I'm ready to send replacements of planes and crews and continue building up our strength. The opposition isn't nearly what it was and we are wearing them down. The loss of sixty American bombers in the Schweinfurt raid was incidental.

For those who survived, life would never be the same again.[27] Eaker knew that his deep penetration missions were finished without a proven long-range escort fighter. The Mustang was the straw that would break the back of the *Jagdgruppen* but for the time being the bomber crews were, for the most part, still very much on their own against the Luftwaffe.

Notes

1. *In My Book You're All Heroes* by Robert E O'Hearn. Privately Published 1984.
2. Jim Bradley completed his 25 missions on 7 November 1943.
3. See *Wrong Place! Wrong Time! The 305th Bomb Group and the 2nd Schweinfurt Raid October 14 1943*. George C Kuhl. Schiffer 1993. Major Normand was promoted to the rank of Lieutenant Colonel on 27 October 1943. He was shot down on 24 August 1944, survived and was taken prisoner.
4. *In My Book You're All Heroes* by Robert E O'Hearn. Privately Published 1984.
5. Vaughter evaded for two days before being caught. The rest of the crew were also taken prisoner.
6. *In My Book You're All Heroes* by Robert E O'Hearn. Privately Published 1984.
7. 1st Lieutenant Ralph T Peters' B-17 had arrived over the target with its No. 2 engine out but had completed the bomb run. After 'Bombs away' the group went into a climb from the 22,500ft bombing altitude and Peters' Fortress, suffering from the strain imposed on its damaged wings, gave up the ghost and he ordered the crew to bale out. All 10 made it before the B-17 exploded. About 20 minutes after the target, 1st Lieutenant William C Bissom's B-17 in the 367th Bomb Squadron was brought down by flak – which scored two direct hits on the engines – and fighters. Staff Sergeant Thompson E Wilson, the tail gunner, was killed. Charles R Stafford, the co-pilot, and four others managed to bale out safely. When the heat of battle eased a little the tail gunner and formation observer, Lieutenant Curtis L Dunlap, who had tried to keep abreast of what was happening, could only tell a shocked Schoolfield that just five ships were left. Schoolfield and his co-pilot, Captain Charles Flannagan nursed their ailing bomber home despite a fire in the No. 3 engine and a failed attempt to bale out when the bale-out button refused to work.
8. See *In My Book You're All Heroes* by Robert E O'Hearn. Privately Published 1984. One by one all of Nettles' crew were rounded up. Eugene Sebeck recalls: 'Later that night we were brought together in a dingy prison. Sitting on a cold floor, feeling pretty miserable with German guards all around apparently willing to shoot us at the slightest move, I had forgotten about my letter and hopes of becoming a pilot. Nettles leaned over and said, "Hey Sebeck, why don't you tell them you're supposed to go home, (to the States)." That brought a laugh, one of the few I would have for the next 19 months as a PoW.' All of Scarborough's crew who were flying Nettles' old ship *V-Packet* were captured after they baled out when their engines had quit too.
9. Davidson's crew continued fighting the controls but two engines were gone (one refused to feather and began windmilling) and they were on fire. Another bomb group was sighted and Davidson pulled up under them but he was unable to keep up with them. The oxygen supply was exhausted and Carl Gibson had a bad bullet wound in his knee. Louis W Koth, the radio operator, had lost an arm. Both the waist gunners and Louis Koth baled out. With no oxygen for the wounded, Davidson hit the deck and flew just above a layer of thick haze.
10. Davidson recalls: 'We hit some cows with a little thud but it did not slow the plane up. (The French were pleased because they had more beef on the black market the following day than since the war started!) We skidded along

the field and we were still going quite fast when we hit the trees on the other side and came to an abrupt halt. Everyone was all right because most of the crew had time to put their seats back and get into their crash positions. We scrambled out and the two Bf 109s made a couple of victory rolls on their passes over us. One of the German pilots delighted in making a couple of strafing runs. Fortunately, none of the crew was hit. We got the wounded out and gave Gibson a shot of morphine since he couldn't walk.'

The crew scattered in groups of twos and threes and started walking. Krueger, Mungenast and Davidson headed in one direction while Charlie Breuer, the bombardier and Stan Chochester, headed in another. Al Faudie took off alone. It was the last they all saw of one another. (Faudie made contact with the French Underground and lived with them for almost a year and-a-half until liberation. Louis Koth, Claude Page, Arthur Howell and Carl Gibson were all captured and though they spent some time in German *Lazarets* [PoW hospitals], all survived the war). Chochester and Breuer made contact with the French Underground and a few weeks later were flown back to England aboard a RAF Lysander. Both men were back in England about 35 days from the time they were shot down. Davidson and Krueger also made contact with the French Underground but were later captured during an unsuccessful attempt to cross the Channel and were sent to *Stalag Luft III*.

11. Early in December 1943 Wilbur Klint checked out as a pilot and he finished his tour with his own crew. His 25th mission on 20 February 1944 was an 8-hour round trip to Bernberg. Klint adds, 'That was the only time that the base at Molesworth looked beautiful.'
12. One of these landed in East Anglia while the other remained in formation.
13. *In My Book You're All Heroes* by Robert E O'Hearn. Privately Published 1984.
14. 'The next morning our plane was brought to the ramp to assess the damage. It looked like a sieve. Still, the control wires and all four engines had not been damaged. Gay had not been kidding about his turret guns being broken. One was bent a full 90°. Spent shells from the radio gun had jammed his turret. We learned our lesson. Never again did we run out of oxygen, ammunition, or have a stuck turret. The plane was declared unsafe for flying. A general visited us while we were clearing out our personal gear. He had been in the tower the night before and he was going to write a letter of commendation for each man of the crew. (We never received it.) When a B-17 from our base picked us up, everybody was ready except our radio operator, Frank Cline, who was lecturing the replacements about the "big picture". The day's mail had been deposited on my bunk. One letter was from a stranger named Margaret Cline. She had written at the request of her mother who wanted the pilot to know she was praying for the safety of the crew and especially for the pilot who had so much responsibility. Her mother suggested that Frank not be told of this letter, as he might resent the intrusion. Margaret added that she, too, was praying for our safety. We had prayed throughout the mission for our lives. None of us was injured on the raid. A bullet spent itself in Frank Cline's clothes. We survived our first seven missions and went on to complete our full tour of duty. Five of the six gunners flew the same 25 missions with me. Did we see God?'

Bill Rose began a second combat tour in 1945 and he returned home to the USA in November. At Pyote, Texas in June 1943 as he had walked over to meet his crew, Rose had wondered: 'Which of these guys has a sister that I'm going to marry?' Frank Cline was the 'guy' whose sister Rose would marry. They married in December 1945 with Frank Cline as best man. They lived happily ever after. Their seven children can attest to that.

15. *In My Book You're All Heroes* by Robert E O'Hearn. Privately Published 1984.
16. One of the 379th Bomb Group B-17s (42-29776) that FTR was piloted by 2nd Lieutenant Samuel A Gaffield Jnr, which split in half when a German fighter crashed into it (9 KIA. 1 PoW). Another was *The Iron Maiden* in the 525th Bomb Squadron flown by 2nd Lieutenant Roland H Martin Jnr, which was hit by flak that blew the nose off just after bombs away. Irving Rittenberg, the bombardier, recalls: 'The pilot ordered us to bale out. The navigator, Dan Maher, threw my chest 'chute to me and started to go out the nose hatch. The plane went into a spin. The centrifugal force pinned us both against the side of the plane. I could not snap on my 'chute. Fortunately, about 500ft above the ground, the pilots were able to pull out of the spin and dropped the landing gear so the Germans would stop shooting at us. We were able to crash-land onto a plowed field with a Me 109 buzzing us. Linden Price, the co-pilot and I took off into the woods. Roland Martin and the engineer went in the opposite direction. I never saw them again. The other six crewmen baled out. We hid in the woods for hours but as soon as we stuck our noses out, some farmers captured us. Nearly all the 525th Bomb Squadron was wiped out that day. I met a few guys from my squadron in the PoW camp.' *In My Book You're All Heroes* by Robert E O'Hearn. Privately Published 1984.
17. *In My Book You're All Heroes* by Robert E O'Hearn. Privately Published 1984.
18. 'The two Schweinfurt raids are etched indelibly in my mind. The challenge and responsibility of being lead navigator of the first aircraft over the target on both missions made me sweat the navigation more than the flak and fighters. I was too busy to dwell long on what was happening to us those days. Most of us non-pilot crewmembers were not decorated for our efforts: I shall always be proud of the words "Navigation was Suberb." which appeared in official narratives.'

    David Williams was shot down near Cologne on 4 February 1944. After two nights in a civilian jail and about three weeks in solitary confinement at *Dulag Luft*, he had a five-day trip in a cattle car to *Stalag Luft III* and saw the effects of a bombing raid from another perspective – the target. One raid was in the middle of a marshalling yard in Frankfurt during an Eighth Air Force day bombing and another in Berlin, during a RAF attack. He spent the rest of the war digging tunnels and adapting to the life of a *Kriegsgefangener* until liberated by the Russians in April 1944. In prison camp he taught navigation to pilots, using his imagination to produce gear to simulate the E-6B computer, Mercator charts and a star compass – tools of the navigator's art. He also became determined to seek a regular commission and become a pilot. He accomplished both goals. After the war he completed pilot training as a major and accrued 23 years of Air Force service time. He flew generations of bombers from B-29s through to B-52s. Continuing flying after retirement, he earned FAA ratings of ATP, CFII, ASMEL, SES and Commercial Helicopter.
19. *The Fall of the Fortresses* by Elmer Bendiner. Souvenir Press 1980.
20. All 10 of 2nd Lieutenant Matthew A Zack's crew in 42-3056 were KIA.
21. *In My Book You're All Heroes* by Robert E O'Hearn. Privately Published 1984.

22. 4 Evaded. 6 PoW.
23. *In My Book You're All Heroes* by Robert E O'Hearn. Privately Published 1984.
24. Schweinfurt soaked up 482.8 tons of high-explosives and incendiaries but losses were high. The 1st Division lost 45 B-17s and the 3rd Division lost 15 Fortresses. Worst hit of all the groups was the 305th Bomb Group, which lost 13 of 18 despatched. Major Johannes Seifert, Kommandeur, II./JG 26, shot down 42-29952 at Limmel, Maastricht, with the loss of five of the crew. Fw 190s of I./JG 1, along with Bf 109s and Fw 190s of II. and III./JG 1, shot down at least six other 305th Bomb Group B-17s over the Dutch–German border. Next highest loss was the 306th Bomb Group with 10. The 92nd Bomb Group lost six, and a seventh was written off in a crash landing at Aldermaston. The 379th and 384th Bomb Groups each lost six B-17s in combat, and three crews from the latter group had to abandon their aircraft over England, making nine in all. The 303rd Bomb Group lost two aircraft. One was 42-29477 *Joan of Arc* , which was shot down just after leaving the target area with nine crew taken prisoner and two KIA. The other was 42-5482 *The Cat o' Nine Tails*, which arrived over Molesworth to find it shrouded in fog. As the B-17 had been badly shot up and was low on fuel the pilot, 2nd Lieutenant A G Grant, ordered the crew to bale out. The B-17 crashed in the back yard of a house in Riseley, Bedfordshire, about 10 miles S of Molesworth. The 91st, 351st and 381st Bomb Groups each lost one B-17. In the 3rd Bomb Division the 96th Bomb Group lost seven, the 94th six and the 95th and 390th, one apiece. The 100th, 385th and 388th Bomb Groups suffered no loss. Of the bombers that returned to England, 142 in both divisions were damaged as a result of fighter and flak attacks.
25. Only 88 out of the 1,222 bombs dropped actually fell on the plants. Production at the Kugelfischer factory – largest of the five plants – was interrupted for only six weeks and the German war machine never lacked for ball bearings throughout the remainder of the war. As in many other German industries, dispersal of factories ensured survival, and careful husbanding of resources meant that some forms of machinery needed fewer or no ball-bearings at all.
26. It was only when the city was finally overrun by US armored divisions that America could at last confirm that it had 'got Schweinfurt'. In recognition of the Eighth's heavy losses and the 305th's in particular, the 'Rainbow Division' presented the German flag captured flying over the Kugelfischer plant to the group at Chelveston shortly before it returned Stateside.
27. The losses and a spell of bad weather restricted Eighth Bomber Command to just two more missions in October. One of these, on 20 October, when 212 B-17s bombed Duren and Woensdrecht airfield, nine B-17s were lost.

Chapter 3

127 Ways to Die

We took off at 10.40 am to bomb a very important target. The Jerries did their damnedest to keep us from hitting it. Our bombload was ten incendiary clusters of 500lbs each. Our job was to burn the town and transportation system. We had P-47s and P-38s for escorts and they sure did their job well. Visibility was damn good and the weather was 37 below. We ran into heavy flak three or four places along the way. There was plenty of it. Our supercharger on No. 3 engine was broken so we had to drop back. Three Me 109s came up and the right waist gunner fired a short burst at them. They threw their bellies up and dove downward. An Me 110 came in at 9 o'clock. I gave him a short burst and he lobbed a rocket into the formation ahead of us. I then gave him another burst of about twenty rounds and he started to smoke. He then peeled off and came in at 7 o'clock where I got in another short burst. A P-38 then jumped his tail and he started down, when I lost sight of them.

John W Butler, left waist gunner *Q For Queenie*

Dawn arrived early at Shipdham on 5 November 1943. The winter felt especially cold and damp to Yanks who came from the South or Southwest or who had been training in Arizona and South Texas before leaving the States. The cold wind blew across the Norfolk Broads and rattled against the huts. Dark brown mud lay over the floors of the barracks. The floors were always wet and the chill damp drove everyone to wear warm socks, even in bed. In a barracks in the 67th Squadron some of Lieutenant Rockford C Griffith's crew were asleep while others waited for 'Alabama' Gilbert, whose job it was to wake them on mission days. On the bases men were called by their States. One from Mississippi would be called simply 'Mississip', or one from Georgia, 'Georgia'. No one knew how this got started but for a long time few of their real names were known. When you lose three out of five men early on it was probably good not to know the names. Staff Sergeant Joseph D Gilbert from Lafayette, Alabama, was the one who got them going, got them to briefings and to the dispersal areas. He was the one who sounded the call to duty at the first faint hints of dawn, a duty that some of them were fearful to answer. 'Alabama's' words rang out like a harbinger of doom: 'Rise and shine, mission today!'

Staff Sergeant Forrest S Clark, the crew's radio operator-gunner from Caldwell, New York, was always up when the gloom of the first light struck the long ribbon of runways, and he saw the mist rise. The 21-year-old's induction into the armed forces had taken place at Fort Dix in October 1942. He was not the first in his family to serve. His father's English ancestors joined the Revolutionary Army about 30 miles away in Rahway and his mother's German-immigrant grandfather trained Union troops near Freehold. Forrest was descended, though, from a generally cantankerous but peaceful lot: ministers, artisans and merchants.

One day in early May 1943 Forrest Clark had climbed into an AT-6 trainer at Harlingen, with a young pilot just out of flight school in the front seat. Off they went into the clear Texas sky heading to the Gulf of Mexico for gunnery practice, firing at a tow target. It was the young gunner's first flight. He was barely out of high school and the pilot looked to be 19 or 20 years' old. Forrest Clark took his turn firing a swivel mounted .50 calibre machine gun at the target. He gave the pilot a signal when he was finished firing. Without warning the plane nosed over and down they went to hit the deck over the beaches of south Texas. Clark hung on for dear life.

At Scott Field, Illinois, 'an austere place with a red brick gatehouse, WPA brick buildings and a huge hangar', Clark was trained for eighteen weeks as a radio operator and he learned Morse Code up to 18 wpm. His mother made the long trip from New Jersey to visit him in St. Louis, about 20 miles from the base. This was not easy because the trains were filled with troops at the time. Gunnery and crew training took place at Clovis, New Mexico and at Biggs Field, a sweltering desert air base outside of El Paso, Texas. The crew flew many practice missions out of Biggs over the deserts of New Mexico but none more memorable than one of those designed to test their night navigational and radio skills. Over the pitch-dark desert they nearly collided with another aircraft.

En route to the ETO in late August the crew stopped off at Meeks Field in Iceland: 'a dour and dismal land, long rows of houses stretching away from the capital city.' 'But,' adds Forrest Clark, 'the girls had icy white complexions, golden hair and slim figures of young Viking women.' No sooner had they left Iceland behind than the order came back from the pilot, 'We're over enemy territory. Please get to your positions. Report any enemy subs down there.' The big B-24 Liberator pointed towards Europe. For the first time Forrest Clark and the rest of the crew were in a war zone. When they got to Ireland, after Prestwick in Scotland was closed in by fog, Forrest Clark saw for the first time the 'startling, brilliant green of the Irish landscape, a Shamrock green.' He thought of Yeats and

O'Casey and the descriptions of the fabled green island. 'It was a shock to see the green after so much ice, snow and ash-colored mountains of Iceland and Greenland. I was reminded of the early trans-Atlantic flyers and their first landfalls. Maybe this is how Charles Lindbergh first saw it. We were bound for war and death and the hostile skies of Europe but we had only thoughts of pubs and girls, a night's sleep and a bottle of scotch before starting our missions.'

Now, almost three months later, the skies were hostile. Griffith's crew had been expecting to fly their first combat mission ever since their arrival at the remote Norfolk base. The losses sustained on the Schweinfurt mission had gradually been made good, and two days earlier over 500 bombers had been despatched for the first time, to the port of Wilhelmshaven.[1] Some groups had carried incendiaries, intent on 'burning up the city'. The P-38 escort to the target had kept losses to a minimum and crews had been quick to praise their 'little friends'. Crews hoped the same would be true on 5 November when the target for over 100 Liberators was Münster, the scene of such devastation a month previously.[2]

Crews took the convoy truck from the mess hall to the briefing shack with the others, huddled against the morning cold. Not a word was spoken. Near the Liberator Forrest Clark pulled on his heated suit, a blue head-to-foot coverall.[3] Over it he pulled his flight jacket and flak vest and then his Mae West life jacket. By then the runways were alive in the yellow dawn and he struggled to load his .50 calibre guns on to the weapons truck. Bright sparkles of sunlight spangled the grass around the dispersal area. Sergeant Harold 'Jack' Harmon, waist gunner and armourer, went off to one side in a ditch to smoke a cigarette to calm his nerves. Clark cautioned him about getting too close to the aircraft. His feet felt heavy in the wool flight boots as he walked to the rear of the B-24, listening in the dawn quiet for any sound. And then he heard it. The sound of a morning lark in the hedgerows. Jack Harmon joined him. 'If we make it back,' Clark said, 'I hope we can hear that sound again.'

Jack was checking his guns to see if they would fire. I know he said a prayer but I tried to be real macho and tough it out. A typical New Englander from Gorham, Maine, complete with accent, Jack was an amateur boxer and athlete in his high school days and an accomplished outdoorsman, hunter and fisherman. Harmon was regarded as being the 'pappy' or father figure because of his age (a few years older than other crewmembers). But he was the life and soul of the party when on leave. We called our pilot 'Grif' or 'Rocky'. He said he was from Coody's Bluff, Oklahoma. A quiet man with curly blond hair and a natural skill as a pilot, he had come up through the ranks and was well respected by enlisted men and officers alike.

Abe Sofferman, another New York metro area boy who came from the Bronx, was the crew's radio operator. He and Forrest Clark had hit it off immediately at Biggs Field because of their love of New York and its history and culture. Forrest Clark became his assistant as well as tail gunner:

> Radio operators had no gun position but when there was no flight engineer they took the top turret guns. Most of the time we sat in a cramped space near the front of the plane behind the cockpit.' Abe took his job seriously. He was the typical street-smart kid of the inner cities of America but he was much deeper than that in character and sensibility. I flew home with Abe on his last leave before going overseas. All the way to New York he talked about his sisters and his brother, his childhood and his ambitions for the future. He wanted to go to New York University or City College of New York. Quite athletic, he aspired to be a Golden Gloves boxer. That was all the rage among teenage youth in the 1930s and 1940s. Sofferman was always carrying sandwiches, which we suspected were from the mess hall and would secret them in his flight suit. He also stuck paperback books in his flight suit and would read them in flight. He would read voraciously about history and the lives of Alexander Hamilton, Abraham Lincoln and Benjamin Franklin. He was studious, deep and profound in his thinking and actually the only scholar on the crew. Although he had the manner of a quiet thoughtful man, under it all was an adventurous spirit and a quest for life in all its complexities. He and Bob Weatherwax, our cheerful, outgoing navigator, formed a close bond.
>
> We took off from the slick runway and formed up with the other bombers over the sea. We passed over the Dutch coast. I had never seen the sky so steely blue and such good visibility. I was flying in the tail gun turret and could see for many miles to the rear. We were in one of the lead groups and I could see spread out behind us most of the entire formations of the Eighth Air Force. What a sight. 'What am I getting into? Wow. I never saw so many aircraft,' I said to myself as I swiveled the turret about to coast as we passed over, a thin line edging a blue sea, the North Sea. We were bound for Germany and the target was the industrial city of Münster. It was an important war-production center and believed to be one of the key targets of the bomber offensive. The RAF had gone there a few weeks before and been severely attacked and suffered considerable losses. However, this day looked serene and deceptively beautiful. Below me the dykes of the Zuider Zee stood out clear and straight. I could see sunlight glinting off the surfaces of the bombers in the sky behind us, elements stacked up high and low, covering a large segment of sky. We were at bombing altitude by this time and I

could see the small farms, little villages and canals of Holland below. It was getting cold in the turret and my feet were stuck so I worried if I could get out in time should there be a bale out. We were on oxygen, having exceeded the 10,000–12,000ft altitude. I could smell the rubber of the oxygen facemask and the faintly sweet odor of pure oxygen. It gave me a little high, a kind of euphoria of the heights. Had I remembered to check everything? Would the guns work when called on to do so if there were an attack? I checked the .50 caliber cartridge belts many times. The air was smooth and there was little or no turbulence. We were making our way inland over Nazi-occupied Europe now and yet no enemy fighters were in sight. I thought this might be a milk run and began thinking of life back at the base.

One of the guys, called Looker, who walked with a slouch and shambled along, was standing in the barracks as I checked in and fingering a .50 caliber shell in one hand and telling stories of Ploesti to scare the hell out of the new men. But it was the stories he told of Marrakech and Casablanca, on leave with Arab women and prostitutes, that shook up the recruits. He said whole crews had to be grounded because they got VD and others got so drunk they ended up in native jails, infested with lice.[4]

Next thing I saw were small clouds drifting by the tail section. I thought, 'that's strange, we must be getting into some cloud formations: perhaps a slight overcast.' I didn't think much about that at first but as these clouds continued and increased in numbers I thought it best to push on the intercom button and report to the pilot and co-pilot. Just as I was going to do so the voice of the co-pilot came over the intercom asking the tail gunner to report in. I had neglected to report as required of all crewmembers. I pushed the intercom button and said, 'Everything okay back here, except for a few small black clouds.'

'Black clouds?' came back the voice at the other end of the intercom.

'They look black to me,' I replied.

'Damn it. That's flak!' shouted the co-pilot, Lieutenant Bill Tinsman. Bill was from Bucks County, Pennsylvania and a natural counterpart to Griffith – cool and collected under combat conditions, he was a Rutgers man and I am sure he wanted to fly fighters. He was very neat in appearance and dress. Even when dressed for a mission he looked sharp and self-controlled. While at Herington Army Air Base in central Kansas awaiting our overseas duty assignment we had discovered there was a golf course nearby and in town we found a doctor who had a set of golf clubs to loan. The crew went into the small Kansas prairie town, borrowed the set of clubs and played golf. There was also a swimming pool in town and that is where we met Sue, the beautiful vivacious wife of Bill Tinsman. They were newly married.

I looked out at the small clouds, closer now, fearing I was really in trouble with the pilot and co-pilot for not being more alert. I noticed now that the clouds were closer to us and each had in the heart of them, a red core, which flashed and then disappeared as the cloud drifted off to the rear 'They're shooting at us,' I called out, not realizing I had the intercom button still depressed.

'How did you know?' came the reply. 'Who do you think they're shooting at?' Just then a violent vibration shook the plane and it seemed to rear up in the front, dipping the tail section downward. 'We've been hit,' came the call over the intercom.

'Check for damages. Any reports. All report in.' Again and again the plane rocked from side to side. From then on all hell broke loose. I saw planes going down, flaming wreckage as planes exploded and others spiraling down leaving a trail of smoke.

Suddenly, I had more respect for the small black clouds. I realized that the war had begun for me and that the enemy was actually after us – after me! I began to sweat through my heated suit and nervously pressed the mask to my face. This was my baptism under fire, in a tiny, cramped turret 25,000ft over Germany on the way to Münster with a load of 500-pounders.

Münster was a heavily defended city near the Ruhr. What they didn't tell us was that it was 'flak alley'. I had never seen flak before and did not report it at first. 'Get out and walk on it, boys,' came Bill Tinsman's voice on the intercom.

'Land on it,' sang back Sergeant John Gibboney, the other waist gunner. 'Gib' came from Saxton, Pennsylvania and came to be well known for his wry wit and steadiness under combat conditions. He was a gunner but also, I thought, an assistant engineer. He became very familiar with the B-24 and later with the B-17. Gib often read scripture or church leaflets and was very close to his family.

Gib and Technical Sergeant Earl Parrish worked together. Parish could not get much from reading the engineering manuals but Gib said he could do very well if shown the various parts of the aircraft. Parrish had a great memory once he tried something. I called Parrish a 'hard headed Hoosier' because he was from Freedom, Indiana. He never spoke much but he was quite responsive in flight conditions and was quick to learn the intricate mechanisms of the B-24.

Out of the clear blue sky, Harmon said, 'Look out there. Fighters – coming this way.'

All I could see was endless blue sky. Sure enough within forty-five seconds enemy fighters came in from the direction he had indicated. Sergeant William T Kuban in the ball turret hanging there below us began firing away. Harmon and Gibboney let loose.

Over Münster I heard the bombs going click, click, click as they left the bomb bays bound for our target. I saw them fishtail down into the clouds. But after a while I did not look anymore. There were sickening seconds or minutes when Dave Edmonds, our bombardier, held the bomber steady on the bomb run over the target. Edmonds was a congenial type who could converse about a number of subjects and was a frequenter of pubs. He was also a serious airman. He had attended Valley Forge Military Academy before entering the Air Corps.

We prayed that the flak gunners would not get our range.

We were lucky and got back to the base. Bill Tinsman took me aside and said he was recommending I take a refresher aircraft identification course. After all, he said, if I couldn't see flak, how could I see enemy fighters? I decided, 'If I see anything with a wing and a propeller and it points its nose at us – I shoot!'[5]

Our next missions were to Frankfurt, Zwickau and Solingen, among others. The greatest and happiest sound came when we heard the squeal of the landing wheels hitting the runway at home base. We knew then that we had survived. It was interrogation and back to the barracks to fall into our bunks to try to sleep for another dawn.

The experience of flying missions has never been adequately told because no one has had the courage to tell it. There is fear – overwhelming and paralyzing fear – with every turn of the prop, every yard over enemy territory. A veteran pilot put it this way, 'You know there are 127 ways to die on a mission and you never know when one of them will come your way.'

Even with the outside temperature at 20–30° below zero at altitude ('cold as a witch's tit,' we used to say) I was sweating through my heated flight suit and sweat ran down my legs and into my flight boots. My hands got so sweaty I had trouble holding the guns or even putting the cartridge belts in. Prayer was never far away in our minds and we followed little safety measures like carrying an extra 'chute pack. We prayed at take-off, we prayed at the RPs (Rendezvous Points), we prayed at altitude, we prayed over the target. And we sweated and prayed on final approach.

Sometimes the connections to my electric heated suit would come loose. I panicked when I could not breathe and thought my oxygen had been cut off, until I cracked the hose connection to free up the flow again. Stupid things happened. Planes collided in forming up, at the RPs or coming back, or they crashed on take-off. Even though we did not know one another well in the beginning, some crewmen stood out. 'Red' was a mid-western kid with burning bright red hair, so innocent we believed him when he said he had never been with a woman. He grew up on a farm in Iowa far from the cities and from women, except for the girls he saw at a distance. On an early mission, Red was in the crew of a plane off our wing. The time came for the bomb run and the bomb bay doors opened. Then a shout went up over our intercom. 'Damn!' The news came back that someone had dropped the bombs through one wing of Red's bomber and it went down. We doubted if they ever got their bombs away. Sometimes later I thought I could see Red's ghost on the airfield in the early morning mist. 'Poor kid,' a crewmate said. 'He never had a chance.' We were all kids. I was 21 when I started flying missions. In fact, the whole crew was very young, just out of high school or college.

For two weeks after the 5 November missions the weather grew worse and resulted in many abortive missions. It was not until 11 November that the Eighth was in the air again, with a return to Münster.[6] Four B-17s were lost, three of them in the 94th Bomb Group, which was flying as the low group, led by Major 'Pappy' Colby, and one in the 385th Bomb Group[7]. Three were victims of Fw 190s of the IInd *Gruppe* JG 26 at Epinoy that attacked the Fortresses repeatedly from 12 o'clock and 6 o'clock. Oberfeldwebel 'Addi' Glunz of the 5th *Staffel* claimed two B-17s southwest of Dordrecht but he correctly received credit for only one.

On 13 November 1943, 272 B-17s and B-24s were directed to bomb targets at Bremen, but bad weather caused many in the 1st Bomb Division to abandon the mission during assembly and only 143 of the heavies were successful. The mission cost sixteen bombers, three of which were B-17s.[8] The 93rd Bomb Group suffered the day's highest loss, losing five B-24s. Next worst was the 392nd Bomb Group, which lost four Liberators.

Throughout the first two weeks of November 1943 England was blanketed by thick woolly fog and airfields were lashed with intermittent showers and high winds. When the bad weather front finally lifted on 16 November, Eighth Bomber Command struck at targets in Norway. *H_2X* and *Oboe* sets had been proving troublesome and the break in the weather would enable crews to bomb visually. The 1st Bomb Division was assigned the molybdenum mines at Knaben while the 3rd Bomb Division was to attack a generating plant at Vermark in the Rjukan Valley. (Intelligence sources indicated that both targets were connected with the German heavy water experiments intended to give the Nazis the atomic bomb.) The round trip to Knaben and Rjukan was slightly shorter than the 25 July 1943 1,800-mile circuit to Trondheim and the 1,600-mile round trip to Heroya. At Molesworth the 303rd Bomb Group's *Knock-Out Dropper* was flying its fiftieth mission. If it completed the raid it would set a new Eighth Air Force record for a B-17.

Meanwhile, the 3rd Division struck at Rjukan, about 75 miles due west of Oslo. As the formation approached the target area there was no opposition, confirming the belief that the Germans would not be expecting a raid so far north. The 94th Bomb Group arrived ten minutes early and had to make a 360° turn. (Crews had been told to make certain that Norwegian workers were not on their shift when the bombs fell.) As the Fortresses crossed the target for the second time thick cloud obscured the plant from view and the formation was forced to make another 360° turn in the hope it would clear. While doing the 360° turns off the coast a B-17 in the 390th began doing slow gyrations in the sky and finally sliced into the water inverted.[9]

On 18 November, 127 heavies were dispatched to Gelsenkirchen again. However, the *Oboe* sets aboard the leading Fortresses gave trouble and directed the formation too far north of the target. After an unsuccessful battle with the elements, the B-17s were forced to return to England. The Liberator groups meanwhile, had enjoyed good fortune in a return mission to Norway. One of the men at Shipdham who flew on the raid was Staff Sergeant Forrest S Clark, the tail gunner on Lieutenant Rockford C Griffith's crew in the 67th Bomb Squadron:

> The night before the Oslo raid, 'Alabama' Gilbert got into a heated and lengthy blackjack game. Finally, he lost all his pay and threw down his wallet. 'I won't be needing that any more,' he said.
>
> Next day 'Alabama' and the rest of our group took off from Shipdham to bomb the Ju 88 assembly plant at Oslo-Kjeller, 18 miles east of Oslo. At about 10.00 hours our plane was in a force of nearly 100 Eighth Air Force B-24s approaching the airbase from bases in England, loaded with 500lb bombs. Bombing visibility was perfect. As we came up the Skagerrak and the Oslo Fjord I could see everything plainly etched in newly fallen snow. There had been a snowfall during the night, and in the morning as we proceeded at 12,000 to 15,000ft I could see for miles from my position in the tail turret. The great city of Oslo lay before me, many buildings outlined in the snow. I saw the huge mountains of the spine of Norway reaching down from the far north, tiny villages and fishing vessels in the fjord. Going into Kjeller the formation passed over another German airbase, one situated on the coast. We saw enemy fighters off to the side as we went into the target area but they had not attacked us. 'They'll be back with their buddies,' Sergeant Harold 'Jack' Harmon, one of our waist gunners, shouted over the intercom.[10]

At 12,000ft the 392nd lined up for the bomb run. The skilled navigator–bombardier team of Swangren and Good systematically checked off the course heading, landmarks, true airspeed, wind drift and minutes to 'bombs away'. Myron Keilman, flying deputy lead, saw the target 'standing out in the late morning sun' and thought that 'it would be a shame to miss it.' 'Bombardier Joe Whittaker was following through with every essential detail of a bombing run,' says Keilman. 'Should anything have happened to the lead airplane and it had suddenly aborted the bomb run, Joe had his bombsight crosshairs on the aiming point of the assembly plant. If he had been given the command 'take over', he could have successfully delivered the bombs.'

Lieutenant McGregor in the lead aircraft held his B-24 precisely on altitude and airspeed and he and the twenty bombers following released the 210 500-pounders on the target simultaneously.

On the return leg the same scattered and broken clouds lay across the Skagerrak, beneath the formation. Suddenly the gunners spotted German fighters skimming across the cloud tops opposite the B-24s' line of flight. A dozen-plus Ju 88s climbed to make fast diving passes as they circled in behind the bombers. Liberator 'outriders' moved into a tight formation, providing the mutual protection of concentrated firepower. Diving in pairs, the German twin-engined fighters lobbed rockets and 20mm explosive shells into the 392nd. Tail and top turrets responded with bursts of machine gun fire and the ball turret gunners opened up below as the fighters broke off the attack. Sergeant T E Johnson, flying with Lieutenant Everhart, shot up one fighter so badly that it burst into flames and was last seen in an uncontrollable dive. Two Liberators were hit and began to lose power. They could not keep up with the rest of the formation and as they fell behind the Ju 88s concentrated their fire on them. The B-24 pilots dived for cover and sheltered in the clouds. For a time they played hide and seek as the fighters circled and eventually the bombers were lost from view. Wave after wave of enemy fighters pressed home their attacks but in the 44th Bomb Group formation Forrest S Clark succeeded in shooting down one Ju 88:

> Sitting in the tail position I could look back and see a line of seven to ten fighters lining up to attack our rear. 'They're waiting in line to get at us,' I called over the intercom, pressing the mike to my throat. Suddenly they attacked from all sides. Two shells went through the turret directly over my head, missing me by inches. I followed one after the other as the Luftwaffe pilots zoomed in at our tail and then dove beneath us to come up in front, swing and line-up for another pass. One after another they came. Closer and closer. I tracked them with my twin .50 caliber guns, but could not get a good lead on any until they passed under us and then shot up again for the waist gunners to get shots at them. Finally, I fixed one in my sights as he leveled out and came in faster and faster. 'So close,' I said to myself. 'He's going to hit us: he's going to ram us.' I gripped the triggers of both guns, leveled them out and pressed down. I kept holding the triggers down, hoping they would not jam the belts. I could see my tracers going out in long lines right into his wing roots. Bright flashes of fire and tracers kept boring into his wings until he came so close I could see the outline of the German pilot's head in the

> cockpit. Just as he slipped under us I saw a thin trail of smoke coming from the engine.

Clark was almost completely out of ammunition and a 20mm shell hit Bill Kuban, the ball gunner, who was bringing him more rounds, in the head, knocking him unconscious and bleeding to the floor. Clark heard the bale-out bell, but at first he had difficulty in getting out of his shattered turret. Two men, John Gibboney and L J McAndrews, were getting ready to jump through the open camera hatch. Clark prayed, because he knew he would not survive long in the ice-cold sea if he jumped: 'I actually went down on my knees and prayed. Much to my surprise, just about that time the fighter attacks suddenly stopped and the Germans left us to what they must have thought was our death.'

Lieutenant Joseph L Houle's B-24, which was severely damaged, tottered gallantly to within 50 miles of the English coast, with safety in sight. But by now his fuel indicators were reading zero and he was forced to ditch. The aircraft seemed to break in two and four tiny figures were seen to slip into the icy waters of the North Sea. Griffith, himself flying on three faltering engines, circled over the scene while his radio-operator called ASR. With his own fuel supply running low, Griffith dipped his wing in salute to his fallen comrades and turned towards his base. ASR was unable to trace any of the crew or the aircraft. Griffith's Liberator spluttered on, just above the sea. Clark adds:

> More than once the call went out from the pilot to prepare to ditch but Kuban would surely have died if we ditched in the icy water. We limped on and more than once it seemed all engines quit and the plane stuttered as if in its death throes. But the plane would not die.[11]

Altogether, six B-24s were lost on the Oslo raid, including one each in the 93rd, 392nd and 44th, which were forced to land in Sweden. Forrest S Clark concluded:

> Sixty-two 2nd Division men were lost. The bodies of Lieutenant Houle's crew were never found. 'Alabama' Gilbert was one of those who never returned.[12] We cleaned out his clothes and found a dollar bill, it seemed the more we faced death, the more superstitious we became about everything, including what we said and thought and even the names and numbers of the planes. Even so the 18 November mission was the most successful of all the American missions on Norway during the war. It let the Norwegians know that the Allies had not forgotten them and it boosted their morale at a critical time. We challenged the German Air Force in Scandinavia at a time when it was strengthening its air defenses.[13]

Bad weather continued over the next few days but did not prevent RAF Bomber Command bombing Berlin on the nights of 18/19 November and 22/23 November.[14] This led to rumours of an American follow-up raid being mounted on the capital the next day but the mission was scrubbed. On Friday 26 November, 633 bombers, the largest formation ever assembled by Eighth Bomber Command, were directed against targets as far apart as Bremen and Paris. Two new B-17 groups, the 401st and 447th, had joined the Eighth during November and the 401st made its combat debut this day. Colonel Harold W Bowman's outfit would swell the 1st Division stream to 505 bombers briefed for the port area of Bremen while 128 B-17s of the 3rd Division would head for Paris where skies were expected to be clear.[15] Unfortunately, the weather forecasters were proved wrong and the 3rd Division was forced to return with bomb loads intact. A 94th Bomb Group B-17 piloted by Lieutenant Johnny Pyles, who had brought *Lil' Operator* back to Bury on one engine two weeks before, was hit between the No. 2 engine and the fuselage by a Fw 190.[16] At Chantilly at 10.40 hours Oberfeldwebel Adolf 'Addi' Glunz claimed a 78th Fighter Group P-47. At 11.03 hours near Beauvais, Glunz claimed 42-31215 in the 349th Bomb Squadron, 100th Bomb Group. 2nd Lieutenant George W Ford, whose crew were on their first mission, piloted the missing Fortress. An eyewitness reported that the Fortress was hit in the No. 2 engine when two Fw 190s attacked the low squadron at 10.45 hours. It fell out of formation and dived for cloud cover. The fighters followed but P-47 Thunderbolts went to the rescue. At 10.48 hours one 'chute was seen to open and at 11.03 hours nine more 'chutes were seen. At 11.05 hours it hit the ground and exploded. During its last few minutes in flight fire had spread over the entire left wing.[17]

On 1 December, 299 heavies led by Colonel Budd J Peaslee returned to Solingen and made a PFF attack. This time, the raid was more successful than the one the day before and 281 sorties were deemed effective. Cloud cover forced the 3rd Bomb Division to abort the mission. The 1st Bomb Division lost nineteen B-17s[18] and the 2nd Bomb Division, five B-24s. Staff Sergeant John W Butler, left waist gunner in *Tennessee Rambler* in the 93rd Bomb Group wrote:

> We took off at 08.30 and had to fly 15 minutes into France before we picked up our P-47 escorts. I was very glad to see those babies. Jerry attacked us and he really pressed his attacks. We were under attack for forty-five minutes and I really sweated it out. There was also plenty of flak. We couldn't see the target, so we had to go around to the secondary. There was plenty of flak there too and *Iron Ass* on our wing had his wing shot off.[19] Red Carey, our right waist gunner, shot a Ju 88 down. Four yellow-nosed Bf 109s came diving down so close I could see the 'chute harness on Jerry. Carey fired at them, but no luck. I fired over ninety rounds at a Me 110, a Bf 109 and a Ju 88

but I really didn't get a good shot at them. I saw one bandit attack *Southwind* and it was in trouble. Three 'chutes came out, then five more bandits came down and they shot off the left wing. It went into a spin and burst into flames.[20] The weather was minus 37 and I really froze. This was T U Collins' twenty-fifth and final mission so he was very happy.

On 5 December, 548 bombers set out to attack targets in France again but bad weather completely disrupted the mission. Just over 200 Fortresses of the 1st Bomb Division were briefed to attack targets at La Rochelle and Paris but thick cloud prevented any bombing and none of the B-17s were effective. The same was true of the 2nd Bomb Division's attempt to bomb targets at Cognac-Châteaubernard and St. Nazaire, while the 3rd Bomb Division fared no better at Bordeaux-Merignac air depot. Only two B-24s in the 389th Bomb Group bombed the target and just one B-17, in the 96th Bomb Group, was successful at Bordeaux. For this wasted effort, eight heavies were lost. Staff Sergeant John W Butler in the 93rd Bomb Group flew tail gunner in *O Carole N Chick* piloted by J V Kemp:

We took off at 07.50 to bomb Cognac airfield in France. It was quite a long ways to the target area, which we reached with no mishaps. We were escorted by P-47s and P-38s. Temperature was minus 30. The weather over the target was 10/10 cloud cover so we couldn't drop our bombs. We were not allowed to drop our bombs just any place over occupied territory as we wanted to do as little damage as possible to the French people, except of course to a direct military target. I had just called the navigator over the interphone that it would be nice if we could run into some flak so we could get credit for a mission, when all of a sudden I had all the flak I wanted. A ship in the 389th received a direct hit. He blew into a million pieces. Two 'chutes came out. The whole wing came off in one piece and it dropped by itself turning lazy circles. It was all on fire and it reminded me of a cartwheel from the Fourth of July.[21]

On 11 December the weather cleared sufficiently for the heavies to set out for Emden, their seventh trip to the city and one of the most costly. Staff Sergeant John W Butler flew his ninth mission, flying tail gunner in *Exterminator* flown by J A Bogan. Butler recalled:

We took off at 08.30 to bomb the city of Emden, a pretty important shipping center. It was 39° below zero. My heated suit worked very good back in the tail. Being a tail gunner was nice as you had armor around you and all the bad stuff has gone by. We ran into a lot of flak at the target and it was pretty accurate. I heard a loud noise in the tail and I got out of the turret to see where we were hit. The flak

> put a large hole in the vertical stabilizer. Then some fighters came in at 6 o'clock and in my hurry to get back in the turret I pulled my heated connection off on my right boot so my gloves and boots were not working. I checked all my circuits and even checked my fuses. I was beginning to become real cold. Then I happened to check my right boot. I put the plug back in and the heat came back to my feet and hands again. A Ju 88 came in on the tail but he was gone before I could get a shot in. I fired around thirty rounds at some Me 109s but no results. Flak also hit us in the waist. The tunnel gunner passed out from lack of oxygen. He fell forward on top of the camera hatch. Flak came through the side of the plane and passed the spot he was in, the lucky stiff. The Red Cross had hot cocoa waiting for us. It sure tasted good. Harry Fargo, flying tail gunner on *N-for-Nan* froze his hands and feet and they had to land at another field so they could get him to a hospital. *Q-for-Queenie* made a crash landing on our home base but no one was hurt. My guns worked OK.[22]

Rocket-firing Bf 110s and Me 210s made persistent attacks on the bomber formations and seventeen heavies were shot down, including *Six Nights in Telergma*, the lead ship piloted by Captain Hiram Skogmo in the 390th Bomb Group. Captain Irving Lifson, one of the two navigators on board, recalls:

> We were feigning a raid on the Heligoland area, hoping to draw the enemy fighter planes up towards Denmark. Then we were to cut back on Emden. Shortly after turning back onto Emden eight Me 110s came through the formation, firing rockets. We were hit right away and set on fire. There were eleven of us on board and only Captain Donald Warren and myself the Group Navigator (who landed on the island of Nordeney) survived. German marines picked us up. Ernest Phillips, a gunner, landed in the North Sea and was picked up by a boat. Among those lost was Major Ralph V Hansell, the 390th Operations Officer, the strike leader who was flying as co-pilot. I spent the rest of the war in *Stalag Luft I* Barth.

On 13 December in a record flight, when 649 bombers attacked port areas of Bremen, Hamburg and U-boat yards at Kiel, P-51s reached the limit of their escort range for the first time. This was also the first time in which more than 600 American bombers attacked targets in one day. The 2nd Bomb Division, which included twelve Liberators of the 445th Bomb Group at Tibenham for their first group mission, attacked the U-boat yards at Kiel. On 16 December 535 bombers, including Liberators of the 446th Bomb Group at Bungay (Flixton) making their bombing debut, flew a follow-up raid on Bremen. Staff Sergeant John W Butler in the 93rd Bomb Group flew as J A Bogan's tail gunner in *Birmingham Express* on his tenth mission of the war. Butler recalled:

> We took off at 08.40 to bomb the city of Bremen. It was a very important target, as the world's biggest submarines were built there. The flak over the target was very good and Jerry wasted a lot of money trying to shoot us down. My right glove burnt out so I had to get out of the turret to get a new pair. Just when I was getting back in I heard our right gunner firing so I started firing at some yellow nosed Me 109s. I counted seven. I fired about 100 rounds but couldn't see any hits. Jerry would attack in pairs on a diving approach from 5 to 7 o'clock. Lieutenant A A Russ flew our plane today on his first mission and had the hell shot out of it. Two of his gunners went to the hospital, plus he had to land at another field [Tibenham]. I also received my first oak leaf cluster to my Air Medal.

On 20 December during the third raid on Bremen in a week bundles of *chaff* were dropped to confuse enemy radar.[23] More than 470 bombers hit the port area but twenty-seven heavies were shot down. The Eighth was stood down on 21 December but the following day 439 B-17s and B-24s attacked marshalling yards at Osnabrück and Münster. The 2nd Bomb Division, its numbers increased by the addition of the 448th Bomb Group, was assigned Osnabrück. Sergeant Francis X Sheehan, armourer-gunner in the crew of *Harmful Lil' Armful*, flown by Lieutenant Alvin D Skaggs, recalls:

> Osnabrück turned out to be heavily defended. Although flak was minimal, the fighters were there in abundance, as we found out. My first encounter with combat commenced with black puffs of flak dotting the sky around us. It was something we never did get accustomed to. The effectiveness of this was shown when part of a ship began trailing smoke and parachutes. As we approached the target the aircraft to our immediate right dropped its entire bomb load on the left wing of a wingman that had drifted down and under him. Stunned, I watched the damaged aircraft fade left and over on its back. I prayed for 'chutes to appear, but none did. I was brought back to reality by the call over the intercom – 'Fighters!' Twin-engined enemy aircraft were lobbing rockets into a formation of bombers to my right. At first they seemed oblivious to our presence. I fired at one of the fighters, who began trailing smoke and fire and went down through the clouds. I was later given credit for this.

Staff Sergeant John W Butler, flying his eleventh mission, as left waist gunner in *Judith Lynn*[24] in the 93rd Bomb Group formation flown by J J Collins, also had his hands full:

> We took off at 11.15 to bomb the marshalling yards. The weather was very cold and I really felt it as it was minus 41. We were at 25,000ft. We lost one supercharger, as we crossed the enemy coast. We had P-38s and P-47s for escorts. Only saw a few bursts of flak but the enemy fighters pressed their attacks. A few planes were lost plus quite a few shot up. There was some Me 110s firing rockets into the formation behind us. One of the rockets hit one of our planes and put a large hole in the vertical stabilizer. Also, a B-24 had about 10ft of her wing shot off by fighters. She went into a spin and pulled out of it, then into a steep dive. There were no 'chutes. A B-24 was hit by fighters, went into an inside loop and started down in a dive. She broke into three pieces when she exploded. No 'chutes.[25] I fired around eighty rounds at silver painted Me 109. No results.[26]

The Eighth was stood down on 23 December but missions resumed on Christmas Eve when the B-17s were dispatched to mysterious targets in France, which went under the code-name *Noball*. It was rumoured in the world's free press and in unofficial circles in Washington that the raids were part of a pre-invasion blitz. Crews speculated what the concrete sites were and many dubbed them 'rocket' installations or Hitler's 'secret weapons'. British Intelligence revealed them to be sites for launching 'V-weapons' – pilotless planes packed with a high-explosive warhead in the nose and aimed at London. Sources revealed that seventy such sites were being constructed and all-out raids were ordered at once.

The 447th Bomb Group at Rattlesden, which made its debut this day, further strengthened the Fortress formations. As it turned out, the 447th could not have had an easier debut.

On Christmas Day the festivities got into full swing throughout the region. Americans dined with their English hosts and deprived and orphaned children were invited to bases for Christmas dinner and afternoon parties. Unfortunately, the war was never very far away and preparations were already being made for the next strike. It came on 30 December when the Eighth journeyed to the *IG Farbenindustrie* chemical works at Ludwigshafen, on the upper Rhine near the German–Swiss border. There was a solid undercast but the clouds topped out at 10–12,000ft and above them visibility was unlimited. The bombers maintained a tight formation with their escorts able to keep them in sight while looking out for enemy fighters below. The route to the target had been planned so as to avoid flying across Holland and the Ruhr, where the German defences were now very strong, and the bombers crossed the Seine estuary into France and then flew due east to Ludwigshafen. Altogether, seventeen B-17s were lost this day. Twenty-three German fighters were claimed destroyed. Six of the B-17s in the 100th Bomb Group returned to Thorpe Abbotts with battle damage. 1st Lieutenant Dean Radkte's Fortress barely made it back after being hit by sustained flak in the target area and was then attacked by two Fw 190s southwest of Abbeville, where a number of 20mm shells riddled the left wing and nose. One shell entered the navigator's compartment and struck the co-pilot, Lieutenant Robert Digby, in the head, killing him instantly. Shell fragments struck Radkte, wounding him in the face, head and in the neck beside his jugular vein. One fragment completely closed his right eye and splinters from the instrument panel were driven into the muscles of his right leg, rendering it useless. The explosion also ripped the oxygen mask from his face and stunned the engineer, Technical Sergeant Van D Pinner, who was hurled against the turret controls. Upon regaining his senses, Pinner thought first to escape, as he was certain that the plane had been blown apart. Through the smoke, he could see the pilot and co-pilot slumped over the controls. Blood was spattered over the shell-pitted compartment. The windows were shattered and broken. At this time, Radkte regained consciousness and saw Pinner about to leave. He yelled to him and the engineer returned to his station. Radkte then called the rest of the crew and reassured them. Most of the crew were never aware that Digby had been killed or that Radkte himself was severely wounded in the face, neck and hands and almost blinded. 2nd Lieutenant William B Agnetti, bombardier, was called up and he moved the co-pilot's body to the navigator's compartment and then returned to assist Radkte. Due to the loss of one engine and severed control cables, the B-17 lagged behind the formation. Radkte doubted whether he could remain conscious long enough to bring the Fortress home, but with fingers useless because of severe cuts, he skillfully used the butts of his hands to manipulate the controls and fought his way back into position in the formation and he reached Thorpe Abbotts safely.

Bombardier Harold Heyneman, who flew with Clement Cowan and his crew in the 100th Bomb Group, summed up the feeling at Thorpe Abbotts in December 1943. On reporting for duty, he was informed: 'Don't unpack your bags. Supply hates like Hell to pack them up again and you won't be here long...'

On New Year's Eve Eighth Bomber Command completed its second year in England with all-out raids on airfields in France. Missions of this nature were usually considered milk runs compared to the ones over stiffly defended targets in Germany but twenty-five bomber crews and four fighter pilots did not return to their bases to celebrate the New Year. Fog and rain then grounded the bombers until 4 January 1944, when the 1st and 2nd Divisions went to Kiel. The 91st Bomb Group lifted off from Bassingbourn to become the first group in the Eighth to reach 100 missions, although it had paid dearly for the privilege, losing more aircraft and crews on missions than any other group. At Molesworth, Russell F Beach, an engineer/waist gunner in the 427th Bomb Squadron, 303rd Bomb Group, reported for the mission having been returned to flying status by the medics after recovering from the badly frozen feet, hands and face he had suffered on his thirteenth mission. Flight operations, however, said that he was still on grounded status. Beach missed out as Lieutenant Fred C Humpreys and his crew took off in *Sweet Anne*.

In the 93rd Bomb Group, Staff Sergeant John W Butler was flying his 14th mission, as left waist gunner in *On The Ball*, which carried twelve M-17 Incendiaries and was flown by J J Collins. Butler recalled:

> We took off at 08.50. Kiel had 180 guns around the city. They reminded you of a neon sign. They'd go off four at a time. The temperature was minus 47. The slipstream was cold as hell. My oxygen mask kept freezing up. The vapor trails were very pretty, but they helped the Germans spot our formation. Jerry was really upset as he used a lot of ammunition trying to bring us down. Three planes behind us were knocked down. We lost a supercharger over the target so we were tail end Charlie again, as we had to drop back. We had P-38s and P-51s for escorts. The Mustangs were very good fighters. It was good to see them around. We were hit in the vertical stabilizer.[27]

The 5 January missions were the last under the auspices of Eighth Bomber Command. The Fifteenth Air Force had now been established in Italy and it was decided to embrace both the Eighth and Fifteenth in a new headquarters called US Strategic Air Forces, Europe (USSTAF). This was established at Bushey Park, Teddington, Middlesex, in the same location as the previous Headquarters, Eighth Air Force.

Two more B-17 groups arrived in East Anglia in January 1944. First to arrive was the 452nd Bomb Group, commanded by Lieutenant Colonel Herbert O Wangeman, which was based at Deopham Green, ten miles southwest of Norwich. Close on its heels were the crews of the 457th Bomb Group, commanded by Colonel James R Luper at Glatton, Huntingdonshire. The 457th was assigned to the 1st Bomb Division, joining the 351st at Polebrook and the 401st at Deenthorpe as part of the 94th Combat Wing. The 452nd was assigned to the 3rd Bomb Division, joining the 96th and 388th Bomb Groups in the 45th Combat Wing. The two divisions now totalled twenty B-17 groups and Doolittle had plans to increase this number.

The first mission under the auspices of the USSTAF was on 7 January when 420 heavies caused heavy damage to war plants at Ludwigshafen and Mannheim. Five B-17s and seven B-24s were lost. On 11 January a maximum effort comprising all three bomb divisions and including 291 Fortresses, was mounted on aircraft factories at Waggum, Halberstadt and Oschersleben in the Brunswick area, a city notorious for its flak and fighter defences. Since the destruction of the Fw 190 plant at Marienburg in October 1943, the Oschersleben plant at Brunswick had become the

w 190s attacking a formation of Liberators. *(USAF via Andy Bird)*

rigadier-General Ira C Eaker, Chief, Eighth Bomber Command (right) with Colonel Frank rmstrong, CO, 97th Bomb Group who later commanded the 306th Bomb Group and led the first ghth Air Force raid on Germany. *(USAF via Andy Bird)*

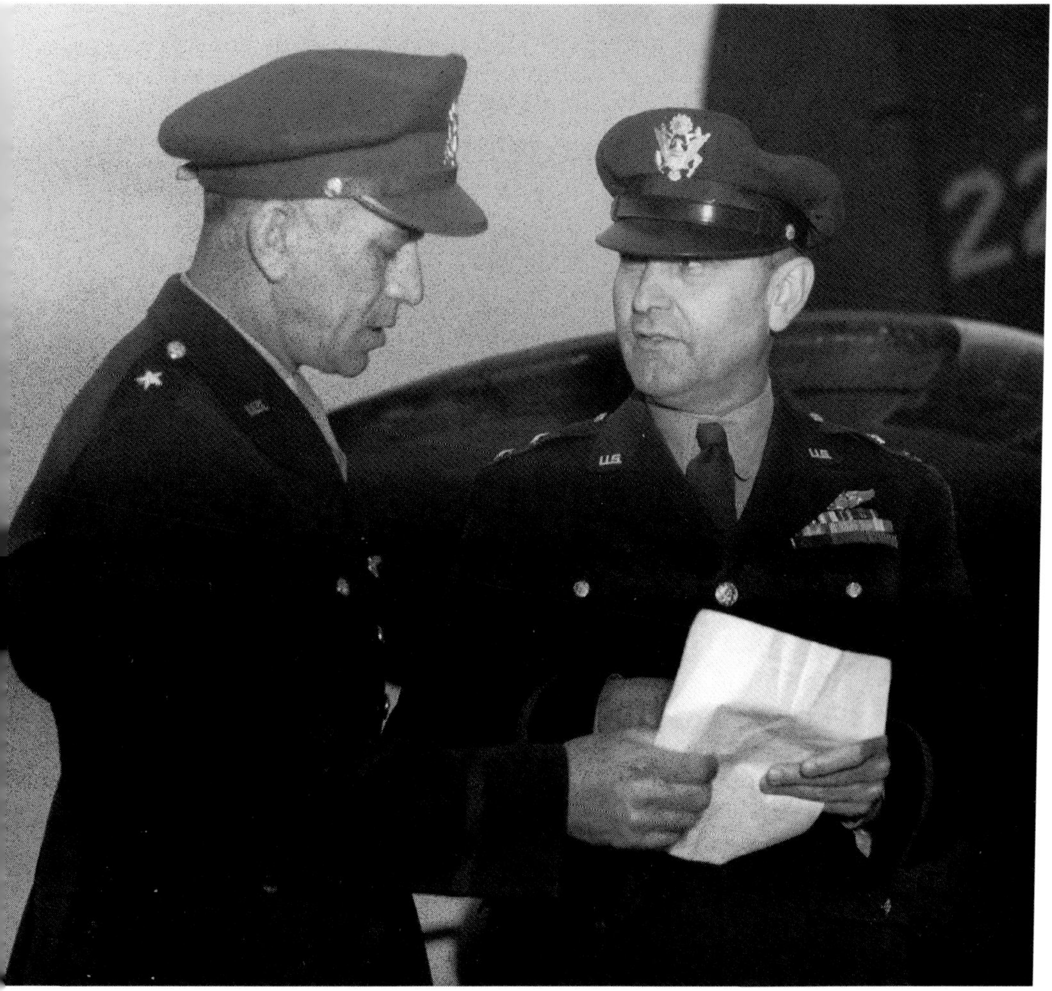

General Follett Bradley, Inspector-General of the US Army Air Forces went as an observer on the Wilhelmshaven raid on 20 May 1942, flying with the 305th Bomb Group. *(via Bill Donald)*

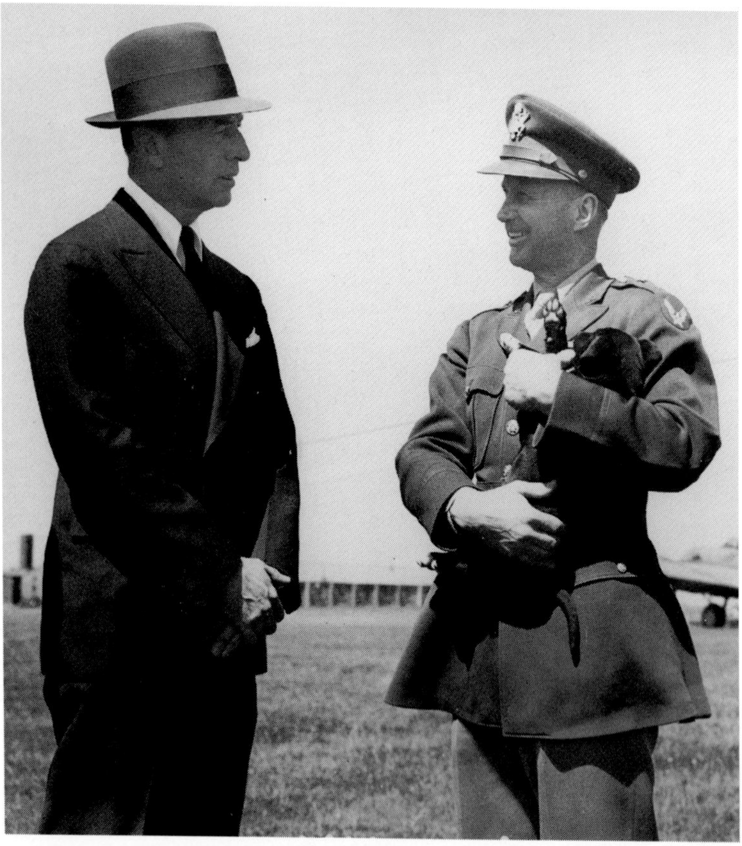

Brigadier-General Newton Longfellow (right) Commanding General of th Eighth Bomber Command of the United States Army Air Corps. *(via Bill Donald)*

igadier-General Hayward S 'Possum' Hansell and Colonel (later General) Curtis E LeMay, CO, 5th Bomb Group after the General's return in *Dry Martini & The Cocktail Kids 4* from Meaulte on May 1943. *(USAF)*

eft) Major Tom H Taylor, CO 364th Bomb Squadron, 305th Bomb Group (KIA 13 January 1943 ing in the co pilot's seat of *Dry Martini & The Cocktail Kids*). *(via Bill Donald)*

ight) Captain Pervis E Youree, 423rd Bomb Squadron, 306th Bomb Group pilot. On the 17 April 43 mission to the Focke Wulf plant at Bremen when the 306th Bomb Group lost ten B-17s, Youree ought *Old Faithful* home 200 miles at wave-top height after fighters put out two engines and shot e aircraft almost to pieces and he crash-landed at RAF Coltishall, Norfolk. Youree completed his mbat tour on 29 June 1943, during the Thurleigh group's 50th mission. *(Richards)*

B-17F *Dry Martini & The Cocktail Kids* in the 364th Bomb Squadron, 305th Bomb Group with Captain Allen V Martini (left). Centre is Ed Kursel, a guy with an infectious smile. This aircraft was the second *Dry Martini & The Cocktail Kids*, the first (42-5057) being lost with Lieutenant Ronald N Dahley's crew on the mission to Stuttgart on 6 September 1943 when it was ditched in the Channel (1 KIA. 7 PoW). (*via Bill Donald*)

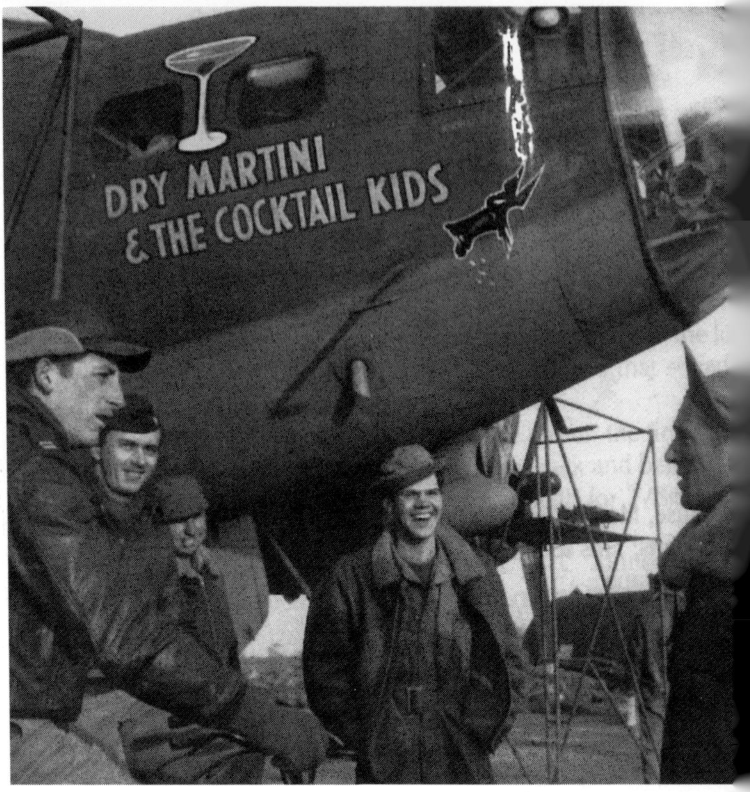

Captain Allen Martini and *Dry Martini 4*. Note the decoy missions signified by the two ducks. (*USAF*)

Daws Hill Lodge at High Wycombe on the green flanks of the rolling Buckinghamshire countryside. *(via Andy Bird)*

'Pinetree' HQ at High Wycombe. *(via Andy Bird)*

Brigadier General Robert B Williams, who at 23.15 hours on 13 October 1943 received a message, sent by General Anderson that the mission on the 14th was 'the most important air operation yet conducted.' Williams, who had led his Division on the first Schweinfurt raid, 17 August 1943, was a Texan who was a stickler for military discipline. He usually carried a swagger stick and was easily recognizable by his moustache and only one good eye; the other was lost while serving as an observer during the Blitz on London. *(USAF via Bill Donald)*

Entertainer Bob Hope and singer Frances Langford and Tony Romano with Sam Johnstone's crew the 364th Bomb Squadron, 305th Bomb Group and B-17F-95-BO 42-30242 *Pappy's Hellions* at Chelveston on 5 July 1943. L–R: Sam Johnstone, pilot; Ellsworth F Kenyon, co-pilot; Martin Licursi, navigator; Arthur Englehardt, ball turret gunner; Frances Langford; Tony Romano (kneeling); Bob Hope; Donald Baer, engineer; Richard Lewis, waist gunner; H M Bagby, tail gunner. R L Hutchinsc bombardier, was crawling around inside the B-17 giving 'Bazooka' Bob Burns a guided tour of the aircraft. Kenyon took over his own crew and they FTR from the mission to Schweinfurt on 14 October 1943. Radio operator Russell J Algren was KIA. Kenyon and eight others survived to be made PoW. (*USAF via Bill Donald*)

B-17F-95-BO 42-30242 *Pappy's Hellions* in the 364th Bomb Squadron, 305th Bomb Group, which was lost with Ellsworth F Kenyon's crew on 14 October 1943. (*USAF via Bill Donald*)

On the Schweinfurt mission 14 October 1943, Lieutenant Joseph Pellegrini was the lead bombardier in the B-17 flown by 2nd Lieutenant Joseph W Kane with Major Charles G Y Normand the Command Pilot. *(USAF)*

2nd Lieutenant Joseph W Kane, lead pilot on the Schweinfurt mission. Kane had the nisfortune of being the only wounded member on the lead ship. A 20mm shell came through the cockpit, peppering his face with shrapnel and burning his hair. The Kane and Farrell rews were the only 305th Bomb Group B-17s to return from the mission. *(via Bill Donald)*

-17F-80-BO 42-29988 *The Uncouth Bastard* in e 364th Bomb Squadron, 305th Bomb Group Chelveston on 13 October 1943, the day efore this Fortress and 2nd Lieutenant Robert Holt's crew FTR from Schweinfurt. Six crew ere killed and four were taken prisoner. *a Bill Donald)*

Crew of the *Eightball* in the 390th Bomb Group beneath their Fortress just before the second Schweinfurt mission. Lieutenant Dick Perry is standing at the extreme right of the picture. (*Perry*)

B-17F-115-BO 42-30727 in the 367th 'Clay Pigeons' Bomb Squadron. 306th Bomb Group taking off from Thurleigh. On 14 October, 42-30727, piloted by Lieutenant William C Bisson, was one of ten Fortresses the Thurleigh group lost on the Schweinfurt raid. Flak knocked out two of Bisson's engines and fighters riddled the rear fuselage, killing S/Sgt Thompson E Wilson, tail gunner. Only 2nd Lieutenant Charles R Stafford, co-pilot, who exited through the side cockpit window, and four crewmen in the aft section, escaped death. (*Richards Collection*)

B-17 under fighter attack. (*TAMM*)

B-17Fs in the 91st Bomb Group at 'Bombs away'. Bottom left is B-17F-5-VE 42-5714, which FTR with 2nd Lieutenant Robert M Slane's crew on 14 October 1943. The aircraft crashed at Nancy, France. Eight men were taken prisoner, one evaded and one was KIA. *(USAF)*

364th Bomb Squadron, 305th Bomb Group B-17Fs en route to their target. Left is 42-30807 WF-K *Katy*, which was lost with 2nd Lieutenant Gerald B Eakle's crew on 14 October 1943 (1 Evaded, 1 KIA, 8 PoW). Centre is 42-3436 WF-R in the 364th Bomb Squadron, which was lost with 2nd Lieutenant Dennis J McDarby's crew on the Schweinfurt raid on 14 October (5 KIA 5 PoW). Top is 42-30666 WF-M *Daisy Mae*, one of two Fortresses destroyed in the mid-air collision at Newton Bromswold on 15 November 1943. *(USAF via Bill Donald)*

B-17Fs of the 366th Bomb Squadron, 305th Bomb Group. Top is 41-24592 KY-G *Madame Betterfly*, which on 6 September 1943 1st Lieutenant Floyd E McSpadden was forced to put down in Switzerland due to fuel shortage and battle damage on the Stuttgart mission. Bottom B-17F is 42-29952 KY-J *Sizzle*, one of two 305th Bomb Group Fortresses that crashed at Maastricht, Holland *en route* to Schweinfurt on 14 October 1943. *Sizzle* was flown by Lieutenant Douglas L Murdock's crew: four men were killed. *(Michael L Gibson)*

Lieutenant David Williams, lead navigator in the 91st Bomb Group. *(Williams)*

B-17F-F-120-BO 42-30831 *Lazy Baby* in the 364th Bomb Squadron, 305th Bomb Group, which 2nd Lieutenant Edward Dienhart crash-landed at Reinach-Aesch, Switzerland on 14 October 1943 after bombing Schweinfurt. (*USAF via Bill Donald*)

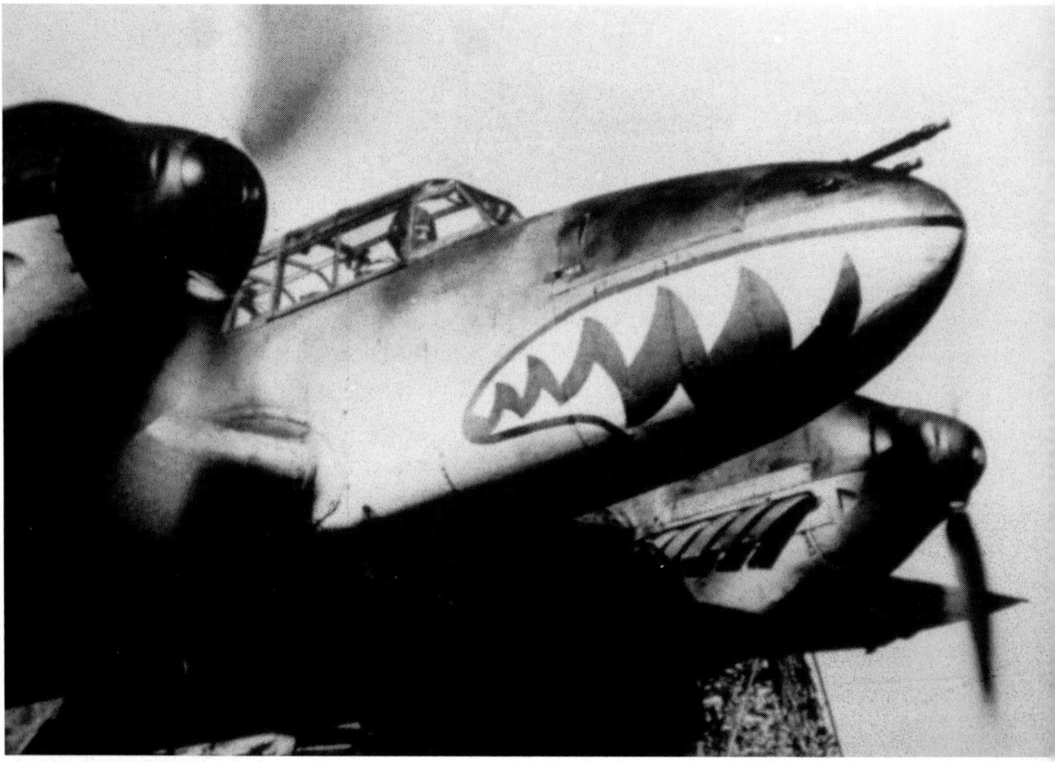

A Messerschmitt Bf 110 *Zerstörer*, which was one of the fighter types defending Schweinfurt. (*via Theo Boiten*)

.t William 'Bill' Rose (third from the left, back row) and his crew of *Sky Scraper* in the 92nd Bomb
Group. *(Bill Rose)*

3-17F-70-BO 42-29784 *Smilin Thru* in the 545th Bomb Squadron, 384th Bomb Group, which crashed .t Blaydon, Gloucestershire on 14 October 1943, returning from the raid on Schweinfurt. This .ircraft had previously served in both the 305th and 381st Bomb groups. *(via Bill Donald)*

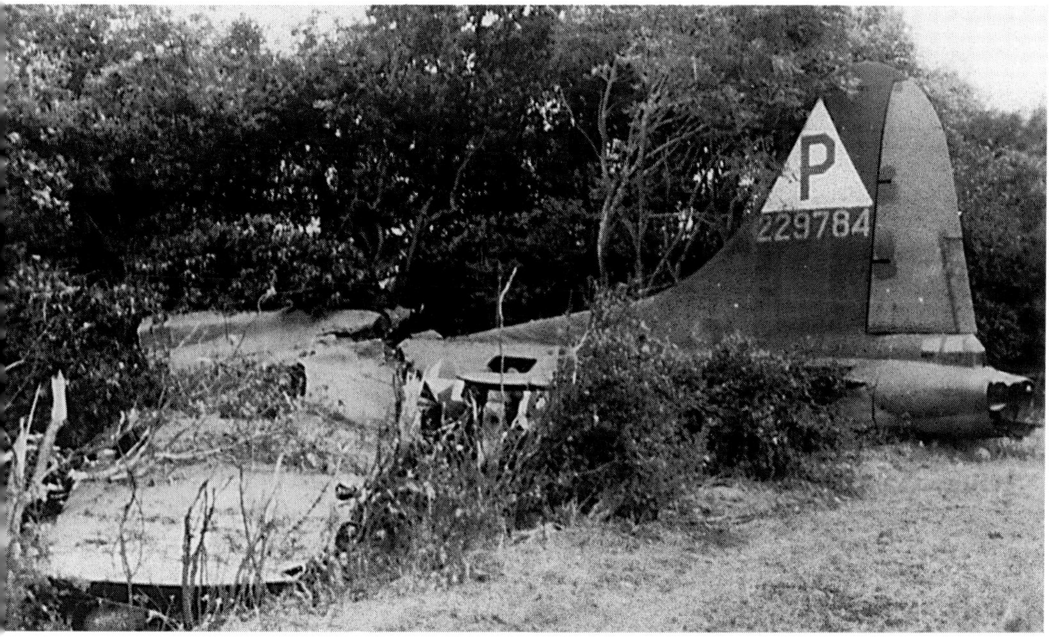

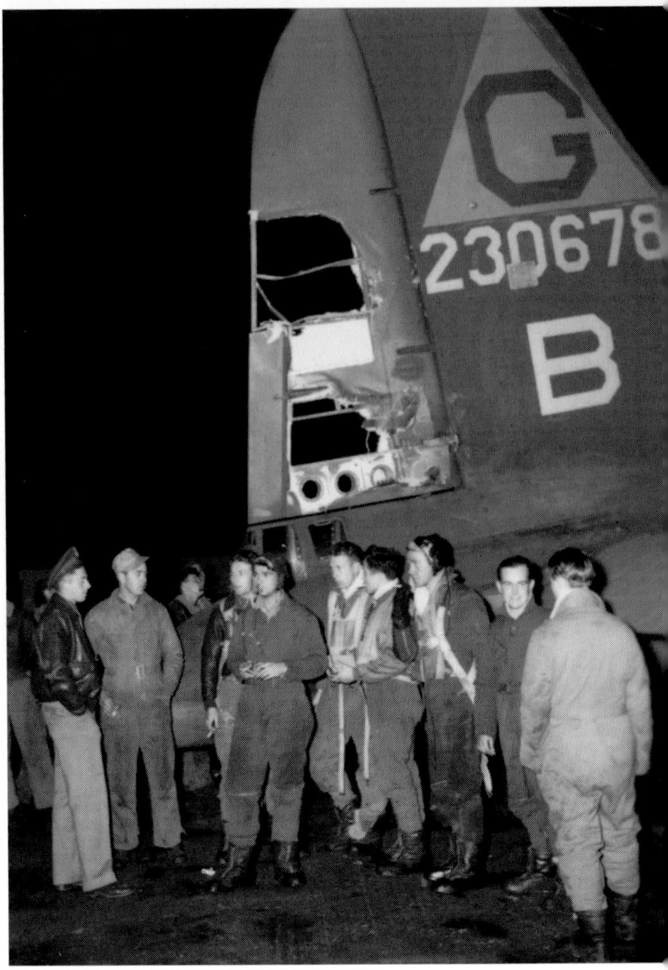

Lieutenant Frederick B Farrell's crew (Farrell is second from right) in the 366th Bomb Squadron, 305th Bomb Group beside their damaged B-17F-115-BO 42-30678 *Rigor Mortis* after returning to Chelveston from Schweinfurt on 14 October 1943. The bombardier, Frederick E Helmick, and navigator, Max Gruber, had been taken away by ambulance to have their wounds treated in hospital. *Rigor Mortis* was lost with Lieutenant Robert H Safranek's crew on 25 February 1944. Three crewmembers were KIA and seven were taken prisoner. (*via Bill Donald*)

(*Left*) Lieutenant Robert 'Bob' Hughes, pilot of *Nine Little Yanks and A Jerk* in the 351st Bomb Squadron, 100th Bomb Group. (*Hughes*)

(*Right*) Colonel 'Mo' Preston, CO 379th Bomb Group, listens to Major 'Rip' Rohr on his return from Schweinfurt. Preston noted that Rohr 'looked harassed, shaken and more agitated that I had ever seen him.' (*Preston*)

B-17F-15-DL 42-3037 was assigned overseas on 1 August 1943 and joined the 366th Bomb Squadron, 305th Bomb Group. It was christened *Windy City Avenger* in memory of *Windy City Challenger*, which was lost on the mission to Villacoublay on 14 July 1943. *Windy City Avenger* transferred to the 384th Bomb Group on 20 September 1943 and was salvaged on 15 October 1943 after damage sustained on the Schweinfurt raid made it only fit for scrap. *(via Bill Donald)*

3-17F-27-BO 41-24605 *Knock-)ut Dropper*, which was flown n the Schweinfurt mission by ieutenant John P Manning, vho led the low squadron in ne 303rd Bomb Group ormation. On 16 November 943 the 359th Bomb Squadron ortress set a new Eighth Air orce record for a B-17 when Ianning flew it on its 50th nission. *Knock-Out Dropper* was crapped at Stillwater,)klahoma in late 1945. *ia Harry Gobrecht)*

This Nazi flag, which fluttered over the Kugelfischer ball bearing plant, the largest of the four plants at Schweinfurt, was presented to the 305th Bomb Group at Chelveston by an Air Force journalist after the US 42nd 'Rainbow' Armored Division captured it on 11 April 1945. The 305th Bomb Group lost thirteen crews on the second raid on the plants on 14 October 1943. *(via Bill Donald)*

(*Left*) Oberfeldwebel Adolf 'Addi' Glunz who is wearing the *Eichenlaub* (Knight's Cross with Oak Leaves). (*via Bill Donald*)

(*Right*) Staff Sergeant Forrest S Clark, radio operator/gunner in Lieutenant Rockford C Griffith's crew in the 67th Squadron, 44th Bomb Group at Shipdham. (*Clark*)

B-17F-20-BO 41-24525 *What's Cookin Doc?* and 2nd Lieutenant Walter E Garner's crew in the 547th Bomb Squadron, 384th Bomb Group, were lost on the 7 January 1944 mission to Ludwigshafen. (*via Bill Donald*)

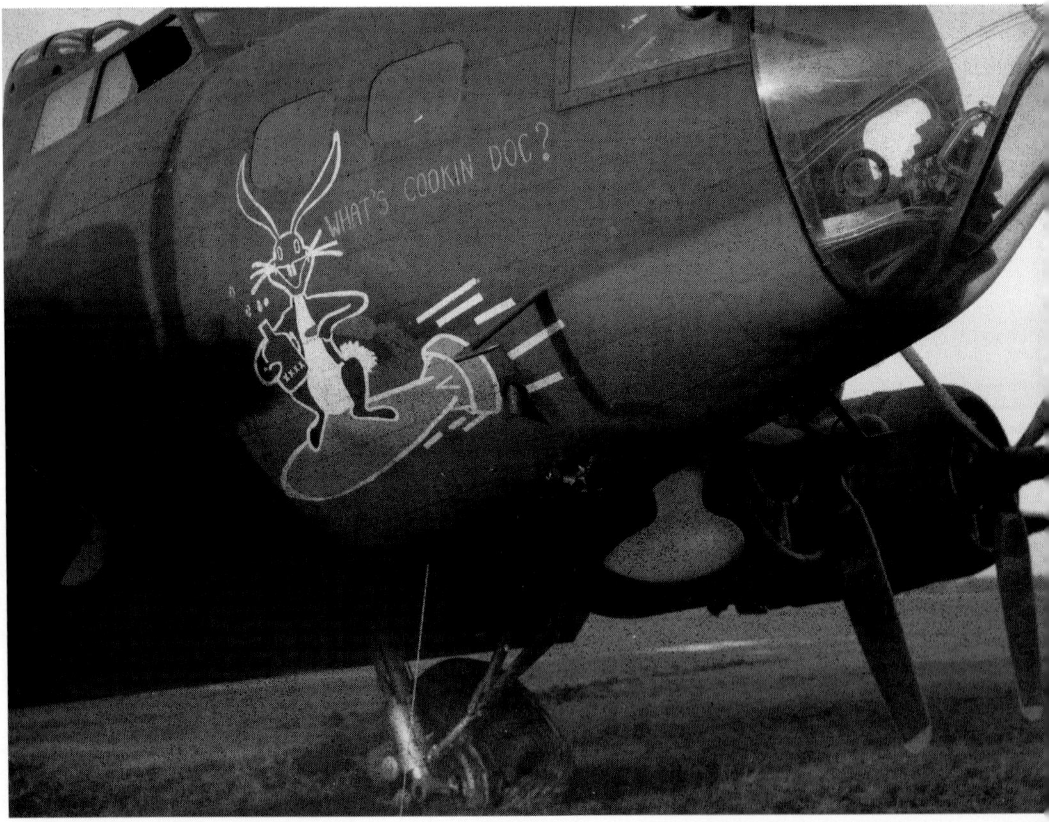

principal producer of this German fighter. All bombing was to be carried out using visual sightings, with the 3rd Division stoking up fires created by the 1st and 2nd Divisions, but, if the weather intervened, crews were briefed to bomb the city of Brunswick using PFF techniques.

Heavy rain pounded the bases in the east of England and heavy cloud began drifting across the Channel, Holland and into Germany. Command allowed the mission to proceed in the hope that the cloud would clear. For two hours the bombers assembled into their intricate formations and then crews ploughed on across the Channel, conscious that the fighter support would be severely restricted or abandoned altogether. The fighters did manage to take off but they soon became lost in the cloud layers over England and many were forced to abort the mission. The Luftwaffe *Gruppen* in eastern Germany were not affected by the cloudy conditions and were able to take off and mass for a concentrated attack, the strength of which had not been seen since the Schweinfurt battles of October 1943. With the American escort seriously depleted the order went out to the 2nd and 3rd Divisions to abandon the mission. The crew of *Dog Patch Raider* in the 93rd Bomb Group formation received credit for the mission because, as Staff Sergeant Butler recalled, 'As we crossed the Dutch coast we ran into quite a heavy concentration of flak. It was my sixteenth mission and the temperature was minus 37°.'[28] The 1st Division, which was about 100 miles from Brunswick, was allowed to continue. The 303rd Bomb Group was leading the 1st Division and Brigadier General Robert Travis flew as Task Force Commander aboard *The Eightball*, piloted by Lieutenant Colonel Bill Calhoun, CO of the 359th Squadron. Just past Dummer Lake over 200 enemy fighters bounced the formation. General Travis was to tell newsmen later:

> The fighters... in spite of our escort, came at us in bunches. Our first attack was from four Fw 190s, the next from thirty Fw 190s. Then twelve and they just kept coming. They attacked straight through the formation and from all angles without even rolling over. They seemed to let up just a little when we started out bombing run. There was a period of three minutes only, from the time the fighters first started to make their attack until they left us, when they were not around.

The 94th Bomb Group, flying at the head of the 4th Combat Wing leading the 3rd Division, was only 25 miles from its objective at Waggum when the order to abort was given. However, Lieutenant Colonel Louis G Thorup in the lead ship decided to press on to the target. Andy J Caroles, a bombardier in the 331st Bomb Squadron recalls:

> The weather over England was very bad when we took off and assembled. The mission was recalled about the time we left the

English coast, but Colonel Thorup did not receive the message. As a result, our Wing and two others that did not receive the message apparently went on into the target, not knowing the mission had been scrubbed and the fighter escorts recalled.[29] It was a costly mix-up and cost us several good crews. The weather began clearing up as soon as we reached Germany and was perfectly clear in the area of the target. We made a 'dry run' and had to do a 360° turn and come in again.[30]

Andy J Caroles continues:

As we started our second bomb run the Me 110s began attacking us. The other two groups in our Wing had dropped their bombs on the first run and headed for home, leaving our group alone, We had a running battle for about an hour – the Me 110s attacking from 3 o'clock around to 9 o'clock with rockets and 20mms. One by one the ships around us would be knocked out of formation. The enemy fighters would then 'gang up' on these cripples and finish them off. Bloyd and Cox were doing violent evasive action all through these attacks and again and again I saw clouds of 20mm shells explode where we had been only a second before. It looked as if our group was going to be picked off one at a time. I was expecting our turn to come at any moment. About 90 miles from the coast six P-47s suddenly appeared and scared away the Jerries. Our formation was a sad sight – only ten planes were left in it out of the original twenty-one. Besides the ships from our group that went down, our formation lost three from the 447th Group,[31] which had tacked on to us. I saw one of the 447th ships go down. It was an all-silver B-17. The entire tail of this ship from the waist back was blazing fiercely and one Me 110 was sitting on his tail not more than 200 yards out, slugging it out with the tail gunner. The tail gunner finally hit the Me 110 and it peeled off and started down smoking heavily. I watched the flames eat their way forward on the ship as it flew on in formation for one or two minutes. Then, it suddenly nosed up, fell off on its back and went straight down. No 'chutes came out of it. It was a fascinating sight and one I'll never forget. Our ship came through the entire battle with one small flak hole. The Lord must have been watching over us and I'm thankful to be back from that raid in one piece.[32]

Vast banks of stratocumulus clouds covering most of Germany prevented visual bombing so attacks on targets in France became the order of the day throughout the remainder of January and early February. When bad weather on 14 January prevented bombing in Germany the bombers were switched to V-weapon sites in northern France, when 527 B-17s and B-24s escorted by 645 P-38s, P-47s and P-51s attacked twenty-one V-weapon sites in the Pas de Calais. The Luftwaffe was hard pressed to deal with the number of bombers – 844 tactical aircraft also hit targets in northern France this day – and the large number of Allied fighters on freelance sorties over northern France.

Of the twenty-nine missions flown during January and February 1944, thirteen were to V-1 flying bomb sites.[33] On 21 January, 795 B-17s and B-24s set out to bomb V-weapon sites and other targets in the Pas de Calais and at Cherbourg. Some of these aircraft bombed targets of opportunity while some combat boxes remained in their target areas too long identifying targets. (One target reportedly required ten runs before the group dropped its bombs!) A total of 628 escorting fighters were to shepherd the bombers and protect them from Luftwaffe fighter attack. However, the delayed runs and constant circling of some of the groups meant that the escorting fighters became low on fuel and had to withdraw, leaving some of the attacking bombers vulnerable to fighter attack. Bombing was also hampered by the weather, which was poor, with heavy cloud over most of northern France. Fewer than half the bombers dropped their bomb loads on the assigned targets. The 44th Bomb Group was assigned two targets: the 66th and 68th Squadrons the V-1 site at Escalles-Sur-Buchy in the Pas de Calais; and the 67th and 506th Squadrons military installations at Agathe D'Aliermont. Normally the mission would have been regarded as a 'milk run' as the targets were so close to the English Channel but it proved costly for the 'Flying Eightballs'. V-1 sites were notoriously difficult to hit and the bombing altitude for the attack was 12,000ft. Conditions therefore favoured the fighters. Once again, it was the 'Abbeville Kids' of JG 26 that took off to meet the Liberators. At 14.20 hours Hauptmann Karl Borris, CO of I./JG 26, and his fifteen fighters, took off from Florrenes to look for the '*Amis*'. Over Poix, Borris saw what he was hoping for – an unescorted *Pulk* (herd) of Liberators. He immediately gave orders for his fighters to attack from the rear, where the seven Liberators of the 68th Bomb Squadron were flying 'tail-end Charlie' position in the formation. Here the JG 26 pilots had the richest pickings. Such was the speed and surgical method employed by the attackers that four pilots achieved all their five victories simultaneously at 15.30 hours. All except one of the victims were from the 68th Bomb Squadron, which returned to Shipdham with only three Liberators.

Staff Sergeant John W Butler flew his seventeenth mission this day when he flew as left waist gunner in *Naughty Nan* flown by J J Collins. 'The Travelling Circus' target was Bois Carre:

> We took off at 12.10. The weather over the target was cloudy so we couldn't bomb it so we just cruised around to see if would clear. We came over Abbeville and they threw up a quite a lot of flak but it was way below so it didn't bother us. One plane received a direct

hit – there was nothing left of it. Those German flak gunners were getting pretty good. They were also shooting rockets up at us from the ground. They left quite a smoke trail behind them. Fighters knocked down some planes. So the whole mission didn't turn out to be a milk run as all the kids thought it would be.

The bombers were stood down for two days following the 21 January missions but operatons resumed again on 24 January when 857 bomber crews were briefed to attack aviation industry plants and marshalling yards at Frankfurt. Bad weather during assembly played havoc with assembly procedures. At Duxford, Earl Payne in the 78th Fighter Group watched the fleets of bombers taking off for Germany. He saw a B-17 flying near the field, which happened to blow up in mid-air before crashing into the hills beyond.[34] Payne counted six parachutes and they seemed to take a long time to get down. Four landed out of sight but two landed near the roundabout out of Whittlesford. One of the 'chutes failed to open because it was burned. 'The poor fellow landed on his feet, which were driven clear up to his stomach and burst his lungs. His entrails coming out of either side of his body beneath his armpits.'[35]

The weather remained bad and the next heavy bomber mission was not flown until 28 January, when fifty-four B-24s were despatched to France. Forty-three Liberators bombed their targets and all of the aircraft returned safely to their bases. The following day the bomber crews were assigned targets at Frankfurt. At Shipdham, Forrest S Clark in the 67th Bomb Squadron was just recovering from a bout of sinusitis and had been in the base hospital. He and Abe Sofferman reported to the flight line for briefing. Radio operators were often called to fill out vacancies on crews. Sofferman volunteered for the Frankfurt mission with the crew of Lieutenant Harold Pinder who was flying *Sky Queen* and Clark stood down. Of the 863 heavies despatched, twenty-four B-17s and five B-24s failed to return. Once again the Luftwaffe seized upon lapses in the bomber formations, which began to go awry soon after crossing the coast at Dunkirk, when navigational errors and radar problems caused several combat wings to fly most of the mission without fighter escort. The Fw 190s of the Ist and IInd *Gruppen* of JG 26 took off at 10.10 and were vectored east to Namur where they intercepted the B-24 formation. While some of the enemy fighters moved on to seek out B-17s in the 3rd Bomb Division formations, the 7th *Staffel* remained with the Liberators and north and northeast of Trier they singled out the 44th Bomb Group formation. Leutnant Waldi Radener later claimed one of the Liberators but this was not confirmed. Unteroffizier Kurt Stahnke singled out another Liberator – it was Pinder's – and the German scored hits near the bomber's right wing tip.[36] 1st Lieutenant Harold H Pinder recalls:

> We were met on the coast and on in by both Me 109s and Fw 190s. I had never seen them mixed before. At about 11.02 hours we dropped out of control after about three separate enemy passes. We took 20mm hits under the flight deck that cut the control cables. I couldn't get the autopilot to take over control – probably a hopeless effort anyway. The aircraft dove out of control. I remember the wing afire and at least the No. 4 engine knocked out. Our B-24 began to lose altitude and fire was seen in the bomb bay. Co-pilot Larry Grono parachuted out and became a PoW. 2nd Lieutenant Alvan E Stubbs, bombardier, died in the nose turret. Milas Green, the left waist gunner, was in shock from a 20mm hit through both lower legs. Staff Sergeant Jack C Robison, the right waist gunner, pushed Green out of the rear hatch and pulled his ripcord but he did not get out himself, possibly giving his 'chute to Green. Robison died in the plane, as did tail gunner Bill Paxton and ball turret gunner Robert L Laucamp. Navigator Donald Boomer and Earl Hall the engineer also parachuted out.[37]

North of Ludwigshafen Oberleutnant Rudolf 'Rudi' Leuschel, *Staffelkapitän* 8./JG 26, shot down the Liberator flown by 1st Lieutenant George H Maynard in the 66th Squadron. Staff Sergeant Derise L Nichols, tail gunner, recalls:

> We were over France and about an hour from the target, with all bombs on board, we were jumped by a flight of fighters and were hit immediately. Shells hit just behind me and made very large holes in the waist section. No. 4 engine was hit and put out of action. So were the controls to the tail section. So the pilots could only control flight with the three remaining engines. With the possibility of getting back to England now so slight, the decision was made to head for Switzerland. The bombs were salvoed, but even then with the trouble of trying to steer with the engines, we continually lost altitude across France. We did finally cross the Swiss border but by then we were less than 1,000ft. We were shot at and hit by (Swiss?) ground fire and No. 2 engine was put out of commission as well. Not being able to gain altitude over the rising terrain of Switzerland, we had to circle back to abandon ship. Only the three of us got out – all from the rear – because we were so low by that time that the others did not have time to get out and open their 'chutes.[38]

Luckily for the 'Flying Eightballs' P-38 Lightnings in the 20th Fighter Group appeared on the scene and JG 26 were forced to break off their attacks and seek cover in the clouds.

On 30 January the Eighth returned to the aircraft factories at Brunswick when a record 778 heavies were dispatched. Bombing was carried out by

701 of the bombers using PFF for the loss of twenty aircraft. Next day 784 B-24s bombed V-1 sites being constructed at St. Pol/Siracourt while seventy P-47 fighter-bombers escorted by eighty-seven Thunderbolts and forty-seven P-38s bombed Gilze-Rijen airfield. They encountered eighty-four enemy fighters and in a fierce battle six P-38s were lost. The US fighters claimed thirteen enemy fighters destroyed.

The bomb groups were stood down on 1 February and missions resumed on the 2nd when ninety-six B-24s bombed V-1 sites in Northern France once more. On the 3rd, 543 bombers bombed Wilhelmshaven while sixty-one others bombed Emden and targets of opportunity. Bad weather caused more than 100 of the bombers to abort their mission. On 4 February 433 bombers in fifteen combat wings of B-17s and B-24s were dispatched to Frankfurt on the Main River.[39] The river presented a clear return on H_2S radar carried by PFF aircraft and it was enough to allow the bombers to drop their loads through overcast with a fair degree of accuracy. However, H_2S failures and high crosswinds prevented completely accurate bombing, while several combat wings came under intense AA fire over the Ruhr. Staff Sergeant John W Butler in the 93rd Bomb Group flew his twenty-first mission of his tour when he again flew left waist gunner in *Naughty Nan*, piloted by J J Collins. Butler recalled:

> We took off at 09.15 to bomb the city of Frankfurt at 21,000ft. The temperature was minus 44, which is very cold. Before we passed the enemy coast my heated boots went out so I went up on the flight deck and borrowed the radio man's before returning to my waist gun position. We ran into heavy flak twice on the way to the target. Over the target it was pretty damn good. You should have seen Carey and I throwing the tin foil out. It is supposed to spoil the German radar equipment. We dropped our bombs and started for home. My heated suit went out for good. I had the ball-turret gunner come back in the waist to take my place as I then went up on the flight deck to try and keep warm. Our bombardier lost his oxygen supply so he came up on the flight deck also. My feet were frozen. The radioman fired a red flare as we came into land and the meat wagon followed us down the runway. We stopped and they took us off to the hospital. There were around twenty fellows in the hospital with frostbite. This was the worst mission I was on to have so many things go wrong.

Fortunately the Luftwaffe was limited in its operations by the weather, though JG 26 claimed seven of the total of ten bombers shot down by the German fighters.

On the 5th, 450 B-17s and B-24s attacked airfields at Châteauroux, Avord, Tours, Châteaudun, Orleans and Villacoublay.[40] Staff Sergeant John W Butler in the 93rd Bomb Group, which was given Tours as its target, flew his 22nd mission of his tour when he flew left waist gunner in 939-E[41] flown by R R Russ. Butler recalled:

> The CQ called me at 06.30 to fly as a spare gunner. So by the time I made the briefing room and out to the plane it was near takeoff time. They didn't pass any candy out today. I didn't have any breakfast either because everything was in a hurry. They had an oxygen leak in the tail turret so they had to replace the regulator. We then had to take off 20 minutes late. We then headed for the rally point where we were finally able to pick up our own group. The weather was nice and clear as we were only at 16,000ft so you could see the ground pretty good. Temperature was only minus 13. My heated suit worked real good. We had good fighter-protection as we had P-38s and P-47s. I saw one P-38 go down in flames but the pilot hit the silk. The plane broke in two and I watched it hit the ground. We got to the primary target and some ships dropped their bombs. We then went on to the secondary where we dropped our twelve 500 pounders. I could see quite a few fires burning. Fighters shot down a B-24 in the 409th Squadron. Four 'chutes got out.[42] It was good mission as a whole. We received a large hole from flak in the de-icer boot.

On 6 February 206 bombers bombed more airfields in France and rocket launching installations at Eclimeux, although bad weather prevented more than 400 bombers from completing their missions. The Bomb Groups were stood down on the 7th. On the 8th, 237 bombers attacked Frankfurt-Main using blind bombing techniques while 127 heavies bombed V-weapon sites at Watten and Siracourt. Another seventy-eight bombers blasted targets of opportunity. In all, thirteen Fortresses were lost. Staff Sergeant John W Butler flew his twenty-third mission, flying as nose gunner in *Naughty Nan* in J J Collins' crew when the 93rd Bomb Group went to Siracourt:

> We took off at 07.15 to bomb the construction works at 15,000ft which we later learned were for the buzz bombs. The temperature was minus 30. I didn't go in the turret until we were at 14,000ft. You needed help getting in and out of the nose turret, as they had to close the turret door behind you. When you wanted to get out you had to call them on the interphone to let you out. Well, I threw my heated and heavy gloves up on the ammunition box and then I climbed in the turret. The navigator then closed the door for me. The four little windows were open and the guns were elevated so the wind was blowing in quite fast. It was very cold. I got my oxygen mask connected. I then tried to close the windows, but my hands were frozen. I couldn't reach my gloves because my guns were elevated.

> The main line was off and it had to be turned on from the outside. I plugged in my heated suit but I had no gloves on and they were beet red. I had no feeling in them. I finally got my throat mike on and I yelled over the interphone to get me the hell out of this turret. The navigator opened the door and pulled me out. I went up to the flight deck for heat. When my hands began to thaw out I really suffered. We shot a red flare as we came in for a landing. The pilot called for a meat wagon, which met us at end of the runway and took us to the hospital.

After another stand-down on the 9th missions resumed again on 10 February, when twenty-eight bombers hit the airfield at Gilze-Rijen, while Brunswick was the target for the 3rd Division. They were escorted by 466 Lightnings, Thunderbolts and Ninth Fighter Command Mustangs. The long-ranging P-51s could accompany the bombers to their targets and back again but they were powerless to prevent German fighters causing carnage on a large scale. The enemy destroyed twenty-nine of the 169 Fortresses despatched. On Friday 11 February, when the first P-51s joined Eighth Fighter Command, 180 B-17s of the 1st Division attacked industrial targets at Frankfurt-Main and a V-weapon site at St. Pol/ Siracourt again, while 130 heavies bombed Ludwigshafen and other targets of opportunity after the blind bombing equipment failed. The 3rd Division was rested and the 2nd Division B-24s bombed targets in the Pas de Calais. At Hardwick, Staff Sergeant John W Butler, now recovered from his ordeal on 8 February, flew as left waist gunner in *Willie's Worry* with J J Collins' crew when the 93rd Bomb Group returned to Siracourt to bomb the construction works again. It was Butler's twenty-fourth mission and he recalled:

> We took off at 07.15. At 14,000ft it was 14 below zero. We met quite a lot of flak at the IP and those flak gunners were right on the beam as you could hear the flak bursting quite close. Turner's plane received a direct hit and then broke in half. The tail gunner fell out of his turret and hit the wing of the plane behind.[43]

The Fortresses bombed Frankfurt through 10/10th clouds in an attempt to hit the target that had been missed three days before. The bombers were protected by fifteen groups of escorting fighters. The strong fighter escort helped keep bomber losses to a minimum and five were lost on 11 February, three of the B-17s falling victim to JG 26. Flak and fighters had harried the 306th Bomb Group formation all the way from the coast to the target, which was bombed by nineteen of the Group's planes. The B-17 flown by 1st Lieutenant Geno DiBetta and his crew in the 423rd Squadron was hit by flak at the IP and the No. 3 engine was put out of action. DiBetta and his co-pilot, 2nd Lieutenant Earl J Wolf Jnr, managed to keep in formation until bombs away, when they turned for home. Flak again hit the left wing and DiBetta tried to reach a cloud bank below but about six Fw 190s caught up with the ailing Fortress, hitting the bomber on the first pass and then queuing up for head-on attacks, one after the other. Near Mons, Belgium, Oberleutnant Erich Scheyda of 3./JG 26 claimed the bomber's final destruction.

Northwest of Poix, *Ain't It Gruesome*[44] flown by Captain John P Carson Jnr in the 351st Bomb Group was claimed shot down by Oberfeldwebel Adolf 'Addi' Glunz, CO 5./JG26. Northeast of Beauvais, *Tenabove* in the 532nd Bomb Squadron, 381st Bomb Group[45] fell victim to Unteroffizier Gerhard Guttmann.[46]

Next day, 12 February, eighty-five Liberators bombed V-weapon sites at St. Pol/Siracourt again. One of the crewmembers who flew on the raid was Staff Sergeant John W Butler, who was right waist gunner in *Reddy Teddy*,[47] piloted by Lieutenant Glenn E Tedford. Butler was flying his twenty-fifth and final mission of his tour in the 93rd Bomb Group. He wrote:

> We took off at 07.30 to bomb Siracourt from 18,000ft. Flak was pretty good, but none was close to us. It was minus 22. When I left the French coast behind I was very happy. I never wanted to see the French coast again except on a postcard or on a newsreel. It was a good mission to finish up on. I was a pretty happy guy when I landed.[48]

Next day the Chiefs of Staff accepted a revision of the CBO Plan. Targets were reduced to a number that could be decisively attacked and target lists were revised to keep up with the enemy's efforts to relocate vital industrial plant. Disruption of lines of communication and a reduction of Luftwaffe fighter strength were now given high priority. General Carl 'Tooey' Spaatz and his subordinate commanders, Major General Jimmy Doolittle (Eighth Air Force) and Major General Nathan F Twining (Fifteenth Air Force), planned a series of co-coordinated raids on German aircraft industry, supported by RAF night bombing, at the earliest possible date. Good weather finally permitted 'Operation *Argument*', the first battle involving the mass use of bomb groups of the Strategic Air Forces (USSTAF), to take place during the week 20–25 February. 'Big Week', as it quickly became, resulted in total losses of 226 bombers. Although the Eighth flew 3,300 bomber sorties and dropped 6,000 tons of bombs during 'Big Week' the destruction was not as great as at first thought. Luftwaffe *Gruppen* were certainly deprived of many replacement aircraft and fighter production was halved the following month, but this had cost 400 bombers and 4,000 casualties to achieve. Unfortunately, the small size high-explosive bombs destroyed only the factory buildings, leaving machine tools, lathes and jigs virtually untouched beneath the wreckage.

It was only a matter of time before this equipment was recovered from the wrecked plants and put into full production again. However, Doolittle and his staff officers believed the Eighth had dealt the German aircraft industry a severe blow, though losses were such that the bomb groups did not fly another mission until 28 February, when 181 B-17s and B-24s attacked V-weapon sites in the Pas de Calais. Half of the bombers dispatched were forced to return without getting their bombs away because of heavy cloud. Seven aircraft were lost, mostly to flak.

Missions against German aircraft industry were resumed on 29 February when 215 B-17s bombed production plants at Brunswick again, while thirty-eight Liberators bombed V-weapon targets in France. Two days later, on 2 March, the Eighth Air Force returned to Frankfurt, sending 481 B-17s and B-24s to bomb the marshalling yards in the city. Only 137 heavies were able to bomb their briefed target because of failures of pathfinder equipment, and 133 heavies bombed targets of opportunity in southwestern Germany, including Mannheim/Ludwigshafen, Limburg and Dürnbach. Some 84 heavies bombed the airfield at Chartres in France.

Doolittle and his staff officers now felt confident enought to strike at 'Big B' – Berlin, the biggest prize in the Third Reich. A raid by the Eighth Air Force on Berlin had been scheduled for 23 November the previous year but had been postponed because of bad weather. RAF Bomber Command had been bombing the capital nightly for some time but Berliners had not yet been subjected to the round-the-clock bombing which had devastated so many other German cities.

'The very thought of making a raid on Berlin was almost terrifying,' recalls Robert J Shoens, a pilot in the 100th Bomb Group:

> Rumours began flying thick and fast several weeks before the day arrived, adding to the apprehension and anxiety. Each day we would walk into the briefing sessions wondering if the tape on the wall map would stretch to 'Big B' that morning. A great sigh of relief could be heard from the crews when the briefing officer pulled back the curtain and the tape went somewhere else. But sooner or later it was sure to come and it did.

Notes

1. 566 B-17s and B-24s and H_2X ships of the 482nd Bomb Group were dispatched. AN/APS-15, usually known as H_2X, or '*Mickey Mouse*' (later shortened to just *Mickey*) was a US-developed version of H_2S. The first use of H_2X was made on the mission to Wilhelmshaven in October 1943. Sets were available in sufficient numbers by late 1943 to mount the first major raids to test its effectiveness and it became the standard device for bombing

through overcast conditions. Using *H_2X* on D-Day, 1,365 Eighth Air Force bombers dropped 2,798 tons of bombs through cloud behind the beachheads 30 minutes before the landing.

2. Also, 374 Fortresses were dispatched to the iron foundry works and marshalling yards at Gelsenkirchen, led by five *Oboe*-equipped pathfinders. *Oboe* was a British technique adopted by the AAF and got its name from a radar pulse, which sounded like a musical instrument. Two ground stations were used, but in contrast to *Gee*, an aircraft's position was assessed at the ground stations, which operated on re-radiation of radar signals directed at the aircraft. Its range was 280 miles.
3. Nicknamed the 'Blue Bunny' suit. Electrically heated one-piece flying suits developed by the General Electric Co. were standardized in 1941. The two-piece F-3A suit appeared in October 1944 and was designed to be worn over long underwear and underneath the A-15/B-11 suit. The F-3 would protect in temperatures as low as minus 60°F.
4. Staff Sergeant Rollin C Looker and the rest of the crew of *Sack Artists* were interned in Switzerland on 18 March 1944.
5. Three B-24s and eight B-17s were lost.
6. A failure of PFF aircraft caused the 95th, 96th, 100th and 388th Bomb Groups to turn back before the enemy coast, leaving just the 61 unescorted B-17s of the 94th, 385th and 390th in the 4th and 13th CBWs to continue to the target.
7. 42-230795 *The Wild Hare* in the 548th Bomb Squadron, flown by Lieutenant John P McGowan, which crashed at Druner. (1 Evaded, 1 KIA, 8 PoW)
8. Oberleutnant Wolfgang Neu, 4./JG 26 CO, was credited with shooting down a 96th Bomb Group B-17 northeast of Arnhem. B-17 42-37830 in the 413th Bomb Squadron, piloted by 2nd Lieutenant Henry E Marks Jnr crashed with the loss of seven crew.
9. The raid, comprising approximately 155 bombers, destroyed the power station in addition to other parts of the facility, resulting in a complete stoppage of the entire manufacturing process. The Germans later decided to ship their remaining heavy water stockpile to Germany. However, all 546 tons of the heavy water was sent to the bottom of Lake Timm when the ferry being used to transport it was blown up by SOE agents over the deepest part of the lake.
10. *Innocence and Death In Enemy Skies: A True Story of WWII Adventure and Romance* by Forrest S Clark. Jawbone Publishing Corp. 2004.
11. Griffith and his co-pilot, 1st Lieutenant L G Grone got the Liberator back to Shipdham where the one landing gear failed to drop. Sergeant Earl J Parrish, the flight engineer, tried in vain to crank it down by hand. Griffith called off the crash landing in favour of a belly landing but the stubborn undercarriage leg failed to respond when Parrish tried to retract the 'down' leg. Griffith refused to panic and ordered everyone except Grone and Kuban to bale out. Forrest Clark baled out, fell to the ground and gripped it with both hands in a gesture of relief and thanksgiving. He was certain he had landed in Holland, but a Norfolk farmer holding a pitchfork soon reassured him. Two hours later repair crews checking the wreckage found two unexploded German shells in the one good engine that had brought the crew home. Griffith won the Silver Star for bringing the bomber back and saving the lives of his crew. He went on to complete 20 missions.

12. Staff Sergeant Joseph D Gilbert was left waist gunner on 1st Lieutenant Edward M Dobson's crew which were lost when *Raggedy Ann Junior* wernt down in the North Sea after fighter attacks.
13. Forrest Clark gradually recovered and was 'trying desperately' to get back on flying status, when on 21 December he flew as a waist gunner aboard *Emmy Lou II*, a Liberator with a distinguished combat record, in a 44th four-plane practice formation from Shipdham to the Wash. The flight was routine enough until there was an explosion in the No. 2 engine and then the other three engines cut. *Emmy Lou II* crashed at 18.30 hours. Clark sustained back injuries jumping out of the waist gun position. Four others were seriously injured.
14. Air Marshal Sir Arthur Harris was in the midst of a campaign of area bombing German cities at night using Lancasters and Halifaxes, while B-24 Liberators and B-17 Flying Fortresses of the Eighth and Twelfth Air Forces stoked the fires by day. From 18/19 November 1943 to 24/25 March 1944, Berlin was subjected to 16 major raids, which have gone into history as the Battle of Berlin. On 22/23 November 764 RAF bombers raided Berlin. *See Battles With the Nachtjagd* by Theo Boiten and Martin W Bowman. (Schiffer Publishing, 2006).
15. 29 B-17s and 5 fighters were lost. Almost all the heavies lost came from the main raid on Bremen. 86 enemy fighters were claimed destroyed, 26 of them by B-17 gunners.
16. Cliff Hatcher, Adolph Delzoppo and Erwin Smith were not flying with Pyles this day. They had been replaced by three other crewmembers for combat indoctrination. The Fw 190A-6 was probably the one flown by Oberleutnant Fritz Falke of 8./JG 26, who was most likely already dead when he hit the B-17. The only survivor was the tail gunner, Harold E Norris. The tail broke free during the impact explosion and Norris managed to bale out before it fluttered like a leaf to the ground. He evaded capture and was passed along the French Underground to Spain, where he recovered from frostbite and was returned to England. Two other 94th Bomb Group B-17s were also lost: 42-3185 *Queen Bee* and 42-37815 *Miss Lace*. Oberleutnant Wolfgang Neu, the 4th *Staffel* CO, claimed a 94th Bomb Group B-17 west of Nantes at 10.45 hours, Oberfeldwebel Hans Heitmann of the 4th *Staffel* another SSE of Creil at the same time and Feldwebel Zirngibl of the 8th *Staffel*, a 94th Bomb Group B-17 near Paris at 10.40. On 29 March 1944 Heitmann, who had 11 victories, was awarded the *Deutsche Kreuz im Gold* (*DKG* or German Cross in Gold).
17. Eight of the crew baled out. Five including the pilot were taken prisoner. Co pilot Jean Pitner, navigator Arno Plischke and engineer Andrew Hathaway evaded. Max Newman, radio operator and George Jones, ball turret gunner, were killed. Waist gunner Carl Glasmeier was WIA. See *Century Bombers: The Story of the Bloody Hundredth* by Richard Le Strange. 100th Bomb Group Memorial Museum, 1989.
18. Four were from the 384th Bomb Group and 5 came from the 91st Bomb Group. Four B-17s were claimed by JG 26 and two were confirmed as 384th Bomb Group machines.
19. B-24 42-40769 RE-S *Iron Ass* in the 329th Bomb Squadron was being flown by Lieutenant Horace R Ketchum. 1 KIA, 9 PoW.

20. B-24 42-63987 in the 409th Bomb Squadron crashed at Herresbach. Six of 2nd Lieutenant Joseph M Wurzer's crew were KIA and four PoW.
21. The ship that Butler saw blow into a million pieces was B-24D 42-40807 *The Oklahoman* piloted by Lieutenant Harley B Mason in the 567th Bomb Squadron. Due to overcast obscuring their view of the target, orders were received to cancel the bomb drop and for the squadron to return to base with their bombs still aboard. During the time the Liberators circled waiting for the order to return, the lead navigator made a navigational error, which brought the Group over land instead of sea. St. Nazaire was France's only deep-water port and home port of a U-boat base and the area was therefore heavily protected by 88mm anti-aircraft batteries. Thinking they were over the sea the B-24s descended to about 14,000ft whereupon they were bracketed by heavy flak. The next thing Mason remembered was that he was unconscious for a few moments and then as he regained consciousness he recalled his body tumbling through the sky. He reached for his ripcord just as his body tumbled into the cloud deck below. The very next instant he remembered being in the water, the wind was blowing and that it was a very cold winter day. A German boat picked up Mason and he was taken to hospital, from where, in the next day or so, he was shipped by train to a PoW camp on the Baltic. The bodies of his nine crewmen were also recovered.
22. *Q-for-Queenie*, otherwise known as 41-24105 *Tupelo Lass* YM-Q in the 409th Bomb Squadron, was salvaged.
23. Strips of tin foil cut to the exact length of the German radar signal.
24. B-24 42-40983 *Judith Lynn* FTR on 1 April 1944 with Lieutenant Joseph M Soznoz' crew. 9 KIA.
25. The 93rd Bomb Group lost five B-24s.
26. Altogether, 13 Liberators were lost, including two each in the 446th, 448th and 445th Bomb Groups.
27. *On The Ball* was lost three days later, on 7 January 1944, when it and Lieutenant Charles W Walters crew FTR. 6 Evaded, 3 KIA.
28. *Dogpatch Raider* was lost on 3 February 1944 when it crashed on take off from Hardwick.
29. Only 49 Mustangs remained to provide support over the target area for the two groups that were left. A squadron of Lightnings managed to rendezvous with the bomber stream but had to turn back before the bombers reached the outskirts of Brunswick.
30. The 385th and 447th bombed the target with devastating results, the former group placing 73% of its bombs within 1,000ft of the MPI. Then it was the turn of the 94th. 19 B-17s placed 73% of their 100lb incendiaries within 1,000ft of the MPI to cause widespread damage to the Waggum plant. The bombing of the Junkers plant at Halberstadt was described as 'good' and the results at Oschersleben were even better. (Lieutenant Colonel Louis G Thorup commanded the 447th Bomb Group 31 March–30 June 1945).
31. The 94th Bomb lost eight B-17s, one of which was flying with the 447th, which lost two B-17s.
32. For its action over Brunswick, the 94th received its second Presidential Unit Citation. The 303rd lost ten bombers and the 351st 7, while the 91st lost five B-17s and the 381st, eight. In all, 34 of the 174 Fortresses dispatched to Oschersleben were shot down while two wings assigned the plant at nearby

Halberstadt came through practically unscathed. Altogether, 42 Fortresses and two fighters were lost. In August 1944 all the 1st Division groups that took part in the raid received the Presidential Unit Citation.

33. These strikes were no longer regarded as milk runs because the Germans, having realized their vulnerability to air attack, moved in additional flak batteries. The bombing altitude was raised to 20,000ft.
34. B-17 42-40009 in the 324th Bomb Squadron, 91st Bomb Group flown by Lieutenant Marco DeMara.
35. Only 58 bombers completed the mission. The 2nd Bomb Division was recalled before being despatched and at 10.20 hours all groups were recalled due to worsening weather en route. All except the leading combat wing in the 3rd Bomb Division, which was at the German border and decided to select a target of opportunity, turned for home as instructed. Two B-17s were lost in action and both were from the 335th Bomb Squadron in the 95th Bomb Group.
36. Pinder's B-24, which crashed into a pine forest a few miles outside Wibrin near Liège, was Stahnke's first victory. Stahnke was KIA on 15 March 1944 when he was shot down by a Spitfire of 401 Squadron RCAF. See *The JG 26 War Diary Vol. 2* by Donald Caldwell. Grub Street, London. 1998.
37. Grono was later repatriated to the USA but died from TB in August 1944. Pinder and Technical Sergeant Abe Sofferman, radio operator, baled out and the latter landed near the tiny farming village of Wibrin and Pinder not far away. A Belgian farmer and a postal worker saw the parachutes of Pinder and Sofferman. They took both men to the *Armee Blanche* (Belgian White Army) that was centred around Houfallize and in the wooded mountainous countryside of the Ardennes. The partisans were blowing up bridges and other strategic facilities to hamper the German Army. Pinder and Sofferman were captured on or about 26 February after a four-day battle, ending in the surrender of those in hiding. Only Sofferman would not allow himself to be taken prisoner. He took his gun and made a run for it and was shot and killed by the Germans while trying to avoid capture. Pinder was taken prisoner and transported to prison in Liège and later to a *Stalag* in Germany.
38. Seven of the crew, including Maynard and his co-pilot John E Norquist, perished, while the navigator, ball turret gunner and Nichols baled out and were taken prisoner.
39. Fifteen fighter groups escorted the bombers. Frankfurt was almost within P-47 range, although target support could only be carried out by the few long range P-38 Lightning and Mustang groups, while eight Spitfire squadrons covered the final stages of the return flight.
40. On 5 February the ranks of the B-17 formations were swelled by the addition of the 452nd Bomb Group.
41. B-24 42-99939 AG-E in the 330th Bomb Squadron was lost on 3 March 1944 when it crashed on take-off from Hardwick.
42. 41-28626 YM-P *Thunderbird*. Nine of 2nd Lieutenant Albert B Austin's crew KIA. 1 Evaded.
43. *Lonesome Polecat* flown by Lieutenant Omar A Turner in the 330th Bomb Squadron crashed at Rouxnesnil. All 10 KIA. *Willie's Worry* in the 328th Bomb Squadron was salvaged on 29 May 1945.

44. Formerly *Kentucky Babe* in the 509th Bomb Squadron (4 Evaded. 1 KIA, 5 PoW).
45. Which crashed at Lauz near Amiens. Seven in 2nd Lieutenant Robert V Laux's crew evaded. 3 PoW.
46. Guttmann was KIA on 27 March 1944 when his Fw 190A-7 was shot down at Chartres by a 359th Fighter Group P-47. See *The JG 26 War Diary Vol. 2* by Donald Caldwell. Grub Street, London. 1998
47. *Ready Teddy* was salvaged on 6 August 1944 and again on 11 June 1945.
48. John Butler had flown 139 hours and 25 minutes of combat time with eight different pilots in 17 different Liberators. On 15 February 51 B-24s again bombed the V-weapon site at St. Pol/Siracourt while 34 P-47s bombed targets of opportunity.

Chapter 4

Big B and Beyond

It was a long day… 8½ hours in flight… sucking in your breath as shards of 88s and 110s pierced our ship's thin, olive-drab skin… checking the fighters to determine if they were bandits or 'Little Friends'… hoping that the oil pressure of No. 4 engine didn't drop any lower and possibly force your ship to be a straggler for E/A to prey on – all that kept the adrenaline surging. The flak over the city was intense and accurate and many aircraft received flak damage. As I straddled the catwalk during the bomb run and pressed the bomb bay anti-creep lever, a chunk of shrapnel ripped through my bunny suit, nearly making an instant soprano out of me as it shorted out my suit. It was a cold flight home. The two-ounce shot of 86-proof hit my empty stomach like an exploding star.

Technical Sergeant Donald V Chase,
radio operator/gunner, 44th Bomb Group

On the morning of 3 March the momentous day when the Eighth at last set out for Berlin arrived. At bases throughout eastern England briefing officers pulled back the curtains to reveal red tapes reaching like groping fingers all the way to Berlin in the heart of Nazi Germany. Whistles and groans greeted the news. The B-17s began taking off in marginal weather conditions. As crews flew on over the North Sea, conditions grew worse. Eventually, the mission was 'scrubbed' but eleven bombers failed to return.[1] Next day, Saturday 4 March, bad weather forced the B-24s to abort early, leaving 502 Fortresses and 770 fighters to continue to the target while 219 B-17s hit targets of opportunity. Thirty-one B-17s in the 95th and 100th Bomb Groups defied the elements to drop the first American bombs on the Big City.[2] Fourteen minutes from the Reich capital, enemy fighters attacked the Forts. The 95th bore the brunt of the attacks and lost four aircraft, and the 100th lost one. On Sunday 5 March crews were briefed again for Berlin but the mission was 'scrubbed' because of bad weather. The Liberators attacked targets in France instead while some B-17 Groups went up and practised bombing after the weather improved over east Anglia.

On Monday 6 March, 730 B-17s and B-24s and 801 P-38, P-47 and P-51 escort fighters were despatched to targets in the suburbs of Berlin. Crews were well aware that the defences in and around 'Big B' had now been fully alerted and that a rough reception could be expected. The Germans knew only too well that any target which was not bombed because of a recall could be expected to be hit again at the earliest opportunity. The column, which stretched for 60 miles, was led by five heavily escorted Combat Wings in the 1st Division, which was assigned the ball-bearing plant at Erkner, a suburb of Berlin. Next in line were the 3rd Division, led by Brigadier General Russell Wilson who flew in an H_2X equipped B-17, which was assigned the Robert Bosch Electrical Equipment factory. The Liberators in the 2nd Division again brought up the rear. The bombers crossed the English coastline and the gunners tested their .50 calibres. The Channel passed beneath then the Dutch coast dropped under the wings and fell away. *Jafü 4* directed some fighters against a formation of B-26 Marauders en route to Poix but decided not to send any fighters to the north. Instead, part of II./JG 26 was ordered to fly east just in case the heavies turned for Frankfurt or targets in southern Germany. The bombers maintained their course and so all three *Gruppen* were told to wait on their bases until the direction of the bombers' return flight could be determined. The bombers meanwhile, sailed over the Zuider Zee and were almost over the German border when the storm broke. Over Dummer Lake the 1st Division was attacked by fighters that concentrated on the leading groups, and the 91st, 92nd and 381st were given a thorough going-over. The 457th Bomb Group was met by head-on attacks. One 109, which did not pull out in time, crashed into 2nd Lieutenant Roy E Graves' B-17 and the combined wreckage fell on 2nd Lieutenant Eugene H Whalen's Fortress. All three fell to earth. Next it was the turn of the 3rd Division groups to feel the weight of the enemy attacks.[3] The unprotected 13th Combat Wing[4] caught the full venom of the enemy fighter attacks. It was another black day for the 100th in particular, which lost the entire high squadron (350th) of ten B-17s. The Bloody Hundredth lost fifteen B-17s in all. In 30 minutes the enemy shot down twenty-three Fortresses in the 13th Wing or damaged them so badly that they were forced to ditch or crash-land on the continent.

The first American air raid on Berlin had certainly flushed out the Luftwaffe, just as Doolittle had hoped it would. The Fortress gunners and the fighter pilots claimed over 170 German fighters destroyed[5] but the Americans had suffered record losses. The 1st Division had lost eighteen B-17s, the 2nd sixteen B-24s and the 3rd thirty-five B-17s. Eleven fighters were also lost, while 102 bombers were seriously damaged. The sixty-nine bombers that failed to return to England represented the greatest loss so far and a loss rate of 10 per cent. And, 347 bombers were damaged, including 121 in the 3rd Division. Six were salvaged after landing. As for the results of the raid, the majority of the bombs fell on a

5-mile stretch of the suburbs, due mainly to overcast, creating huge fires and destroying the gas, power and telephone services. Oslo Radio, which was German controlled, regarded it 'as a catastrophe...' Even the Berlin News Agencies admitted, that 'several hundred bombers had reached the city, despite intensive flak and unceasing fighter attacks.' Air Chief Marshal of the RAF Arthur Harris sent a message to his opposite number Carl Spaatz at High Wycombe: 'Heartiest congratulations on first US bombing of Berlin. It is more than a year since they were attacked in daylight, but now they have no safety there by day or night. All Germany learns the same lesson.'

At Thorpe Abbotts when it became clear that the Hundredth had suffered the highest loss of any group, for the rest of the day, the crews 'remained quiet and subdued.' Few of the men wanted to talk and if they did, it was in a low tone, or in a whisper. Some wandered off, wanting to be on their own, or rested on their beds, while others drank singly, or silently in small groups. Some in their grief at losing their friends openly cursed the desk-bound Generals for sending them to Berlin, when it was obvious the Germans knew they were coming. Even Colonel John Bennett, who within the last 24 hours had taken over as temporary Group CO,[6] confessed, 'We were a sad group of men that evening... I'm afraid I didn't appear too confident before my men...' On Tuesday the 7th the weather was bad so there was no mission. Colonel Bennett said:

> Thank God we had a day off to lick our wounds. I talked to the Division headquarters about some replacement crews, which were to arrive at the end of the week. We were alerted on Tuesday evening and at 10 o'clock I knew that the target was again Berlin. It's hard to describe the feeling that came over the few of us who knew the boys were going back over the same route which had cost us 50 percent of our forces on Monday.

On 8 March when 623 bombers in ten combat wings were made ready for the third raid on Big B, that week the 100th could only scrape together fifteen Forts, led by Colonel John Bennett.[7]

Smaller scale raids on targets in France and Germany followed the early March Berlin strikes. Münster, a *Noball* site at Wizernes, aircraft component factories at Brunswick, Lille and Florennes, were all bombed. On 16 March 740 B-17s and B-24s went to factory and airfield targets in Germany and 679 of the bombers bombed Augsburg, Ulm, Gessertshausen and Friedrichshafen. The Luftwaffe was up in force and twenty-three bombers were shot down. A mission to Frankfurt on 17 March was abandoned but the heavies were out again on 18 March, when 738 B-17s and B-24s were despatched to aircraft plant and airfield targets at Oberpfaffenhofen, Lechfeld, Landsberg, Memmingen and Munich in southwest Germany and the Dornier works at Friedrichshafen. Starting at 10.00 hours, twenty-eight Liberators began taking off from Wendling. Four returned early with mechanical problems, leaving the remaining aircraft to continue over France. 2nd Lieutenant Gerald M Dalton's crew in *Amblin' Oakie* – a Gotha veteran – got caught in prop wash and collided with *Late Date II* flown by 2nd Lieutenant Ellsworth F Anderson, slicing off the tail and its turret. Both aircraft collided again as they went down and exploded in sheets of flame before crashing.

As the bombers neared Friedrichshafen, the leading 44th Bomb Group at the head of the 14th Wing made an unscheduled 360° turn. The leading elements in the 392nd bombed the target, but the second block, disconcerted by the manouevres ahead, chose to attack the rail yards at Stockach instead. The Liberators became strung out and heavy flak dispersed the formation to such an extent that many B-24s flew over Swiss territory on the opposite side of Lake Constance and drew fire from the Swiss guns. The Liberators were running nine minutes late for their rendezvous with P-38 fighter escorts, which was missed, and the 14th Wing was left to fend for itself against an estimated seventy-five single-engined enemy fighters. They attacked in line abreast, five and six at a time and harried the Liberators for over 100 miles. The 392nd was decimated, losing fifteen Liberators and nine other ships damaged by fighters and flak, all totalling 154 casualties. The 44th lost eight B-24s.[8]

Colonel Joseph Miller, CO of the 453rd Bomb Group, was leading the 2nd Combat Wing on only his fourth mission. He was in the lead ship with Captain Joseph O'Reilly, the newly appointed Group Navigator, and Captain Stock, a pilot in the 733rd Squadron. Jim Kotapish, the co-pilot of *Reluctant Dragon*, flying below Stock's B-24, recalls:

> Our astute group navigator had led the group over the harbor and everyone was waiting for us. The first flak burst hit the bomb bay of the lead ship and it immediately burst into flames. All I could think of was, 'Please God, don't blow up right now or we'll get the whole plane in our nose.' It didn't. It banked right in a low spiral and several men baled out of the plane, which was streaming flames from the bottom and the waist windows. The second burst hit our left wing. While I heeled over to follow the deputy leader out to sea, Ray Sears, pilot, was busying himself with No. 2 engine, which had taken the brunt of the burst. I followed the flight of the lead plane as long as I could, but I fell behind.[9]

Next day the bombers carried out 'milk runs' to V-1 sites in northern France and 172 heavies unloaded their bombs over the *Noball* sites. On Monday 20 March, bad weather and malfunction of blind-bombing equipment caused nearly 300 heavies to abandon the mission and only fifty-one B-17s bombed industry and transportation targets at Frankfurt/

Main and 99 heavies attacked targets of opportunity. It was however a memorable day for the crew of *Smoky Liz* in the 731st Bomb Squadron, 452nd Bomb Group, at Deopham Green, who were flying their first mission, as Ralph Reese, the left waist gunner, recalls:

> Target for today was a propeller factory at Frankfurt. We were awakened at 01.30. Breakfast was at 02.30 and briefing began at 03.30. Takeoff was scheduled for 07.15. Our bomb load was thirty-nine demolition bombs. At 11.55 hours we dropped twenty-nine bombs. The nine remaining bombs were dropped in the English Channel as they failed to release over the target. Flak was very heavy over the target and we encountered flak over the French coast. The group became lost on the way out from the target and we headed for the French coast to follow back to England, as Norman Wright our navigator didn't have a map of the territory we were now over. We were being shot at all along the French coast and as we neared land we were running low on gas, Fred Whitlinger our pilot gave the signal to prepare for ditching and to lighten the ship. We started throwing out ammunition, guns and any equipment we could lay our hands on. We even threw out our parachute harnesses and even my pair of GI shoes, as we were a little excited. We spotted land and an English fighter base was near by so we made for it. It was a very small space to have to set a B-17 down in, but our pilot did it. As soon as the plane stopped rolling we jumped out and kissed the ground, as we never expected to see land that day. Our engineer checked the gas supply and found the tanks very dry. We had landed on the very most southern tip of England and Bolt Head was the name of the Spitfire fighter base. We were housed at a nearby naval base. We remained there for two days and received excellent care. Finally, another ship from our Squadron came after us and we left *Smokey Liz* behind. It was later repaired and returned to base, where we continued to fly her. For being Mission No. 1 it was a very exciting way to start our missions.

Marvin J Byer, Ed Hartman's navigator in the 730th Squadron adds:

> We were flying deputy lead. At sometime during the bomb run, a bomb dropped through the nose of Jim Reynolds' plane, also in the 730th, killing the bombardier. After we left the target, the lead navigator did not catch the drastic wind shift. Instead of going home, I knew we were heading southwest of Paris. We called the lead ship and Hartman relayed the information I was using. The wind had a drastic shift from our forecast and we were far off course. The Lead Command Pilot asked if we wanted to take the lead. I didn't want to take it away from the lead navigator. If he had the correct

coordinates, he could get us home. We gave our coordinates in the open. After all, the Germans knew where we were; we didn't. Our route would have taken us to Bordeaux if we didn't change course and our group would never get home. The lead ship still did not change course. We called the Lead Command Pilot and he asked us to reconsider and take the lead. I am assuming his navigator didn't believe he could be 250 miles off course, particularly when no one else complained that we were off course. We took the lead and my options were to cut north across the Brest Peninsula or go west out over the water and then turn north to England. Hartman and I supposed our Command Pilot decided we should do the latter. When we took the lead, Reynolds pulled underneath us into the No. 4 position and told Hartman he had confidence in us and let's get home. When we were abreast of Brest, I used my drawing compass to find the closest beach in England. We made it to a RAF base in southern England. Reynolds landed at a different location.

On 21 March, fifty-six B-24s bombed a V-weapon site at Watten and about 650 B-17s and B-24s bombed the Berlin area. Twelve bombers were lost. Next day the heavies again sought the rich industrial targets of 'Big B'. Almost 800 B-17s and B-24s, including the 466th Bomb Group, which made its bombing debut, were dispatched, led by H_2X-equipped bombers flying their last mission under the control of the 482nd Bomb Group.[10] The 466th Bomb Group lost two B-24s in a mid-air collision.[11]

Altogether, the Eighth dropped 4,800 tons of high explosive on Berlin in five raids during March 1944. The raids cost the Eighth scores of experienced crews and valuable aircraft, to say nothing of the mental scars on those who survived. Berlin would be indelibly printed on their minds for days, months, even years, to come.[12]

On 1 April the number of missions to complete a combat tour was increased from twenty-five to thirty. Thick cloud grounded the 1st Division but the 438 B-17s and B-24s of the 2nd and 3rd Divisions continued on to the chemical works at Ludwigshafen. All 192 B-24s of the 3rd Division were forced to abandon the mission over France, leaving fifty-four B-24s to continue to the target, while 162 B-24s bombed targets of opportunity at Pforzheim near Karlsruhe and Grafenhausen. Unteroffizier Albert 'Adi' Boeckl of the 12th *Staffel* JG 26 and two pilots in JG 2 were credited with the destruction of B-24 *Judith Lynn* flown by Lieutenant Joseph M Soznoz in the 329th Bomb Squadron, 93rd Bomb Group, northwest of Reims at 11.50 hours.[13] Return fire from the Liberators in the 20th Combat Wing hit Unteroffizier Kurt Hofer in the 3rd *Staffel* JG 26 and he died in the wreckage of his Fw 190A-7 while trying to force land north of Reims-Pont Faverger.[14] One by one the remaining German fighters, low on fuel, landed to refuel and rearm and await the returning bombers, which could be expected later in the afternoon. En route to Ludwigshafen the 44th and 392nd Bomb Groups veered off course when the command pilot in the PFF lead ship, whose *Mickey* set had malfunctioned as the formations departed the English coast, decided to carry on to the target. Colonel Myron Keilman wrote:

> Without visual reference with the terrain, the lead navigator[15] had to rely solely upon pre-briefed estimates of winds aloft to carry out his dead-reckoning type of navigation... There must have been quite a change in both the direction and velocity of the winds aloft [because] the formations were blown 120 miles to the right of course and 50 miles further in distance.[16]

On the return journey the 448th Bomb Group, which was flying unescorted after bombing Pforzheim, and those who dropped out of formation, became easy prey for enemy fighters. JG 26 claimed three Liberators in the 448th Bomb Group in the Reims-St. Pol area. Two of these had run almost out of fuel and the crews had already decided to bale out. *Black Widow,* which was being flown by Lieutenant Jack Black, was alone after flak had damaged an engine over Roubaix. Oberfeldwebel Erich Schwartz knocked out the other three engines and was convinced he had destroyed the Liberator. However, Black flew *Black Widow* towards the Channel where he ditched the aircraft in the sea, fifteen miles off Dunkirk. Black and his co-pilot Joseph Pomfret were badly injured in the ditching because 448th Bomb Group B-24s were not fitted with shoulder harnesses. Pomfret was in fact thrown out of his seat in the impact. The others scrambled into the only life raft available. Pomfret, weakened by the cold, drowned before he could be taken aboard one of the life rafts. Sergeant Charles Nissen, who was injured and suffering from shock, died later. The eight survivors spent forty-four hours adrift on the surface of the sea until they were spotted by Bert May, skipper of the *The Three Brothers* fishing boat. Miraculously, favourable winds blew the dinghies across the Channel to within 5 miles of the English coast and they were rescued. After this tragic loss of aircraft and crews the 448th did not return to full combat status until 8 April.

The weather in the first part of April was atrocious and on the 8th the cloudy conditions abated to allow the bombers to assemble in force and send thirteen combat wings consisting of 644 heavies, including 192 bombers which attacked Brunswick, to aircraft depots throughout western Germany. On Easter Sunday, 9 April, the 1st Division was assigned the Fw 190 plant at Marienburg; the 3rd Division, Poznan; and the 2nd Bomb Division, the aircraft assembly plant at Tutow. The Marienburg plant had been the scene of a successful bombing attempt earlier in the war but the component part of the plant had escaped bombing because a thick layer of cloud had obscured it from view. In all,

104 Liberators took off for Tutow. At 09.00 a 392nd Bomb Group B-24 and *Might of the Eighth* in the 389th collided at 8,000ft while forming up over north Norfolk.[17] At Horsham St. Faith nineteen Liberators had defied the elements and taken off for Tutow but bad weather caught up with them over the continent and forced the majority to seek their secondary target at the airfield at Pachion. Bombing was ineffectual and the Group lost four Liberators. Meanwhile, the 1st Division was *en route* to the Fw 190 plant at Marienburg. Despite the loss of one combat wing and some combat boxes from another, ninety-eight B-17s placed 71 per cent of their bombs within 1,000ft of the MPI. Leaving the target, the B-17s received radio orders to join thirty-three B-17s of the 3rd Division, which had bombed the Fw 190 plant at Poznan, for mutual protection but before they could rendezvous the 3rd Division came under heavy fighter attack. The leading 45th Wing bore the brunt of the attacks but stout defending by the Fortress gunners kept losses down to just two aircraft. Meanwhile, a further eighty-six B-l7s bombed the Heinkel plant at Warnemünde, while forty B-17s bombed the airfield at Rahmel and forty-six B-17s bombed airfields at Parchim and Rostock. Altogether, the Eighth lost thirty bombers.

On 10 April, 730 crews were 'rewarded' with milk-run missions to airfield targets in France and the Low Countries. On Tuesday 11 April, 830 bombers were dispatched in three separate forces to bomb aircraft production centres in eastern Germany. 1st Lieutenant Edward S Michael and 2nd Lieutenant Franklin Westberg in the 364th Bomb Squadron, 305th Bomb Group, brought *Bertie Lee* home to England after it had been devastated by cannon fire and had plummeted into a 3,000ft dive. They were awarded the MoH. Bombing results were good but enemy fighters outnumbered friendly ones and the flak was accurate, varying from moderate to intense, and sixty-four B-17s and B-24s were lost in one of the heaviest single-day losses of the war.

Crews barely had time to catch up on some much-needed sleep when 455 crews in East Anglia were told to prepare for another long mission on the 12th. Once again the targets were aircraft plants in central Germany. Men dragged themselves out of their beds and took off but the weather intervened and the bombers turned back early. Although some crews came under fire none were sorry the mission had been 'scrubbed'. It meant another day to live. Colonel (later General) Maurice 'Mo' Preston, CO of the 379th Bomb Group, flying at the head of the leading 41st Wing, led the 1st Division to the ball-bearing plants at Schweinfurt, while the 3rd Division went to the Messerschmitt plant at Augsburg in southern Germany. The 2nd Bomb Division was assigned German aircraft manufacturing installations near Munich.

Thereafter, the weather intervened once again and provided a much-needed respite for weary fighter pilots and bomber crews, ever conscious that soon they would be flying yet another mission, days, maybe even hours later. The waiting was agonizing for old and new crews alike. Most crews were fatalistic. Some missions were regarded with superstition. Staff Sergeant Forrest S Clark, radio operator-gunner in the 44th Bomb Group was superstitious and feared flying a mission on 13 April:

> We had all nearly finished our missions and had some rough ones. The pilot, Lieutenant Rockford C Griffith, had a particularly rough time in combat. By the time we went on the 13 April mission to Lechfeld we had cut in the roughest and most dangerous period of the Eighth Air Force combat missions, the time when the Luftwaffe was very strong, the flak was heaviest and the losses were highest. The chances of surviving twenty-five or twenty missions were indeed slim. We had seen many of our friends go down over Germany. We lost our bombardier, 2nd Lieutenant Dave Edmonds, and Sergeant Abe Sofferman, our first radio operator.[18] I had suffered frostbite, sinusitis, combat stress and injuries to my back and legs in combat flying but I was determined to go on. I had crashed, parachuted and narrowly missed being hit by enemy fighter fire. I would have preferred another date than 13 April but the crew and I had no choice. As we prepared for take-off I said, 'Why me on the 13th?' Anyway, it proved to be quite a mission among many I had flown to that date.
>
> It was a long haul, a deep penetration, as they called it. I can still see that clear steely sky over Germany, the farmlands and the small villages shining in the sunlight, looking so peaceful, yet so deadly. We knew that to come down in that part of Nazi Germany would likely mean being beaten by a hostile civilian population because our officers at previous briefings had warned us of such incidents. The decisions we made that day shaped the rest of my life and my survival in WWII. We were at about 20,000ft over Lechfeld, a strategic Nazi airfield in southern Germany, when all hell broke loose. Flak came up at us from all sides and we scrambled to get out of the target area after 'bombs away'. I saw them go, fishtailing down on the runways and saw the Nazi planes parked on the dispersal areas go up in a thousand splinters of steel and flames. Later, we learned the bomb pattern was 'excellent' and we had bombed what was a key German jet fighter base of the dreaded Me 262 and others of the once famous Luftwaffe. We found we were losing fuel at a rapid rate and falling inexorably behind the rest of our formation. It was impossible for us to maintain air speed. To try to make it over 600 miles of enemy territory in a shot-up bomber losing fuel by the gallons would have been foolhardy and costly in manpower and in equipment. There is no question that we would not have made it and would have crashed or exploded in mid-air. The flight engineer, Sergeant Earl Parrish, checked the fuel gauges and found he had lost

so much fuel we barely had enough to make the Swiss border. We would have to either crash, a very risky business, or if successful, land and be taken prisoners of the Germans. The other possibility was to fall into the hands of a cruel crowd of pro-Nazis. Adding to our woes there suddenly appeared Me 109s following us as if waiting for the kill. We learned later that some of these aircraft were Swiss Air Force 109s.

I fired off distress flares to alert the Swiss Air Force but we had to make an emergency landing at Dubendorf near Zurich. Our plane received four bursts of flak as we passed over the German–Swiss border. One of these flak bursts wounded Sergeant Harold 'Jack' Harmon, one of our waist gunners. As soon as we got down a dozen armed soldiers surrounded our plane, one pointing a gun at my head. I thought we had come down in Germany. Our navigator, Lieutenant Ralph Jackson got out and the first thing he did was hang his parachute harness over the rifle of one of the soldiers. He said he was so disgusted because he had lost his original crew and had flown only three missions with us. The soldiers closed in around us and soon a Swiss colonel in full dress uniform stepped out of a car and told us we were in neutral Switzerland. This was our welcome to a neutral country in the midst of WWII, a not totally friendly welcome party. I had a sense of elation, yet sadness, because I had wished to finish my tour of duty and return to the US. Now my future was in doubt because no one knew then how long the war in Europe would last.[19]

The Hamm mission on 22 April was the first flown by 2nd Lieutenant Charles D Peritti's crew in the 68th Bomb Squadron, 44th Bomb Group.[20] The navigator was 2nd Lieutenant John W McClane Jnr, from Niagara Falls, New York, who though he turned twenty-one years' old on 18 March 1944 looked more like seventeen. He had to get used to being asked by perfect strangers, 'How old are you?'

McClane recalled:

My pilots were ideally selected, as were our flight engineer, radio-man and gunners. I had the one job that I was born to hold. I loved navigation and nothing was more enjoyable to me than my position. One could walk into a room full of airmen and in a short time pick out with considerable accuracy who held what position just by observing the mannerisms of those present. Navigators were easy to sort out. Just look for a hypersensitive guy, someone who can't hold still one minute, an eager beaver asking questions unrelated to the interest of everyone else. It helped to be a little odd but I loved my job. The 'old man' of our crew was Staff Sergeant Paul M Corlew at age thirty-two and the baby was Staff Sergeant Otho H Freeman, age nineteen. 2nd Lieutenant John F Warga, our bombardier, and our belly gunner, Staff Sergeant Charles J Alexander (who we called 'Swoose' after the popular song of the day, 'Alexander the Swoose') were the whiskey drinkers in our crew. On our way over the South Atlantic while we were at Fortalaga in Brazil, Warga bought a 5-gallon wooden barrel of whiskey. But even they could not drink the Brazilian rot-gut, as it was too strong. The only thing it was fit for was to start the coal fire in the pot belly stove in our hut at Shipdham; it must have been 500 percent proof, as it was as effective as gasoline.[21] Warga, who was as strong as an ox, not only could hold his liquor better than any one else in our crew (and perhaps the whole squadron) but the girls seemed to fall all over themselves about him. Every crew has to have someone who can be AWOL for three days and show up one minute before roll call. Anyone else, especially me, could be AWOL one minute and miss the same roll call. Warga often came to briefing with a severe hangover. He would stay awake long enough to get his bombing instructions and reach the flight line.

At briefing I was told to look for 'light lines' the British had set up on the ground to lead us home. Each light had its own code. Before take off I spread my navigation equipment out on the ground. While going over the maps, perhaps talking to the bombardier, I became cognizant of someone trying to get my attention. Just as I looked up, I caught a full slash of water in my face. It was the Group Chaplain asking God to look after us as we began our combat tour. Later I was to know why there are no atheists in combat. On many missions I had good reason myself to pray for God to spare us just this one more time. I will never understand why God answered this prayer for some and so many others were required to give their all.

As navigator, it was not my duty to man a gun but I certainly did like the nose turret as it gave my navigation compartment much protection from frontal attack. On both take off and landing, I vacated my forward navigation compartment to stand behind the pilot. I would hold on to a steel protection plate at his back. This gave me an excellent view of take off and landing. If a crash situation were to develop, I was to sit on the floor with my back to the steel plate, my knees pulled up and my hands behind my head, which I would brace also against the steel bulkhead. Flak was moderate and fighters were few but the 68th Squadron did claim one. The thing that stands out was the return trip. As our formation approached the Channel, a single B-25 twin-engined plane was flying about 10,000ft below us and on the same course. We were at 20,000ft. Smoke and flame were coming out of its port wing. I watched the crew bale out but the plane continued to fly on autopilot for several minutes before it exploded and a huge ball of orange flame and black smoke filled my sight. 'Poof', the plane was gone. This B-25 was the first of many planes I was to see on my tour of combat explode before my eyes.

We crossed the sea as dark settled in. I soon began to pick up the 'light lines' and I had no problem whatsoever in navigating. We reached our field and Peritti landed using his wing lights. We had flown six hours. None of us thought this unusual until we saw what was happening. As we got out of the plane, we could see planes landing at nearby fields also using their wing lights but a number were exploding on the approach at their home bases east of us. At the time we could not imagine what was happening. The next day we were told that fifteen Me 410 fighter planes had infiltrated our bomber stream as we crossed the Channel. They simply lined up their gun sights between the wing lights of a bomber on its approach to land and had a field day, like shooting fish in a barrel.[22]

The wreckage, considerable at some bases, was cleared away and conditions returned to normal. Time was now fast approaching when the Allies could look ahead to the momentous day when they would invade 'Festung Europa'.[23] The Eighth Air Force was further strengthened and preparations were begun immediately to get the new Groups operational in time for D-Day. When that day was no one knew for certain. But it was imminent and the three Bomb Divisions and fighter groups had to be prepared for a maximum effort when the fateful day finally arrived. During April, despite the obvious drawbacks in mixing two different types of heavy bomber – the B-17 and the B-24 – six new B-24 groups joined the 3rd Bomb Division. Doolittle wanted to bring the Eighth up to full strength using just B-17s but there were simply not enough to go around. In contrast, by the late spring of 1944, five B-24 plants in America were producing more than enough Liberators. This uneasy marriage was to last only four months, by which time Doolittle had gone some way to achieving his all B-17 force.[24]

On Monday 24 April, 750 bombers were despatched to bomb aircraft plants in the Munich area while in Italy another strong bomber force hit targets in the Balkans. Ralph Reese, left waist gunner in *Smoky Liz* in the 452nd Bomb Group, recalls the mission, his ninth, to the Focke Wulf and Dornier plant:

We were awakened at 03.30. Breakfast was at 04.15. Briefing 05.00. We took off at 08.05 and departed the coast at 11.10. Our forty-two 100lb incendiaries were away at 13.15 from 24,000ft. Flak was very heavy over the target as our No. 3 engine was hit, so our pilot tried to feather the prop but it failed. The prop kept windmilling and vibrating like a threshing machine. Finally the cowling and part of the prop hub flew off. Everyone grabbed his 'chute and was ready to jump upon the command. With the loss of one engine, we could not keep up with the formation, so became a straggler. Fortunately, we had fighter escort, as our No. 1 engine had a two-inch flak hole and No. 2 engine was leaking oil. We were in a tight situation, like 'Coming in On a Wing and A Prayer.' We were gradually losing speed and the fighter escort had to leave. Shortly, we saw fighter planes coming in on us at 6 o'clock and we started firing away. The fighter planes tipped their wings to signal they were friendly instead of enemy. They turned out to be British fighters and they escorted us home. We thought we would have to crash land but the pilot brought *Smoky Liz* in to a fine landing at 17.15 hours. Battle damage was 101 flak holes, one large hole near my foot and two holes in the bombardier's dome.

The 41st Bomb Wing, which bombed the Dornier repair and assembly plant 15 miles south of Munich, bore the brunt of the attacks carried out by an estimated 200 enemy fighters. Of the wing's fifteen losses, the 384th Bomb Group suffered the worst casualties, losing seven aircraft before the Luftwaffe turned its attention on the 40th Combat Wing. The 92nd Bomb Group, which achieved excellent results in the bombing of the Dornier plant, lost five bombers in the resulting aerial battle. Thirteen B-17s landed in Switzerland this day from the total loss of thirty-nine bombers.

On 25 April almost 300 bombers blasted marshalling yards at Mannheim and airfields in France. The next day 292 heavies bombed Brunswick after thick cloud prevented bombing at primary targets. Nearly fifty more bombed targets of opportunity in the Hildesheim–Hanover areas. For the first time, on 27 April, when the Eighth flew two bombing missions in one day and the following day, the heavies bombed targets chiefly in France. The 44th Bomb Group's afternoon mission was to the key marshalling yards at Châlons-Sur-Marne, south of Rheims, 60 miles east of Paris, one of the most vital marshalling centres between Paris and Germany. 2nd Lieutenant John McClane recalls:

We launched twenty-five planes as our part of almost 600 for the total of the day. (The morning effort was twenty planes to Moyenneville, France with the loss of one to enemy action.) A total of seventy-two aircraft attacked, from the 44th, 392nd and 445th Groups. Intelligence had reported a loaded ammunition train there. Our bomb load was twelve 500lb bombs. Take off was after 16.00 hours. The trip to the target was uneventful with no enemy aircraft attacks. The weather was beautiful and visibility unlimited. As we approached at 20,000ft the flak was moderately heavy but our bombardiers held us steady on course. Because the bombs fell in a large arc the bombardier released them some distance before we would fly over the target area. I heard 'Bombs away', felt the plane lurch upwards as the load lightened and as one of my duties, pushed the salvo handle under my desk to release any bombs that might fail to fall as a result of water freezing the electronic latches.

I never failed to watch the bombs fall as I had the best view to see in all directions of any crewmember. My bubble windows on either side of my navigator compartment afforded full visibility straight down as well as forward, outward and to the rear. Just as our bombs began to walk across the assigned MPI, a most astonishing thing happened. I can't really describe what I saw but I'll try. Suddenly a blinding flash of light of brilliant silver, yellow and red exploded before my eyes. We were directly over an ammunition train when it blew to bits. Many locomotives and 600 railroad cars were disintegrated. A mile of track 200 yards wide was torn from the earth. I let out a yell and tried to describe to the rest of the crew what I was witnessing. I must have been very excited as my pilot asked me to calm down but I couldn't. As we left the target area, a huge mushrooming cloud began to rise. It was at 15,000ft in a few minutes and finally reached our flying altitude of 20,000 before we lost sight of it. No one else in the crew saw it explode – not even Warga our bombardier. For days I kept trying to tell the crew what I had seen until they all got fed up with my foolishness.[25] There were no incidents on the return to home base and we landed at 21.00 hours after 5 hours and 40 minutes in the air. This was a bit late, as the experience of 22 April had taught us.[26]

On Saturday 29 April, 768 bomber crews throughout East Anglia were awakened early for briefing. At Great Ashfield, one of the 4th Combat Wing B-17 bases, 385th Bomb Group crewmen Carlyle J Hanson was one of those who made the mission. Hanson recalls. 'We got up at 01.30 for target study. The target was Berlin!'

Lieutenant John W McClane was the navigator in 2nd Lieutenant Charles D Peritti's crew in the 68th Bomb Squadron, 44th Bomb Group at Shipdham. McClane recalls:

The first two were not too rough and we were a little too complacent. After stumbling through the blackout to the breakfast that morning, the usual question was on everyone's lips, 'Where are we going today?' Was it going to be a 'milk run' over the coast of France or a deep penetration to the heart of Germany? As we filed into the large Nissen hut used for briefing, the men gathered together, as crews, sitting facing a stage with a huge map of Western Europe above it. However this map was securely covered with dark draw curtains. Suddenly the command, 'Attention' was sounded. In unison, all snapped to their feet and in walked the Commanding Officer, Colonel John H Gibson and his staff. The briefing officer stepped forward with a long pointer and the map curtains were quickly drawn open. At this movement we all knew what was our target for the day. The ribbons pinned to the map led straight to the heart of Hitler's Germany, the 'Big B' – Berlin. The howl and commotion could have been heard a block away.

Finally, everyone settled down and the briefing officers proceeded to detail our objectives. The predicted weather, the expected fighter opposition and flak concentrations were outlined. The various pilots were assigned positions in each section of each squadron of the group. Some were to lead, others were to be wingmen, some were assigned high and others low positions in the formation. And of course, someone had to fly coffin corner, low left rear with the least protection from the guns of the fellow planes in the formation.

The pilots, bombardiers, navigator, flight engineers, radio men and gunners all went to their own briefing for further details and instructions pertaining to their specific duties. The pilot was in command of the ship but the success of every mission depended upon close teamwork. No one man, crew, flight, squadron, group or division did it all. In toto we were a powerful Air Force out to do battle with a determined enemy. Our objective was to do maximum damage to today's target. Theirs was to prevent us from reaching the target or to inflict such painful punishment that we would cease trying. The stage was set; the battle would soon begin. Hundreds of men would be either killed, wounded, or missing this day but nothing could stop the mission once it had been set in motion.

Briefing over, we gathered as crews to be taken by truck out to our planes. Now began an extremely tense period. We would busy ourselves preparing for flight, each man checking what pertained to him. At the same time, we kept an eye on the tower because if the mission was aborted, a red flare would be sent aloft. If it were 'Go', a green flare was used. Today, the mission was 'Go'. The engines were started and we mounted the plane. The moment of truth was at hand. There was no option but to go and only God knew who would return.

Part of the 4th Combat Wing strayed off course and near Magdeburg the enemy fighters wreaked havoc among the unprotected formation, shooting down or fatally damaging eighteen Fortresses in twenty minutes. Seven of them came from the 385th Bomb Group.

Technical Sergeant Clarence L Mossman, left waist gunner in the *Worry Bird*, flown by 28-year-old Cleveland, Ohio pilot, Lieutenant Richard A Spencer in the 549th Bomb Squadron, recalls:

> We were flying a tight formation and all the squadrons seemed to be in their right positions when the German fighters attacked. We did evasive action to help us from head-on attacks. We first spotted about 200 fighters about 12 o'clock high and in a few minutes they attacked us head-on, coming down out of the sun in waves of forty and sixty at a time and doing barrel rolls right through the formations. They made three passes. Our left and also our right wingman went down. We had a lot of flak damage on our aircraft and also damage to our wing from 20mm shells fired by Me 109s that came down through our formation. All of the crew came through the mission without being wounded or killed.

Carlyle J Hanson again:

> This undoubtedly was the worst day in my life to date. God answered my prayers for sure. After turning on the IP, about 150 enemy fighters struck at us. They looked like a swarm of bees. They made three passes at us, knocking down seven out of our group. Flak was accurate and heavy. We didn't even get over Berlin, as the weather was too bad. It would have been twice as bad if we had have tried it. We dropped our bombs on a town about 30 miles southwest of Big B. I think we plowed up a field. Fred and Bob kept the plane going after No. 1 engine was knocked out and another was smoking. We got a little flak on the way home.
>
> One waist gunner was hit in the head by flak but wasn't too serious. A 20mm shell hit No. 1 engine. Flak flew all over the plane (it looks like a sieve), knocking out the radio compass. I had my flak suit off and parachute on once and really thought I would be using it. One of the fellows in our barracks went down and it was his first mission. This was Fred's and Tony's thirteenth and my fourteenth. Now we sweat out Bob's twelfth. It can't be any rougher. Our group lost more planes today than any other day other than their third mission last summer. Brandenburg was the place we hit. Humor for the day was when Jerry was coming in like bees. King hollers out, 'Flak at 3 o'clock!' we had been flying through flak for half an hour. We'd make seven trips to Berlin and they were all nasty.

Worst hit of all the Bomb Groups was the 447th whose eleven losses took its monthly total to twenty-one aircraft lost. The 94th and 96th Bomb Groups losses for April 1944 were also twenty-one bombers apiece; the Eighth's heaviest of the war. The 2nd Bomb Division, flying thirty minutes behind schedule, brought up the rear of the bomber stream and was also met in strength by the Luftwaffe. After leaving Celle airspace the only protection afforded the B-24s was a solitary Mustang group, which was forced to retire just after the Liberators completed their bombing run. At the IP *Play Boy*, piloted by 2nd Lieutenant Franklin F Cotner in the 466th Bomb Group, received a direct hit from an 88, which knocked out the No. 3 engine. Cotner completed the bomb run but *Play Boy* was attacked by fighters after the target and went down over Holland.[27] It was not until the Liberators reached the Dummer Lake on the homeward journey that P-47 Thunderbolt escorts reappeared. German ground controllers, however, seized upon the time lapse and directed over 100 fighters to the Hanover area to intercept. Lieutenant William Moore's B-24 in the 467th Bomb Group, which carried Major Robert Salzarulo, CO of the 788th Bomb Squadron, was shot down over Holland.[28]

2nd Lieutenant John W McClane in the 44th Bomb Group formation, which sent twenty-one planes up this day with no aborts, continues:

> According to *Stars and Stripes*, our ETO newspaper, this was the heaviest daylight assault in history on any one target. The Force was made up of 600 four-motor bombers carrying almost 1,500 tons of explosives and incendiaries. We were escorted by 814 fighters but the Germans were ready with some of the heaviest opposition encountered to date on daylight operations. One wing alone reported being attacked by at least 200 fighters. The resistance met by the various elements of the massive bomber fleet varied widely. Fortunately the 44th Bomb Group was well known by the Luftwaffe pilots as being a seasoned combat outfit and best left alone as long as there were less experienced groups that would be an easier target. A number of German interceptors did test us however, approximately thirty on the way to Berlin and forty to fifty on the way out. My most vivid memory of the war was burned on my mind when we were approximately halfway to Berlin. Over my earphones came the voice of Paul Corlew, our engineer and top turret gunner, 'Fighters high at 1 o'clock.' I looked out of my astrodome and saw three German fighters circling. One could almost hear the lead pilot say, 'Watch me boys, I'll show you how it is done.' He peeled off into a wide arc so he was at an altitude headed straight for our formation. At this I switched positions so I could look out of my right bubble window, which afforded an excellent view forward, down and to the whole right of our line of flight. As he flew towards us he began to slow roll. I became very fearful as I was looking down his two 20mm wing cannons and with each burst, I saw the orange-red flash of the guns. He appeared to be aimed directly at me and I could not help but wonder where the shells were going. I fully expected the next one to explode in my navigation compartment. I was extremely fearful and yet spellbound at the same time. But what followed in the next second or so really put fear into me. As the scoundrel slow rolled towards us, closing at rapid speed, I really became upset. It

appeared to me that he was going to crash into our plane with a head on collision. I was petrified. Then suddenly Peritti lifted his wings in a vertical position so he could slice between our right wingtip and the left side of the plane on which we were flying wing. I jerked my head as he flashed by at which time I could easily see the German pilot at our wing tip; he just missed it by inches.

An awesome sight caught my attention. At the base of the wing of the adjacent plane, right at the inboard motor and fuselage, a large ball of orange flame exploded before my eyes. The whole left wing peeled off and to me, it seemed like an eternity that the plane stood there as if it were flying. It could have only been a few microseconds but the vision was burned in my memory like a still photograph. Then in a flash the plane flipped over on its back as the right wing was still flying. It was a violent motion that skewered the whole axis of flight. As the plane flipped, the force of the action catapulted the waist gunner on the right side out of the gun opening and towards our plane. The arc of his flight through the air put him towards our right wing and he fell between where I was standing at my bubble window and our right inboard motor. He wore only a harness with two nipples. Needless to say, this unfortunate waist gunner had no such opportunity to grab his parachute before he was thrown through the window. As he passed me, at most only a few feet away, he was kicking both feet and grabbing the air with his hands in desperation. Maybe he thought he could grasp our plane in some way to hold on. I watched him plummet towards the ground until my attention went to the wreck of the one-winged B-24 falling through the sky. It was cartwheeling nose over tail over the one wing in a huge windmill spinning motion. All of the other nine men were trapped due to centrifugal force in the plane with no hope whatsoever of getting out, I thought. My eyes were glued to this action, as I watched the wreck tumble end over end for at least 10,000ft.

I had lost all track of time or anything else that was going on around me when I heard on my helmet earphones, 'Second fighter coming in.' I looked up and saw a second enemy craft repeating what his leader had done. At this point my mind went blank. I was too absorbed in my own thoughts and fears. When I came back to reality we were approaching Berlin. The flak was intense. The defenders had 520 anti-aircraft guns trained in a 20-mile arc on us. The sky was one huge black cloud of exploding metal. The guns fired in batteries of four, or so it seemed to me. When it was bursting at some altitude other than our own, we had little to fear but as soon as they zeroed in, trouble was at hand. I never did get over the fright of seeing a flak burst right in front of us. Then a second a little closer and a third even closer yet. With each burst, the plane would almost instantly fly through the black cloud. One could easily sense the cordite smell. At this point you knew the next burst would be inside your plane but with God's help, the burst would be directly behind the tail. This mission was the first time I prayed out loud for God to let me live through the battle. I asked him to let me survive the day. I promised I'd do anything he asked of me if only he would spare me.

Many planes went down. One slid off to the side in a rather steep dive. (I heard later that it was because they had lost their oxygen supply and had flown low level back to base). We did survive the flak barrage somehow and headed back to England but our troubles were not over by a long shot. We turned into a 100-knot headwind. Our indicated air speed was about 165mph and at 25,000ft and as cold as it was (–60° F) our true air speed was over 200mph. However with a headwind, our ground speed was something just over 100mph. Talk about eternity. This was it. We had 600 miles to go and it would take hours at the ground speed we were flying. Our fighter escort had turned back due to fuel consumption. Many planes were damaged and just would have made it home under the best of conditions but with the delay caused by this strong head wind some just could not make it. I don't know how many planes I saw go down that day on the way to target, over the city and on the way home! I know it was a great many. I saw some explode, others trailing smoke, others with wings on fire and many, many parachutes open as the crews baled out. But one sight stands out above all others on the way home. As we crossed the North Sea, I began to see planes ditching in the water. It was like watching a motion picture. I was so detached from the action! Some of the planes would glide to the gentlest stop and the men would climb onto the wings but others would hit a swell in the water and seem to dive nose first in a crumpled heap. It was obvious that almost no one could survive the shock. British PT boats were on hand to pick up survivors. This was one of the worst days ever for the Eighth Air Force.[29] When we reached base and landed at 17.30 hours I actually bent over and kissed the ground, as I was so pleased to be back. I had been in the air 8 hours and 15 minutes. Now I knew why we were told that if we flew twenty-five missions at an average of four losses per mission that we had a 100 percent chance of being shot down.[30]

The losses had a telling effect on those who returned. At Bury St. Edmunds, Leo C Riley, a co-pilot in the 94th Bomb Group wrote:

Things are pretty sad around the Nissen 91 today. We started on a raid to the heart of Berlin and had to turn back over Amsterdam. Chism and crew stood by but took off at last minute and have not been heard from since. There is no way to explain our feelings when men we knew and loved as brothers go down. Of course, there is a chance for them. There is always a chance, except for a direct hit and explosion. I never knew before how many times a day one could find time to pray, if one will try.[31]

May marked the beginning of all-out raids on the enemy's railroad network in support of the *Pointblank* Directive, although raids also continued against V-1 sites in France. During the morning of 1 May more than 500 heavies were despatched to twenty-three *Noball* targets in the Pas de Calais but most of the bombers were forced to abort because of bad weather. In the afternoon, 328 B-17s and B-24s bombing in individual combat wings attacked marshalling yards and railway centres in France and Belgium. It was John W McClane's fourth mission:

In the afternoon the 44th Bomb Group dispatched fifteen aircraft; there were no aborts. Our target was the marshalling yards at Liège. We were part of the second wave of heavies to proceed over the continent that day. A total of forty planes of the 2nd Bomb Division were effective over the target. All told 157 tons of bombs were dropped; our load was eight 1,000lb bombs. Flak was moderate and the 44th Bomb Group encountered no enemy planes. The bombing accuracy was fair to good. All aircraft returned safely at 18.45 hours after 5 hours in the air. The Eighth Air Force sent out 328 heavy bombers for the day to seven different targets, of which three were MIA along with the loss of three of our escort fighters. This was the seventeenth straight day of the pre-invasion aerial offensive. General Doolittle announced that US heavies dropped more than 24,000 tons of bombs on German targets in April. There was considerable debate about using heavy bombers on rail targets. One school of thought said light bombers and fighter-bombers should be used in order to save the B-24s and B-17s for more strategic objectives. Also there were concerns for the civilian population in the occupied countries. In the light of 20/20 hindsight, we now know we followed the correct course. One change was made in the bomber formation, however: instead of large groups, a six-plane formation was used. Raids such as on my second mission to Châlons-Sur-Marne, large numbers of planes were required but later such as my twenty-eighth mission to a road junction near Rouen it would have been utter folly to use more than six planes in any one formation.

On 3 May the 2nd Division dispatched the only Eighth Air Force planes for the day and then only by three Bomb Groups, the 44th 93rd and the 382nd. Take off was after the noon hour. The total number of planes was fewer than fifty all told, of which twenty-four were 44th Bomb Group aircraft. Our particular target was a V-1 site near the railhead of Wizernes, 35 miles west of St. Omer. Bombing was by GH radar led by Pathfinders from the 93rd Bomb Group. There was no Luftwaffe opposition. However flak damaged fifteen of our twenty-four planes but none so seriously that it could not be put back in action within 36 hours. No planes were lost by the Eighth Air Force and only three airmen were wounded. Heavy cloud cover prevented an assessment of bombing results. We arrived back to base at 17.15 hours after 4 hours and 30 minutes of flying.

Bad weather fronts over the continent halted deep-penetration missions like the one to Brunswick and Berlin on 4 May when 851 B-17s and B-24s were forced to abandon the mission over the Low Countries. John W McClane recalls:

Today was my first experience at flying through clouds so dense that we were forced to turn back when approximately half way to our intended target, an aircraft factory near Brunswick. Cirrus clouds up to 23,000ft so frustrated our navigation that the mission was recalled. Some groups encountered stiff enemy aircraft opposition but the 44th Bomb Group saw none nor did we have any flak damage. Our group of fourteen planes, with Colonel John H Gibson in command, led the 14th Combat Wing, which led the 2nd Bomb Division. Not one of 231 B-24s reached the target but forty of 360 B-17s did bomb. No planes were lost but sixteen were damaged with two airmen killed and one wounded. All told, this was a frustrating day. There was much confusion and the day seemed to me that we were in a dream world. The clouds were everywhere; we could not find an opening. The planes in our squadron weaved back and forth due to turbulence but there was a certain beauty due to the very dense contrails. We were credited with a sortie as we penetrated enemy territory for a considerable length of time. I was glad to get home after 4 hours and 45 minutes in the air.

The only raid on 5 May was mounted by thirty-three B-24s which bombed a V-1 site at Sottevast and on 6 May seventy Liberators bombed another *Noball* site at Siracourt. Over ninety bombers were prevented from bombing other V-1 sites by thick overcast. It was hardly an inspiring debut for the 398th Bomb Group at Nuthampstead, who made their combat debut this day, just thirty-one days after leaving Rapid City, Dakota and only fourteen days after arriving in England.

During the morning of Sunday 7 May, when 1,000 American bombers were dispatched for the first time, the B-17s headed for Berlin. They were joined for the first time by B-24s of the 486th and 487th Bomb Groups.[32] Another 342 heavies bombed Osnabrück, Münster and targets of opportunity. In the afternoon twenty-eight B-24s bombed targets in Belgium. John W McClane flew his seventh mission, to Osnabrück:

The 44th Bomb Group dispatched thirty planes to the target, a marshaling yard and locomotive repair shops. Take off was 06.30 hours with no aborts. We carried fifty-two 100lb oil bombs. A total of 165 B-24s carrying 146 tons of bombs reached the target of which one was lost and twenty-three damaged. The 44th suffered no losses although the flak was heavy over the target and one German fighter did pass through the formation. This was my second mission that was led by a PFF ship carrying *Mickey* H_2X radar. We never saw the target due to heavy cloud formation, which blanketed the area. Bombing altitude was 24,000ft and the temperature ranged at −42° F.

We landed at about 14.00 hours after 7 hours and 30 minutes in the air but the day was not over yet. Not only did we have to go through debriefing and critique but Jerry gave us a little scare that night. 'Bed check Charlie,' as we called the German night bomber, paid us a visit about the time we had settled in our barracks for much needed rest. I ran for the air raid shelter, as did most everyone. We were tired after four missions in seven days. Just this day alone in order to take off at 06.30 hours, we had been awakened between 3.00 and 4.00 am. The orderly, who got us up, shone a flashlight in our eyes when he shook us. I never did get used to it and certainly did not relish it. (The old story goes he also woke up anyone else if he had a smile on his face.) The Eighth Air Force also sent the 1st and 3rd Bomb Divisions to Berlin with about 600 B-17 Flying Fortresses. This force dropped 1,344 tons of bombs on the Nazi capital, losing only eight planes to enemy action. It was the eighth raid by the Eighth Air Force on Berlin. All told, it was a good day for the Eighth, sending out a grand total of 922 planes with 865 effective in deep penetration of the German homeland, losing only nine planes (1 percent). This day was special in another way for the Eighth Air Force. It was the first time that over 900 heavy bombers were dispatched in one day. For some reason, the Luftwaffe chose not to oppose us as only nine enemy planes were sighted by all groups. 3,500 planes of all types struck at the Nazis from England and Africa, inflicting severe punishment to the Axis.

The next day Berlin was again bombed in the morning – this time by 378 B-17s, while 287 B-24s and 49 B-17s hit aircraft factories in the Brunswick area and another twenty-nine heavies attacked targets of opportunity.[33] For John W McClane in the 44th Bomb Group it was his first mission to Brunswick after they had been turned back by weather four days earlier, although on that occasion they were given a sortie credit.

Brunswick was an aircraft manufacturing center as well as a major rail center, 125 miles southwest of Berlin and with a population of

201,000 people. In spite of the Allied bombings, German fighter production was producing the planes they needed. One plane turned back so thirty-two were effective over the target, along with another 256 2nd Division Liberators. As we approached the target area, between 150 to 200 enemy defenders made a strong defensive effort, thirty-five attacking us at one time. Flak was always frightening at Brunswick and today was no exception. We had a good escort of P-38, P-47 and P-51 fighters from both the Eighth and Ninth Air Forces. The Germans were determined to defend the Reich's skies after their dismal showing the day before. Reports were made that some of the Luftwaffe planes tried to ram our bombers in deliberate collisions and a few succeeded. In all my missions, I never saw a fighter collide with one of our bombers but often I would deliberately not look at the battles going on around me as it frightened me and distracted my navigation. We wore steel flak helmets over our headgear. I would pull the front lip down so I could not see out but I was able to look to the ground to navigate. Peritti would wait until a fighter was lined up to fire at us, then at the last moment lift or drop our plane. The planes behind us would follow his lead in a wave motion. Only God knows where the cannon shells went that missed us. I do not know how many enemy fighters the gunners of our crew claimed but I'm sure we got our share of licks in. When we were in a battle and the guns were firing. I could smell the cordite. It was long after the war before the smell of gun smoke would not bring fear back to me. Also the excitement would make me sweat. I would have a cake of ice on my forehead where my perspiration was coming out from under my helmet. I pulled it off in little chunks.

We returned to Shipdham about 13.00 hours. Our actual flight time was 6 hours and 40 minutes. We were tired as this was our fifth mission in only eight days but little did we know what was to come before we got any relief. The 44th Bomb Group lost one plane when it crashed at Halvergate killing two of the crew. None were shot down in the air battles over Germany. All told eleven B-24s were lost and the B-17s going to Berlin and other cities lost twenty-five more for a total of thirty-six for the day. Another 205 bombers were damaged, eight beyond repair. Men known KIA was eight, fifteen wounded and 373 missing. Our fighter losses were thirteen in some very fierce dog fights. I would often watch these dogfights. They were usually off at a far distance and at a higher altitude. The contrails would show us the path of the planes as they maneuvered in violent arcs through the sky. Oh, what a beautiful sight to see our fighter escort catch up with us as we winged our way into enemy territory or pick us up on the way out.[34]

We were awakened early on Tuesday 9 May for our third combat mission in three days. This was the fifteenth straight day the heavies had hit the Third Reich. Fortunately for us, it was not going to be the deep penetration of Germany of our Osnabrück and Brunswick raids on Sunday and Monday. The target was an airfield thirty-five miles east of Brussels. The Germans had been using it to strike at the RAF with nightfighters. The 2nd Division sent out 290 B-24s, with 101 going to St. Trond, carrying a total bomb load of 227 tons. We were carrying fifty-two 100lb bombs with instantaneous fuses. (This was the maximum we could carry as we only had 52 bomb shackles in the bomb bay; otherwise we would have had 6,000 to 8,000lbs of bombs of 500 to 2,000lbs each.)

This was a straightforward mission. The sky was very clear with almost unlimited visibility. Our bombardier, John Warga, as soon as we took off would curl up in the passageway between the forward compartment and the tunnel to the rear. The forward compartment is where the front gun turret, his bombsight and my navigation desk were located. When necessary, Warga manned the gun turret; otherwise he dozed at my feet. As we would gain altitude, the atmospheric pressure decreased until at 10,000ft we were required to put on our oxygen masks. In the meantime, he would supply us with all the gas we could stand. The fragrance would penetrate my navigation area and go up through the maze of pipes and wires separating my desk from the pilot's and co-pilot's feet and fill the pilot area and back into the radio and flight engineer's room. Needless to say, we were glad to breathe pure oxygen again. How Warga could be so relaxed as we approached the target area, I'll never know. When we were close to the IP, the initial point before the target where we would begin our bomb run, usually about 15 to 30 miles before bombs away, I would kick him with my left foot and say, 'Warga, wake up – we are coming to the IP.' At this he would become alive. He had to be one of the best bombardiers in the Air Force. He almost never missed. The flak would be exploding all around us and I'd be a nervous wreck but not Warga. He was completely calm. He stayed alert just long enough to see the bombs hit the target and promptly relax on the floor again. Planes could be burning and exploding all around us but who cared? Not Warga. The truth is that he was ideally suited for his job, certainly not navigator or pilot.

As we were on the bomb run to the airfield at St. Trond, the flak was moderately heavy and at our altitude, which was bad news. This always 'scared me bad.' Why our bombs were set to explode as soon as they left our bomb racks, I do not know. All other times the bombs had a small propeller on the nose that would unscrew as it fell through the air thereby arming the bomb on it's way down. The sight of bombs leaving the nearby planes always fascinated me. We reached the drop point and the bombardiers released the bombs

> using an interverlometer, a device that let the bombs out one at a time. As they fell, it would appear the bombs were stacked one above the other suspended in space in a long stream, especially when they were stacked fifty-two high. I was looking directly at one plane when flak set off the bottom bomb. It exploded and set off the one above it which in turn set off the next higher and so on until the last exploded in or very close to the bomb bay. The plane fell out of formation and began to go down with the men baling out. I assumed then that the plane and all the crew were lost but the plane I saw explode was *Northern Lass*, piloted by Lieutenant J P Ferguson who did bring the badly damaged aircraft back to England and crash-landed at Attleborough. However five crewmembers baled out before the plane was brought under control. We landed before noon after being in the air 5 hours and 45 minutes. We still had to go through debriefing and critique, which took at least two more hours. I was pretty excited over what I had seen.

In all, 772 heavies were dispatched to enemy airfields and transportation targets on 9 May. The B-24s bombed airfields at Florennes, St. Trond, Nivelles and Hody and the marshalling yards. Major Ronald V Kramer, 448th Bomb Group, was flying in the co-pilot's seat of Captain Robert T Lambertson's B-24[35] when it was hit by flak and burst into flames just as they released their bombs on the marshalling yards at Liège, Belgium. All attempts to control the fire proved futile and the crew were ordered to bale out. Kramer wrote:

> We were at 18,000ft. It looked a long way to the ground but I did not hesitate. I jumped and dropped several thousand feet on my back. There was a terrific jerk after pulling the ripcord. Everything seemed very quiet after the terrific noise a few minutes before. I saw the burning pieces of our aircraft falling and tremendous palls of fire and smoke coming from the target. It was a lonely feeling to see our bombers disappearing in the west when in another hour I knew they would be back at Seething.[36]

On 11 May, 973 bombers were dispatched to marshalling yards in Germany and the Low Countries. The 44th Bomb Group 'Flying Eight-balls' were part of the bombing effort directed against the marshalling yards at Mulhouse, but the primary target was obscured by clouds, so several targets of opportunity were hit. The Liberator[37] flown by 2nd Lieutenant James H Walsh Jnr, was singled out northeast of Châteaudun by 'Addi' Glunz, CO 6./JG 26, who set the No. 1 engine afire. The B-24 left the formation 'in difficulty' but still under control. Sergeant Joseph O Peloquin, engineer recalls:

The time of day was very close to 14.20. It's always been a habit of mine to look at watches when things occur – and I do recall that very well. We were shot down by Me 109s. Our position in the formation was Purple Heart Corner. It turned out to be just that! As an engineer, my position was the top turret and that is where I was just before it all started. Things were rather quiet and as we had a fighter escort, Lieutenant Walsh suggested that I go back and transfer my fuel. It would seem to be a good time as we had used enough from our main tanks to transfer in from the outer cells. And the fuel would be out of the way in case we ran into trouble later and couldn't spare the time. So I went back to the waist section and told Sergeant Lawrence Richards to cover my position while I was doing my job of transferring the fuel. I could take his position if anything happened.

Well, I had just had time to finish and was on my way back to the waist position when all hell broke loose. There was flak banging around us as well as fighters firing at us. One Me 109 hit us in the No. 2 engine, setting it on fire. Another shell exploded in front of us and blasted my headgear off just as I was scrambling to get my chest 'chute. Sergeant Puksta helped me to snap it on and that's when I could see that he had been hit also. I opened the escape hatch and told him to jump. He looked at me and said, 'You go first!' The plane was going down and he didn't look too good, so I told him to be damned sure to follow me. Puksta baled out, was captured and become a PoW.

My experiences are ones that I still have nightmares about. When I jumped, I counted to about ten – enough to clear the plane. We were at about 15,000ft at that time and I pulled my ripcord – and nothing happened. No 'chute came out! So I was falling free at 120mph and I tugged and pulled at the flaps on my 'chute – and finally pulled out a little of the silk or nylon. As I kept pulling, the pilot 'chute came out and it, in turn, released the main 'chute. All of this took so long that when it finally blossomed out, I was about 300 feet from the ground! This is one of the reasons why the Germans did not spot me coming down. When I landed, I injured my left heel and I, too, had been hit by the shrapnel from that exploding shell that had hit Puksta. I had one in my arm above the elbow and several small ones in my face and another one in my neck, which just missed my jugular vein. This all took place near Patay, a little village about 20 miles from Orleans and known for its association with Joan D'Arc. I met up with Richards a couple of weeks or so after we baled out. To my surprise, we met on a bus, along with our Free French escorts, going to a farm camp in the Forest of Freteval, where the Germans had an ammunition dump and these men all hid out successfully, right under the German noses. When the camp was

> started, there were only about eight or ten of us, but things changed rapidly and soon there were several hundred of us evadees.[38]

JG 26 next turned their attention to the seventy Liberators of the 486th and 487th Bomb Groups of the 92nd CBW, which was on only its fourth mission. The formation had been briefed to bomb the marshalling yards at Chaumont but the leading 487th Bomb Group had flown into a flak area near Châteaudun. Both the lead and deputy lead aircraft were shot down and a third was crippled. Among the missing was the Group CO, Colonel Beirne Lay Jnr.

On 12 May almost 900 B-17s and B-24s were dispatched with 980 escorting fighters in the first attack on the five main oil plants in the Leipzig area in central Germany. This simultaneous attack on oil and aircraft was in keeping with Eisenhower's policy of pounding two of Germany's most valuable assets. Both had to be knocked out or crippled if the invasion of the Continent was to succeed. The bombers would fly a common course in trail to the Thuringen area where the bomb divisions would peel off and attack their targets. Brux was the target for the 13th and 45th Wings of the 3rd Division. (This was the first time that the Eighth had been assigned a target in Czechoslovakia). The 1st Division sought the synthetic-oil plants in the Leipzig area.[39] In the 2nd Bomb Division at Shipdham Technical Sergeant Don Chase and John W McClane were among those who sat through the briefing expectantly. Flight Officer Metz' crew were minus a radio operator so Chase flew his twenty-fifth mission (and his final three) with the crew. John W McClane, whose tenth mission this was, recalls:

> When the briefing curtains were pulled back so we could see the large map of Europe, the ribbons indicated our target to be in the Leipzig area. For the first time, the Eighth Air Force had set its goal to wipe out the synthetic-oil plants so vital to the German war machine. This was a new kind of objective in the campaign to paralyze Hitler's Europe. There were three synthetic-oil plants in the Leipzig area of which one was Zeitz, 20 miles to the southwest and our target for the day. Zeitz lay approximately 550 miles from our base at Shipdham but we flew many more miles than this as we never went straight to a target but took a 'Cook's Tour' of Europe, zigzagging from France to Denmark in order to keep the Luftwaffe guessing where to concentrate their defences. We would faint towards a potential target only to turn in another direction about the time the Germans had alerted their AA batteries and fighters. Sometimes the city we pointed towards would already be throwing up a flak barrage even though we had no intention of making this our target. Somehow this seemed to amuse us. To proceed, as the bird flies, to the target and back (about 1,100 miles) would take less

than six hours but we were in the air 8 hours and 20 minutes due to the assembly time and the evasive flight course.

The 2nd Bomb Division dispatched 716 B-24s to Zeitz of which nineteen planes were ours. Each carried nineteen 250lb bombs, however one of our planes had to abort and return to base, making eighteen over the target. Take off was approximately 09.00 hours and we broke the English Coast about one and a half-hours later. We did not expect this to be an easy mission and we were not disappointed. The enemy fighters were out in great force but with over 1,000 bombers to attack, they were spread pretty thin for which we were grateful. Flak was another thing. The Germans knew the importance of oil refineries so they set up an elaborate complex of anti-aircraft batteries. The refinery itself had sort of a trapezoidal shape and was set out in the middle of farm country. The visibility was extremely clear and even from more than 20,000ft the outline of buildings and oil storage tanks were clearly discernible. There were several villages within a mile of the refinery. The target stood out like a sore thumb with farms all around. The flak was intense: not one plane escaped damage. We were down to 18,000ft to achieve maximum accuracy. One of the 67th Squadron's planes was hit so badly that it had to drop out of formation where it became easy prey for the enemy fighters to pick off. This was the only 44th loss for the day.[40]

When we departed the target area at Zeitz, the refinery was severely damaged and on fire. The great majority of all bombs dropped by the attacking 116 Liberators landed well within the strike zone. To me it appeared that we had destroyed the objective completely. 'So much for one synthetic-oil plant,' so I thought, but little did I know that the Germans had a fantastic ability to rebuild. We landed shortly after 17.00 hours.

The 13th Wing, comprising the 95th, 100th and 390th Bomb Groups, and the 45th Wing comprising the 96th, 388th and 452nd Bomb Groups, meanwhile carried out the long and gruelling mission to the oil refinery complex at Brux.

Wilbur Richardson, a ball turret gunner in the 331st Bomb Squadron, 94th Bomb Group, was on his eighth mission. The pilot, John Moser and the rest of the crew were unaware they would also be flying such a war weary B-17 until they taxied out at Bury St. Edmunds:

061, the 'F' we were assigned, had been shot up, repaired, crash-landed and repaired again. This queen had seen her best days. It just didn't fly that well. This all became apparent as we started our roll down the runway. We were at maximum load and 061 just barely got off. John Moser used up all of the runway and I saw green grass as we just lifted off in time. Close? Shades of Lindbergh. We were off for what was to prove an historic operation. We weren't long into Belgian airspace when all hell broke loose. The yellow-nosed 'Abbeville Kids' and the German Air Force rose to the occasion. Upward of 400 fighters attacked. In our area there were only six P-51s. Not much help with such odds. I watched as a '51 and a '109 collided head-on. We flew eastwards towards our target area, fighting all the way. The fighters came from all directions – the tail as well as the effective nose-on attacks. In some cases there were 25–30 abreast and even attempts at ramming by using a wing so the pilot could bale out, as we later learned. Attacks were made from 12 o'clock, circled and charged from 6 o'clock level so neither ball or top turret might get a line on them. As the upper and lower turrets could fire in all directions Bruton and I were kept busy twisting and turning constantly. The navigator, Les Ulvestad or the bombardier, Frank Sarno, called out 'Bandits 10 o'clock low' or 'Straight in at 12 o'clock.' If I weren't shooting to the rear, assisting the tail gunner, Gilbert Gabriel or some other direction, I'd swing forward ready to follow through coming from the nose. It was a busy time returning the fire of those fast-moving targets with winking flashes on the wings coming our way.

Clifford D Jones, navigator in Lieutenant Lourie's crew in the 96th Bomb Group recalls:

It was a beautiful clear day and the usual forming of groups into wings took place over England and then proceeding over the Channel to our various destinations. We picked up heavy flak near Koblenz but to my knowledge no planes were lost or delayed; however, for the 96th Bomb Group, this was just a harbinger of things to come. In no time at all we observed our fighter cover above us being drawn off to defend us against German fighters. Almost simultaneously, our crew was reporting attacks by enemy fighters from almost all points of the clock. With the exception of the tail gunner, who wore a flat, back-type parachute at all times, the remaining crewmembers had detachable chest-type 'chutes. Obviously, attaching a chest 'chute on a buckle harness under a flak vest was extremely awkward. However, considering the pressing attacks on our group from the German fighters, in a brief lull, I decided to loosen my flak vest and put my 'chute on. Quite frankly, with all the bombers going down around us, I felt it was just a matter of time and if worse came to worse, I could, at least, make an immediate attempt to escape. It seems like a very short time thereafter, when tracking an Me-109 and firing my .50 caliber machine gun as he came in from 12 o'clock high and as he passed my line of vision

> there was a sudden jolt and shuddering of our aircraft. It seemed to stop in mid air and then fell off into an uncontrolled fall. As explained, with the exception of myself and my tail gunner, none of the other crewmembers would have had their 'chutes on and when our plane went down out of control, there would have been no chance, whatever, to recover any of the 'chutes. Through a miracle I escaped through the B-17's nose hatch and the tail gunner was blown out the rear. I personally believe the German fighter was out of control and had struck our B-17 amidships, as I do not recall any explosion.[41]

Wilbur Richardson continues:

> We were hit in the No. 1 engine. It lost a lot of oil and we had to feather it just prior to the target. It was a struggle to keep up with the group with bombs still aboard. The flak over the target was moderate, which incidentally, I almost welcomed because we had a brief respite from the fighters. We received some flak damage including the loss of some oxygen in my ball turret as well as some on the left side.

Ralph Reese, who was flying left waist gun position in *Smoky Liz* in the 452nd Bomb Group, recalls:

> Everything went smoothly until fifteen minutes from the IP. Then we saw some planes on our wing go down in flames. To our delight, they were enemy planes being shot down by our P-47 fighter escorts. We saw one P-47 shoot down three enemy planes. The flak was very heavy over the target and beyond. We saw one B-17 shot down and I saw ten 'chutes open and glide towards the ground. The group behind us [100th] was attacked by Bf 109s, who stayed out of range and were able to reach our planes. We lost fourteen ships out of our group.

Meanwhile, Wilbur Richardson's B-17F was fighting a grim survival battle:

> Soon after bombs away we endured the second half of the German fighter attacks. Twin-engined fighters joined the 109s and 190s. They sat out behind the bomber boxes in groups of 10–20 to fire rockets and cannon just out of effective range of our .50s. With the loss of oxygen we could not remain long in our group formation and we had to lose altitude relatively fast to make it with the oxygen we had left. Stragglers always attracted attention and on our way down 109s and 190s came at us and we received many hits. Bruton claimed one

fighter and the tail and I claimed two apiece. As I was in the rear firing at one below, another fighter hit the top turret with cannon fire. I saw the plexiglas and Jim Bruton's empty special leather flak helmet go over the right horizontal stabilizer. I thought he had had it. I later learned that he lost consciousness for a few moments and came to on the deck before Lieutenant Leo Riley, the co-pilot, could get to him. Jim wasn't hurt. Just highly put out and using four-letter words, as he couldn't vent his anger by returning their fire. The shells that knocked him out of the turret damaged both .50s and they were beyond repair. He was very lucky. We also took cannon damage from the rear. One hit the right elevator severely limiting its travel. Moser used the trim tab while Riley exerted pressure on the yoke to maintain a little level flight. He locked his left arm around the control column and held on tightly to his left wrist with his right hand while he propped both feet against the instrument panel. The shell that damaged the elevator was followed immediately with another that went on through the elevator. The right waist window was hit and the left waist gun was put out of action. Ken Rasco was uninjured. We managed to join another group coming from another target until the fighter attacks let up. We couldn't get in too close because of the difficulty in flying level but we did get some help in covering the attacks. By the time we reached the coast we were somewhat behind and below our foster group. We kept losing altitude across the Channel and Moser thought we might need to land at the first opportunity. Riley felt he could hold on a little longer, as we seemed to have enough altitude to make just one attempt. Being alone and late we were able to make a straight in approach. This was fortunate because we lost No. 3 engine through fuel starvation as the '17 was nosed down and lined up with the runway. For us, 11.45 hours in the air, according to John Moser. Because we were late and the crews at de-briefing had reported seeing us go down in trouble we were listed as MIA. We returned to our barracks just in time to stop our belongings from being picked up. '061 never flew again. It became a hangar queen to keep others in the air.

Lieutenant Leo Riley wrote:

God has been good to us again today. It is 7.30 and we have just finished a mission that started out at 8.00 this morning. Once again, I am so tired I can hardly sit up. Wish I could write. After going through what I have today, I feel that I can't. Saw many big Forts go down in flames. Our ship was shot to pieces plus a ship in our own squadron shot out our No. 1 motor. But God brought us back. Must be up again tomorrow. Too close.

Altogether, 470 Luftwaffe fighters had opposed the formations and in one of the fiercest air battles of the war, forty-six bombers were shot down, mainly over the Rheine–Main area.[42]

At Shipdham, Don Chase heard the news that Lieutenant Lewis I Vance's aircraft had gone down. The young radio operator had also seen, off in the distance, about 2 o'clock level, a B-24 that had had its top turret plastic bubble shot completely away. Chase kept thinking:

> Headless Horseman... Headless Horseman... The crippled ship had continued flying but slowly fell behind the group formation. As a straggler he was a prime E/A target. I hoped he made it.
>
> When a crew went down, foot lockers were pried open and personal belongings minus any objectionable material or firearms, were collected and shipped to their next of kin. Their beds were stripped and the thin mattresses folded. Soon newly assigned young men would arrive and the beds would be made again.
>
> Next day I flew my twenty-sixth mission and the Group's seventh in a row. The top turret gunner got off several bursts, the empty casings clinking against one another as they fell onto the cabin deck. I crouched behind the armor plate that protected the co-pilot's back, only my helmet and eyes above the armor as I watched the action. Oh, how I wished I could shoot back... please don't let them strip my bed....[43]

Notes

1. 79 of the 748 heavies despatched attacked targets of opportunity including Wilhelmshaven and Heligoland.
2. The formation, led by the 95th Bomb Group went for a visual run but the clouds closed in again and at 13.42 hours the bombs were released under the direction of the leading 482nd Bomb Group PFF aircraft flown by Lieutenant William Owens. The 95th Bomb Group was awarded its third Presidential Unit Citation and the 100th was similarly awarded later.
3. The leading 385th Bomb Group at the head of the 4th Combat Wing came in for persistent fighter attacks. Brigadier General Russell Wilson was flying in a 482nd Bomb Group *H_2X*-equipped Fortress and his crew included Medal of Honor recipient John C Morgan, now a 1st Lieutenant. Just as the formation approached the Berlin area the flak guns opened up and bracketed the group. Wilson's aircraft was badly hit but continued on the bomb run with one engine on fire. Major Fred A Rabbo, the pilot, gave the order to bale out after the bomber began losing altitude, but before they could take to their parachutes the aircraft exploded, killing six of the ten-man crew. Incredibly, Morgan survived, being somersaulted out of the aircraft with his parachute pack under his arm. He managed to put it on after several attempts and was saved from injury when a tree broke his fall. Morgan was captured and sent to *Stalag Luft III.*

4. Comprising the 95th, 100th and 390th Bomb Groups.
5. US fighters claimed 81 enemy fighters shot down and the bomber gunners claimed 97 destroyed; the Luftwaffe actually lost 64 fighters destroyed and 2 damaged beyond repair. This was a loss rate of 12.5% of those committed to action.
6. Colonel Neil 'Chick' Harding was suffering from gallstones but had refused to report to the medics. Over the past few days his health had deteriorated and preparations were being put in hand to send him back to the United States for an operation. Colonel Robert H Kelly became 100th Bomb Group CO on 19 April.
7. The Bloody Hundredth's only casualty was *Nine Little Yanks and a Jerk*, which was salvaged with a badly wrinkled skin.
8. Altogether, 43 bombers and 13 escorting fighters were lost on the 18 March raids.
9. Captain Stock's crew were taken prisoner and although Colonel Miller evaded he was caught trying to cross the Pyrenees into Spain. After being interrogated by the *Gestapo* he was finally sent to *Stalag Luft III*. Meanwhile, Colonel Ramsey D Potts assumed command of the 453rd Bomb Group. In all, 43 bombers and 13 of the 925 fighters dispatched were lost. USAAF fighters claimed 13 victories, while the bomber gunners put in claims for 45 destroyed, 10 probables and 17 damaged.
10. Thereafter, each of the three bomb divisions operated one pathfinder squadron apiece. The 1st Division assigned the task to the pioneer 305th Bomb Group at Chelveston while PFF responsibilities in the 3rd Division were allocated to the 96th Bomb Group at Snetterton Heath.
11. Two days later the weather was responsible for the loss of two more 466th Bomb Group ships which were involved in a second mid-air collision, near Osterburg. On 27 March two more collided, shortly after take-off from Attlebridge.
12. By 19 May 1944 John A Miller in the 100th Bomb Group would complete six missions to the German capital; the greatest number of Berlin missions in one tour by any Eighth Air Force member: 'Altogether, we started out for Berlin seven times. Twice our co-pilot went nuts and tried to crash us into the sea. These times the crew fought him off the wheel and we aborted. After the second time he didn't return to our crew. He wasn't a coward; he just couldn't go back to Berlin.'
13. *Judith Lynn* crashed at Bougemeron. All nine crew were KIA.
14. See *The JG 26 War Diary Vol. 2* by Donald Caldwell. Grub Street, London. 1998.
15. Captain C H Koch.
16. 26 B-24s in the 392nd had dropped 1,184 100lb bombs on a forested area 3 miles southeast of the Swiss town of Schauffhausen, over 120 miles from Ludwigshafen, and the CO, Colonel 'Bull' Rendle, had some explaining to do. The mistake led to America paying the Swiss thousands of dollars in reparations. Koch was rebuked and never again allowed to perform the function of lead navigator. Keilman concludes: 'As a personal friend, I felt sorry for Captain Koch. He had flown as my navigator on numerous 8- and 10-hour ocean patrol missions between Ecuador and the Galapagos islands in 1942... When the radar set malfunctioned, the odds were against precision

navigation and the command pilot should have recalled (aborted) the mission.' The 1 April mission cost the 2nd Division 10 B-24s.

17. Nine men in the 392nd Liberator were killed and seven men in the forward section of *Might of the Eighth* were killed instantly when five 500lb bombs and the full fuel load exploded.
18. Edmonds went on a mission with the crew of 2nd Lieutenant John I Scarborough in the 67th Squadron to Friedrichshafen on 16 March 1944. He was killed when *Shark Face*, returning from the mission on two engines, crashed at Kingsnorth near Woodchurch, Kent. *Shark Face* had lost an engine just before the target and the crew could see Switzerland across the other side of the lake but Scarborough had said, 'Let's go home.' Six of the crew were killed and Scarborough, Edmonds and Loren M Bean, co-pilot, were laid to rest at Cambridge. See *Innocence and Death In Enemy Skies: A True Story of WWII Adventure and Romance* by Forrest S Clark. Jawbone Publishing Corp. 2004.
19. In December 1944, Forrest Clark escaped from Switzerland with the aid of US agents in Berne and the French Resistance, making his way to Lyons, France, just before Christmas 1944 during the Battle of the Ardennes.
20. On 15 April the crew had left the replacement and indoctrination centre in North Ireland for Tibenham in an old war-weary B-24D which had been stripped down and made into a transport. Fifty men and their entire B-4 bags etc were thrown in the belly of the plane and they were ordered to sit wherever they could find space to squat. They all knew that the plane was badly overloaded and there was great relief when they finally touched the runway late in the afternoon at Tibenham, the home field of the 445th Bomb Group, 15 miles south of Norwich. They were fed and given a place to spend the night. Peritti's crew were to be assigned to a squadron the next day. However in the morning, word came for four crews to transfer to another Bomb Group, 15 miles west of Norwich, which had just suffered severe losses and needed replacement. On 8 April the 44th Bomb Group had lost 11 out of 27 planes due to flak and fighters. In short order the 44th was decimated. Peritti's crew were not too happy to be a replacement under these circumstances but as it turned out, they would be eternally grateful that they were assigned to the 44th Bomb Group.
21. 'Later, when the ball turrets were removed from our Liberators we hated to lose "Swoose" Alexander. He was the "character" of our crew and a fun person to know. Swoose was assigned to another crew and soon completed the required 30 missions. What happened to Alexander, I do not know as he volunteered for a second tour.'
22. Twelve Liberators crashed or crash-landed as a result of KG 51's actions. 38 American crewmen were killed and another 23 injured.
23. Overall command of the Combined Bomber Offensive and the Eighth Air Force officially passed on 13 April to General Dwight D Eisenhower, the newly appointed Supreme Allied Commander.
24. Also in April 1944, Generalmajor Adolf Galland, the Luftwaffe fighter commander, revealed to his superiors that since January that year the day fighter arm had lost more than 1,000 pilots. He estimated that each enemy raid was costing Germany about 50 aircrew and at that rate the time was fast approaching when the Luftwaffe would lose air control over Germany.

25. 'It was not until September when words and pictures finally convinced my crew that I had not dreamed my wild story. A confidential report published by the 2nd Bombardment Division entitled: *Target Victory* came to group operations. As squadron navigator of the 68th Squadron I was in a position to obtain a copy, which described in great detail the destruction that I had witnessed. Not a train moved through the Châlons marshalling yard for two months. By this time, the invasion was three weeks old and this important rail community was denied the German defenders. At long last I was vindicated.'

    McClane was appointed Squadron Navigator on 30 August 1944. He adds: 'The position of Squadron Navigator called for the rank of Captain and I was recommended for promotion to this grade on 4 October, but I was not given my Captaincy. The 'Table of Organization' called for only one Captain Squadron Navigator. The dates reported could not overlap even one day, which it did in my case. I never let it bother me. I was so young and looked like a kid; I never expected it to happen anyway. It would have been almost embarrassing to have been a Captain in my training after I returned home to the ZOI and besides, I was happy just to be alive.'
26. Eighth Air Force heavy bomber losses from all missions this day were four planes. 254 others were damaged, two beyond repair. 3 airmen were KIA, 16 WIA and 40 MIA.
27. Sergeant Falk, flying his first mission with the crew as waist gunner, was killed instantly by a shot through the head. Two of the crew evaded for the rest of the war. Cotner was sent to *Stalag Luft III*.
28. He and the crew were later reported to be prisoners of war. Lieutenant John L Low, the Group Bombardier, evaded capture for 296 days in enemy-occupied Holland and was liberated on 29 April 1945. 25 Liberators were lost, including a 458th Bomb Group B-24, which was forced to land in Sweden. In all, 579 bombers hit Berlin while 38 other heavies attacked targets of opportunity in the area, including Magdeburg.
29. Of the 679 B-17s and B-24s dispatched, 618 were effective. They dropped 1,498 tons of bombs. 63 bombers were MIA. Two planes were interned and 432 damaged. 18 men were KIA, 38 WIA and 606 MIA. Of 814 fighters dispatched, 13 were MIA.
30. 'They raised it to 30 missions before I completed my tour just to be sure none of us made it and then I volunteered for a 31st against all current wisdom to never volunteer for anything. I did survive the 31 missions and GOD WAS WITH ME!'
31. *Passionate Witch II* flown by 2nd Lieutenant Kenneth Chism crashed at Hassenberg with the loss of 1 KIA and 9 PoW.
32. These two groups, commanded by Colonel Clendon P Overing and Lieutenant Colonel Beirne Lay (who had been one of Eaker's original staff officers in 1942) at Sudbury (Acton) and Lavenham respectively, had arrived in England in April to join the 92nd Bomb Wing. Lay had taken command of his Group on 28 February 1944.
33. In the afternoon 81 B-17s bombed *Noball* sites, while 56 B-24s bombed marshalling yards at Brussels.
34. 'A strange thing happened on this mission. The 96th Bomb Group B-17s stationed at Snetterton Heath, about 20 miles south of Shipdham, were

scheduled to go to Berlin along with the rest of the B-17s but they became lost. They fell in with the B-24s going to Brunswick. The enemy fighters attacked them savagely, shooting down 10 of their number. We were called the Eightballs because we were a jinxed outfit suffering losses out of proportion until the jinx was broken after the ill fated mission of 8 April. Then the 492nd Bomb Group took over our misfortune and even the 100th Bomb Group was called the Bloody 100th. The prize for the worst hard luck goes to the same 96th that followed us to Brunswick this day. They had the unenviable title of having the greatest loss rate of any bomber group in the USAAF.' (In additon to the 36 bombers shot down on the morning raids five more were lost in the afternoon).

35. 42-100287.
36. Nine of Lambertson's crew were captured and 1 was KIA. Kramer was hidden by some Belgian farmers, given a civilian suit and, accompanied by a Belgian who was presumably an underground agent, struck out for France. *En route* two German soldiers examined the Belgian's papers, but they were not in order and he was later shot. Kramer was taken to Luftwaffe headquarters in Brussels, where he was threatened with execution before being sent to *Stalag Luft III*. Altogether, two B-17s and 4 Liberators FTR.
37. B-24 42-94999, 506th Bomb Squadron.
38. Most of the evadees were liberated by the US Third Army on 13 August 1944.
39. Two composite 4th Wing formations meanwhile went to a Fw 190 repair depot at Zwickau. Also, 823 B-17s and B-24s were despatched to bomb marshalling yards and airfields in France, Luxembourg and Belgium, escorted by 668 fighters.
40. 42-110042 in the 67th Bomb Squadron flown by 2nd Lieutenant Lewis I Vance (1 KIA 9 PoW).
41. Jones and tail gunner Lewis Lanham were the sole survivors. Incidentally, the area Jones went down in on that fateful day was Bad Camburg, about 28 miles NNW of Frankfurt, Germany.
42. Total Eighth Air Force heavy bomber losses were 46 B-17s and B-24s and a staggering 412 bombers damaged. Worst hit was the 45th CBW. The 452nd Bomb Group lost 14 B-17s, the 96th 12, including two which collided whilst under attack, and the 388th, one. As a result of this raid, oil production at the Sudetendeutsche plant was completely stopped during June 1944.
43. Finally, Don Chase could not resist anymore. He just had to do something positive. As an enemy aircraft came barrelling through the formation he pulled the trigger of his Verey Pistol and fired a signal flare at him. Useless? Foolish? Certainly. But he did get to fire one futile 'shot' at the enemy.

Chapter 5

Assaulting the Westwall

Everyone knew the invasion was close at hand and we were going to the marshaling yards as part of the pre-invasion offensive against the enemy transportation system. There had been a heated debate among the planners of our war strategy as to which would be the better use of our heavy bombers. One group thought the 'Transportation Offensive' was urgent to break the Germans' ability to supply their Western front once the invasion had taken place. Another equally vocal group said the Strategic Oil Offensive should take first priority. To me it seems now that we did both, we were knocking out Hitler's oil capacity and at the same time striking at any form of transportation.

John W McClane, 44th Bomb Group

In May, long penetration missions were the order of the day. On Saturday 13 May, the Eighth Air Force dispatched 749 bombers to targets in the Reich: the 1st Division going to Politz on the Baltic coast to bomb more oil refineries; while the 2nd was assigned Tutow; and the 3rd, the marshalling yards at Osnabrück. John W McClane in the 44th Bomb Group recalls:

> For a second straight day we were assigned to fly deep into Germany. Our target was a Fw 190 fighter plane assembly plant 1 mile north of Tutow near the Baltic Coast, about 60 miles northwest of Stettin and approximately 100 miles due north of Berlin. Take off was just after 10.30 hours with a total of seventeen 44th Bomb Group planes. We took a southern route across Holland and Germany, feinting towards Berlin, which always aroused the Luftwaffe. The day before, when our group went to Zeitz, the enemy fighter command had lost 150 planes defending their synthetic-oil plants. Therefore they were licking their wounds and hesitated to throw their full remaining strength against us, especially since we had over 700 of our own P-51, P-47 and P-38 fighter escorts protecting us. All told the Eighth Air Force dispatched over 700 heavies, of which 228 were B-24s

reaching Tutow loaded with 572 tons of high explosives. Our fighters were very effective in keeping the interceptors away from us. I saw many dog fights going on at a distance however. Several enemy planes swept through our formation inflicting no serious harm to any of our planes. The 44th suffered no loss on this mission in spite of rather intense flak over the target and again on the way home.

I saw something on this mission I had never seen before and never saw again. It was the practice of our defending fighters at times to fly escort along side of us. Because of the great similarity of our P-47 and the enemy Fw 190 and our P-51 and the Me 109 fighter planes, our escort pilots had to be very cautious on how they approached our bomber formations. Our gunners were a little trigger-happy so if a fighter pilot came in toward us without identifying his plane, it was assumed he was an enemy and fair game for our gunners. The method our friendly pilots used to identify themselves was to get out of reach of our .50 caliber machine guns and rock their wings so we could get a silhouette. Every airman, even myself who never manned a gun, was highly trained to recognize the subtle differences in shape between our planes and the enemy's but woe to one of our pilots who failed to make this maneuver. Once the pilot was sure we knew who he was, he would move towards us rocking his wings over and over just to be sure. Only then was it safe to get near us.

A group of about twenty Liberators were just ahead of the 44th, maybe less than a mile away, as we approached the IP and were ready to start the bomb run. I could see these planes very clearly and was watching them when a fighter plane swooped in towards their tail. Like the gunners of that group, I too thought it to be one of the enemy's, as the pilot attempted no recognition. Of course every tail gunner in the formation opened up. The fighter began to smoke and go into a spin. Not until then did I recognize it to be a P-47 Thunderbolt, one of our escort planes. The pilot baled out with his 'chute in full bloom. His plane continued to plummet towards earth until I lost sight of it. We were soon over the spot where all this had happened. I looked down where the pilot landed deep in northern Germany and thought how mad this guy was about now. I don't know who he blamed but I firmly believe it was his own carelessness. This whole action was like watching a movie, as I was so detached. Every so often we were warned at briefing to be careful about who we shot at. It seemed HQ had gotten messages from the Fighter Command that their planes were coming back to base with .50 caliber holes in them (no German aircraft used this size gun). Anyway, it made them a little angry and there were some valid threats that they would not protect certain groups if something were not done to stop it.

Our bombs dropped squarely on target, AA fire was moderate. It was time to head home. It might be helpful if the reader were to look at a map of where the German, Danish, Baltic Sea and Swedish areas came together in order to get a better idea of our flight path back to England. We proceeded out over the Baltic Sea and turned westerly so we passed within view of the southern tip of Sweden then over the entire width of Denmark and finally to the North Sea where we took a south westerly course back to East Anglia, site of our home base.

Neutral Sweden had Bulltofta airfield near its southernmost coast. Many times US planes were forced to land there due to battle damage, with no hope of being able to reach England. Of course the crews were interned for the duration of the war. We were briefed on how to reach this haven if the occasion arose but were told that the US had inspectors there to look over every plane as it came in. Any plane they judged to still be airworthy enough to have made it back or if there was not sufficient evidence in their mind's eye for the pilot to have landed, he would be court-martialed when he was repatriated. Anyone could understand what a temptation it could be to cop out of the constant danger we faced day after day. With this background one can only guess what was in everyone's mind when I pointed out this emergency landing field as we passed by.

The flight over Denmark, such a peaceful looking land to be occupied by the hated Nazis, was beautiful and uneventful. We broke the coast and when I felt it was safe I told everyone that they could remove their flak vests and helmets. We were out over the water and I had no reason to believe that any more danger existed from anti-aircraft fire. I was wrong: about the time we pulled the straps that let these heavy protecting vests fall to the floor, wham bang, four very accurate flak bursts went off close to us. It frightened the holy heck out of us. I looked down to the water to see where the AA was coming from and low and behold, the scoundrels had stationed a barge off the coast fitted with an AA battery. By the time we got our vests back on, it was too late. This taught me a lesson I never forgot; from then on I looked to be sure all was safe before announcing time to drop our vests. We still had 350 miles to go to get home. Total losses for the day were twelve bombers out of 691 to reach their various destinations. Of these one was from our force of 228 Liberators attacking Tutow. We landed shortly after 18.00 hours having been in the air for 7 hours and 45 minutes. On this day I was awarded my first Air Medal.[1]

On 14 May the weather grounded all three divisions and missions were scrubbed. At Molesworth 2nd Lieutenant Richard R 'Dick' Johnson, co-pilot to 2nd Lieutenant Theodore R 'Bud' Beiser in *Buzz Blond* in the

427th Bomb Squadron, 303rd Bomb Group, waited to fly the first mission since the crew had arrived in England in April. He was bussed to Molesworth as he recalls:

> It was the famous 303rd Bomb Group known as 'Hell's Angels'. As we drove past Molesworth and turned onto the base, which was a little over a mile from the village, we were greeted with some strange sights. There were so many B-17s that they couldn't be easily counted. The 427th Squadron to which we had been assigned was on the base, while the other three squadrons were just off the base. As we approached the barrack area of the 427th, some wag had hung a sign on the first billet area. The sign said, 'GIRLS WHO VISIT ON A WEEK END MUST BE OFF THE BASE BY TUESDAY.' Along the taxiway near the armament section row upon row of bombs were out in the open. Some of these larger bombs were fitted with wings and empennage to be used as glide bombs. After we got settled in and after hearing 'You'll be sorry,' a few times, we did the latest schooling and two short flights to familiarize us with the area. On 15 May we started earning our keep and learned why we had been trained so hard all these months. On our first mission I was to fly co-pilot for 1st Lieutenant Phillip W O'Hare in 42-97391. He was almost finished with his tour and was to train me in all aspects of combat flying.[2]
>
> My first combat mission was to Mimoycques, near Calais, to finish off a German project.[3] Our bombardier, Lieutenant Ed Cooper, had the job of arming the six 1,000lb bombs after we were in the air. Each bomb had an 8-inch vane or propeller on the nose fuze, which was prevented from turning by a cotter pin through a hole. Each cotter pin had a bomb tag with warnings. As the pin was removed, a wire attached to the bomb bay was inserted through the cotter pin hole. When the bombs were dropped, they slid off the arming wire, which allowed the propeller to turn in the wind. After falling about 500ft, the propeller wound itself off the fuze, which was then armed and would explode the bomb upon contact. After he removed the bomb tags from the nose fuze, Cooper walked to the front of the airplane and gave each officer a tag to use as a souvenir. Charlie Latta did the same with the tail fuzes for the rest of the crew. I kept my mission diary on mine. On this first mission each B-17 carried 1,700 gallons of gas and six 1,000lb bombs. The bombs were fuzed at one tenth second at the nose and one fortieth second at the tail. One fortieth second would allow the bomb to penetrate a roof before exploding and the one-tenth second fuse would assure that the bomb would explode before deep penetration.
>
> This day's mission started with a 04.00 wake-up call. Breakfast and briefing followed quickly and we were in our plane with the engines running by 06.00. The lead plane took off at 06.15 and all twenty

> B-17s were over the field and in formation at 20,000ft at 07.40. Our squadron, the 427th, was assigned the high position, behind and to the right of the lead squadron, the 358th. The 359th Squadron was low left. The 360th Squadron did not fly this mission. Each squadron furnished seven B-17s to the group formation, except the lead, which had six. Our squadron also furnished two spares that were to take up any position that might be left empty by an abort. They were to return to base before reaching enemy territory and if there was an abort later, the other B-17s moved into the empty slots, leaving the tail position empty. On this day there were no aborts and the spares returned to base. O'Hare's position in the squadron was No. 7, 'Tail End Charlie.'[4] Just after 'Bombs away' from about 25,000ft we encountered some flak. However, it was light and inaccurate, the nearest burst being at least a quarter mile away. The German gunners may not have had their radar working and so were shooting at the noise of our engines. None of our aircraft sustained damage and all planes returned to base and landed before 10.30. Total flight time was just over 4 hours. We were over enemy territory barely 7 minutes.

John W McClane in the 44th Bomb Group also flew a mission to France on 15 May. He recalls:

> After two deep penetrations of Hitler's Germany on the previous Friday and Saturday, what a relief to be informed that our mission on this Monday would be to the Pas de Calais area. No one jumped with joy however. We all knew that even though our course would carry our aerial task force over enemy held territory for a relatively short distance of only 109 miles, we could expect an intense and accurate flak barrage at most targets equal to many in Germany itself. Luftwaffe opposition was not a major worry as our fighter escorts were plentiful by this time but our gunners had to be constantly on the alert in case one or two enemy airplanes slipped past our 'little friends'. The Germans had been constructing launching sites for their V-1 'Buzz Bombs', which were soon to be sent against England and London in particular. We had no idea what we were bombing, as we had never heard of a buzz bomb. Generally these missions were thought of as 'milk runs' because of the short duration over enemy territory and with almost no aerial opposition, but they could be rough from flak.[5] The 44th Bomb Group launched seventeen planes, of which sixteen joined seventy-three others of the 2nd Division to bomb a V-1 site under construction at Siracourt, two miles southwest of St. Pol, 45 miles due south of Dunkirk. All told we carried 352 tons of bombs. Our load was eight 1,000 pounders. Our course took us due south from Shipdham to Clacton on the

> English coast, 50 miles east of London. From there we flew southeast to our famous entry point on the Belgian coast half way between Dunkirk in France and Ostend. Going south 36 miles put us 10 miles west of Lille. We took a southwesterly course for 28 miles to our IP. The bomb run was 12 miles northwest to the target. After unloading our bombs, we headed due west 33 miles where we broke the French Coast, went out over the Channel until we headed north again back to 'Jolly Old England'.
>
> If there ever were a 'milk run' this was it. We encountered no flak and the P-51 escort fighter spotted not one enemy plane. It was a most enjoyable trip. However we never saw the target due to a heavy cloud layer but this did not keep us from bombing. Usually the Germans jammed my *Gee* box with spurious radio signals as soon as we crossed the enemy coast. This resulted in a multitude of blips on my screen to the point where I could not tell the true course from all this 'grass'. (It was called 'grass' as the phosphor on our cathode ray tube emitted a bright green color.) For some inexplicable reason, the Germans were not jamming our signals and my *Gee* box was working perfectly. Warga had no idea where to drop the bombs. I asked him to calculate how far in advance of the bomb drop that would be required in order to hit the target from our 23,000ft altitude. He made this calculation which I plotted on my map. I then set the *Gee* box controls to these coordinates. I watched the blips come closer and closer. When they got exactly one over the other I said, 'Bombs away' at which time he released our load of explosives. Only 'Heaven above' knows where those bombs went. Of course we reported this at debriefing at which time we got the impression that we had performed a 'job well done.' I often wondered over the years what the Germans thought when these bombs came out of nowhere. It's difficult to believe that we were in the air 5 hours. We landed approximately 11.15 hours. I was sure proud of myself.

Technical Sergeant Don Chase, whose twenty-seventh and penultimate mission this was, agreed with McClane that 'at last' it was 'a *Noball* milk run aptly named.' The radio operator hoped that 'maybe, just maybe' his final mission might be another one like it. However: 'Weather-bound, the Group was stood down for the next four days. It was a trying time. I wanted to fly that final mission quickly. Yet I didn't want to fly it at all. I knew of at least one man (and I heard of others) who was killed on what was supposed to be his tour finale. After three days of rest, operations were resumed in a big way.'

On Friday 19 May, 888 B-17s and B-24s were despatched, the B-17s attacking targets at Berlin and Kiel and the 300 Liberators, Brunswick. 2nd Lieutenant John W McClane in the 44th Bomb Group recalls:

It had been four days since our 'milk run' to St. Pol on Monday. This would be our thirteenth mission. We could not hope for another easy one and when the curtains were drawn, we knew this was going to be another rough day. For the second time in eleven days, we were headed for Brunswick. Need anyone be reminded of the stiff fighter opposition we could expect and the accurate flak barrage over the city itself? Brunswick was known as the second 'Big B' – Berlin being the more noted. Lift off was 09.00 hours with twenty-eight of our planes, two of which were PFF. Our load was six 1,000lb bombs. Ten other bomb groups and we made up the 272 B-24s of the 2nd Division to reach the objective. We hardly reached German airspace when the battle began. The Germans sent up two groups of fighters, one to distract our escort and the other to attack the 14th Combat Wing. We three groups flew together perhaps a half a mile apart. All hell broke loose when between 150 and 200 of the enemy planes swarmed all over us. Most of the enemy action was aimed at the 492nd Bomb Group.[6] Our 44th gunners were very busy; they shot down thirteen of the attackers, four of which my 68th Squadron accounted for. No 44th plane was lost but what I saw happening to the 492nd Bomb Group was like watching a motion picture, as they were ahead of us within easy view. Enemy fighters in mass saturation swung in for the attack – some head on, others from up and into the rear of the formation. It looked like a massacre. One after the other of their bombers was shot out of the sky. I saw the whole thing and before it was over, the 492nd had lost eight of their number. Little could any of us know this was to be their lot as long as the Group remained in combat. They had inherited the Eightballs' jinx.

We were still on the way to Brunswick. Our objective was the marshaling yards in order to disrupt traffic through this most important rail center. Being 125 miles west of Berlin, it was a vital junction for goods flowing from the east and north. Our B-24s all together had 700 tons of bombs and when we finally got there we delivered them on target with excellent results, due to the fact that the cloud cover had dissipated so that our bombardiers were able to make a visual bomb run. But we were not there yet: we still had many miles to go when suddenly one of our motors began to smoke. Peritti feathered the prop and gave more power to the remaining three in order to keep in formation. We had apparently caught some enemy fire and were losing oil. This was bad news. Luftwaffe pilots just loved to see a plane fall out of formation. They were reluctant to come at us again as we had shot them up badly on their attack before, but brother, watch out for any bomber that left formation. Many times I saw one of our bombers leave formation and before long the enemy would be on the attack. They would swoop down on the crippled ship. It always seemed to me like a cat playing with a mouse. Most times I would watch our fellow airmen bale out before the plane made the final plunge to earth.

We did not want to be one of these unfortunates so Peritti and I devised a plan. As I said before, we never flew in a straight line for long before we would alter course in order to not alert the Germans as to our final destination. Peritti ordered Warga to release our bombs to lighten our ship so we could keep up with the others. I was to plot a new course about ten minutes before the whole formation turned in order to 'cut the corner' and rejoin the group before the German pilots had a chance to get at us. In all my missions I never saw another plane do what we did that day. At every turn, to the target and on the way home, we cut the corner. It must have appeared odd to the rest of the squadron but they obviously could tell what we were doing and could see we had lost an engine. I feel it saved us from being shot down. Warga did release our bombs. If I lived to be a hundred years old, I'd still be able to close my eyes and see it again. He picked out a German farmhouse in the middle of nowhere. The bombs started walking across the barnyard, through the barn and into the house coming out the other side of the yard. No one on the ground could have survived this completely unexpected disaster. When questioned at interrogation why he picked this target, his reply was, 'What's the difference in destroying a farmhouse or a city house?' I never have had a bad conscience about it, as the Nazis had no qualms about sending V-2 rockets into England that plummeted out of the sky at 3,000mph exploding with no warning whatsoever. This was war and we were just young boys playing the game.

Finally we did reach the target and one can only imagine how helpless we felt going through the terrific flak barrage with no bombs to drop. We did not want to be exposed to this terrible danger but neither could we leave formation and as usual, we picked up our share of flak holes. With their bomb loads gone, the other planes in our formations now were able to fly faster than we were using only three motors. This put us in a tight spot. We continued to cut corners until we started to pass a nearby B-17 formation. Peritti left our Group and joined onto this Flying Fortress outfit. The B-24 could easily fly as fast with three motors as the B-17 with all four. We were told later that we really did look out of place with our square body, twin tailed Lib flying among the round bodied single tail Forts. We could have cared less; we needed the protection of a formation to keep the fighters off our backs.

In spite of all that the Germans threw at us, the 44th lost not a plane or man this day but in turn we had punished them severely. We landed at 16.00 hours having been in the air exactly 7 hours. To put the day in prospective, for the whole Eighth Air Force, 888 heavies were dispatched, of which 818 reached their targets. In the process twenty-eight of our bombers and nineteen of our fighters did not return. In the fierce aerial fighting, the Luftwaffe took a severe beating, as did the German cities.

No one at Shipdham was more relieved than Technical Sergeant Don Chase:

We were lucky; others were not. The brunt of the E/A attacks was borne by the newly arrived 492nd Group. Attracted perhaps by the non-painted, silvery finish of the brand new planes that glinted in the sun, Me 109s and Fw 190s evaded the cordon of American fighters and pounced on the fledgling Group, which was flying in tight formation off to our left and below us. I watched as E/A, lined up six or eight abreast, made a frontal attack that felled four, maybe five, bombers. I saw no return fire from the B-24 gunners who, possibly, held their fire thinking the oncoming fighters were friendlies. Few 'chutes were sighted as the 24s spun earthward in increasingly tight circles which caused an upward G-force that few men could overcome. Later, other B-24s fell but I looked away, feeling nauseous, as each began its fatal spiral. So, after twenty-eight missions of varying intensity and the loss of many friends, I was through with combat. There were no easy missions. And I wished that nobody, anywhere, ever had to go to war again.

Dick Johnson, who flew with Bud Beiser on their second mission this day, recalls:

The 427th Squadron was assigned lead and we flew in position No. 5. Berlin was the primary target, with Kiel as the secondary target in case Berlin was socked in.[7] Our route north over the English Channel was hampered by dense and persistent vapor trails of the preceding groups. Our cloud ceiling at take off was 2,000ft, which altered our forming up a bit. However we departed the English coast with eighteen aircraft plus two radar ships from another group. Soon, the lead ship of the low squadron aborted due to a supercharger problem. Our route to Berlin took us up the English Channel past Hamburg and across the Jutland peninsula to a southeasterly heading. This took us about midway between Hamburg and Kiel. Our escorting fighters were P-38 Lightnings and a few P-51 Mustangs. Their fuel range would not allow them to escort us all the way to Berlin and they dropped off just past Hamburg. Fortunately, we saw no enemy fighters close enough to identify and so our main problem was flak.

As we approached the target, the flak was unbelievable. It was as if someone had painted a thin black line across the sky and it was exactly at our altitude of 26,000ft. As we approached Berlin, clouds covered over half the earth below us, which made the target difficult to see. Many of our aircraft dropped *chaff*. This only helped during cloudy weather, as the German anti-aircraft gunners preferred visual sighting. Their 'Final Aimer' usually aimed for the left wing root of the lead plane. These 88mm cannons were all on turntables and all six guns turned in unison. The gunners were so good that they could fire a burst of six, every three seconds or so. While the aim was done from a control site, all six guns pointed parallel to each other and did not converge on the target. This allowed a wider pattern of bursts, which could cover an entire group of airplanes. The big disadvantage for the flak gunners was the necessity to lead the target by two or more kilometers. That was how much they had to allow for the interval of travel by the target until the explosive shell arrived. The gunners had to assume that the target would be at a given point when the explosive shell arrived. A slow turn by the target aircraft usually was enough to cause the flak to miss.[8]

On this day, however, Lieutenant E L Roth and his crew of '*Sky Duster*' in the No. 3 position of the high squadron was hit by a direct burst shortly after bombs were dropped, and went down. Only five parachutes were seen to emerge from the stricken aircraft. As co-pilot I was able to see this loss for a short while but our ball-turret gunner, Charles Lana and others got a first hand view. We had heard rumors that civilians had murdered some of our crew-members that had baled out and this was confirmed after the war. After leaving the hell in the air, many were faced by an equal hell on the ground.

Our Group Commander, Colonel Stevens was leading this mission against Berlin. He was flying with Lieutenant Bordelon of our squadron, which led the group that day. Of the nineteen aircraft from our group, one was shot down by flak, three received major damage, eleven suffered less severe damage and only four B-17s came back unscathed. Our aircraft had several flak holes in the leading edges and a few in the sides. Ours was listed as 'major damage' due to the fact that during the bomb drop, our B-17 was forced out of position by a neighboring aircraft. This put us directly behind the lead plane, so that when he dropped his bombs, his 'Sky Marker' bomb enveloped our plane with a white acid fog and flying home was difficult due to the milky looking windshield. Due to 6/10th cloud cover over Berlin, our bombing results were not very good. We felt let down, feeling that our effort was largely wasted after facing such battle conditions. Total flight time over 8 hours. Over enemy territory, 3 hours and a half. We reported 'Hot News' of a German naval convoy in the Hamburg Fjord on the way in, but couldn't see it on the way out, because of the ruined plexiglas.

Fighter opposition was heavy and twenty-eight bombers failed to return. Three of them came from the 100th. Clarence F Cherry, left waist gunner in *Rogers Raiders*, piloted by Julian Rogers, recalls:

We left Thorpe Abbotts before daylight on 19 May. Our flight was to Berlin. We were hit with light to mild flak over the target. So we thought we had a good flight. On our way back over Denmark we were flying low squadron and 'tail-end Charlie' position when we were attacked by Me 109s and Fw 190s. They made about six passes at our position before my left waist position gun was completely blown out and I was wounded in the head. They removed me to the radio room for aid. They began to throw out equipment to lighten the ship. Already, two engines were gone. Finally, the pilot, Julian P Rogers, told our crew to prepare to ditch in the sea. We made a rough landing. They threw me out of the top window in the radio room and I came out on the wing and started to float away from our sinking Fortress. They pulled me into the life raft. It was shot with cannon holes. We were close to two islands off Denmark. We could hear the small engines on the boats in the harbor. Julian said to us, 'Row out to sea.' We were not going to be PoWs. I don't know how far we rowed. Later on a Fortress came low and made a fix on our position. Forty hours later an RAF ASR plane came over us and dropped a smoke flare on the water for wind drift. They dropped a wooden boat which had three parachutes attached to it. It dropped very close to us in the sea. We climbed aboard and started towards England. We ran into two Danish fishing boats and they interned us on their boat. They were going to take us back to Denmark as PoWs, but the British flying above us told them to stay put or be sunk. An ASR launch was on its way for us. We were taken to Great Yarmouth Hospital. All of my crew was saved. I stayed at Great Yarmouth hospital for a few days and then went back to flying and completed my tour.

On 19 May Lieutenant John Moser's crew in the 94th Bomb Group flew their first mission to Berlin,[9] as Wilbur Richardson recalls:

What made the 19 May trip memorable was that on the bomb run the ship above us [*Trudy*, flown by Lieutenant John Winslett] missed us with his bomb load. One of the 1,000-pounders fell behind No. 3 engine (I saw this one go by my ball turret). I quickly followed it down only to see it hit the left stabilizer of *Miss Donna Mae*, which was out of position below us. Apparently, it jammed the elevator in a down position. It lost altitude rapidly and began a steep dive. I watched in vain for 'chutes. None appeared.[10] Others indicated that the Fort started to break up although I didn't see it. The flak was heavy and some fighters were in the area but Brux had been much worse.[11]

On 20 May it was back to France again, when 367 B-17s and B-24s were sent to pound targets in France, while 271 B-24s and B-17s of the 3rd Bomb Division were despatched to bomb Liège and Brussels. Heavy cloud caused the 3rd Bomb Division to abandon its mission and part of the 2nd Bomb Division to be recalled. Bomb Groups were stood down on the 21st but the following morning, after bad weather had ruled out targets in France, the heavies struck at Kiel and Siracourt. Five B-17s were lost. With the good weather continuing the heavies made visual bombing attacks on several targets in France on 23, 24 and 25 May. On 23 May, 804 B-17s and B-24s, including for the first time B-24s in the 34th Bomb Group at Mendlesham, commanded by Colonel Ernest J Wackwitz, bombed several targets including Hamburg, Saarbrücken and French airfields for the loss of only one bomber.[12] The next day 447 B-17s bombed 'Big B' while 72 more attacked targets of opportunity and 400 Liberators bombed airfields at Orly, Melun, Creil and Poix in France. John McClane in the 44th Bomb Group recalls:

We were allowed to rest for five days after that frightening experience of Brunswick on Friday the 19th. Today turned out to be another 'fun day' as our target was an airfield 22 miles southeast of Paris and 5 miles North of Melun. Our course took us directly over the center of London. At briefing we had been told that the balloon barrage would be pulled down so we could make a low pass over the city to let the long suffering Londoners get a close look at the tremendous power of 'The Mighty Eighth Air Force'. Take off was early at 05.00 hours. Our group was divided into three separate squadrons of twelve planes each. We assembled over clouds with another 132 B-24s of the 2nd and 3rd Divisions, making a total of 168 Liberators carrying 500 tons of bombs headed for the Melun airfield. After assembly we headed straight for London. There was no cloud cover over the city. It was a never to be forgotten sight as we traveled this huge city at approximately 1,000ft. The roar and vibration was something to behold. I doubt that in the foreseeable history of mankind that this sight will be repeated again. We continued on to the Channel then broke the coast of France in Normandy. From here we circled in around Paris from the west making our bomb run south of Paris to the target which lay between Paris and Melun. Our strike photo showed that the 68th Squadron's bombs landed squarely on target. Each plane carried twenty-four 300lb bombs or

> approximately 3½ tons of high-explosives. The flak was light and inaccurate inflicting no damage to our plane. Fighter support was so effective that we saw no sign of the Luftwaffe. Our outbound flight took us to the same old area between Dunkirk and Ostend where we crossed the Channel homeward bound. Generally we did not refer to a penetration of enemy territory as deep as a run around Paris as a 'milk run' but for all practical purposes this was a 'milk run'. We landed at 11.15 hours after 6 hours and 15 minutes in the air.

Altogether thirty-three bombers were lost on 24 May. Cloud and thick contrails caused the 381st Bomb Group to lose contact with other groups in the 1st Wing and fighters shot down eight B-17s. The 'Bloody Hundredth' suffered even worse. 1st Lieutenant Francis 'Frank' J Malooly, pilot of *Powerhouse*[13] in the 350th Bomb Squadron described the mission, his twenty-seventh, as 'a complete disaster from beginning to end'. His ground crew chief, Sergeant George Pullar, who had given the Fortress its name, never had a crew finish their tour, and he was getting more nervous as his crew were closing in on thirty. Malooly recalls:

> This was the period when the Air Force was moving flying officers from long stateside duty into Eighth Air Force combat groups. These people were captains and field grade officers, some of whom were given positions of responsibility without, in my opinion, the required experience. My crew and I had already completed six or seven Berlin missions and our Squadron CO, Captain Jack Swartout, had assured me that we had filled our quota of Berlin missions (more 'Big B's' than any other crew in the Group). However, a new and apparently inexperienced Major Maurice Fitzgerald who was going to be our new Squadron CO was scheduled to be Command Pilot for the Group and Swartout wanted his most experienced crews on the mission. I was a lead pilot and on this mission led the high squadron and was deputy group lead. The Group lead pilot was Captain James Geary who had completed a tour with the 390th Bomb Group and then been assigned to the Hundredth.

After take-off the Hundredth had difficulty forming up with the Wing and when the B-17s started across the North Sea they were badly strung out and behind the rest. They entered enemy territory in this same condition and the low squadron was badly strung out and behind by several hundred feet. They were 'meat on the table' for the Luftwaffe and enemy fighters decimated the low squadron. *Powerhouse* had a bad fire in the right wing and was badly shot up, and Malooly's crew baled out. Geary's ship was 'hit by a shower of lead' and flak and went down. The plane flying on Malooly's left wing, piloted by Lindley Williamson, burst into flames and eight of the crew baled out to be taken prisoner. The co-pilot and radio operator were killed. The B-17 piloted by Lieutenant Delbert S Pearson and Wilbert Lund was also knocked out by the fighters and disappeared into the clouds. Nine men baled out and were taken prisoner. The tenth man, a replacement ball turret gunner, was killed. By this time, eight of the 100th Bomb Group's Fortresses had turned for home, leaving the rest to release their bombs through a hole in the clouds with fairly good results then to turn away in an attempt to avoid the heavy flak. The formation was then attacked by a succession of enemy fighters. *Nelson King*, piloted by Lieutenant Emil J Siewert, who was killed, was shot down. The bombardier and tail gunner also died. The rest of the crew baled out and were captured. Four more losses came from the 349th.Squadron. The first was a B-17 piloted by Lieutenant Martin T Hoskinson and Marvin Apking, who with their crew were on their first or second mission. All ten men were killed. Next to go was the B-17 flown by Lieutenant Robert G Roeder and Paul Lammers. Both men were killed, as were the navigator, engineer, radio operator and toggelier. Although wounded, the two waist gunners managed to bale out with the ball turret gunner and tail gunner. *Times A Wastin'*, piloted by Lieutenant Henry F Jespersen and Robert Atkins was shot down. Both men and the engineer, waist gunner and bombardier were taken prisoner after baling out. The rest of the crew were killed. The ninth and last B-17 lost was piloted by 2nd Lieutenant Clarke T Johnson and Raymond Lund, who with their crew were on their first mission. Seven of the ten men aboard were killed, including the pilots and the navigator.[14] At the de-briefing back at Thorpe Abbotts the only good news was that Colonel Ollen 'Ollie' Turner and Captain Jack Swartout had finished their tours.

The next day, 25 May, crews correctly anticipated a 'milk run' to the Low Countries. 2nd Lieutenant Dick Johnson in the 303rd Bomb Group flew his third mission of the war:

> Target for today was the marshaling yards at Blainville, France. Since this would be a rather long mission, our take off time was a little earlier than usual. The first B-17 took off at 05.47 and the last at 05.58. The 303rd Bomb Group was to supply only twelve aircraft, with two spares, for the 41st Combat Wing, of which we were a part. London is 60 miles south of our field at Molesworth and our departure course took us straight south, past London. At that point we turned east and passed over a suburb of London, climbing to 19,000ft at 07.31. From here we crossed the English Channel in a climb so that we penetrated the French coast at 23,000ft. Our penetration was at a point about half way between Le Havre and Boulogne as there were no flak guns nearby. Just out of range, we saw a few bursts of flak as we continued on a course which took us within sight of Paris, which lay to our south. At the target we had taken an earlier lead, since the other combat wings had overshot the

penetration course, which put us almost first to the target. We were low group on this mission and since the lead group overshot the IP we had a longer than usual bomb run. During the bomb run, the formation is most vulnerable to enemy action, as the bomb bay doors are open for the entire trip from IP to target. This alerts the German anti aircraft gunners that we will be flying a long, straight course to the target. This day, the bomb run was eleven minutes and we expected to have a great deal of flak come up. But nothing happened. Evidently the 88mm guns that we thought were there had been moved elsewhere. The weather was CAVU[15], therefore if there had been flak guns we would have been 'sitting ducks'. This was first that I saw bombs exploding on the target. The extended bomb run allowed the lead bombardier to kill his drift to perfection and the Norden bombsight did its job flawlessly. There were no damaged aircraft and no aborts on this mission and all twelve returned to base just after noon. Total flight time, five and one half-hours. Over enemy territory, almost exactly three hours. We did our part to damage the German war machine for the upcoming invasion.

Despite perfect weather some Fortresses in the 390th and 401st Bomb Groups bombed using radar. Command needed to know how successful PFF could be on D-Day if targets were obscured by cloud. It all served to increase speculation, at Framlingham and Deenthorpe at least, that the invasion of *Festung Europa* was imminent. 'Invasion fever' was on everyone's lips. At Shipdham after fourteen missions, Charles Peritti's crew had become a seasoned crew. Peritti had already been advanced to 1st Lieutenant and on 25 May the remaining three officers, co-pilot Burr W Palmer, bombardier John F Warga and navigator, John W McClane, Jnr, were promoted to the rank of 1st Lieutenant. McClane had been awarded the Air Medal on 13 May after his eleventh mission and the first of three oak leaf clusters on 22 May, and he was beginning to feel 'like a real vet':

Already we were being put in a lead position having worked our way up through the formation. Soon Peritti would be the 'A Flight' leader and I would be directing our course as a lead navigator. We no longer flew in low position. We were becoming leaders, not followers. The group had four squadrons of which three usually flew on any one mission. Each squadron had a lead navigator with a deputy on his wing. At this stage of the game we were deputies, but on D-Day and thereafter, we were leaders. We had been assigned a new NMF B-24H (42-95260), which Peritti selected the name of *Lili Marlene*. How he came by this name I have no idea. He also arranged to have the picture of *Lili* painted on the right side of the nose of the plane. She was sitting on a bomb and, as one might expect, mostly nude. This plane had been especially equipped with a Gee box. At this time only lead navigators had Gee boxes. *Lili Marlene* was a beautiful plane – bright and unpainted with our squadron code letters of WQ in large letters on either side of the fuselage just aft on the side gunner windows. I was sure she would fly until old age sent her to the 'Great Haven in the Sky' where old bombers go. I know she is there now – even if she did meet with a premature death.

On 27 May the Eighth switched to German targets when the rail network once again came in for a pounding by the Fortresses. Colonel James Luper, CO, 457th Bomb Group led the 'Fireball Outfit' and the 1st Division to Ludwigshafen in *Rene III*.[16] The flak was heavy and fighters made head-on attacks that verged on the suicidal. *Rene III* was badly shot up but Luper managed to nurse her back to Glatton.[17] 2nd Lieutenant Dick Johnson in the 303rd Bomb Group meanwhile, flew his fourth mission, to Mannheim:

We were assigned to position No. 6 in the low squadron, known as 'Purple Heart Corner' because it is lowest in the squadron and farthest out. Mannheim was a heavily defended city on the Rhine River near Ludwigshafen, just a few miles northwest of Heidelberg. Mannheim was a bottleneck for transportation in that area. Our mission was to destroy the marshalling yards that would feed supplies to defend the coast during the D-Day invasion. We did not yet know when the invasion would be but knew it would be soon. Our assigned secondary target was the nearby city of Ludwigshafen. If overcast, PFF on Ludwigshafen. Target of opportunity Florennes/Juzaine airfield. Last resort, any military installation in Germany not adjacent to built up area (!). We were trying to spare German civilians. This phrase was usually reserved for use in occupied countries only. Thirty-seven of our B 17s were loaded with ten 500lb bombs each. Engines were started at 08.15 and takeoff started at 08.45. We assembled the group over Molesworth at 6,000ft and departed base at 09.45. We were two minutes late, due to keeping Division battle order. The logistics of forming up, joining your Wing and staying on course is almost mind-boggling. The Eighth Air Force put up almost 1,000 bombers that day, using about 2 million gallons of gasoline. We departed the English coast at Beachy Head at 10.39 and 16,000ft. We climbed as we crossed the English Channel and crossed the enemy coast in France at 11.00 at 20,000ft. At the Initial Point we made a 30° turn to the target and opened bomb bay doors. Ten minutes before the target, the code word for visual bombing, 'Stud Horse', was given by radio. A six-minute bomb run was made on a straight line to the target and the flak started coming up. As we approached the city of Mannheim, the flak became intense and shell

> fragments struck many of our B-17s. The ceiling and visibility was unlimited, so the German flak gunners were aiming visually. The radar jamming *chaff* that we dropped did little good. Only a few German fighter aircraft were seen in the distance, but didn't attack, as our escort kept them at bay. Our thirty-five B-17s dropped a total of 350 bombs on the target with good results. One B-17 jettisoned his bombs over Germany after they failed to release over the target. One B-17 received major damage and seven had minor damage. None were shot down. In my diary I have underlined the words, 'Very Lucky', as our plane escaped damage. Total flight time, 7 hours. Time over enemy territory, 3 hours and 35 minutes.[18]

The 457th's tale of woe continued on 28 May. The group lost three more crews when a record 1,341 heavies were despatched to seven oil targets in Germany. The Luftwaffe again concentrated their attacks, in this instance on the leading wings of the 1st and 3rd Bomb Divisions. The escorting fighters were overwhelmed and over 300 fighters assailed the 94th Wing at the head of the 1st Division. Altogether, thirty-two bombers were lost, including seven in the 401st Bomb Group.

Lieutenant John R Shaffer, the bombardier in *Naughty Nan* in the 93rd Bomb Group, was flying his second mission, to the synthetic-oil refinery at Merseburg, the second largest of its type in Germany. 'Flames reaching to 2,000ft were proof enough that the Liberators had found their mark.' Even 200 miles from the target, crews could still see a pall of smoke, which rose 12,000ft into the air.

John W McClane flew his fifteenth mission in the 44th Bomb Group:

> On Sunday morning of 28 May I had the surprise of my life. When I went to early briefing (I was a lead navigator now) I could not believe what I heard. We were going to Zeitz again. The very same synthetic-oil refinery 20 miles southwest of Leipzig, Germany that we had left wrecked and burning just sixteen days before on our tenth mission of May 12th. My question was, 'What are we going back to Zeitz again for?' Well, little did we know of the German's ability to repair and even completely rebuild industrial plants that our intelligence people had considered destroyed. At this time of my limited knowledge, I thought we were going on a wild goose chase, which made no sense. We all knew better now and before the day was out, I was to once more look down on this refinery to see with my own eyes that it had been completely rebuilt and back in production.
>
> While rebuilding their oil refineries, the Germans also put around them some of the strongest concentration of anti-aircraft guns in all of Hitler's Europe. We no longer could expect just four gun ack-ack batteries to track and fire at us. These 'Grossbatteries' of 88mm as

well as 105 and 128mm calibre were in groups of twelve to twenty-four guns that gave a 'shot gun' effect. The tighter our formation, the more effective they were. We dispersed *chaff* to jam the radar, which aimed the flak guns. This was very effective except for the lead formation throwing out the first of the stuff. The first groups caught all hell, as I was to really find out on my twenty-sixth mission to St. Lô when we led the Air Force. The mission was a major effort by the Eighth Air Force. In all, over a thousand 4-engine bombers were sent to more than thirty different targets in Germany; 864 of these reached their objectives. Of all these planes, our 2nd Division Liberators made up the largest single force. The 44th Bomb Group's twenty-six planes were part of 187 to strike Zeitz with almost 450 tons of bombs, whereas on 12 May we had only 250 tons. We were out to destroy this oil refinery once and for all.

Take off was 10.00 hours. Our fighter escort was so effective we never saw an enemy on the way in or out.[19] The AA gunners at Zeitz must have been low on ammunition or asleep because the flak was much less intense than we expected. However the flak that they did send up was accurate as our 506th Squadron lost one of its planes for the only loss of the day for the 44th Bomb Group. The 389th Bomb Group lost two more. Our bombing results were excellent. Visibility was unlimited. The black smoke was almost to our flight altitude before we were out of sight of the target. This time, 'we tore them up bad.'[20] We arrived back in Shipdham air base at 17.30 hours, having been in flight some 7 hours and 30 minutes.

2nd Lieutenant Dick Johnson in the 303rd Bomb Group in the 41st Wing flew his fifth mission this day, to the Eifeltor marshalling yard at Cologne:

The weather over Europe was predicted to be mostly clear and targets would include fuel and transportation systems. Our crew was assigned a special mission this day and would not participate in the regular effort to neutralize Nazi war materiel. In the night the armourers attached two strange bombs to the belly of each bomber, using special bomb shackles.[21] The bombs were side by side, with their wingtips only four inches apart. They had a 12-foot wing span and were almost 12ft long. The three groups in the 41st Combat Wing[22] were expected to put two battle formations in the air. The 303rd put nineteen planes in the glide bomb formation, which left the base an hour earlier than the second element going to oil targets. Our take off time was about 09.30, so that we could be out of the way of the next element. We crossed the French coast two miles south of Nieuport at 19,500ft and proceeded to Cologne. Our squadron, the 427th, went in first. Starting at 140mph we started a dive until we reached 208mph. At this point, we leveled off for a few seconds and released the bombs nearly 18 miles from the target. Unfortunately, our bombs, as well as those of the other two groups following, mostly spun in and exploded in fields 15 miles from the target.[23] Upon our return to base, one engine on our *Bet Jane* had to be replaced due to flak damage on the way to the target. Later that evening on German radio, which we always listened to, William Joyce, or 'Lord Haw Haw,' as we called him, reported that Cologne had been bombed by allied bombers from an altitude of 40,000ft. We had quite a laugh about that, since the B-17 wasn't designed to fly quite that high.

On 29 May, 993 B-24s and B-17s were despatched to several targets, including the oil plants at Politz and the Junkers Ju 88 plant at Tutow and three Focke Wulf 190 factories in the Reich. Some 888 of the heavies made visual attacks on aircraft plants and oil installations in Germany. Russell A Grantham, 836th Bomb Squadron Operations Officer in the 487th Bomb Group at Lavenham who was flying his fifth mission, flew the group lead:

Being a staff officer, I did not have an assigned plane, but substituted with assigned lead crews and did not, therefore, have a regular assigned plane. We approached Politz with three squadrons of Liberators (approximately thirty-eight planes). At the IP we were met by Me 410 twin engined fighters. They made repeated attacks into and past the target from a position of 11 o'clock high and aiming at my plane. The target was partially obscured by clouds and smoke from previous hit. However, we were able to place bombs on the target by a simple and effective device. We had developed a simple plastic sheet with elongated cross hairs that by over-laying the intelligence photos, we could select aiming points outside the obscured area, which lined up with the target and naturally, the cross hair intersection would automatically line up on the target. Our group received an Eighth Air Force Commendation and I received the Distinguished Flying Cross.

2nd Lieutenant Dick Johnson flew his sixth mission this day, to Posen (Poznan): 'Slugging it out for ten hours':

Part of our mission to prepare for *D-Day* was to decimate the German fighter force. Had this been accomplished earlier, the invasion would have been in early May. In order for the invasion to succeed, the Allies had to have mastery of the air and this had not yet occurred. We were to bomb a Focke Wulf assembly plant and airfield in Posen where the dreaded Fw 190 was being built. We were assigned No. 3 position, behind and to the left of the high squadron leader. Our group furnished eighteen planes for the wing formation. We were in our aircraft at 07.10 and started engines at 08.00. We started taxi at 08.10 and took off at 08.25. It took one hour for all planes to get into formation at 8,000ft over Molesworth. Climbing to 13,500ft we crossed the English coast at Cromer. Over the sea we climbed to 21,000ft, picking up friendly fighters. We crossed the enemy coast near the Dutch town of Ijmuiden, not far from Egmond, at 10.44. Our course was due east, aimed directly at Berlin. While still out of range of their flak guns, we made a dogleg to the south. We then took a direct flight to Posen and drew a bead on the Fw factory in the suburb of Erzesinki.

The sky was cloudless and so our bomb run of 38 miles gave the lead bombardier plenty of time to kill the drift, which was 5° to the right of our track. This caused our true heading to be at a compass heading of 64° while our track over the ground was at 68° magnetic. The intervolometer was set at the Salvo position and when the bombs first appeared out of the lead plane, all the other planes dropped in unison. Despite considerable flak, the Norden bombsight did its job well on this mission. Much of the plant was destroyed, as were several buildings nearby. Coming off the target, we headed due north for 25 minutes, while letting down to 14,000ft from our bombing altitude of 22,000ft. This was done to conserve fuel, as this was a critical problem on such a long mission. At the lower altitude, the superchargers could be turned off and the engines leaned out for better fuel efficiency. After letting down to 14,000ft, we turned to the northwest and crossed into the Baltic Sea. At this point we crossed over an island that we thought was undefended. We were wrong. The island contained a four-gun battery of 88mm flak guns and we flew directly over them. Four bursts at a time were coming up every three or four seconds and the only thing that saved us was a quick turn to throw off their aiming lead. The second burst destroyed an engine on one of our planes and he started dropping back.

We no sooner got over the open Baltic again than we noticed a small formation of planes off to our right, going in the same direction. They were German fighters trying to simulate our own P-51s. After they passed us a couple of miles, they made a turn to the left and their profiles gave them away as Me 109s and Fw 190s. There were three of each and they made a diving left turn to attack us from the 1 o'clock high position. One Me 109 chose our plane as his target and came in firing his 20mm canon too soon, as they were exploding ahead of us. Beiser grabbed the yoke and pulled up a bit. I was convinced that the German pilot had drawn a mental Bullseye on the co-pilot's windshield, so I grabbed the yoke to assist Beiser. All our forward guns were firing at this point, but our gyrations prevented any serious damage to the Me 109. More importantly, it

> also prevented the German pilot from inflicting any damage on us. Our B-17 was very light at this time, having dropped our ten 500lb bombs and having burned most of our eight tons of gas. This Me 109 duplicated our every move, but was behind the curve, as he could not anticipate what we were going to do. At the last moment, I was sure that he was going to ram us, but he veered off our right wing tip so close that I could see his face and was startled to see that he was not wearing an oxygen mask. It was our rule to use oxygen above 10,000ft in daylight and from the ground up at night. He probably removed his mask at the start of his attack. Whether it affected his aim, I'll never know. We expected the fighters to come back, but they spotted our straggler and decided to finish him off. It didn't work, as two of the enemy planes were shot down and a third was damaged. On the way back to base we saw a B-17 go out of control and explode. Eight parachutes were counted. In the North Sea we saw another B-17 ditch, having run out of fuel. We saw one of the inflatable life rafts that had several men in it. Air sea rescue came and picked them up a couple of hours later. None of these downed bombers were from our base and we all got back safely, including our straggler who made it on three engines. Nine B-17s of our group sustained minor damage, while our straggler was listed as major. One aircraft was listed as damaged by friendly fire. This was our aircraft, as another B-17 firing at 'our' Me 109 fired a 50 caliber, armour piercing, incendiary bullet through our left wing. Fortunately for us, it missed our gas tank, which would likely have made us into a fireball. Guns on the B-17 cannot shoot parts off their own plane because of stops built into the mechanism, but it cannot prevent 'OOPS' from your neighbors. On this mission, the return flight took us very near neutral Sweden and from other groups, eight bombers sought refuge from the war by landing at two fields there. Total flight time for this mission was just over 10 hours. Time over enemy territory, 4 hours and 40 minutes.[24]

Beginning on 30 May,[25] American and RAF Bomber Command crews made all-out attacks on the invasion coast. Both were careful to place twice as many bombs on targets further afield as they did on the Normandy coast, for fear that the German defenders would learn where the assault would come. The enemy knew that invasion was imminent but suspected that the first wave of troops would land in the Pas de Calais, further north. So, while the German defenders on the Atlantic Wall played their guessing game, the heavies continued their strikes on *Noball* sites in the Pas de Calais.[26] Operation *Cover* called for raids on coastal defences, mainly in the Pas de Calais, to deceive the Germans as to the area to be invaded by the Allied armies massing in Britain. On 31 May 1,029 heavies, including for the first time B-24s in the 490th Bomb

Group at Eye, Suffolk, led by the CO, Colonel Lloyd H Watnee, were despatched and only one bomber and three fighters were lost.[27]

John W McClane adds:

> The 44th put up twenty-six planes and in all, the 2nd and 3rd Divisions assembled an Air Armada of 491 B-24s loaded with eight 1,000lb bombs to disrupt the marshaling yards in Brussels. Take off was shortly before 08.30 hours but we were back a little after noon having been in the air only four hours, the shortest combat flight time of all my thirty-one missions. The reason being clouds. They extended up to 26,000ft and there was no way we could see the target visually even though we came within 10 miles of it. It would have been far too dangerous to the Belgium population of this large city to take a chance of bombing by Pathfinder lead without being precisely sure of our aim. There was nothing to do but turn for home. We encountered no fighters and flak was very light and inaccurate. Of over 1,000 bombers dispatched for the day, only one third were able to bomb their targets. The rest of us carried our bomb load back home. This was the thirteenth mission we had flown this month and we were tired. Fatigue was showing on everyone including the ground personnel who got less rest than the combat crews. They were up day and night keeping our bombers flying. Not enough can be said for these men. At the rate we were knocking off missions, it would have taken only another six weeks to complete our tour. Because we became a lead crew, we later only flew when it was our time to lead. Also we were due some rest leave sooner or later but as of now, the invasion was imminent and there was no rest for the weary.

On 2 June the Eighth Air Force mounted two strikes on V-weapons sites in the Pas de Calais. In the first raid, 776 B-17 and B-24s were involved. In the second raid, 293 bombers struck at airfields and railway targets in France. No bombers were lost.[28] On this date – his mother's forty-fourth birthday – 2nd Lieutenant Dick Johnson in the 303rd Bomb Group flew his eighth mission, to the large marshalling yards at Juvisy in the south-western suburbs of Paris. The aim of the mission was to delay German movement to the front lines during the upcoming invasion. Johnson's diary for that day reads. 'Paris, France (Marshaling yards) five tenths cloud cover. Moderate flak no damage. Saw hundreds of landing craft on English coast. Invasion soon maybe.'

> Fourteen aircraft were furnished for the 41st Combat Wing from our group. The 427th Squadron was to lead our group. Our B-17s had been loaded with six 1,000lb bombs and 1,700 gallons of gas. Our time schedule for this mission was pretty tight, as we were to take

> off at around 17.30 and arrive at the target before dark. The days were long at this time of year, so we were confident that we could make this schedule. We departed the English coast over Selsey Bill, at an altitude of 18,500ft. Selsey Bill is a point of land just east of Portsmouth. We crossed the English Channel, climbing to 22,000ft, hitting the French coast just across the harbor from Le Havre. We encountered a layer of clouds at our altitude and decided to drop down to 18,000ft. We made a feint toward Chartres and just before reaching their outer defences, made a dogleg to the left and made a direct flight to our target. We bombed at 20.32 just before the sun went down. We flew a circle around Paris at 21,000ft and headed toward Le Havre, where we departed the enemy coast a few miles north of that town. It was dark by then and no lights could be seen anywhere on the ground. Just before dark we saw a large group of British Lancasters heading out to do their nightly bombing. Our track to Molesworth took us about a mile west of London, which was so totally dark that it could not be seen. We landed at nearly 23.00 and headed to the mess hall for a late snack, having eaten our box lunches on the way out. I was somewhat miffed to find that the mess hall personnel had gone to bed, leaving a large pot of coffee into which they had put too much cream and too much sugar. I was unable to drink it, since I always drank mine without sugar. This was my only gripe about food, since the Mess Sergeant had always done a great job.[29]

For the next three days hundreds of Eighth Air Force bombers flew two missions a day to the Pas de Calais area. On 4 June *Sack Rat*, piloted by Lieutenant Clifford R Galley in the 491st, developed a high speed stall while forming up and crashed near Sizewell, Suffolk, killing everyone on board. That evening the 361st Fighter Group accompanied five B-24s in the 753rd Bomb Squadron, 458th Bomb Group making their second attempt to knock out a series of bridges on the Seine River with the radio-controlled *Azon* glide bombs. On Monday 5 June, 629 bombers attacked coastal defence installations in the Cherbourg–Caen and Pas de Calais areas and three *Noball* sites and a railway bridge were also raided. 2nd Lieutenant Dick Johnson in the 303rd Bomb Group flew his ninth mission to the Cherbourg Peninsula and its heavy gun batteries. He wrote:

> We made three bomb runs. Meager flak, no damage. Four tenths cloud cover on target. Saw hundreds of ships on English coast. Things may pop open very soon now. This was a short mission so we traded fuel for bombs. Each B-17 was loaded with sixteen 500lb SAP bombs. We took off at 06.15 with twelve B 17s and one spare. Since there were no aborts, the spare returned before reaching enemy

> territory. We departed England at Selsey Bill at 24,500ft and headed to our IP in the Channel, which was determined by LORAN.[30] Due to clouds, we tried three times to hit the primary target, each time returning to our IP, to no avail. Just ahead of our last attempt was a heavy gun emplacement next to a landing strip. They received 144 semi-armour piercing, 500lb bombs of the nine aircraft in our part of the group just because the weather was bad elsewhere. After bombing, we let down over the Channel, through clouds and crossed the English coast at Portland Bill at 2,700ft. We flew a direct course to Molesworth, arriving just before noon. Over the target area, there was moderate flak in several places but none close enough to damage any of the B-17s of our group. Only two fighter planes were seen and they were both ours. We were in the air four and half-hours with 35 minutes over enemy territory.

Six B-24s, including *Missouri Sue* (a 44th Bomb Group PFF ship), which carried the 489th Bomb Group deputy Commander Lieutenant Colonel Leon R Vance, were lost. A malfunction prevented bomb release on the target, a V-1 site near Wimereaux and, despite protests, Vance ordered the crew to go around again. This time the bomb drop was made by hand but two bombs hung up. Now the flak had increased in intensity and a 88mm salvo burst directly under the port wing. Captain Louis A Mazure, the pilot, was killed instantly when he was hit in the temple and Earl L Gamer, the co-pilot, was seriously wounded. Three engines were put out of action and *Missouri Sue* rose menacingly on the verge of a stall. The tall, rangy, colonel, who was standing behind the pilots' seats, looked down to see that his right foot had been virtually severed from his leg and was attached only by the Achilles tendon, which was jammed behind the co-pilot's seat. Despite his terrible injury, Vance managed to reach the panel and feather the three useless engines. Gamer cut all four engines and turned the B-24 towards England. When the shoreline came into view Lieutenant Bernard W Bale, the radar navigator, ordered the crew to evacuate the B-24. Although he was suffering from shock, Bale managed to get the colonel down into his navigator's seat. He took off his belt and wound it around Vance's thigh to stop the blood spurting. His quick thinking undoubtedly saved Vance's life. Bale told him they would have to jump because there was no way they could land the B-24, especially since the two bombs were ready to go off on impact. The colonel shook his head and said he would not jump. Bale knew that he could not possibly drag Vance to the bomb bay and push him out and he was also aware that the aircraft was rapidly losing altitude. There was little time left to save himself. Bale checked the tourniquet one last time, shook Vance's hand and jumped from the open bomb bay. Vance managed to get into the cockpit and succeeded in ditching within reach of the English coast. The impact blew him clear of the aircraft and ASR, who gave him immediate medical attention, quickly picked him up.[31]

That night at Hethel just outside Norwich, Lieutenant Duane A Hall's nine-man crew in the 566th Squadron, 389th Bomb Group, which had been one of the replacement crews to arrive in May, had been assigned to a B-24H in good condition, called *The Little Gramper Jnr*. She had finished up one crew, a good sign, but the Hall crew were still waiting to fly her on a combat mission. On 5 June they were alerted to fly their first combat mission next day. That night the enlisted men in their hut listened alternately to the BBC and the enemy propaganda station. Both came in loud and clear. Lord Haw Haw, the traitor William Joyce, was in great form. 'Shove it sideways,' someone yelled. Each member of the hut had contributed a one-pound note to a pool to correctly guess the date for D-Day. Staff Sergeant Robert H 'Bob' Sherwood, the top turret gunner, had drawn 29 May, a date that came and soon passed by. Someone else would collect the £120.

Planning the final date for the invasion involved a certain amount of guesswork and it had kept the planners at SHEAF[32] awake for several nights. Only a select few knew that a stretch of the Normandy coastline from Quineville to just south of Caen had been selected for the long-awaited Second Front. The invasion had been due to take place in May 1944 but General Dwight D Eisenhower, Supreme Commander at SHAEF, then postponed the date by a month to enable extra landing craft to be built. On 8 May he selected 5 June as D-Day but the weather conditions had to be right. A local storm front, forming suddenly east of Iceland forced Eisenhower to postpone the invasion for 24 hours but the forecast for the 6th was better so Eisenhower said, 'OK, we'll go.'

At Deopham Green Gus Perna and Ralph Reese, tail gunner and left waist gunner respectively on *Smoky Liz*, were in the base theatre when Norman Wright, the navigator and James McLellan, the bombardier were called to go to target study at the 452nd Group Headquarters. Reese recalls:

> We suspected that something was in the air. We went back to our barracks and were told to report to briefing at once. During briefing, we were told this was 'It' and that our target for today would be Le Havre. There would be wave after wave of planes to hit the coast. We could not drop any bombs after 07.30, in case we hit our own troops. All planes after the bomb run were to turn to the right, so as to make one way traffic pattern because many planes were in the air. Every airfield in England had lights on at 02.00. This was the first time since England had been at war. There was a solid overcast, so we had to bomb PFF. After we had landed at our base, the *Smoky Liz* would be loaded with 500 lbs for another mission.

It was common knowledge that the Allies were preparing to invade the Continent. But where and when? As a 21-year-old junior flying officer, it was not John W McClane's concern:

> I knew when the orderly awakened me that morning that something unusual was afoot, as it was not our day to lead. At briefing I found the answer to my question. We were not going to fly the usual large squadron and group formation but rather small groups of six planes each. Every lead navigator that could be rounded up was required for this maximum effort. The rest of my crew were held in reserve for a later raid but for this early effort, I was assigned to another crew. I'm sure they were not pleased to have a strange navigator forced on them and I did not relish flying without my crew. A strong bond of trust developed among crewmembers, as it was a life or death situation on every mission.
>
> There was great excitement when the curtains concealing the route map were drawn back at briefing and we were informed that, 'This is it' – D-Day and that the landing was to be made in Normandy. Surprise? No, but fear of the unexpected? Yes. I fully expected the Wehrmacht and the Luftwaffe to resist with every ounce of strength available to them. My concern was fighter opposition to our bomber force. I was really fearful that this might be my last mission. Little did I know how overwhelming our air strength was and that the German defenders had no chance whatsoever of inflicting any serious losses, much less of turning this aerial armada back. Take off was at 03.00 hours. We were told in no uncertain terms that we were to fly a fixed and preset course to and from the target area. Once we broke the coast of England and passed over the Channel, there could be no alteration in course for any reason whatsoever that would be tolerated. We were told that British fighters had instructions that any plane flying out side of the narrow prescribed corridor or any plane aborting and flying the wrong direction would be shot down without exception. The point was made so clear that I believed it 100 percent and so did everyone else. One thing that did please me was the fact that I was not going to miss out of the invasion. I really wanted to be a part of the show and would have been greatly disappointed had I not been selected to lead the flight.

At Molesworth, 2nd Lieutenant Dick Johnson went to briefing. 'Today is D-Day,' the briefing officer announced. 'The invasion has already started and we are going to try to prevent the Germans from bringing up reinforcements. The weather is very, bad and we may bomb by radar,' he said.

The Eighth was required to fly three missions. The first was primarily concerned with neutralizing enemy coastal defences and front-line troops.

Subsequent missions would be directed against lines of communication leading to the bridgehead. The bombers would be in good company with no less than thirty-six squadrons of Mustangs and Thunderbolts patrolling the area. Initially, they would protect the 'big friends' but would later break off and strafe ground targets. It was evident that there could be no lay and that any stragglers would be left to their fate. Any aborts were to drop out of formation before leaving the English coast and then fly back to base at below 14,000ft. It was a one-way aerial corridor and the traffic flow intense. Aircraft would fly to and fro over the length of England dropping various coloured flares to denote the aerial corridors. If a plane had to be ditched, only those ships returning to England from the bridgehead would stop to pick up crews. Crews were told that if they were shot down they were to wait in uniform until they could join their own troops in France. Finally, an 'inspirational message to the departing troops' from General Eisenhower, the Supreme Allied Commander, was read out. At briefings throughout East Anglia American fighter pilots and bomber crews tramped into the briefing rooms to be told what their mission on 6 June would be.

2nd Lieutenant Dick Johnson in the 303rd Bomb Group recalls:

> Each B-17 was loaded with twelve 500lb and two 1,000lb bombs and we were off at 06.00 with thirty-four aircraft. Two aircraft aborted due to mechanical problems – Lieutenant Baleie of the 358th Squadron and Lieutenant Fackler of the 359th Squadron. This was my tenth mission with the 427th Squadron, and Colonel Snyder, the commander, led the low flight. Walter Cronkite flew with Bob Sheets in *Shoo Shoo Baby* of our squadron on this mission. We were to bomb a bridge near the invasion coast, but the cloud cover at the target was total, so we were to bomb by PFF. Sixteen aircraft of the lead group dropped 192 500lb GP bombs and thirty 1,000lb GP bombs on the target, with unobserved results. Our flight had a radar failure and dropped no bombs. We flew our bombs back to base and made ready for our second mission of the day.
>
> Our target near the invasion coast was a bridge near Caen that we were unable to bomb because of an equipment failure on the lead aircraft. We saw flak again at a distance but we were not affected. The weather over the French coast was bad with 5/10th cloud cover but we could see bits of the invasion activity. The number of wakes from ships and landing craft covered the entire English Channel for miles. We could see smoke on the French coast from all the artillery. To prevent being fired upon by our own gunners, the fighters and medium bombers had a wide, white stripe painted across one wing and around the fuselage. The heavies didn't bother with this, as we were too high to be seen. We had achieved the desired mastery of the air by this time and the Germans had a bitter joke amongst

themselves: 'If you see a camouflaged airplane, it's British. If you see a shiny, unpainted airplane, it's American. If you don't see any airplane at all, it's German.' Much of our mission at this stage of the war was the attrition of experienced German fighter pilots. As they rose up to defend their country, our fighters shot them down. And so, on this day, the destruction of Hitler's Third Reich began in earnest and the outcome is in the history of Earth's greatest war.

All told, four B-24 Liberators were lost on D-Day. Throughout East Anglia crews rightly felt pleased with their contribution.[33] An indication of the success of the operation was contained in a message from Lieutenant General Doolittle sent to all bomber bases. 'Today the greatest effective strength in the history of the Eighth Air Force was reached; an overall effectiveness of approximately 75 percent of all crews and airplanes assigned. Please extend my congratulations to all members ... for their untiring effort in achieving this impressive strength.'

At Hethel Bob Sherwood noted the sense of anti climax after the thrill of D-Day. The 389th was alerted to fly every day after 6 June. Every day Hall's crew was slated to fly; each day there was a stand down. The weather was impossible. Fog and rain. Anything that was not paved turned into brown mud. The crews stayed in their damp, dark huts. They dashed out only to get meals. The humid mess hall smelled of powdered eggs, stale grease and wet wool.

Notes

1. Twelve B-17s and B-24s were lost. The fighters claimed 47 enemy fighters shot down for the loss of five of their own.
2. 'My pilot, Lieutenant Beiser, was to fly with the rest of our crew while he flew co-pilot for an experienced pilot, Steven Bastean, who finished his tour in mid-June. All crews were thus flown on their first mission. This policy of flying experienced pilots with new crews was necessary in order to teach the "green" crews how to get into formation. After this first mission, the new crew was reunited for subsequent missions. Little did I know at that time, that on my last eight missions I would be flying seven or eight new crews on their first mission, using their pilot as my co-pilot.'
3. 'Most are aware of the V-1 "Buzz Bomb" and the V-2 suborbital rocket. What most people don't realize is that Hitler had under way a V-3. This was the so-called "London Gun" being installed in western France, at Mimoycques. It was to consist of two batteries of 25 guns each; the barrels of which were each 416 feet long. Installed along a steep incline, they would be capable of firing a 55lb shell into the city of London. If the Allies had allowed this weapon to be completed, it would have eclipsed the damage done by the V-1. The explosive propellant would have altered the range and direction so that the entire city of London could be targeted. Unfortunately for the Germans, the earth removal

scars caught the attention of Allied reconnaissance planes and the site was periodically bombed.'

On 15 May 166 B-17s and B-24s bombed V-weapon sites in France. No bombers were lost and 128 of the heavies dropped 485 tons on the *Noball* sites.

4. '"Tail end Charlie" is one of the most vulnerable positions in the formation. "Purple Heart Corner" is the next plane on the outside of the formation. There was an undercast at the target and we bombed by radar. The lead plane was equipped with this system and all following planes dropped at first appearance of bombs from the lead plane.'
5. 'As a matter of fact, on 12 June 1944, when we first heard that these pilotless "Flying Bombs" were being launched by the Germans, we thought it was an act of desperation on their part, that they had no more pilots or planes to strike back with. In other words, it was very funny to us but later we changed our tune when we went to London on rest leave only to be brought back to reality by five of them exploding close by.'
6. 'On 11 May, the 492nd Bomb Group, a new addition to the 14th Combat Wing, flew its first mission. They were stationed at North Pickenham, 12 miles to our west. These guys had come to England as the first group ever to have the new all silver Liberators. These "Hot Pilots" prided themselves as being unusually good at formation flying. Before their combat began, we were told to watch a "fly over" by this new group so our pilots could see how it was done by "experts". Needless to say, they resented this display and said so in no uncertain terms but not loud enough for General Johnson, head of the 14th Combat Wing, to hear them.'
7. 'Each B-17 was loaded with 2,700 gallons of gas and twelve 500lb bombs. At 6lb per gallon the weight of fuel for each plane was 16,200lbs and bombs weighed 6,000lb for a total of over 12 tons. The B-17G carried over 5,000 rounds of ammunition for its 13 machine guns. The weight of these .50 caliber machine guns, plus oil for the engines and oxygen for the crew often brought the take-off weight of these aircraft to over 65,000lb. Empty, they weighed about 35,000lb.'
8. 'Berlin had large numbers of 88mm flak guns all around the city. Also, many fixed guns of larger caliber were deployed in the area. Many of these were 105mm and some were 128mm. They were not as accurate as the 88s but made a larger explosion. When the target aircraft couldn't be seen, these guns fired a burst that would explode at or above our altitude, thus forcing us to fly through a rain of shell fragments.'
9. They had to abort their first scheduled run to the 'Big City' on 29 April. First, *Luscious Duchess* had developed turbo problems and then the second ship had a runaway prop at altitude. 2nd Lieutenant Kenneth L Chisum's crew that took their place were shot down.
10. There were no survivors from Lieutenant Marion Ulysses Reid's B-17G-20-BO, 42-31540 *Miss Donna Mae* in the 331st Bomb Squadron.
11. US fighters claimed 70 enemy fighters for the loss of 19 of their own The 2nd Bomb Division encountered 150–200 enemy fighters between Dummer Lake and the IP and again after leaving the target area. At Waggum airfield 30 Fw 190s and Bf 109s attacked from 12 o'clock, skidding through the

formation head-on. At Steinhuder Lake, more then 220 enemy fighters were encountered. A total of 12 B-24s and 4 P-47s were lost.

12. B-24 *Sweet Lorraine* in the 458th Bomb Group collided with a Fortress over Eye, Suffolk, while forming up for the mission to Bourges. All 10 crew aboard the Liberator were killed.
13. Formerly *Shilayee* in the 349th Bomb Squadron.
14. See *Century Bombers: The Story of the Bloody Hundredth* by Richard Le Strange, 100th Bomb Group Memorial Museum, 1989.
15. Ceiling And Visibility Unlimited.
16. The 1,000th B-17 built by Douglas and named after Luper's wife.
17. During final approach, however, only one undercarriage leg would extend despite repeated attempts to lower it. Finally, Luper had to land *Rene III* on only the one wheel, skillfully keeping her straight and level for as long as possible before the left wing began to sag. The Colonel killed his ignition switches just before the Fortress dipped and plowed an arc across the airfield. The entire crew was unhurt and was able to walk away unscathed. *Rene III* was repaired and flew again but three other B-17s in the 457th FTR and 19 were severely mauled.
18. In all 923 B-17s and B-24s pounded the German rail network on 27 May. 24 bombers were lost, including B-24 42-95159 in the 755th Squadron, 458th Bomb Group, which collided with *Briney Marlin*, another 755th Squadron B-24, north of Cromer in undercast during assembly. 42-95159 went into a spin and only one crewman, who left by the waist window, was seen to escape. Two men aboard *Briney Marlin* baled out but those who remained with the aircraft managed to bring it home safely to Horsham St. Faith.
19. However the 1st Division B-17s had 300 fighters attack them with rather severe consequences, especially to the 401st Bomb Group which lost one-fourth of the 32 bombers MIA for the day from all three Air Divisions.
20. 'Anyone who has read Albert Speer's *Inside The Third Reich* will recall that he said that as long as we struck at his factories, he could keep production going by repair, dispersal and going underground. But on May 12th, the day we started bombing the oil refineries, he knew the war was lost. Production of gasoline and oil dropped from 182,000 tons in March 1944 to 39,000 tons in July to 12,000 tons in August and less than 5,000 tons by September 1944. After the war, many German leaders said that no single thing greater than the Eighth Air Force's attacks on their oil resources was responsible for the collapse of the Nazi war machine.'
21. Experimental GB-1 *Grapefruit* glide bombs, developed by fitting small wings and empennage to a 2,000lb GP M34 bomb.
22. 303rd, 384th and 379th Bomb Groups.
23. 59 B-17s released 116 GB-1 glide bombs. None came within a mile of the yards but 42 hits were scattered throughout Cologne, killing 82 people and injuring over 1,500 others.
24. For the second day running strong enemy fighter formations opposed the bombers, whose gunners claimed 62 of them shot down. 673 US fighters were airborne and they claimed 39 enemy fighters destroyed for the loss of 10 of their own. Actual *Luftwaffe* losses on 29 May amounted to more than 50 aircraft shot down, 44 aircrew KIA (including two leading aces) and 19 others being injured in air combat. 17 Liberators and 17 B-17s FTR. The Leuna works

suffered a 50% drop in production after the raids in May; the Pölitz works was even worse hit on 29 May.

25. On the morning of 30 May 911 heavies, including, for the first time, the B-24s of the 489th Bomb Group at Halesworth, were despatched in six forces to attack aircraft targets in Germany, marshalling yards in Belgium and France and *Noball* sites in the Pas de Calais.
26. 928 heavies in six forces escorted by 672 fighters continued the pounding of aircraft industry targets in Germany, marshalling yards in France and Belgium and *Noball* sites in the Pas de Calais. 12 bombers and 9 fighters were lost.
27. Four specially equipped Liberators in the 753rd Bomb Squadron, 458th Bomb Group attempted to bomb five bridges at Beaumont-sur-Oise, Melun and Meulan in France with the revolutionary *Azon* glider bomb. The device could be released by an aircraft at a distance and then directed on to the target. Basically, it was a conventional 1,000lb bomb fitted with radio-controlled moveable tail fins. Visibility had to be good to enable the operator in the B-24 to see it right to the target. For this purpose a smoke canister was attached. Each bomber could carry three such bombs, but had to circle the target as many times to release them, which was an obvious disadvantage. The 30 May raid ended in failure with none of the bombs hitting the target. Experimental raids continued in June, with, at most, 15 Liberators being used on any one mission, but results did not improve and General Doolittle abandoned the project. Later versions of the radio-guided bomb included the *Razon* and the 12,000lb *Tarzon* used by B-29s in Korea.
28. In the afternoon mission, 319 B-17s and B-24s, including for the first time B-24s of the 489th and 491st Bomb Groups flying the first full 95th Wing mission, were despatched to bomb airfields and railway targets in France. The two 95th Wing groups bombed Bretigny, Creil and Villeneuve airfields near Paris for the loss of one 491st Bomb Group Liberator and 4 489th B-24s. Flak also caused varying degrees of damage to 59 other machines. 35 491st Liberators approached their home base at Metfield, Suffolk in gathering darkness and landed safely, but at Halesworth three of the returning 37 489th Liberators crashed and had to be written off.
29. 'Recon photos the next day showed that we had done a good job on the railroad marshalling yards. Our total flight time was 5 and half-hours, with 1 hour and 40 minutes over enemy territory.'
30. This was a less sophisticated version of modern LORAN (Long-Range Navigation), which could take crews within a quarter mile or so of their destination.
31. Vance was awarded the Medal of Honor. He was the fifth and final airman in the 2nd Bomb Division to receive the award (the other four awards were for Ploesti on 1 August 1943). He underwent amputation of his right foot and was later invalided home in a C-54. Somewhere between Iceland and Newfoundland the Skymaster with its crew and patients disappeared without trace. Bale was later shot down, on a mission to Stuttgart, his 25th operation, and made a PoW.
32. Supreme Headquarters Allied Expeditionary Forces, whose HQ since 28 May 1944 was at Southwick House near Portsmouth.

33. Altogether 2,362 American bomber sorties involving 1,729 B-17s and B-24s were flown on D-Day, dropping 3,596 tons of bombs for the loss of only three bombers. Eighth Fighter Command flew 1,880 sorties and claimed 28 enemy fighters shot down. In the period 6 June–31 August the RAF flew 224,889 sorties, losing 2,036 aircraft (983 of which were from Bomber Command and 224 from Coastal Command). Aircrew KIA/MIA totalled 1,035 from 2nd TAF and ADGB (Air Defence of Great Britain), 6,761 from Bomber Command and 382 from Coastal Command.

Chapter 6

The Oil Campaign

Merseburg was the first time I saw colored flak. I remember it as red, although there are those who remember it as pale blue. I still think it was red. Someone told us; probably someone who didn't know either, that it was to call in the fighters. Since we already had more fighters than Custer had Sioux, I thought that it was gilding the lily somewhat to call in something that we already had in abundance. But to me, one fighter was plenty for the day.

Fred Huston, bombardier,
337th Bomb Squadron, 96th Bomb Group

'As we approached the Rhenania Ossag Mineralolwerkes AG at Harburg, a suburb of Hamburg, the flak was unbelievable. The Germans were determined to protect their oil supplies at any cost.' Dick Johnson was one of the pilots when the Eighth Air Force put up 853 B-17s and 695 B-24s for a total of 1,548 heavy bombers on 20 June:

> The flak explosions were constant and unrelenting, being so close that many could be heard to explode and throw fragments against the sides of the airplane. The angry, red center of some of the explosions meant that they were very close. To hear flak explode, it had to be within 50ft of our plane, otherwise the very loud engine noise would drown out the noise of an explosion farther away. Likewise, to feel a jolt from a flak explosion, it would have to be within 25ft or less from the plane. I saw plenty of red centers and heard several of them during our 41 mile (!) bomb run. Our ground speed against the wind was barely over two miles per minute, allowing the German defenders a good chance to track us in the straight and level flight from the Initial Point to the target. Just before the IP, the B-17 flown by 1st Lieutenant J T Parker, nearly dead ahead of us, suffered a double engine failure due to flak damage. He was able to keep up for

a short while and dropped his bombs with the formation. He could not keep up with the homeward-bound formation but lost altitude while still under control. When we last saw him he was down near the ground, still under control, but he never made it back to base and all nine crewmembers became guests of the German Government for the rest of the war.

We busted the target wide open. One group ahead of us had also hit the target and smoke was visible during the entire bomb run. There were many great explosions among the oil storage tanks and on the cracking plant itself. From our vantage point at 26,500ft we could see clearly that the target was completely covered by bomb bursts. We hadn't bothered to carry any incendiary bombs on this trip, but it seems that they would have been redundant. It was surprising that there would be a target of this importance still in existence in the city and suburbs of Hamburg, since it had already been razed by British night bombing, causing a firestorm of tornado intensity that covered most of the city.

Only two of our B-17s escaped damage on this mission. Eleven suffered major damage, three crewmen were wounded by flak and the one plane was lost. It is remarkable that only one plane was shot down. Our plane suffered over 263 flak holes of various sizes and yet not a crewmember was hit and the airplane flew as if nothing had happened to it. Our bombardier, Ed Cooper in *Old Ninety Nine*, almost lost it on this mission.[1] Flak was so thick that it fell like rain at times from explosions above the formation. One of these pieces of shrapnel came in the nose window and struck Ed on the breastbone and drove him six feet back into the navigator's compartment. There is no doubt that the flak suit saved his life, because when we returned to base we helped him cut the piece of flak from the suit. The flak suit is composed of small plates of tantalum steel that overlap each other like scales on a fish. There were always three thicknesses of these plates. The first layer had clasped the flak fragment so that it could not be removed. The second layer was bent sharply around the first and the third layer was only slightly bent. Ed sported a large bruise on his chest for several days, but was not injured enough to take him off flying status.[2]

Ralph Reese in the 452nd observed:

The target was really flaming and smoking as we dropped our bombs and closed the bomb bay doors. Smoke reached as high as 5,000ft. On the way back to the coast we saw many targets which had been bombed. They were burning and smoking and smoke reached as high as 10,000ft.[3]

Wednesday 21 June was notable for a raid on Berlin and also for the second Eighth Air Force shuttle mission of the war. The 4th Combat Wing and a composite from the 3rd Division led the Eighth to Berlin with the 1st and 2nd Divisions behind. After the target, 163 Fortresses of the 13th and 45th Combat Wings of the 3rd Division, each B-17 of which was equipped with a long-range bomb bay tank, would fly on to landing fields at Poltava and Mirgorod in Russia, while the rest of the force returned to East Anglia.[4]

Staff Sergeant James H McMahon, a B-24 nose turret gunner on his twenty-eighth mission in the 409th Bomb Squadron, 93rd Bomb Group, was part of the mission to Politz (Stettin) on 21 June:

> It was very clear all the way in and out. We lost about forty-five bombers and we were attacked in force by the GAF. Many of the bombers were hit very hard by flak over the target area and by fighter fire as we went in to the target and after we began our return to base. There were over 1,000 heavy bombers attacking, supported by over 700 fighters. We were attacked in waves from head on. The enemy attacked in long lines abreast. They dove under the formations as they went through. I believe that I destroyed one Fw 190 that almost crashed head on into our ship. I fired a very long burst at him and he exploded under the formation as he dove under our ship. I saw many B-24s blowing up during the fighter attacks and many spiraling down like falling leaves in flames, or out of control. Some of our ships received direct hits directly over the target and the fighters came through their own flak to get at us.[5]

Wilbur Richardson was in the ball turret of *Kismet* in the 94th Bomb Group formation in the leading 4th Wing. He recalls:

> The flak was extremely heavy at the target and we were bounced around by the flak bursts. Holes were appearing everywhere. Just before bomb release, John Moser, who was concerned about damage, asked all of us to assess the situation. At that moment I saw fuel in a large stream coming from No. 2 turbo. 'Feather No. 2 quick,' I yelled anxiously. My heart was pounding. It was done. Moser then asked why, because his instruments had given no hint of danger.[6]

Leo C Riley, *Kismet*'s co-pilot, was far from happy. He wrote:

> Today we have just returned from a so-called retaliation raid on Berlin. It was very rough indeed and to my notion uncalled for. Our ship was shot practically into a sieve by flak. No. 2 gas tank punctured but thank God it did not catch fire. No. 3 pierced but kept running. We came home on three motors, but made it very nicely.

> Have quite a few flak frags I picked up in the ship. More scattered all over it. Left tire was blown out on landing, but we made it OK. Lead ship went down. Think the crew baled out. Fighters were there, but did not get to us. God has been kind to us again today. (On landing we found that No. 2 motor had been on fire and for some unknown reason had gone out.)

Ken Weisl, in the *Nevada Avenger* in the 384th Bomb Group, made it back to Grafton Underwood, as he recalls:

> At the base, because we were lost from the rest of the formation, they never thought that we were crazy enough to go to the target by ourselves! So they tried to say that we dropped our bombs in the Channel and then just flew around to use up the gas. They would not give us credit for the mission. The fact that no one on the crew was hurt was not the way that old 013 brought its crews back! Well, the pilot remembered that we had a camera in the camera well and this camera started operating when the bomb bay doors opened. They got the pictures developed and they found that we hit the target but the main group missed it! All we got for the extra effort was credit for the mission. Of course this broke the jinx of the *Nevada Avenger* – 'Old 013'. Then we reported the two enemy planes that we shot down but the intelligence officer wanted confirmation from other crews and we pointed out that there were no other planes from our group around. He insisted that we had to have confirmation, so we told him to forget it. After that we never reported any planes that we had shot down or thought we had shot down.

Meanwhile, the 163 Fortresses in the 13th and 45th Wings headed for their target, the Ruhland-Elsterwerda synthetic-oil plant 50 miles south of 'Big B'. The shuttle force flew the northern route to Germany, climbing northeast to a point above the Friesian Islands, then heading due east as though to southern Denmark. When the Fortresses reached the German coast near Cuxhaven four B-17s in the 452nd Bomb Group were involved in a mid-air collision. During the trip to the target the most impressive sight was a glimpse of Berlin and some of the B-17 crews saw a few B-24s go down as their turn came.[7] Over 'Big B' bombs fell from the bellies of the 388th and 452nd Bomb Group Fortresses and they were joined by those of the 100th Bomb Group.

During the shuttle force's absence combat tours were raised from thirty to thirty-five missions. Headquarters also announced that deep penetration missions would rank equally with the short-haul raids in the table of missions per tour. Eventually, a fairer method was evolved when headquarters took into account the greater risks involved in flying deep into Germany. One of the more immediate ways of shortening a tour and earning a 30-day rest and recuperation leave was to 'volunteer' for a second tour.

For all intents and purposes the Luftwaffe failed to make any serious attempt in the first few days of July to challenge the awesome number of B-24s and B-17s being hurled against them. But finally on 7 July, when over 1,000 heavy bombers attacked three synthetic-oil plants, eight aircraft assembly plants and engine works and other targets, Sturmgruppe JG 3 led by Wilhelm Moritz in the Leipzig area viciously attacked the 2nd Division B-24 Liberators again. For the second time the 492nd Bomb Group suffered severely, losing eleven of the thirty-seven heavies lost that day.

On 7 July Nick G Plackis in the 390th Bomb Group flew his first deep penetration after making a few short haul sorties that proved to be milk runs, giving the crew the false impression that combat flying was a 'piece of cake'. But that was to change quickly on 7 July when they were exposed to their first 'blood-bath' before ever getting near the target at Merseburg. Plackis says:

> We had just crossed the English Channel and still over the Zuider Zee above Holland when our two wingmen on the right collided due to propwash turbulence while tightening up our formation, one directly on top of the other. It was like a slow motion movie. When the upper '17[8] descended into the wings of the lower one,[9] its props chewed into the aluminum while the lower '17's props were disintegrating the belly of the upper one. Gasoline was spewing everywhere and immediately ignited both aircraft into bright orange flaming torches. The No. 2 prop of the upper plane broke off cleanly at the shaft in one piece and as it came off, it laid flat on the top of the wing as it slowly slid off into space. We watched in horror, as both flaming B-17s gently peeled off to the right, together, prior to going into a joined spin. We counted five 'chutes before both planes separated. The lower one exploded in a tremendous blast with a full load of bombs, maximum long haul fuel and ten crew. The other Fortress blew up a short distance from the first, but we heard that some of the crew who baled out were captured and became PoWs.

Lieutenant Leo C Riley, co-piloting a B-17 in the 94th Bomb Group, saw the two ships go down in flames over the Zuider Zee. He wrote: 'Such is fate again. Six 'chutes came clear, but fourteen men burned to death. It all happened directly in front of us and we had to dodge the pieces to keep from getting hit.'[10]

Nick G Plackis again:

> As rough as the rest of the mission was, with fighters and flak, it all seemed anti-climatic after seeing our friends going down in flames.

> Though, as young and as impressionable as we were, our somewhat reckless and adventurous resilient spirit recovered us from this setback, anxiously giving us an optimistic attitude to eagerly look forward to boarding our Fortress for each subsequent mission and reaching our ultimate goal of thirty.

For three successive days, beginning 11 July, the heavies blasted industrial sections of Munich. The Bavarian city was important to the Germans at this stage of the war because of the many aircraft industrial facilities nearby, where engineers and designers were building new weapons for the final aerial battles between the Luftwaffe and the Allied air forces. Jet aircraft and experimental works dotted the vicinity of Munich. The hub of the complex was the massive Allach aero engine works, which, with assembly plants and Luftwaffe airfields close by, made Munich a top priority target. The Thursday 13 July mission to Munich was Wilbur Richardson's and some of the rest of the crew of *Kismet* in the 94th their thirtieth and final mission of their tour. Wilbur Richardson remembers the mission well:

> No. 30 would be remembered for just that, no matter what. Mine, again just a bit different. I was seriously wounded over the target by 155mm flak. There was one very small hole in the wing and a very large one in my turret and me. Just the two. *Kismet* – fate. I stayed in the turret to count the bombs away. I thought I could stick it out longer but I was losing too much blood. I reported to the pilot and he said to get out and the waist gunner could take my place as bandits were reported in the area. The radio operator, Bernard Jeffers, and the right waist, Milo Johnson, stripped off my flight clothes and new pants and shirt I had just purchased. I was treated and placed in a survival electric blanket bag. A short time later fighters hit us. I jumped up at the sound of shooting and grabbed the radio gun. I didn't have any intercom so I wasn't sure what the action was. I saw only one that I could shoot at from that position. After a bit I realized I had nothing but a T-shirt and shorts on and I was getting awfully cold so I hit the blanket to get warm. It was three and-a-half hours back to the base and I was still losing precious blood. We left the formation to get back to base as soon as possible. Another ship joined us as a waist gunner had an arm wound. Upon landing I was strapped on a stretcher, placed in an ambulance for a ride to an Army hospital. I didn't get back to the base for over five weeks. A nurse tossed away the large piece of flak that hit me.[11]

On the 16 July mission to Munich, the 1st Scouting Force of Mustangs and Mosquitoes, developed and led by 42-year-old Colonel Budd J Peaslee, was used for the first time. Peaslee's scouting force flew just ahead of the main bombing force, transmitting up-to-the-minute weather reports back to the task force commander to prevent him leading his bombers into heavy weather fronts which could disrupt the mission and, in some instances, lead to its cancellation. Peaslee's weather scouts again proved effective on the 18 July mission to the principal German research and development centre at Peenemünde on the Baltic coast, where German scientists were trying to create the atomic bomb. The MPI was well covered with bomb hits and smoke was reported rising to 12,000ft. The bomb pattern brought acclaim from General Spaatz, among others, who described it as, 'one of the finest examples of precision bombing I have seen.' General Williams added, 'On this vital operation the 1st Division again demonstrated its ability to destroy the assigned objective regardless of its location or enemy opposition.' Peenemünde was the furthest penetration into northeast Germany and it was not until after the war that its importance was fully realized.[12]

During July the Eighth flew seven tactical missions in support of the Allied armies in northern France. On Monday 24 July Operation *Cobra* was scheduled to penetrate German defences west of St. Lô and secure Coutances but bad weather prevented all but 352 of the 1,586 bombers from bombing the primary for fear of hitting their own troops. The 379th Bomb Group made three runs over the target before it found a gap in the clouds to bomb through. Accuracy was essential and many bombers returned with their bomb loads intact rather than risk dropping them on their own troops, as John W McClane recalls:

> The mission of 24 July was a complete flop as to its intended purpose. It was to be a repeat of our effort at Caen on the 18th except at St. Lô, 34 miles west of Caen and with a much larger number of planes. We were to drop in advance of the US 1st Army in a carpet bombing tactical attack. 1,586 B-24s and B-17s were taking part, of which thirty-seven were from our 44th Bomb Group. Take off was early and we reached the drop zone in mid-morning. This type of tactical bombing, being only a few hundred yards in front of our own ground troops, required absolutely clear visibility of the drop area. This was not in the cards for today as there was 10/10 cloud cover over the target area. Under no circumstance were we to drop our bombs under these conditions so we took our flak bursts and returned to base. For the 44th, it was a very uneventful day but little did we know what was in store for us tomorrow. This day affected the Germans very little but two mishaps turned this abortive mission into disaster for some of our own ground personnel. The first was an accidental tripping of the bomb release switch by a B-24 bombardier. When a large quantity of *chaff* being thrown out by a forward plane hit his compartment, it startled him. His bombs fell on one of our own landing strips killing four men and wounding fourteen

others. In addition he destroyed two P-47 Thunderbolt fighters. The second unfortunate happening was even more disastrous. Another bombardier who was leading his squadron was trying to free a faulty release mechanism, which in turn salvoed his bombs accidentally. When they left the bomb bay, it was a signal for twelve following planes to drop their bombs, which they did. This incident killed sixteen of our ground troops and wounded sixty more. After 5 hours and 45 minutes, we landed at Shipdham unaware of these tragic mistakes.

An even worse accidental bombing of our own troops occurred the following day when we returned. It had been one week since our ineffectual carpet bombing in front of the British and Canadian troops at Caen. Only twenty-four hours had passed since our 'dry run' over the same target we were assigned to bomb today. This was to be a massive tactical carpet bombing in support of our armies fighting in the St. Lô area. Since the invasion six weeks before, our ground forces had not been strong enough to break out of the small beachhead area roughly extending from Caen on the east to St. Lô on the west and only fifteen to twenty miles inland from the English Channel. General Eisenhower decided the time had come to make a major 'breakout' effort. He ordered the Eighth Air Force to bomb just in front of his 1st and 3rd Armies.

The weather had cleared considerably since the abortive attempt the day before. An even greater force of heavy bombers than before were scheduled for this mission. There would be 850 B-17 Flying Fortresses and 650 B-24 Liberators (1,503 in all) carrying 3,400 tons of bombs, destroying the enemy's ability to fight before this day was over. As lead navigator for the 68th squadron on this mission, I went to early briefing to prepare for this critical flight. After breakfast, all flying personnel assembled for the main briefing. We were instructed in great detail, as our target area was [the Marigny–St. Gilles region] a small rectangular section behind a road leading north and west from the city of St. Lô. The order to the pilots and bombardiers was to fly as low as necessary to keep below the clouds. This had to be a visual bombing as the target area was only a few hundred yards in advance of our troops, who had pulled back behind this road. We were told to look for red smoke artillery shells to be fired by our forces into the drop zone.

Our plane, *Lili Marlene*, was the lead plane for the 68th Squadron. We had a Command Pilot on board as well as our own pilot and crew. All went well in the assembly and the flight to the English coast near Brighton, south of London. There is approximately 100 miles of open water over the English Channel at this point to the French coast north of St. Lô, and another 20 miles over land to St. Lô. The 2nd Air Division was leading the Eighth Air Force, the 14th Combat Wing was leading the 2nd Division, the 44th Bomb Group was leading the Combat Wing and the 67th Squadron was leading the group. Our 68th Squadron of twelve ships was behind and to the right of the 67th. After we had broken the English coast and flown some distance over the Channel I became concerned, as I knew we were off course to reach out target and so advised the Command Pilot and Captain Peritti. It was an unforgivable sin to break formation, as this was part of our protection from enemy fighters but time and distance were running out the further we went. Everything depended upon the proper approach on the bomb run. Being a typical hypertensive navigator type, I began to stress over and over that we had to alter course if we were to reach the IP. I really do not know what I said or how I said it but my concern must have been convincing. I can only imagine the anguish the Command Pilot and my pilot must have gone through in wanting to keep formation on the one hand and my urging them to correct course on the other. It seemed like an eternity to me but finally I was asked for a new heading. I directed a change of about 20° to the right.

After the change in flight direction, we began to pull away from the lead formation. They continued straight while we moved off to their right. After a few minutes it was obvious to anyone in either squadron that we would soon be far apart. What was going through the mind of the Lead Command Pilot and the lead navigator, I do not know. There must have been some soul searching. As for me, I was almost sick from concern that I had possibly made a mistake and had talked my pilot into committing an unforgivable disobedience of standing orders.

The 68th Squadron kept to my course. The closer we got to the French coast, the more I realized my navigation was accurate. In the meantime, the lead squadron had pulled far off to our left but suddenly they realized the error in their course and made a large correction to parallel ours. Now the 68th Squadron was in the lead with the former lead behind us and to our left. We were now the lead for the entire Eighth Air Force and naturally this would put us over the drop zone first.

Now we had a new problem: the clouds were getting lower. Due to our orders to bomb visually Warga requested we follow the clouds down which we did. This put us at 14,000ft by the time we reached the drop zone. All hell broke loose. Every anti-aircraft gun the Germans could muster that could reach our low altitude was concentrated on us. Peritti had turned control of the plane over to Warga's bombsight. We had to fly straight and level. I pointed out to Warga the road from St. Lô and the red smoke shells, which were clearly visible. Like all bombardiers, he had nerves of iron, never became excited and had an excellent rating on most bombings. Today was no exception. I watched the bombs land squarely on target.

Our job was done. Peritti now put the squadron into violent evasive action. Even over Berlin, the flak was neither as concentrated nor as intense as we were going through. Holes were being ripped through us at every explosion. I gave the order to correct course to the right and just as we made the turn and straightened out, a flak shell exploded directly under us. The concussion suddenly lifted *Lili Marlene* at least 20ft and just as quickly, we began to fall. I was thrown to the floor of my navigation compartment. Under my desk was a lever that opened the nose wheel doors, which was my escape hatch. I was not waiting around to assess the damage. I thought we had lost a wing and a combat flyer only has to see this happen to a nearby plane once to know there is no escape due to centrifugal force once the plane begins to spin and tumble. (This type of fear accounted for frequent premature bale-outs.) I had my hand on the lever ready to jump. I did not take the time to disconnect my electric flying suit, the oxygen supply nor ear phone plug. Just as I was ready to go I heard Peritti say, 'Stay on board; the plane is still flying.' I stood up. We were still on the westerly course and beginning to leave the flak area. Our plane had been severely damaged. The flak shell had exploded directly under us spewing out steel in a cone shape. We had caught the concussion in the centre of the cone and received over 400 flak holes from this shell and the AA barrage. We knew our two wingmen were hurt badly also but only after we landed did we know that the plane on the left of us had 600 holes and our deputy on the right had almost 1,000. Believe it or not, not a man in any of the three aircraft received a scratch.

Resuming my navigation duties, at the appropriate place, I ordered a turn to the right, which would put us on a northerly course up the Cherbourg Peninsula. At this point, something happened that I did not understand. Instead of turning as directed, Peritti asked, 'Mac, are you sure you want me to turn to the right?' Never had he ever questioned my navigation before. I was mystified and told him, 'Yes, turn as directed.' Peritti came back, 'But I see the English Channel ahead. We will fly back into the combat zone again.' I looked out. Sure enough there was water ahead but to my amusement it was the Atlantic and not the Channel. After assuring my pilot that it would take several minutes of flying up the peninsula before we could see the Channel, he made the turn to the right.

Now we were flying north and could look to our right, easily seeing back into the battle area. There was a tremendous billow of dust up to several thousand feet being blown back over the American front lines by a south wind. I did not get the significance of this terrible turn of events until after we had landed. Our planes were loaded with 100lb fragmentation bombs set to explode on contact; the purpose being to kill enemy personnel, not to dig big holes that our tanks could not get past. This was the reason for this huge volume of dust being churned up.

About this time I looked at the planes in the bomber stream when suddenly, one of the aircraft exploded, falling into a nearby plane and into one or two more. It appeared that four planes came burning and exploding all at once in a jumble of wreckage falling through the sky. It looked terrible.[13] Finally we left the area and the English Channel did come into view. Needless to say, we were badly shaken up. We knew our plane had been severely damaged. There were holes all through my navigation compartment. I could see daylight through the fuselage as if it were a sieve. But thanks to the Grace of God, all our planes were flying and no one killed in our squadron. The 68th Squadron had paid the price for having taken the lead, ten out of our twelve ships were damaged. As so often happened, the excitement of the battle caused me to perspire so greatly that the sweat ran from under my helmet and froze into ice cakes on my forehead. We had about two hours of flying to return back to base. Our course took us around the city of London and we had time to think about the mission. A great concern gripped me. What was going to happen when we landed and were made to account for leaving the formation over the Channel?

We reached our base and landed after 5 hours and 30 minutes in the air. Peritti was instructed to pull up in front of Group Headquarters rather than go to our usual hardstand. When I lowered myself out of the plane and looked up, the first thing I saw was Colonel John Gibson, Commanding Officer of the 44th Bomb Group. My heart sank. I could see a very serious look on his face. He stepped out of his Jeep and looked straight at us. With a wide rapid motion of his right hand starting at knee level swinging up over the top of his head, he demanded in a loud voice, 'YOU FOLLOW ME'. He also ordered that the camera be taken out of our plane and the pictures be developed at once.

Needless to say, we did follow Colonel Gibson into the debriefing room. He spread a map in front of him and pointing to me said, 'WHERE WERE YOU?' In a stammering voice filled with trepidation, I began by explaining what had happened over the Channel and why we had changed course away from the lead squadron. Suddenly I was greatly relieved because Colonel Gibson said to forget about what happened on the way over the Channel. He wanted to know where we had dropped our bombs. All this time I thought we were in big trouble for having left the formation and now he did not give a hoot about that. I knew exactly where Warga had dropped our squadron bombs and pointed out the spot on the map, as did Warga.

> Intelligence came up with the pictures taken from our plane. They had even penciled lines over our designated strike area and almost every bomb was inside the lines. At this point Colonel Gibson's whole personality changed back to the usual good natured and likeable person he was. A smile broke over his face from ear to ear. The 44th was not at fault for a grievous error, word had filtered back that bombs had fallen short of the drop zone, crossing the road coming out of St. Lô and into the American lines, killing many of our men. Later I was told it was 260 men including General McNair.[14] Ours were the first bombs to drop so the target area was very visible. But the Groups following us could see nothing through the dense dust and dropped their bombs into the cloud until corrected by P-51s flying to indicate the correct drop area. History records that the Allied forces did break out of the beachhead as a result of this bombing. It was the greatest tactical bombing of the war.[15]

On 28 July, 653 B-17s bombed the synthetic-oil plant at Merseburg while fifty-seven others bombed Wiesbaden marshalling yards and an aircraft engine factory at Taucha. They were supported by 437 fighters, which later broke away to strafe ground targets. Seven B-17s and two P-51s were lost.[16] A J Sinibubb, navigator in Lieutenant Pullen's crew in the 323rd Bomb Squadron, 91st Bomb Group, which flew deputy lead, low squadron to Merseburg, was flying his fifteenth mission. Sinibubb wrote:

> We ran right into Leipzig and all hell broke loose. Flak bursts were so close that we could see the flash as they exploded. Six out of the twelve ships in our squadron came back on three engines. Our oxygen was shot out on the right side. (When we landed we found 'fist' sized holes in Nos. 3 and 4 engines. Why they didn't go out on us I still don't know. They had to be taken off.) On the turn off from the target we ran into an experimental flak station and those Jerries really know how to shoot.

Dick Johnson in the 303rd Bomb Group flew his twenty-sixth mission, to Merseburg:

> This mission would take us deep into Germany to the Leuna oil works where enemy resistance was always encountered. My second new crew was going with me in the B-17 named *Betty Jane* that I had flown several times before, including the glide bomb attack on Cologne. My new co-pilot for the day was J A Drewry with all his crew, except his co-pilot who was flying with yet another experienced pilot. This morning the 303rd Bomb Group put up thirty-seven aircraft, taking off between the hours of 05.50 and 06.19 to make assembly over the Harrington Buncher at 9,000ft. Each B-17

> was carrying ten 500lb bombs. During assembly my aircraft was approached by another B-17, which caused me to fly a 360° turn to stay out of his way. By the time I returned to the assembly area the 303rd Group was too far ahead for me to catch up so I latched onto the 379th out of Kimbolton, which I knew was going to the same target. Many pilots aborted when they couldn't find their group and I didn't want this stigma attached to me. Had I not known the destination of the 379th, I would have had no choice but to abort. During the mission the 303rd saw no enemy fighters but the 379th that I was flying with encountered a few. Our top turret gunner, Sergeant E H Koch, fired at a Fw 190 that seemed to be trying to drag a bomb on a long wire through our formation. That bomb didn't explode and Koch didn't seem to hit the Fw 190, who was about 3,000ft above us flying in the same direction. The fighters were not pressing any attacks for some reason not clear to me since there were no P-51s in the immediate area. We encountered flak at seven different locations on this mission but the *Betty Jane* only suffered two minor wounds for this trip. We had been discharging *chaff* to foil the German radar and it seemed to do some good. The target was overcast, so the German gunners could not sight visually, nor could we bomb visually. Most of the heavy concentration of flak seemed to always be behind us. Evidently we didn't do such a good job on the synthetic-oil plant, as we later learned that we would go back tomorrow. Our flight time was 8 hours and 10 minutes, with 4 hours and 20 minutes over enemy territory.

Lieutenant George P Fory, a pilot in the 100th Bomb Group, had his introduction to the Leuna flak on 28 July:

> Many times I had expressed that flak-wise, Merseburg was worse than Berlin. I suppose the worst condition for comparison was Berlin. There the flak was in curtains and of a barrage type where an area was filled with it, but Merseburg flak was mostly tracking type and always four bursts at a time. There was tracking type at Berlin too, but it wasn't so noticeable with all the other. The flak would come up in four bursts, generally 50–75 yards apart and usually staggered in elevation. If you saw three bursts, you wondered if you were in the fourth. The worst part of being in the lead was waiting for the flak to start. On one occasion we were in the lead and had passed the 'three minutes to go' point and no flak. About the time I asked the bombardier, 'Where's the flak?' a great big black, brown burst, seemingly big as the airplane, went off directly ahead of us on our level and immediately we were in it. For an instant I was in a pure 'puckering' state, as were the other crew who saw it. Merseburg flak was brownish-black. Berlin flak was black. Munich flak was mixed

·24 going down in flames. (*USAF*)

(*Left*) 1st Lieutenant John W McClane Jnr, navigator in Lieutenant Charles D Peritti's crew in the 68th Bomb Squadron, 44th Bomb Group. (*McClane*)

(*Right*) On 22 April 1944 1st Lieutenant Gordon E Clubb's B-17 in the 325th Squadron in the 92nd Bomb Group was hit by bombs jettisoned from another Fortress on the raid on the Dornier aircraft assembly plant at Oberpfaffenhofen near Munich. F C Leonard, radio operator looks at the second bomb on his jacket, which represents the raid on Oberpfaffenhofen. (*Leonard*)

Tour completed!

24 Liberator going down on fire. *(USAF)*

ıe jubilant crew of B-24D-90-CO 42-40722 *Little Gramper* taken the day they completed their final ission in February 1944. Top row, left to right: Russ Hayes, ball turret gunner; Leonard Boisclair, aist-gunner: Captain Howard 'Ben' Walsh, pilot; Marcus DeCamp, engineer: Charles Cavage, aist-gunner. Bottom row, left to right: Tom Campbell, navigator; Robert Schroeder, bombardier; 'nest 'Jack' Cox, tail-gunner and Arthur Marsh, radio operator. Soon after this photograph was ken Captain Tom Campbell was killed in a plane crash in Sweden. It was he who had originally lled the reptiles in the African desert 'grampers' from which the ship got its name. *Little Gramper* as retired in the summer of 1944 for conversion to the Group's assembly ship. *(Russ D Hayes)*

On 22 April 1944 the Liberators were sent off late in the day to bomb the marshalling yards at Hamm, Germany. Their return, in darkness, was shadowed by Me 410s of KG 51 who shot down several B-24s in their circuits and generally caused mayhem over the bases. One of the worst hit wa Seething where five 448th Bomb Group Liberators crashed at the end of the runway. *(Francis X Sheeha*

An 832nd Bomb Squadron, 486th Bomb Group B-24 Liberator passes over Allied shipping off the Normandy beachhead near Caen on *D-Day*, 6 June 1944. *(USAF)*

The first indication for the majority of crews that 6 June was *D-Day* came at early morning briefings on that dramatic Tuesday morning, although at many bases that night wave after wave of RAF aircraft could be heard overhead. Many Groups flew three missions on 6 June. (*USAF*)

Wilbur Richardson in the 331st Bomb Squadron, 94th Bomb Group. (*Richardson*)

The wing of B-24J-140-CO 42-110187 in the 467th Bomb Group breaks off after a direct hit in the fu
tanks over the target at Oschersleben on 29 June 1944. The pilot, Lieutenant William H Counts, wh
was blown out of the aircraft, was the only survivor. *(USAF)*

B-24 Liberator under attack from fighters from the rear. *(USAF)*

arnage after a mid-air collision. (*USAF*)

. Liberator filled with fuel and bombs blows up after a direct hit. (*USAF*)

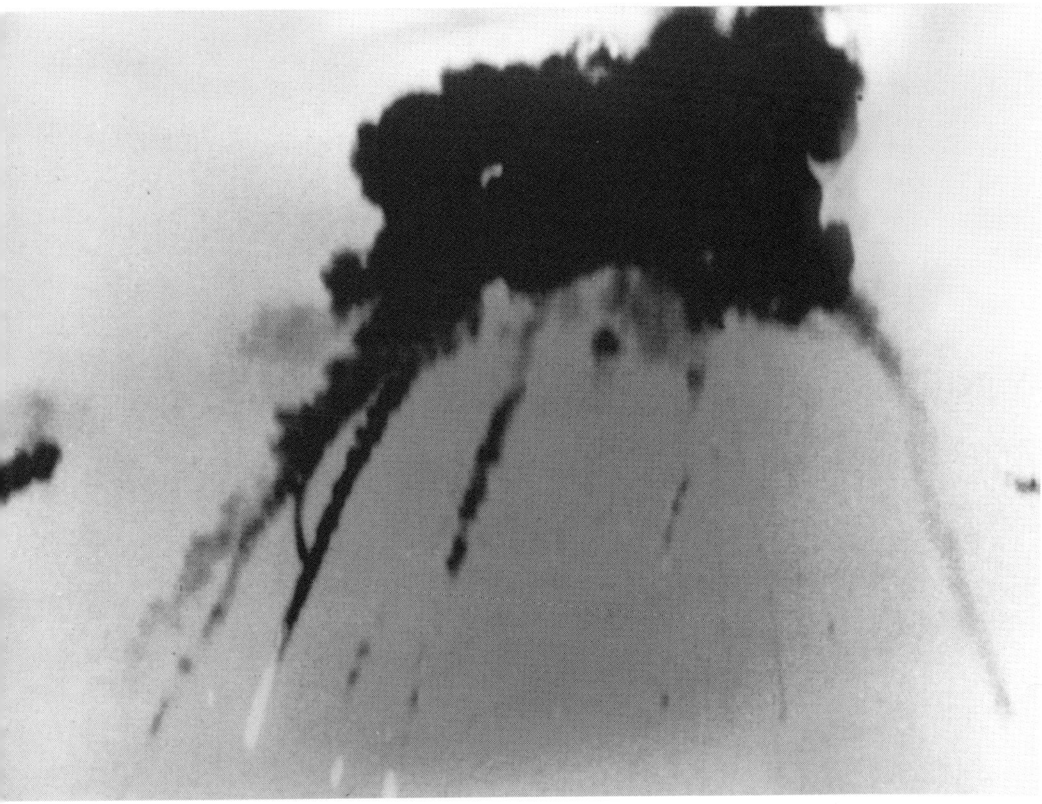

Pangbourne Rest and Recuperation Centre in Berkshire. *(via Andy Bird)*

1st Lieutenant Donald J Gott and 2nd Lieutenant William F Metzger, in the 729th Bomb Squadron, 452nd Bomb Group, whose actions on 9 November 1944 resulted in posthumous awards of the Medal of Honor.

Fw 190 attacking a B-24 formation. *(via Andy Bird)*

On 15 October 1944 a direct flak hit over Cologne, just after 'Bombs away' literally tore off the nose of the B-17G piloted by 1st Lieutenant Lawrence M deLancey in the 603rd Bomb Squadron, 398th Bomb Group and instantly killed the togglier, Sgt George Abbott. Without instruments and maps the navigator managed to navigate the bomber back home, where deLancey and his co-pilot set the Fort down at Nuthampstead without further mishap. *(USAF)*

3 February 1945, Major Robert 'Rosie' Rosenthal, flying his 52nd mission, led the 100th Bomb Group and the 3rd Division to Berlin. (*TAMM*)

Rum Dum, a veteran Fortress of many missions in the 385th Bomb Group at Great Ashfield. (*USAF*)

A PFF Liberator in the 392nd Bomb Group over the smoking target at Braunkhale synthetic-oil refinery on 3 March 1945. *(USAF)*

B-17G-35-BO 42-32090 *Silver Dollar* in the 418th Bomb Squadron, 100th Bomb Group, which by mid April 1945 had completed 102 missions. On 18 April *Heavenly Angel* ran into *Silver Dollar* and flattened the tail fin but the veteran bomber was given a new tail section and continued to be used as a 'hack' aircraft and flew several *Chowhound* missions at the end of the war. (*TAMM*)

Witchcraft in the 467th Bomb Group was one of the most famous of all Liberators and flew its 100th mission, all without once turning back, on 5 January 1945. *(via Paul Wilson)*

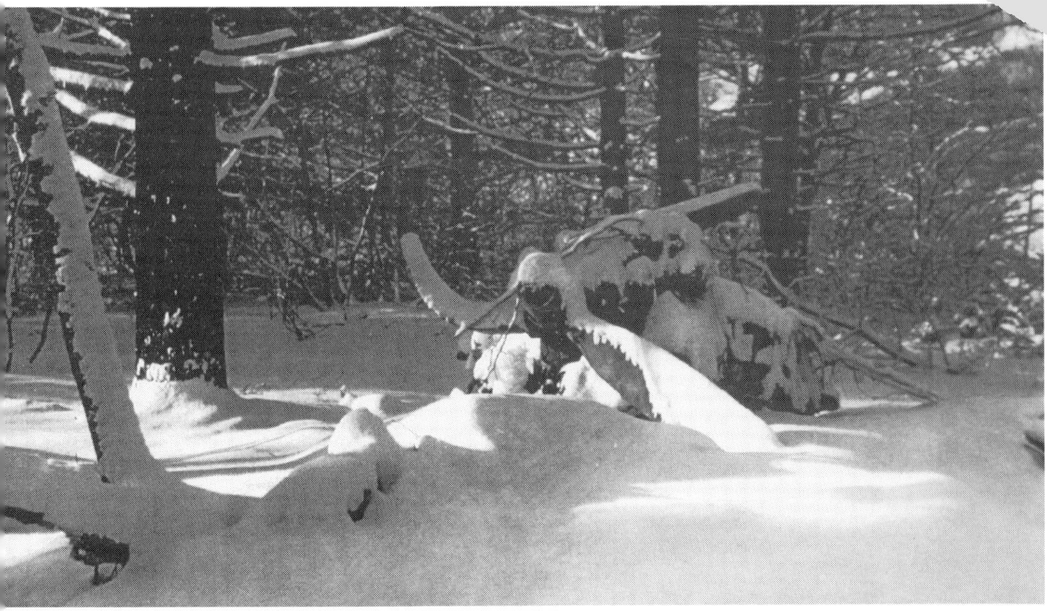

'he wreckage of B-17G-65-VE 44-8444 *Treble Four* in the 836th Bomb Squadron, 487th Bomb Group, ›iloted by Brigadier General Frederick Castle (leading the 3rd Bomb Division) with Lieutenant ₹obert W Harriman's crew, which was shot down and crashed in Belgium on Christmas Eve 1944. ;astle and six others were KIA. Castle was posthumously awarded the Medal of Honor. *₹ougham Tower Assn.)*

ˌbandoned Me 262 at the end of the war. *(USAF)*

VE Day, 8 May 1945. *(USAF)*

RAF airmen wave 'cheerio' to a departing B-24 of the 44th Bomb Group at St Mawgan, Cornwall in May 1945. *(USAF via Philip Kaplan)*

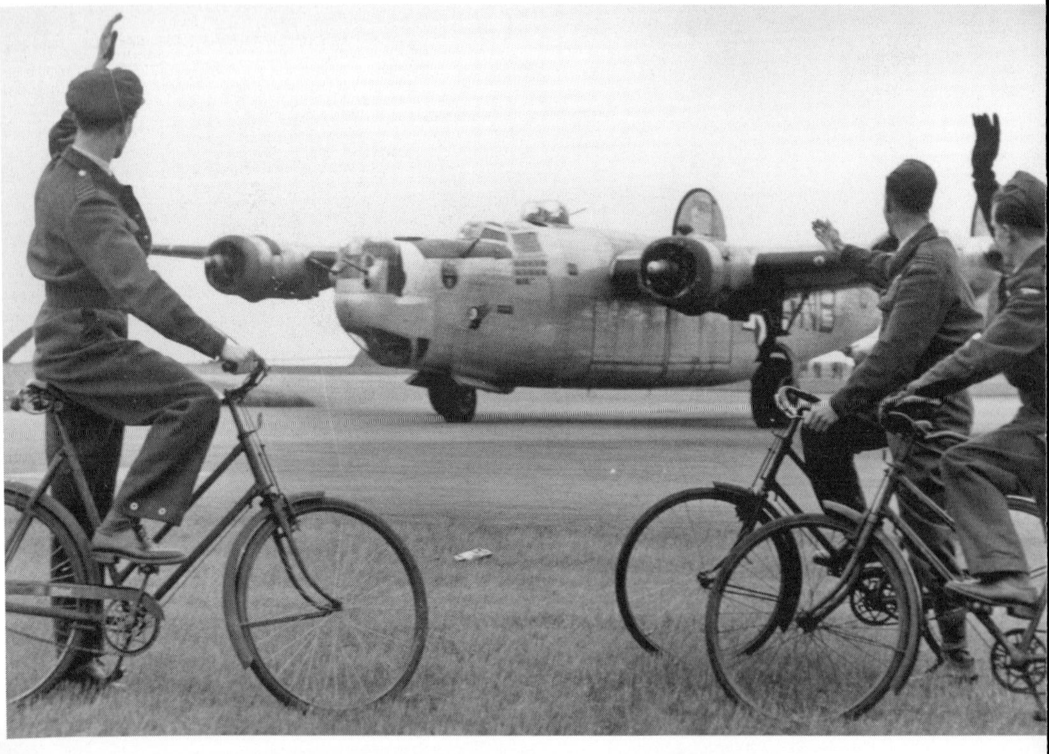

> brownish and pinkish centers. That was the way it looked to me anyway. The 28 July mission did not give me anything unusual to go on. I did not see any ships go down. Maybe I just didn't see them, or I was too busy. However, I saw black oily smoke above the undercast and by the time we passed the rally point it must have been at 20,000ft so I had assumed that we had hit it hard, but again, we went the next day.

Command Pilot Captain Herbert Howard who flew with Lieutenant Austin Dunlap led the 100 'A-Group', which filled in behind the leading 390th Bomb Group. The formation went over Leipzig by mistake and the bombers flew towards Merseburg on a southerly course. At the target a very heavy flak barrage bracketed the B-17s. In the next few minutes the low squadron of 100 'A-Group' lost five out of six B-17s. The first to go down was *Buffalo Gal*, piloted by Lieutenant William T 'Buzz' Fitzroy. Of the nine men aboard five baled out and were taken prisoner, including the pilot. The rest were killed. Another B-17, *Sparky*, was finished off by a fighter as it lagged behind. Of the nine men aboard only the tail gunner survived to be taken prisoner. The B-17 piloted by Lieutenant Eden C Jones was next.[17] The fourth loss was piloted by Lieutenant Carl C Gustafson Jnr, whose crew were on their twenty-second mission.[18] The Fortress piloted by 2nd Lieutenant Morris E Clark, most of whose crew were on their first mission, was the fifth and final B-17 in the low squadron to be shot down.[19] *Regal Eagle*, piloted by Lieutenant Gerald H Steussy, the high squadron lead, also went down. All nine men baled out and were taken prisoner. In the meantime, the 100th 'B-Group' led by Major Joe Zeller and Charles E Harris had flown on course to Leuna.

George P Fory recalls that the flak 'started sooner than the day before. Maybe the planes ahead had stirred them up, but they were there. The elevation was just on us and tracking was on our left and crossed over us before "Bombs away". It stayed with us until we turned off the bomb run.'

Charles E Harris recalls:

> The word Merseburg always brings back the memories of flak and more flak! To our crew, *Sack Artist* and I dare say most of the 100th, Merseburg was one of the worst targets, if not THE worst. Our crew hit that place three times. In each case, the missions were rough, primarily from the heavy concentration of 88mms.
>
> The 29 July mission is perhaps the most vivid in my memory as the flak that day was the worst ever. Until we hit the bomb run, it was pretty much like other missions. But as we started down the run I looked straight ahead and the sky was a continuous flak burst.

> Being the lead plane, there were no other planes to look at; the preceding Group was far ahead. I think that this was the only mission where I honestly thought to myself: 'We'll never make it through,' and I said a quick prayer. Major Zeller was on the radio, in contact with the other groups, and his apparent coolness helped settle me back into the routine of flying. The pilot of the lead plane was essentially on instruments. Maintaining exact altitude and speed was vital, also the heading provided by the navigator. Once the bombardier took control, the heading became his responsibility. After that one good look forward, I went back to the business of flying on instruments. For the pilot that was a blessing in a way, as it kept his eyes on the instruments and not on what was going on around but the Command Pilot, with no actual flying responsibility, got to see everything (poor guy). During the bomb run there were several 'bangs' that indicated flak bursts all too near but we didn't come home with any holes in the plane. At 'Bombs away' I made a fast, descending turn to get out of the flak. At that time, getting away was primary and I left the instruments so that I could see where we were going so as to avoid conflict with any other groups in the area. Because of the evasive action, the group formation always loosened up a bit due to the manuever. When a Command Pilot was in the right hand seat, the normal crew co-pilot was 'promoted' to tail gunner. My navigator, Lloyd Coartney, said that the target was smoked out. He was leaning over John Dimel, bombardier, trying to point out where to hit, when he looked through the nose and saw all of those fighters headed right at us with tracers, making it look like the 4th of July.[20]

Lieutenant George P Fory again:

> Being in 100B, we were not aware of what was going on with 100A at that time. About ten minutes after the Rally Point we saw a straggler below at about 10 o'clock, appearing to go very slow. As we came by him we could see two engines feathered and someone called, 'Bandits at 3 o'clock high.' The bandit was a Messerschmitt 262 jet. It peeled off and dove straight down on the straggler. The straggler blew up and the jet went on down out of sight. There were no parachutes seen by us. I heard later that this was the first mission in which jets were used by the Germans to attack bombers. Many believed that the German fighter pilots were radioing our attitude to the flak guns and this may be true; it sounds feasible to me. They had some very accurate fire at Merseburg and there must be a reason for it. The best words I know of to describe Merseburg flak was that it was 'intense' and 'accurate'.

Dick Johnson's diary entry for 29 July read:

Same target as yesterday. (Leuna Oil Works). Saw terrific dogfights over target between our P-51s and the enemy fighters. Target CAVU. And flak was terrific. Got several holes this time. Had third new crew. Carried twenty 250lb GP bombs. Flight time, 8 hours and 35 minutes. Over enemy territory 4 hours and 20 minutes.

I was flying the *Bet Jane* again today for an assault on Germany's most heavily defended city. My new crew for the day was that of Lieutenant P F Curetan, Jnr.[21] The 303rd Bomb Group supplied thirteen aircraft for the 41st 'C' Wing, High Group. We did a plan 'D' Group assembly over Harrington Buncher at 17,000ft and flew in Combat Wing formation while slowly climbing to 26,000ft. At the IP we took Group interval for visual bombing and dropped our bombs from a magnetic heading of 95°. At the target we saw about fifteen Me 109s trying to attack the lead group but were being harassed by our P-51s. Just after bombs away, four of the fighters managed to elude the P-51s and made a single pass through the lead group without shooting any down. After we dropped our bombs we made a sharp right turn to avoid flak and at this time rejoined the wing formation for our return to Molesworth. At the target there were no photographs of the actual bomb bursts as they were concealed in smoke and shadows in the target area. The Germans always tried to conceal their important targets with smoke screens but with limited success. The lead Group's bombs appeared to fall a little short of the MPI. They approached the target at 103° magnetic. The low Group's bombs appeared to fall right on target. They flew to the target at 102° Magnetic. Our heading of 95° gave us a good separation from the prop wash of the other groups and our bombs were right on target. The lead group of the 'D' Wing following us headed to the target at 98°. Their lead bombardier didn't quite kill the drift and their bombs fell a couple hundred yards to the left of the MPI. Over England we dropped down to 1,000ft and eventually had to fly at 300ft because of low clouds. Of the fifty-one aircraft furnished by our group for this mission, thirty-two sustained battle damage, but none were shot down, thanks largely to the effort by our P-51s over the target. Several of our B-17s had major damage from flak and many had flak holes, including my poor old *Bet Jane*.

A J Sinibubb flew his sixteenth mission as navigator in *Nine-O-Nine*,[22] flown by Lieutenant Pullen, who flew low flight lead in the High Squadron in the 91st Bomb Group. Sinibubb wrote:

Bomb-load twenty-two 250lb GP. Route Base–Caxton Gibbet–Ely–Spalding–SP#4. Most of the trip was 10/10 undercast. We had

> fighters in the area and a dogfight commenced. Saw a couple go down in flames and hit the ground. Target was hit good. Flak was heavy and fairly accurate. On return trip across North Sea saw a ditched B-17. Crew were all out in dinghies. Hit coast and ceiling was '0'. After going in for 50 over coast we decided to go back over North Sea, gain altitude, fly over precip and make instrument let-down. As we made 180° we ran into a squadron flying behind us and we almost collided together. It was really scary. We saw a field and they shot up flares to guide us in. Pilot made a wonderful emergency landing. We waited till the sky cleared before taking off again. Landed 13.38.[23]

On 31 July Dick Johnson flew his twenty-eighth mission with a trip to Munich. His diary for this day reads: 'Munich, Germany (Rough). Carried incendiaries this trip. It looked like we made big fires too. The flak was really intense. Saw several B-17s go down. I carried quite a bit of flak back with me. Saw a few Fws but none attacked. Carried ten M17 Incendiaries of 500lb each. Over enemy territory 4 hours and 35 minutes.'

Johnson recalls:

> The 303rd Bomb Group scheduled thirty-eight planes to bomb the Aero Engine Works by radar. Two aircraft aborted and the mission was flown by thirty-six B 17s for an 8 hour and 10 minute flight. We had a late breakfast for this mission and finished briefing and were at the airplane at five minutes past eight. I was flying another new crew for this mission; their first. We were loaded with 2,700 gallons of gas and ten 500lb M17 incendiaries. We assembled over the Harrington Buncher at 7,000ft and departed in Combat Wing formation. Since we were bombing by radar, we remained in Wing formation for the bomb run and dropped our bombs in the target area with the leader. We could see fighters through an occasional hole in the clouds. The flak was always bad at Munich and many B 17s were hit by fragments. Of the thirty-eight planes of the group, twenty were damaged by flak, of which eleven were major. I was flying from the left seat on this mission and learned a little lesson on this date.

Late in July the ball turrets were removed from many Liberators to improve stability and altitude performance. During the last week of July General Doolittle carried out the first stage of his plan to convert all Liberator groups in England to Fortresses.[24] At first crews resented the changeover but they quickly grew to like the improved flying characteristics inherent in the B-17 and they praised the more spacious nose compartment and improved heating. There was also a downside, as Lieutenant Francis S Milligan in the 493rd Bomb Group recalls:

> Changing over to Flying Fortresses was practically a guarantee from the Eighth Air Force that from now on we would be visiting the Reichland – definitely the 'Big League'. Bremen, Merseburg, Magdeburg, Ludwigshafen, Münster and other German cities became our targets. Hitting the Hitler gang's back yard was a bit different than bombing V-1 launching sites in France. They really loved to shoot at us over the Fatherland. I think they must have given the school kids recess at Merseburg and each one had a flak gun. Flak and rocket trails were heavy over practically every one of the German targets. It was almost impossible to visualize how black the sky became when Jerry started to throw his stuff up at us. Flak always scared me but I think rockets made me just a bit shakier. Sitting there in the nose one saw a hell of a lot and watching those rocket trails start at the ground and head up towards me wasn't the most fun I've had in my life, yet never in all my missions did I see a plane hit by rocket.

August followed the same operational pattern as July with bombing raids on airfields in France and strategic targets in Germany. On 1 August, while bomb groups struck at airfields in France, 191 B-17s escorted by three P-51 groups again parachuted supplies to the French Resistance movement. Meanwhile, seventy-five B-17s escorted by a P-51 group bombed the airfield at Tours, and 387 B-17s escorted by another Mustang group attacked five airfields and a railway bridge in an area south and southwest of Paris. A fourth force of 320 B-17s was despatched to bomb targets in the environs of Paris itself. Bad weather caused over 100 aborts but 219 planes bombed four airfields, five bridges, railway facilities and a rail and highway junction. The fifth force of B-24s sent against eight V-weapon sites in northwestern France also ran into bad weather, which caused multiple aborts, and only thirty-four Liberators managed to bomb their targets. Another force of 156 Liberators was despatched against seven V-weapon sites in the same area and an oil storage depot at Rouen. Bad weather again prevented raids on the V-weapon sites but eighty-five B-24s bombed the oil depot and the railroad junction nearby. Four fighter groups strafed rail and ground vehicles during the course of the day, which cost five bombers and three fighters.

Next day the 2nd and 3rd Bomb Divisions flew two late afternoon missions against targets in France again. In all, 289 B-17s and B-24s attacked twelve targets including oil dumps and depots and supply depots, railroad bridges, junctions, canal lock, airfields and marshalling yards. Three P-51 groups flew escort for the bombers, two of them later strafing rail and highway traffic northeast of Paris. In the second mission over 390 bombers attacked fifteen V-weapon sites, five bridges, an airfield and a rail junction and bridge. Five Mustang groups flew escort and three of them later strafed rail transportation targets. In total the day's losses numbered six bombers and six fighters, mostly to flak. No enemy aircraft were encountered. On 3 August in early afternoon nearly 400 B-17s and B-24s bombed marshalling yards in France and one in Germany, an oil refinery in Germany and an airfield, road and rail junctions, bridges and a few individual targets in France. Three of the six P-51 groups, which provided escort, later strafed transportation targets and airfields. On 4 August the Eighth Air Force bombed several targets,[25] including a return to Peenemünde. For Dick Johnson it was his twenty-ninth mission:

> This was one of the most successful missions that I participated in. I was flying another new crew, in *Jigger Rouche, Kraut Killer*. We carried five 1,000lb bombs and 2,700 gallons of gasoline for this 9-hour trip. The 303rd furnished thirty-seven aircraft for this mission and we had two radar ships from the 305th Bomb Group, which was a PFF Group that supplied these aircraft to many different groups. It later developed that we would not need to bomb by radar, as the weather had cleared at the target. We had made a plan 'D' assembly at 6,000ft over Molesworth and took our thirteen B-17s into the high group of the 41st Combat Wing formation to which we were assigned. We departed the English coast at Louth at about 11 o'clock and intended to fly at low altitude for a while to save gas. However, over the North Sea there was a cloud layer that caused us to start our climb to altitude a little early. We crossed the enemy coast at 22,000ft and maintained this altitude to the target, which was on the Baltic coast north of Berlin. Just before the IP we got a radio message that visual bombing would be done, so we took proper interval so that groups could bomb individually. We made a seven and a half minute bomb run from the IP to the target and bombs were away a few seconds after 14.42 from 23,000ft, us being the high squadron for today's mission. The bombs from my airplane had delayed-action, or 'Long Delay' fuses. This is how we added insult to injury. Some fuses of this type had a device built in, so that when the bomb struck the ground, a plunger broke a vial of acetone. The acetone slowly dissolved a celluloid diaphragm that was spring loaded. When the diaphragm was dissolved, a striker set off the bomb. The celluloid discs were of different thickness so that the thicker they were, the longer it took for them to dissolve. Thus there were no moving parts to the fuse and sound detectors could not hear anything except the final movement of the firing pin. By then, everybody within two miles could hear it.
>
> My bombs didn't explode with the others, but one was designed to explode three hours after impact. Each bomb had a different delay, so that the last bomb didn't explode until three days after the initial drop. My aircraft was in position 9, which is near the center of the

formation. This same position in the other groups had the same fuses, so that there was a total of fifteen delayed-action bombs dropped onto the target. These were intended to harass the clean up crews and I have no doubt that they were quite unnerving. We had at least one aircraft carrying these bombs on most big industrial targets in Germany.

We had taken off and climbed through a solid overcast in England, but over the target area the clouds were almost absent and visibility was 40 miles. The bombardiers flew the lead planes with the Norden bombsight, which was hooked to the autopilot and the bombs dropped automatically at the proper instant and position. The seven and a half-minute bomb run gave the bombardiers plenty of time to kill the drift.[26] As the bombs started falling, a speedboat on the canal turned and sped away in the opposite direction. It was just as well for him, because several of these 1,000lb bombs hit the canal, damming it. We even thought that we might kill some of the big rocket scientists at the facility. We later learned that Werner Von Braun was at the facility that day. One non-operational Junkers 52 was seen near the west end of the east-west runway but the executive transports were nowhere to be seen.

As we headed back home, going over the Baltic we flew over the Danish Island of Falster and immediately over the island of Lolland Maribo. At this point, the tail gunner of this new crew, Staff Sergeant E S Brown reported on the intercom: 'Tail to pilot, there's a Me 410 coming up behind us. No, I believe it's a 110.'

'Are you sure it's not a B-25?' I asked.

'No, it's definitely a 110 and he's closing.' The ball turret gunner, Staff Sergeant J A Czerwonka, confirmed that it was indeed a Me 110.

'How far back?' I asked.

'About two miles and closing' the tail gunner answered.

'Well,' I said, 'we are on our way home and haven't fired a shot, so let him have it.' With this, the tail gunner and ball turret gunner started firing. After thirty or forty seconds of almost continuous firing, the ball turret gunner yelled on the intercom, 'He's diving away! He's going straight down. He's picking up speed and still going straight down! He's crashed! He's crashed! I didn't see any parachute!'

After this action we got a little too close to Germany's northern-most city, Flensburg, and flew within range of a battery of 88mm flak guns and a battery of larger guns that was fairly accurate. This after the target where the flak was fairly intense and accurate. Also at Eckernferde, where a single battery of three guns peppered a few of us with fragments. Of the thirty-nine B-17s that participated in this mission, seventeen had battle damage, with eight major and nine minor. We were lucky that none of us was shot down. Even

> the Me 110 that we shot down had fired rockets at our group, but missed.[27]

On 5 August, the Eighth returned to strategic targets with all-out raids on eleven separate locations in central Germany. Dick Johnson, who flew his thirtieth mission, recalls:

> The 303rd Bomb Group had been flying two missions per day for quite a while and today each squadron planned to put up ten B-17s each. Beiser was leading our squadron for this rush job and only six of us made formation with their assigned group. A few of the planes were so rushed that they were not fully loaded with bombs. We were to bomb six different targets in France in support of the ground troops. We were in the 'E' squadron of the 41st Combat Wing and we assembled over the Harrington Buncher at 3,500ft. Since we were late in taking off, we took a short cut to Splasher 10 and then direct to Beachy Head at 20,000ft. As a result of this short cut, three of our planes couldn't catch up and tacked themselves onto another squadron. Our squadron's target was Crepieul, France where we did a ten-minute bomb run. We were not fired on by flak gunners as were some of the other squadrons, and none of our squadron were damaged. The 'A' squadron lead ship was hit by flak, which knocked out the manual aileron controls and tumbled the gyros that operated the autopilot, just forty-five seconds before bombs away. The bombardier recovered in time to do a fair job in his bombing attempt.
>
> The 'D' squadron was twenty minutes late to their target when they had to circle to avoid a large formation of British Lancasters in their path. At the target one plane was hit by flak, which disabled two engines. That squadron flew a direct course to England so that the disabled plane could land at Ford, near the White Cliffs of Dover.
>
> We saw two of the German rocket planes, the Me 163 *Komet*, but with their five to six minute fuel supply, none could reach the 303rd formations. P-51s shot down several German fighters that day.
>
> Today was Beiser's last mission, as it was for most of our original crew. I had two more to go. I had the same co-pilot as yesterday's mission but was flying a mixed crew of enlisted men who were making up missed missions. My old favourite airplane, *Bet Jane* had to abort this mission when the pilot had to turn off both inverters due to an electrical short caused by a urine 'spill'. Many crewmen didn't like to use the relief tube that was located near the forward bulkhead of the bomb bay and simply relieved themselves on the bombs or in the bomb bay. Usually nothing happened, but this time the amplifiers were shorted out and no boost could be obtained for the superchargers. This practice was forbidden, but was often

> violated, as in this case. The pilot brought the *Bet Jane* back to base with the wet bombs and the culprit was disciplined by having to fly an extra mission. The official report was softened to indicate that a urine can was accidentally knocked over instead of what actually happened. Thus, the culprit might have lost rank as well as having to fly another mission, if the whole truth were known.

The 5th August marked John W McClane's twenty-seventh mission and it was back to Brunswick for his fourth time:

> We expected the worst anytime we headed to Brunswick. It was the second most feared target after Berlin due to flak but especially the excellent German fighter groups in the vicinity. Today's mission turned out to be an anticlimax to our fears. The 44th Bomb Group launched thirty-four aircraft for this mission. Twelve of the 68th Squadron planes made up the second section, with the 67th in the lead and the 506th squadron in the third section. The group was led by PFF. In spite of the reputation of the German fighters they were notably absent on this day both flying into the target and back to base. All three Bomb Divisions dispatched a total of over 1,200 planes to fifteen different targets in Hitler's Germany. Just under 100 B-24s in the 14th Combat Wing were assigned to bomb an aircraft factory. Each plane was loaded with thirteen 100lb and nine 500lb bombs. We were protected the whole distance with very effective fighter escort. The clouds broke at the target so our bombardiers were able to drop their bombs visually. Our squadron achieved excellent results hitting squarely on target. The flak did not seem as intense as we had expected, our 68th Squadron receiving no serious damage.
>
> The flight home was uneventful except for one interesting thing. As we headed back towards the English Channel, a lone B-24 was flying perhaps 5,000ft below us and off to our left. Its No. 3 motor was on fire. The pilot put the plane on autopilot and we watched everyone bale out. (One of my jobs as navigator was to record how many and where men baled out.) The gunners were counting as they watched the crew abandon ship. The plane was now on its own without any crew when just like nothing had happened, the fire went out. All of us watched with fascination as the 'ghost ship' sailed merrily along. The course of the pilotless ship and ours paralleled each other for maybe twenty minutes when it came time for our formation to make a turn to the right. I'll forever see the image in my mind of this derelict flying off to eternity as our paths separated and we lost view of it. I wonder if it is still flying? It made me think of the song, *Ghost Riders in the Sky*.

Next day the B-17s struck at Berlin and oil and manufacturing centres in the *Reich*. On this occasion, seventy-six Fortresses in the 95th and 390th Bomb Groups hit the Focke-Wulf plant at Rahmel in Poland.[28] Dick Johnson in the 303rd Bomb Group flew his thirty-first mission on 7 August with a trip to Paris, where the target was a large fuel storage area in an area inside the city limits, almost on the banks of the Seine in the St. Ouen section of the city. His diary reads:

> Flak really rough. They tracked us all the way. I was luckier than most as I only got a few holes. Target CAVU except for haze. Carried thirty-eight 100lb bombs. Over enemy territory two hours and five minutes.

He recalls:

> I was flying in the No. 2 position on the right wing of the lead plane. My new co-pilot for today was 2nd Lieutenant G C Lawrenson and we were flying 42-102569, which had no nose art. Thirteen airplanes were able to bomb this target while the rest went to Chartres to bomb the airfield there, as a target of opportunity. From our bombing altitude of 25,000ft the visibility was fair, with the target being obscured for a time with a thin layer of clouds. Another group from our wing turned in front of us at our altitude, giving us some violent prop wash, but twelve of our thirteen aircraft bombed the primary target, with only fair results. The new airplane being flown by Lieutenant Walker in the No. 4 position failed to bomb because the bombardier failed to turn on the selector and salvo switches. They brought their thirty-eight bombs back to base.
>
> We were in a ticklish situation where we had to be extremely careful not to bomb built-up areas in occupied France. The bombs that we dropped had no nose fuses and had a one fortieth second fuse in the tail to give them instantaneous ignition. We were carrying 2,000 gallons of gas for this 5 hour and 45 minute mission. There was intense flak throughout our seven-minute bomb run and just after bombs away it became very accurate until we took evasive turns. The German gunners were slow in getting our range while on the bomb run and by the time they got us in their sights the bombs dropped and we turned away to foil their two and a half kilometer sighting lead. Of the thirteen planes in our low group, only three escaped damage. We had five planes with major damage and five, including mine, with minor damage.

On his eighteenth mission navigator A J Sinibubb in the 323rd Bomb Squadron, 91st Bomb Group, flew in *Cheri*, piloted by Lieutenant Stunf, who flew High Flight lead, deputy squadron lead, to an oil depot on a river. They carried twenty 250lb demolition bombs. Sinibubb recalled that the mission was 'pretty easy. We went over battle lines at 20,000 but descended to 15,000 for bombing. A little flak was encountered over lines. Bombs fell short but hit a bridge. We flew over target. Rest of mission was uneventful. Large allied convoys were in Channel.'[29]

On 8 August Dick Johnson in the 303rd Bomb Group flew his thirty-second and final mission of his combat tour:

> We were to try a tactical attack on German ground troops in an area 11 miles south of Caen. Captain Bob Sheets was leading the raid with a ten-man crew. This used to be standard for the Flying Fortress but they had lately been reduced to a nine-man crew. Bob Sheets was in *Shoo Shoo Baby* in our 427th Squadron. Technical Sergeant Frank X Neuner was in Bob Sheets' top turret. He was a good buddy and roommate of my regular ball turret gunner, Charles W Latta.[30] I was assigned to 'tail end Charlie' for this raid, which was also 'Purple Heart Corner,' since there was nobody behind me. I had the same crew as on yesterday's raid, but with two different gunners on makeup missions. My erstwhile pilot, Theodore 'Bud' Beiser, was 427th Operations Officer, while Sheets flew the lead position. Beiser had just finished his tour of duty and was doing this office work while waiting transport to the States.
>
> This 41st 'B' Combat Wing, Lead Group with twelve B-17s did an assembly at 5,000ft over the Harrington Buncher Beacon and departed the English coast at Portland Bill at 14,000ft, which was to be our bombing altitude. The combat wing ahead of us didn't turn on the briefed IP and we had to follow them around to avoid flying a collision course. There were no clouds over the target, but the haze was so bad that we couldn't see the bright red and yellow markers that our ground troops had put out to identify the target that they wanted bombed. We made a bomb run, but the lead bombardier didn't drop because of this problem. The high group was the only one of our three groups to bomb the primary target and they missed it by over a half-mile. Luckily their bombs still fell in German occupied territory, destroying a lot of apple trees where a lot of vehicle tracks were visible.
>
> Our secondary target had a cloud bank over it at 12,000ft, so we finally picked a railroad siding and made a five minute bomb run and dropped 446 100lb bombs on that target with fairly good results, cutting the rail lines and a highway. According to the mission summary, flak was 'moderate and inaccurate at the Primary.' This was written by Bob Sheets at the front of the formation while I was a quarter mile back and 500ft lower. My diary reads: 'Caen, France. German front line defenses. Flak was really rough as we were at 14,000ft. Didn't drop on primary and finally dropped on railway

yard, but good. CAVU. I'd rather go to Berlin. Finis. DFC.' Only one B-17 received minor damage. Guess whose? At one time the flak was bursting all around our plane but several hundred feet away most of the time. I could see the angry, red center of these explosions several times. I often wondered if I was overly sensitive because it was my last mission and thought that they were determined to get me on this one last chance, but I thought at the time that one of those bursts might actually have my name on it.

After we returned to Molesworth at fifteen minutes past three, I did the necessary paper work and came out of the airplane, only to find the crew lined up in front of the airplane by the nose art, *Miss Lace*, to congratulate me. My co-pilot, 2nd Lieutenant George C Lawrenson who just finished his second mission asked me:

'How does it feel to finish your missions?'

'Wait a minute and I'll show you,' I replied.

With this, I took off my 'Fifty Mission' hat, removed my 'Flak Beanie' and handed them to Lawrenson.

'Hold these for me, will you?' I said. I untied and dropped my flak suit, which I picked up and handed to Lieutenant John P Emmet our navigator who also acted as our bombardier. I removed my oxygen mask and throat mike and handed them to Technical Sergeant Leroy H M Foerster, our engineer-top turret. I unhooked and removed my parachute harness, which I gave to Sergeant Robert H Hitchcock, our radioman. I lifted my 'Mae West' life preserver over my head and handed it to Staff Sergeant Myron M Musyka, the other waist gunner. I removed my leather A-2 jacket, which I handed to our ball turret gunner, Sergeant Joseph A Czerwonka who had shot down the Me 110. My flight gloves I handed to Sergeant Donald L Garlick, waist gunner who had just finished his first mission. I took off my flight coveralls with its escape kit and handed them to Sergeant Wayne L Rughe, our tail gunner, also on his first mission. This left me with my uniform pants, shirt and shoes. I walked to the middle of the line of crewmembers and faced them.

'How does it feel to finish my missions, you ask?'

With this, I did a standing back flip and landed on my feet. The crew applauded as I took a bow like a ham actor, the same as I did in my High School plays. The standing back flip was a standard with me that I learned at McLeansboro, Illinois High School. I never told the crew how scared I was on this mission when the flak started bursting around us. But now it was over and I could actually look forward to going back home where instructors wouldn't yell at me and other people wouldn't shoot at me. Utopia, here I come! I lacked a month and two days of being 22 and a half years old, a combat instructor with thirty-two missions under my belt. They were giving me credit for three more missions, so that my official records would indicate that I actually flew thirty-five missions. I guess my job of flying new crews on their first missions made me earn it.

Notes

1. Cooper was flying with 1st Lieutenant G T Savage Junior in 42-107099.
2. 'Several crewmembers each received an extra DFC for this mission. For my part, I lived through the mission and received an Oak Leaf Cluster to my previously awarded Air Medal. The Air Medal was given to each airman upon completion of six missions and an oak leaf cluster given to signify another of the same. This was my third Air Medal. Our 7 hour and 2 minute flight had us over enemy territory 1 hour and 50 minutes.'
3. The main 2nd bomb Division thrust was a 9½-hour round trip to Politz and Ostermoor, while 130 Liberators bombed V-1 sites in France. The Luftwaffe intercepted the Division en route to Politz and Ostermoor while it was temporarily without adequate fighter cover. The 355th Fighter Group had been delayed by its new type drop tanks, which failed to jettison, leaving only the 339th Fighter Group to protect the entire 2nd Bomb Division. Bf 110s and Me 410s ripped through the formation over the Baltic with rockets firing and cannons blazing.
4. The shuttle force touched down at Poltava, where, later that night, 60 Luftwaffe bombers destroyed 44 of the 72 bombers.
5. 'The mission lasted eight hours. I talked to the Chaplain and told him that I felt that the "law of averages" was catching up on me and I felt that I was going to "go in". I flew the next day however and nearly bought it. I was interned in Sweden the next day after taking a hit in the gas tanks over Berlin. I met some of the men who had also been on the Politz raid who had made it to Sweden the day before I got there and we talked about the mission. We all felt very good about destroying the target.'
6. '*Kismet* made it back to Bury St. Edmunds but was out of action for two days for repairs. One of the spars had received a direct hit. As we left the ship on the taxiway with a flat tire, I picked up my 'chute and found it riddled with holes.'
7. Despite intense fighter cover the Luftwaffe made a few attacks on the Berlin force. Near the capital, Me 410s swooped on the rear of the 1st Division formation and made several attacks on the B-17s. Altogether, 44 Fortresses and Liberators were shot down on the raid.
8. 42-97983 in the 570th Bomb Squadron flown by 2nd Lieutenant Larue F Cribbs.
9. 42-107070 *North Star* in the 571st Bomb Squadron, flown by Lieutenant Lawrence J Gregor.
10. Eight of Gregor's crew were KIA and two survived to be taken prisoner. Five of Cribbs' crew were KIA. Five survived to be taken prisoner. Both Fortresses crashed at Hoorn, Holland. Leo C Riley completed his tour in August.
11. The Eighth lost nine aircraft on 13 July.
12. On 19 July 1,200 bombers attacked targets in south-central Germany again and two days later the Eighth went to Schweinfurt. Peaslee's weather scouts were instrumental in preventing the 1st Bomb Division entering a cloud belt

that towered to 28,000ft. The 2nd Bomb Division did not receive the radio signal put out on the fighter-bomber frequency and 26 Liberators FTR as a result of collisions and enemy action. In sharp contrast, the 1st Division lost only three bombers. The 2nd and 3rd Divisions wasted no further time in forming their own scouting units.

13. *Miss Shirley* and 42-95026 in the 567th Squadron, 389th Bomb Group, went down. 20 men parachuted out of the two Liberators. *Jo Jo's Special Delivery* was among the others damaged in the collision and crash-landed at Manston.
14. Bombs from the last few B-24s in the 2nd Bomb Division hurtled into American forward positions, killing 101 men and wounding 308 others. Among the dead was Lieutenant General Leslie J McNair. Five bombers were shot down.
15. Operation *Cobra*, the breakout of the American forces from Normandy, was heralded by air attacks by 3,000 Allied aircraft, which paved the way for the breakout, and several days later Allied and German troops clashed in the Battle of Brittany.
16. 111 B-24s sent to bomb targets at Brussels and an escorting fighter group were recalled because of cloud cover at the targets and another 180 Liberators dispatched to bomb targets in France also failed because of heavy cloud. Fighters flew 237 sorties supporting the B-24s and strafing ground targets. No aircraft were lost on these missions.
17. Five of the crew including both pilots were killed while four baled out and they were taken prisoner.
18. Of the nine men aboard, only the engineer survived to be taken prisoner.
19. Five of the crew, including both pilots, were killed and four were taken prisoner. Some of those who died were killed on the ground by the Germans, and one crewman who was taken prisoner was beaten with clubs and rifle butts.
20. Charles E Harris adds: 'Our crew had a real rough beginning: badly mauled on two missions and in the Red Cross flak shack after only six missions. But soon after that we were designated a lead crew and were only touched on one mission after that, when my Command Pilot got shot up.'
21. He was to be KIA on 21 November at this same target. The only survivor of this nine-man crew would be radio operator, Technical Sergeant J A Ellis. Civilians would murder some of the others.
22. B-17G 42-231909 whose last three digits suggested the Fortress's name.
23. In all, 569 B-17s in the 1st and 3rd Bomb Divisions attacked the Leuna plant, where they released 1,410 tons of bombs. In the previous day's attack, 652 Fortresses dropped 1,601 tons of bombs.
24. The 486th Bomb Group at Sudbury and the 487th Bomb Group at Lavenham, which formed the 92nd Wing, were taken off operations and by the end of the month, were ready to begin combat missions in Fortresses. During the period end of August–mid September the three B-24 groups of the 93rd Wing (the 34th, 490th and 493rd) also changed over to the B-17. The 95th Wing, which had begun with only two groups, ceased to exist on 14 August, when the 489th was transferred to the 20th Wing as a fourth group.
25. In the late morning and mid-afternoon raids, over 1,250 bombers attacked four oil refineries, four aircraft factories, four A/Fs, the Peenemünde experimental establishment and torpedo plants in Germany, two coastal batteries in

Pas de Calais area and two weapon sites, two A/Fs, a M/Y, a railway crossing and a bridge in NW France. All the Eighth's 15 fighter groups supported the operations, flying 782 sorties.

26. 'Of the three groups doing individual bombing on this mission, our high group had the best score, having 100% of our bombs fall within 2,000ft of the MPI. 95% fell within 1,000ft and 60% fell within 500ft. The low group did nearly as well with 95% of their bombs falling within 1,000ft of the MPI and 30% within 500ft. The lead didn't do quite as well, with 93% within 2,000ft and 25% within 1,000ft. They only got 5% within the 500ft circle. Our high group also had the most concentrated bomb pattern, it being 1,230 feet by 900 feet, which indicated that we were flying a tight formation at bombs away. The lead group's pattern was 1,800 feet by 1,150 feet. The low group's pattern was 1,700 feet by 1,350 feet.'
27. The bombers claimed three aircraft destroyed and fighters, 39 destroyed in the air and 15 on the ground. Strafing claims included numerous items of rolling stock. Fourteen bombers and 15 fighters were lost during the day.
28. After the bombing the two groups flew on to their shuttle base at Mirgorod in Russia, scene of such devastation two months before. During their stay they flew a raid to the Trzebinia synthetic-oil refinery and returned to Russia before flying to Italy on 8 August, bombing two Romanian airfields en route. Four days later they flew back to Britain on the last stage of their shuttle. Toulouse-Francaal airfield was bombed on the flight back over France. This third shuttle by the Eighth Air Force proved more successful than the disastrous shuttle of June 1944, with not a single Fortress being lost.
29. On 7 August also the 492nd Bomb Group, 2nd Bomb Division was withdrawn from combat, having lost 54 aircraft in May–July 1944. This was the heaviest loss for any B-24 group for a three-month period. The 491st Bomb Group moved from the 45th Combat Wing to take the place of the 492nd in the 14th Combat Wing.
30. 'We knew Frank from his experience of swimming in the English Channel on 1 December 1943. His aircraft, piloted by Lieutenant A Eckhart, ran out of gas after a mission to Solingen, Germany. They had to ditch in the Channel, but were all saved by ASR.'

Chapter 7

Milk Runs to France

This was not Channel hopping but it was a milk run. Variety, it's great. Our target was a railroad yard at Belfort in the southeast corner of France. I saw no flak on this trip and that defines a no ball to me. A milk run. How many more like this can we get? I rolled another seven today although in the front of the plane they said they saw flak in the distance.

Technical Sergeant Robert T Marshall,
radio operator/gunner, 385th Bomb Group

As he stepped out of his barracks building on 8 August when the 'Eightballs' were taking off for the mission to Le Perthe, France, Lieutenant John W McClane saw smoke rising beyond the perimeter of Shipdham airfield. He realized that one of their planes had crashed. He found out later that the pilot of *Pregnant Peg* had committed the ultimate sin in a four-motor bomber. He had banked into a dead engine, could not recover and rolled the plane onto its back, where it fell straight down on the Yaxham Road near the base. On board was a full load of gas and bombs as well as nine other men. Later that afternoon, McClane decided to cycle to the site of the crash, which he found easily by following the back roads leading to the still rising smoke. When he came upon the scene, the utter destruction of a once proud bomber was difficult to describe. Wreckage was scattered over a large area. McClane was the only person there except for the British Bomb Disposal Crew. The area was roped off, which he ignored. He proceeded to within a few feet of one of the craters caused by an exploding bomb. Not all bombs went off as he saw several scattered about, still unexploded. The bottom cone of the hole was filled with aluminium that had melted from the intense heat of the burning wreckage. Not too far away was a crew of three men. They had placed a rope around the trunk of the body of one of the pilots. Both of the unfortunate pilots were still sitting in their heavy metal bucket seats, their arms had been burned to stumps as were their legs. All their bodies including their heads were burned charcoal black. The clean-up crew gave a tug on the rope, expecting to extract the body but instead, the torso simply pulled apart like an overdone roast. He saw no other bodies, but on the way to his observation point, McClane saw an unburned electric flying glove. An extra glove was always useful so he was not above usurping this one for his emergency bag. When he picked it up, it took him no time to let it go again, as he noticed that it still had a hand in it. One of the men pointed to his feet and said, 'Look what you are standing on, Governor.' McClane looked down. His left foot was on top of a man's skull, cut off at the hairline. Another man said he should move further away as they were going to defuse some bombs. By this time, he had seen more than he had bargained for, so he cycled back to the 68th Squadron area.[1]

Next day B-17 and B-24 crews were summoned to the usual daily briefing. At Lavenham Norman K Andrew, navigator in Jack Stanley's crew in the 837th Bomb Squadron, 487th Bomb Group, prepared to fly his first mission. Philosophically, he wrote in his diary:

> First mission today, thirty-four to go. They woke us at 1.50am. Briefing time 3:00 am so we knew it was pretty sure to be a long one. Had pineapple juice, fresh egg, hotcakes, sausage, cold cereal and coffee. Target Schmitt ball bearing works, Nurnberg. Took off 07.15 – left England 08.56. Over enemy coast 09.21. Ran into overcast and cloudy weather. Turned back approximately 50 miles southeast of Aachen. Picked a target of opportunity – dropped on lead ship and leveled the town of St. Vith in Belgium. Encountered flak at Liège – moderate. Landed 12.20. Logged five and a quarter hours.'

Bob Maag in the 94th Bomb Group was flying his twentieth mission this day:

> We learned that our target was Stuttgart again, though it seemed highly unlikely to me that the mission would come off as planned. The weather officer informed us that the cloud cover over the target would extend to 40,000ft, at which altitude bombing would be impossible. Furthermore, they told us that, when we returned to base, all of England would be socked in from zero to 20,000ft, making landing impossible!
>
> We'd be taking our own *Skinny*. We didn't know at that time that she was something of a legend (the first B-17 in the 94th to complete 100 missions), but realized that she was a venerable veteran. We assumed she got her name from the fact that she was an anomaly – a B-17G with no chin turret. We sometimes speculated whether *Skinny* had lost her chin turret in an earlier battle, or had been built that way. We all felt at home on *Skinny* and liked having her for our

missions because her missing chin turret gave us the advantage of lower fuel consumption.

When we arrived at the hardstand we weren't surprised to learn that take-off had been delayed, first for one hour, then another. We were still dubious when we received orders for take-off and fully expected to be recalled. The forming and flight to the target area were routine and uneventful. When we approached Stuttgart we found that the cloud cover did indeed extend to 40,000ft. Since we could not bomb the target and no secondary target had been communicated to us, the formation turned for home. In Luxembourg we were led over some flak guns mounted on railroad cars and all hell broke loose. I don't know how many hits *Skinny* took but one that came through the plexiglas caught me on the left side of the face and wounded George Bycxkowski, the top turret gunner, in the leg. I lost my left eye and the co-pilot, Ivan Walker, had to take over the controls. Lyle Haines and Smitty, the bombardier and navigator somehow managed to get me into the nose of the plane where they did what they could to keep me alive.

During the trip back under these emergency conditions the crew performed magnificently. Since this was the sixth consecutive day we'd flown a combat mission with only two or three hours' sleep a night, it was all the more remarkable that everyone handled the emergency so well.[2] I know Ivan and I were so wiped out at that point that we had been alternating at the controls at the same time! I was conscious during that hairy trip home and remember lying in the nose and worrying about the weather over England and the fact that this would be Ivan's first attempt to land a B-17! I needn't have worried. Not only did Ivan get us down safely, he made sure that *Skinny* was the first to land, thus ensuring that George and I would get medical attention at the earliest possible moment. For their actions, Walker, Smith and Haines were awarded the DFC.[3]

On 11 August, 956 heavy bombers escorted by 578 fighters attacked transportation targets in France. Villacoublay airfield near Paris was the target for the 13th Bomb Wing. The air raid sirens sounded over Paris as the 54-ship formation flew overhead, spreading as the pilots jockeyed for bombing position. At 12.14 a furious anti-aircraft fire broke out as the Germans put up a box barrage of 88mm shells, which filled the airspace nearly 4,000ft deep. Shortly after bombs away, while the last of the anti-personnel fragmentation bombs left the bomb bays, *Royal Flush* in the 100th Bomb Group formation was hit. The first shell hit the No. 3 engine. The second and third shells hit – the second just behind the cockpit and the third in the bomb bay. Fire broke out immediately. A massive smoke trail moderated to a steady black, sometimes grey, plume as Alf Aske and his co-pilot, Lieutenant Charles S 'Chick' Barber, featured the No. 3 prop and cut off fuel to the engine. For a few seconds *Flush* held its position. A shudder went through the B-17 as the automatic pilot was put into operation. Then perceptibly, the ship began to lose altitude. As though under full control, *Flush* began a slow turn to the right. Down below twelve-year-old Leon Croulebois, who was staying with his grandmother, saw an object fall from the *Flush*. It was the waist door. A second object hurtled down then checked its descent as a white canopy of parachute opened above. Armanda Consorto was the first to leave the stricken aircraft. Now a second hatch door was seen to fall, followed by a body. Lieutenant Jim Magargee, the bombardier, left the ship. Then followed the tail gunner, Sergeant Stuart Allison, Barber and Sergeant Chuck Nekvasil, the radio operator.[4]

R D Russell and his crew in the 702nd Bomb Squadron, 445th Bomb Group flew their twenty-third mission this day, to Strassburg, Germany where they were to bomb oil storage tanks. Russell wrote:

> Today 'we had it.' We slept late, got up at 06.45 and went to breakfast. Returned to the hut we found a note telling us to be at briefing at 08.45. We took off at 11.30 with twenty-four 250lb GPs in the *Green Hornet*. The formation was a mess and we had to use maximum power to stay up with them. The flak wasn't bad over the target but it was accurate! We had No. 4 engine shot out as the bombs were dropped and it caught fire. We had to feather it and couldn't keep up with the formation. We lost No. 2 engine shortly after and started losing altitude immediately. I had the boys start throwing out anything that was loose. We kept dropping so they kept throwing out flak suits, guns, ammunition, radios, and Whitey even threw the 'put-put' out, which was a shock to all of us when we needed it for the top turret (the only one with guns and ammo). No one was overly excited and all acted as though it was a routine flight. We determined to go home by way of Belgium rather than try for the beachhead. We were down to 7,500ft and chugging along at 110mph. We dodged flak at Brussels, Antwerp and Ghent and then flew circles off the coast over a downed B-17 until Air Sea Rescue arrived. We made it home without further incident and even made a fair landing. Flight time 7:00 hours.[5]

On 13 August over 1,300 heavy bombers escorted by six fighter groups attacked targets in France for the loss of thirteen bombers. At Lavenham Norman K Andrew, navigator in Jack Stanley's crew in the 837th Bomb Squadron, 487th Bomb Group, flew his second mission of his tour. He wrote:

> Woke us up at 05.45 for mission No. 2. On the way to breakfast we piled out of the truck and saw a buzz bomb. It was really moving

along – stringing out flames behind it. It sounded a bit louder than an outboard motor. What a gliding angle! It hit about a mile and a half from the field. The briefing for the mission was the real Army stuff. Gave us series No. 3 charts and the *Gee* signals were series No. 2. Mission was three-ship element bombing behind the German lines about 25 miles west of Paris, 1 mile south of the Seine. We went into France between Cherbourg and Bayeaux. We skirted the lines (on the Allied side). We were lead ship of our element. I was really sure that we stayed on course. Between St. Lô and Uire there was a twelve-ship formation flying on our left about 8 miles. They plowed right over a flak battery at Falaise. I was looking right at them when one of the ships got a direct hit in the right wing. The wing broke off between No. 3 and No. 4. Wing fell in flames – the ship fell in flames, tight spin to the right. No parachutes observed. Three minutes later another one got a direct hit. All I could see was shiny bits of aluminum – just a ball of fire. No one had a chance. The formation did not try evasive action. As near as I could spot the flak it was close to Falaise. We turned on the IP and made a 15-minute bomb run. Hit a road – purpose of raid was to interrupt Jerry's supply lines. We dropped thirty-six 100-lb GP bombs. About 20 miles SW of Rouen there were about twelve rocket bombs. They really leave a trail of smoke. Jack called out four planes down in flames before I saw what he meant. Van Nostrand called five parachutes – it was a high formation that the sun just hit at the right angle. After the rally point I called Jack to tack onto a formation. As usual Jack said, 'Hell Andy, let's go home by ourselves – get there quicker.' So we dragged into England with a formation on our tail. I can still see that B-17 in a tight right spin. I knew they couldn't get out – it was spinning too tight. I'd rather get a direct hit.

Over 800 fighter-bombers attacked marshalling yards and other transportation targets in a wide area northeast of the Seine. Ninth Air Force fighters covered the ground forces and flew armed reconnaissance in the Alençon, Le Mans, Domfront and Chartres areas.

August 13th was John W McClane's twenty-eighth mission and he went to Rouen:

After our tactical bombing at St. Lô three weeks before, our 1st and 3rd Armies had put General Von Kluge's Wehrmacht into disorganized retreat. The broken German Army was caught in a pincer trap near the small town of Falaise, some 20 miles south of Caen. Their army was fleeing eastward toward this narrowing gap. All the time our Eighth and Ninth Air Force, especially the fighter-bombers, were pounding anything that moved unmercifully. These savage attacks were creating pandemonium in the German Army. The job of the heavy bombers was to block any route of supply or escape surrounding the battle zone. Our Groups were dispatched as squadrons of six to twelve planes, each with some road junction, river bridge, rail transport or communications center as its target. Today the Eighth Air Force targets were to be transportation choke points between Le Havre and Paris. Specifically the target for the 44th was a road junction near the city of Rouen. This city lies astride the Seine River some 70 miles down stream from Paris and 45 miles east of Le Havre on the Channel. The 44th put forth twenty-five aircraft divided among three squadrons, the 67th, the 68th and the 506th. We were the lead for the eight planes of the 68th. For the life of me, I never did understand what our target was except a 'road junction'. If Warga our bombardier knew, he kept it a secret and judging by the strike photo taken from our plane, I'm not sure he knew. We flew for five hours just to bomb some miserable country road near the Seine River. But this was no 'milk run'.

Our squadrons were lined up one in front of the other as we approached the Seine. The 506th Squadron was perhaps a half-mile or less ahead of us. As they approached the river, very heavy and accurate flak burst in their formation. I was looking directly at it when one of their planes started to burn. The plane fell out of formation and the crew baled out just before it exploded in front of us. There was a monstrous explosion, the plane literally disintegrated before my eyes. This was a bright cloudless day with unlimited visibility and the sun was shining bright. The plane blew to bits. The motors were torn from the wings and went tumbling through the sky with their props windmilling, as they fell in a large non-linear arc. The wings and the fuselage and the tail were torn to shreds. As the pieces of aluminum drifted and twisted while they fell, with each turn the sun would be reflected off their surface back into my eyes as if they were mirrors. It was like watching a thousand suns turn on and off in a rapid random fashion. But the most spectacular sight was the gas tanks, which had been torn from the wings. They did not explode their gasoline but rather it burned in huge orange flames streaming out behind the tanks as they fell in a wavy fashion towards the earth below.[6]

I was fascinated with the sight that I was witnessing until all of a sudden I realized that our squadron would be over the exact same spot in a minute or two. It sounds cowardly but I became obsessed with an uncontrollable fear. I got it in my mind that we would be the next plane to be literally blown out of the sky. As the flak began to reach us, I was paralyzed until we passed beyond their range. I never experienced such an intense emotion before or since.

On 15 August when the Liberators went to bomb the hanger area at Vechta, Germany south of Bremen and north of Dummer Lake, 2nd Lieutenant Ralph Elliott, a pilot in the 467th Bomb Group flew the mission, his fourth:[7]

> We took off at 09.00 loaded with four 1,000lb GP bombs and four 500lb incendiary clusters. At assembly time I counted hundreds of B-24s and B-17s in the air and on-course across the Channel – they looked like flies. We crossed the North Sea and into Germany over the Friesian Islands and into the target, which the formation hit dead center. Only two of our bombs went out and the salvo handle wouldn't work at first so that we dumped six bombs on the town of Vechta itself I saw a large fire after the explosion so we must have hit an oil dump accidentally. We must have raised hell with 1,500lbs of incendiaries in the town as well as 3,000lbs of TNT and steel. There was no flak but the boys saw about twenty-five scare bombs near the target. They came up leaving a trail of white smoke and then exploded but didn't seem to do any damage. The fun began just as we came back out and were nearly to the Zuider Zee. Fw 190s and Me 109s hit the formation just behind us and my boys saw four B-24s go down. A couple blew up and the other two spun out of control. The P-51s began chasing them and got some. A P-51 came up alongside and made the bad mistake of pointing his nose at us. My nose gunner, top turret and waist gunner opened up on him as did some other ships and my boys hit him, as we saw some smoke. Sorry, but he should know better than that. The Germans had some captured equipment and used our planes against us so we'd been told not to take any chances. The pursuit boys knew we'd shoot and knew better for the most part. Today was the biggest raid in history and between ourselves and the RAF we dumped between 6,000 and 7,000 tons of bombs on targets over enemy territory. Over Germany we could look out and see fires for miles after the bombing and there was smoke in all directions as far as I could see. I never again expected to see as many or as extensive fires as today.

On Friday 18 August Technical Sergeant Terry Parsons, a radio operator/gunner in the 862nd Squadron, 493rd Bomb Group, went to an airfield, 'Rue de Balcourt – or something like that' near Amiens:

> Rough! Wooee! Those ack-ack gunners have really been checked out. We lost two planes and the 34th Bomb Group, three. The Germans' first shot blew our leader's tail clean off. He just went straight down – poor devils didn't have a chance. Washington got it too but I guess they all got out.[8] Hansen was really scared I guess, but so were we

all. Our formation just split from hell to breakfast. 'A' Group didn't get much flak at all.

This same day, 2nd Lieutenant Philip G Day flew his first mission, as co-pilot in the 467th Bomb Group, which bombed an aircraft engine plant at Woippy, near Metz. Day recorded: 'No flak – no fighters – excellent results ... The 100-mission party of the Group was on 19 August and it was a wild, glorious, all night drunk out time. The Group had been stood down for 20 August; I am sure no one was fit or able to fly.'

Meanwhile, in the 44th Bomb Group, John W McClane flew his twenty-ninth mission, to Nancy-Essey airdrome, 170 miles east of Paris, just south of Luxembourg:

The weather was beautiful with unlimited visibility. This mission turned out to be my last for the month. The Luftwaffe had been forced to withdraw there after the capture of their field in north-west France. We had twenty-three aircraft make it to the target. We carried fifty-two 100lb bombs each. We were the lead aircraft for the group and had been assigned an intelligence officer as an observer. This officer had been hanging around Group Headquarters for several days waiting for the right opportunity. It appears that in order for an intelligence officer to be allowed as an instructor at our training bases back home, he was required to fly at least one real combat mission in order to be qualified as an 'expert'. Common sense tells you that he would not pick a deep penetration into the heart of Germany as his first choice. This mission looked like an 'easy one' so he requested that he be allowed to fly with us. This guy was a real 'eager beaver'. He was all over us. At briefing, he asked a thousand questions and when we reached our plane and were preparing for the flight, again he was everywhere. I usually laid my charts out on the ground to study them or to go over the bomb run with the bombardier. I got a bit aggravated when he picked up my papers so he could 'study' them. Finally the flare came from the tower. It was time to board *Lili Marlene*. Peritti and the officer agreed in advance where he would be during the bomb run so he could get maximum visibility when the bombs were released and follow them down to the target. He was to lie on the 'catwalk' that ran the length of the bomb bays with his head to the rear of the plane and his body towards the flight deck.

As lead navigator I had a great responsibility during the assembly. It was a complicated and exacting task. I really did not have time to fool with this 'observer' but that did not bother him. Again a thousand questions and he was taking notes. He wandered from one end of the aircraft to the other, asking each man about his duties. He almost ran us nuts but finally we reached the vicinity of Nancy and the IP and he took his pre-selected position. Nancy-Essey airdrome was well protected by anti-aircraft guns and they had us in sight as we were only at 15,000ft. The flak began to burst close by and before Warga was ready to release our bomb load a piece of flak came into the bomb bay striking one of the smoke bombs.[9] This bomb was only a short distance in front of the observer's head. Smoke began to pour out of the bomb and in short order our whole plane was filled with this white stuff. I could hardly see my navigation desk and I don't know how Peritti kept control of the plane.[10] Warga released our bombs when he was ready. He did not let little things bother him. (As our strike photo later showed, our bombs landed dead center of the airfield. He of course received an excellent rating for the day.) The smoke finally blew clear of our plane. (The crews in our fellow squadron planes said later that we looked like nothing they had ever seen before with all the smoke streaming from us.) On every mission Peritti made a check of the crew to see if anyone had been hurt. He received a negative response from all positions except the observer lying on the 'catwalk'. He did not respond. Peritti asked the radio-man, John Schneider and our engineer, Paul Corlew to check on our passenger. He knew we had been hit in the bomb bay and feared the worst for our 'new crew member'. Schneider and Corlew got to the officer and reported back to Peritti that he was alive but would not talk nor let go of what he had been holding onto. They could not bring him back onto the flight deck as long as he held on. The bomb bay doors were closed so Peritti decided to leave our observer where he was.

It was a long way back to base and we flew a total of eight hours, of which at least three hours were required to arrive back to Shipdham. This intelligence officer never said one word on the way back. I was busy navigating and did not have time to worry about him. I was glad not to have the aggravation that I had on the way to the target. Landing was late afternoon. When the plane finally rolled to a stop at our hardstand and the props stopped turning, I got out through the nose wheel door opening. I walked back to the open bomb bay and saw several of the fellows lifting our 'observer' out of the plane. A more pitiful sight, I've never seen. He could not stand up by himself and he was shaking all over. Boys will be boys, we began to razz him and ask if he would go with us on our next mission. In a very stammering, high pitched, quivering voice he said, 'I - I - I - I'll never-never-fly-fly-fly-fly again.' They put him in a jeep and we never saw him again.

From 19 to 24 August a low-pressure system gathered over the British Isles and Western Europe. During the stand-down it was announced that

Paris had been liberated and it was reported that the Romanians wished to seek peace.[11] On 24 August Norman K Andrew, navigator in Jack Stanley's crew in the 837th Bomb Squadron, 487th Bomb Group flew his third mission of his tour. He wrote:

> Was awakened at 01.45 this morning by Dick Giles. They were on their way to briefing. I thought to myself 'Missed us this time' but the CQ woke me at 02.00 for 02.30 briefing. So after a breakfast of canned grapefruit, two eggs over easy, bologna (ugh!) and cereal and fresh oranges and coffee, I was well prepared for the shock of the rising curtain (on the mission route). Holy Smokes! Whoever planned this one should have given it to the Russians – it was sure a lot closer to them. Anyway, take-off was 07.45. Target was a synthetic-oil plant at Dresden. The secondary, an airplane assembly plant. Last resort, an airfield. It rained off and on until take-off. The apron to my flak suit was wet (really frozen stiff at 25,000 [–25° C]). We departed Splasher No. 7 at 09.08, left England and headed for Heligoland at 09.32. Just before Heligoland, Dick lost his oxygen and aborted so the deputy lead took over. Saw a hell of a lot of flak all along the route but the nearest to us (except at the target) was approximately 300 yards. They used rockets. Not even close and saw one burst of red flak. The rest was black. Every town we went by was smoke screened but Bremen was getting quite a pasting. They were putting flak all the way up to 30,000 but I observed no hits.
>
> We made a very fancy bomb run – evasive action for all but about three minutes – then the bomb bay doors would not open electrically. So Rector cranked them open. Then on 'bombs away' only half the load dropped, five 500lb GPs, so Chuck hit both the salvo and the toggle switches. That did it, but it threw the other five 500lb bombs about three sec over the target – approx. 1,000ft. Hope we didn't kill any women or children with those wild bombs. Then Rector had to hand crank the doors shut while we were making just about a 180 and diving. There were fifty-one sure guns at the target. The ride home was just a ride. Some flak, but all of it wild. Logged 8½ hours – 5:05 on oxygen and traveled 1,204 nautical miles, not counting evasive action. On that oxygen – I had to move to the Bomb–Co-pilot line so Jack would have enough to get home – landed with the red light on and 75lbs on the gauge. We darn near ground-looped when we landed. The pin in the tail wheel sheared and we took off across the infield. To top it off it started raining like the devil and everybody got wet. There was one ship (B-17G) that landed at Lavenham that made it all the way back from Dresden on two motors. They had thrown everything they could out, including the parachutes.

Bishop E Ingraham recalls the mission to Merseburg on 24 August:

> This was the first day that the Eighth Air Force was hit by jet fighters. It was our sixth mission I believe and prior to that day our ball turret gunner had remained in his turret from take-off until the return landing. However he had been talking to his buddies, other gunners and they had told them that once they arrived at the 'IP' they got out of the turret until after the bomb run because enemy fighters 'NEVER' flew through their own flak. Therefore on this day he was not in position. We were on our bomb run when the tail gunner announced, 'Something coming in on our tail!' Almost immediately after his announcement the turret gunner got into his turret. A few seconds later we sustained a direct hit in the bomb bay. We still had not arrived at the target so we still had full bomb load, 500lb bombs and the hit was partly under the floor of my radio room. The flak had knocked out some of the bombs but some were still in the bay and fusing. Several of us managed to release the rest. There was a fire in the cockpit and in the radio room, which we extinguished. Fortunately, we had dropped from about 35,000ft to approximately 12,000. I say fortunately, because our oxygen system had been punctured so we had no oxygen. Also one of the wing tanks had been hit and so it was another miracle that we did not have any problem there.
>
> Of course there was a radio check immediately after we were hit and the only crewmember not to respond was our turret gunner. A fragment had gone through his gunsight and critically injured him directly in his head. We had taken him out of the turret but even when the emergency oxygen mask was placed on him he did not revive. Later the Flight Surgeon told us that there was nothing more we could have done because of his injuries.
>
> All of the radios and navigation equipment with the exception of the 'Gibson Girl'[12] was destroyed. Fortunately I was able to run out the trailing wire antenna and attach it to the 'Gibson Girl'. I must have cranked on it for nearly thirty minutes and it was a welcome sight to see a P-51 just above us in, again I estimate about thirty minutes from the time I first began transmitting our SOS on the emergency radio equipment. Another miracle was the fact we never encountered another enemy fighter from the time we were hit. The P-51 guided us to a crash landing field on the coast, I believe was Woodbridge. I have not mentioned yet that many of our plane's controls were so damaged that it took both Captain Bosko and our co-pilot, Curt Kohnert, to maintain as level flight as possible. Consequently when we arrived over Woodbridge it was impossible for the pilot and co-pilot to bale out. Because of the damage to controls and possible brake damage the pilot ordered the rest of the

crew to bale out. It turned out that he had neither flaps nor brakes but due to the field length they had no problem. We all were picked up at various points by the RAF and taken to their hospital where the injured were treated. A miracle for me personally was the fact I did not sustain even a scratch on this mission, even though my radio room was a shambles.[13]

On 25 August over 1,100 heavy bombers attacked four aircraft plants, three airfields, two experimental stations and fifteen targets of opportunity for the loss of nineteen bombers. Fifteen fighter groups flew over 600 sorties in support of the bombers and four of these later strafed ground targets including numerous parked aircraft, of which thirty were claimed destroyed. In a follow up raid ninety-two heavy bombers attacked five liquid oxygen plants in Belgium and Northern France.

Norman K Andrew in the 487th Bomb Group at Lavenham was rudely awakened at 04.30 hours for 05.00 briefing for what would be his fourth mission. He wrote:

Looked like a short one but it was sure longer than yesterday's. Left Great Yarmouth at 09.32 and headed over the North Sea. Right through a stationary front. It really scattered the formation. We were reforming for 100 miles. Came over Germany at the Denmark peninsula about 5 miles left of course. Everything was smooth – solid undercast – when, with no warning the Flensburg flak batteries opened up. They must have tracked us for 10 minutes because the first bursts were right off our left wing in the formation. The plane would jump up about six inches every time a burst would let go underneath and there were several. One of the ships got his, jettisoned his bombs and headed home. We got the hell out of there. From Flensburg we cut across Kiel Bay to Nykobing on one of Denmark's islands. Angled across the Baltic Sea and hit Germany again near Stettin. Two flak batteries took shots at us going by but we were just out of range. We flew west of Stettin where the flak forced us to fly 4 miles off course. That flak wasn't very well figured out. Turned on a 6-minute bomb run and hit an experimental airfield (Rechlin, the Wright Field of Germany) on the SE shores of the Muritz Sea. Had about fifteen flak guns at the target and they were good. One of the boys went down in flames – the stories vary from three to nine 'chutes came out. It was the deputy lead – six officers and five enlisted men.[14] We had seventy-one holes from flak. Went north to Nykobing and home the same route as we flew out. Plane out for four days. Logged 9¾ hours but only 2¼ hours on oxygen. I'll dream of that bomb run – there were three bursts of three right across the nose. If that gunner had loaded just a little slower, he

> would have had us. Well, four down and thirty-one to go. Wasn't quite as scared today as yesterday – but that's not saying much. Better get some sleep – we're alerted for tomorrow – if we do three in a row is rough.

Eino V Alve, a B-24 pilot in the 453rd Bomb Group, was one who went to a V-2 fuel dump in Belgium:

> Flying alone, we became sitting ducks for German fighter planes. An easy target, this crippled B-24. Indeed, a fighter plane did pick us up, but thank God, it was American and not German. He was flying a P-47 and came within eyeball range. He called over the radio, 'Hello Big Friend, this is your Little Friend. How much fuel do you have?' Just then a flak battery had our range again and began firing – hoping to finish us off. Our 'Little Friend' dove earthward, heading directly toward our enemy. His courage and skill put a stop to the German firing. We were saved. At this point, we could have headed for Sweden and internment for the rest of the war, but with the P-47 at our side as escort, I was determined to get our old B-24 safely back to Old Buck. The aircraft had stabilized by now; it was losing altitude steadily, due to the loss of the No. 3 and No. 4 engines but once we reached 10,000ft it leveled off and maintained level flight. We were confident now, that 'Big Friend' would return us even though the two right engines were inoperative. In the distance, I could see a sight that never looked better to those weary eyes: the White Cliffs of Dover. We were home! We landed without any problems but our faithful B-24 was full of holes. It had no brakes or flaps and was damaged beyond repair. She never flew again.

On 26 August 956 bombers escorted by 897 fighters attacked targets in France, Belgium, Holland and Germany. Thirteen bombers and thirteen fighters were lost and 148 bombers and fifteen fighters were damaged. Soon after take off from Framlingham, Suffolk, *Ding Dong Daddy*, flown by 1st Lieutenant George E Smith, and 42-102936 in the 390th Bomb Group, collided over Hertfordshire near Hitchin and exploded, scattering pieces of aeroplane over a two and a half mile area. Everyone aboard *Ding Dong Daddy*, which crashed into woodland minus a wing and without its tail section, was killed, while five of the crew of 42-102936, which exploded in mid air, including the pilot 2nd Lieutenant Paul H Bellamy, died. One of the crew on Bellamy's plane had managed to bale out safely but as he was gathering up his parachute, a jagged piece of metal fell from the plane and pierced his chest, killing him instantly. 2nd Lieutenant Raymond A Klausing, the navigator, survived after being blown clean through the plexiglas nose.[15]

Norman K Andrew, navigator in the 487th Bomb Group at Lavenham, flew his fifth mission in Jack Stanley's crew in the 837th Bomb Squadron. Andrew wrote:

> Up at 04.00. Briefing at 05.00. It sure looked good to look at the flak map and see Brest for the target. Not Brest itself, but a flak and coastal battery across the bay. Nice trip but there isn't such a thing as a milk run. We went over the target at 20,400. There were clouds about 9/10 but we had a beautiful hole and about a 1½-minute bomb run. The Air Leader had jumped the gun and decided to go under the clouds so we didn't drop. Damn it! So we circled around and came in at 17,400. I could see a battery in Brest winking at us. The ship jumped about a foot once but the only flak observed was at 7 o'clock level and close in. Found out later they were shooting gray flak and it blended with the clouds. Anyway I wish they would do that more often – it has its psychological advantages. Dropped thirty-eight 100lb GPs. I think we dumped them in the bay. However someone ahead of us has put a load on the target. I saw the smoke the first time over. Logged 7 hours. The best part of it was only 3 hours on oxygen and only 45 minutes carrying that flak suit. My shoulders are really sore from the last two long trips. So ends Mission No. 5. Travelled about 680 nm not counting the 2nd run. Make it 700 nm.

On 27 August Robert H Tays flew his first B-24 mission in the 392nd Bomb Group to Hanover. He wrote:

> Aircraft are everywhere for the entire Eighth Air Force is out this day.... Upon arrival at the IP... a flak burst hit our No. 3 engine. It stopped running almost immediately with just enough time to feather the prop. I added power to the remaining engines, stayed with the formation in position.... Then it was bombs away. The sky was dark with flak bursts, some bursts close enough to hear over the roar of the engines and see the little orange flame in the center of the bursts.[16]

On 1 September Norman K Andrew, navigator in the 487th Bomb Group at Lavenham, flew his sixth mission in Jack Stanley's crew in the 837th Bomb Squadron. Andrew wrote:

> Up at 02.30 for 03.45 briefing. However I've had so much sleep the last three days that I hardly slept at all. We are beginning to get some benefit from the occupation of France. We were scheduled to bomb Mainz, a supply depot. Going over we were behind the lines. However we ran into some pretty soupy weather. It went up to about

> 30,000. We circled around and over Paris trying to get through. Our position was No. 3 on the lead element; No. 1 and No. 2 were pathfinder ships. We milled around in the overcast for about 1½ hours. Ships and formations were everywhere. At one time one formation went right across over us and one went under. Really gave us a scare. The mission was finally recalled. Two ships, not from our field, had a mid-air collision – coming around a cumulus build-up from different directions. Some of our boys, on the way home, weren't quite on the ball and went over Le Havre. Got some flak but no damage. Logged 7 hours. Plus a few more gray hairs. Temperature went to –31° C.[17]

Bad weather in September severely limited missions and only fourteen were flown during that month. On 8 September Lieutenant Norman E Freidman, a co-pilot in the 493rd Bomb Group at Debach near Ipswich, flew his seventeenth mission and his first in a B-17 since the group converted from Liberators:

> Our crew had been designated a lead crew. Therefore our navigator, Lieutenant Billy McVicker from California, was back with us permanently. Briefing was held at 03.00 for a mission to Mainz, west of the city of Frankfurt. We were always awakened early enough to be able to do our personal and get to the mess hall for breakfast. Our next stop was the main briefing room. All crews alerted for the mission assembled there for general and individual briefings. The very first thing that occurred always took our strict attention. The curtain was pulled back and a long string showed the route to and from the target area. The longer the string, the farther to the target, which meant more time in the air and more chances to get shot down. The Operations Officer briefed on the mission's general facts, where we were going, what type of bombs we were carrying and what we were going to hit. He also briefed on the formation procedures to use and gave us the number and type of fighter groups, which would provide escort all the way in and out of enemy territory. He gave us the times they would appear. All of this of course was printed on forms for us to take along. All times, start engine, taxi, take-off, forming up etc were also noted on the briefing form. The next briefer was the Intelligence Officer. He gave us the target information, why we were hitting it, the amount of enemy flak and fighters we could expect on the route in and out and over the target He explained the latest in escape and evasion procedures for the area we were flying over. Our target was an ordnance depot. We climbed on course to 29,000ft flying deputy lead to Captain George Field. We were supposed to drop on PFF but the bombardier was able to drop

> visually. All the bombs landed well within the intended impact area. A good job. Light flak and no enemy fighters. Target destroyed.
>
> Next day there was no rest for our crew. We were briefed early in the morning for a mission to Düsseldorf, directly in the center of 'Happy Valley', so-called because of the concentration of flak guns. This area was the home of much of Germany's heavy machine industry. We were flying deputy lead in the low group off the wing of Captain George Bruck. He climbed on course to 29,000ft for our bomb run. The flak was very intense and accurate. Fortunately, our only casualty was the heel of Billy McVicker's shoe. A piece of flak entered the nose compartment and lodged in his shoe. There were no enemy fighters to harass us or our escort of P-51s. The bombing was fair and the target partially destroyed. Many planes had flak holes in them.

On 10 September over 1,000 Eighth Air Force heavy bombers escorted by several hundred fighters attacked targets in Germany. The 96th Wing went off operations and the 458th, 466th and 467th began 'Trucking' operations. Philip C Day, co-pilot of *Lil' Peach* in the 467th Bomb Group recalls:

> We hauled boxed goods and five-gallon Jerry cans of gasoline initially but soon we were hauling 80-octane gas only, in our plane's outer wing 'Tokyo' tanks, in tanks installed in the bomb bays and in fighter drop tanks carried in the waist area of the ship. These loads were about 2,700 gallons, which were pumped off at the landing fields in France. In addition, we carried enough 100-octane in our wing tanks for the approximate five hours round trip. At the height of the operation there were 150 airplanes at Rackheath. All armament was taken from the planes except the Martin upper turret guns and ammunition and we flew at altitudes of 1,000ft or less, ready to go 'on the deck' if attack by enemy fighters occurred.[18]

On 11 September over 650 heavies, escorted by fourteen fighter groups, were sent to bomb six synthetic-oil plants and other targets in the *Reich*. An estimated 525 fighters atatcked the formations and fifty-two bombers and thirty-two fighters were shot down. One of the worst hit groups was the 'Bloody Hundredth', which went to Ruhland. Fighters tore the 350th Squadron apart shooting down nine Fortresses. The low element of the 'C Group' was also badly hit and it lost three of its number in quick succession. Two Fortresses in the high element were also destroyed.[19] Next day it was the turn of the 493rd Bomb Group to suffer unmercifully in the onslaught by the enemy fighters. Thirty-eight B-17s took off from Debach for Magdeburg where they experienced very heavy flak. As the Group left the target they were jumped by fighters. It seemed to take forever for the Low Squadron to make it through the intense flak since they were flying directly into a vicious headwind. Fortunately, all twelve aircraft emerged from the flak intact but Fw 190s and Bf 109s seemed to appear out of the flak and attacked from the rear. In moments seventeen B-17s were either spiraling down or descending on fire. The arrival of P-51s finally forced the Germans to break off their engagements with the bombers. The dispersed, crippled Forts then set course for Allied occupied territory while tending to wounded crewmen and assessing their damage. Two of the five landed at Brussels to get aid for critically wounded crewmen and to get their damaged aircraft on the ground. The other three elected to return the wounded to England since their aircraft seemed airworthy for the flight across the Channel.

The most disastrous period in the 92nd Bomb Group's history occurred on 11 and 13 September when twelve B-17s were lost in consecutive missions to the city. Merseburg was the target on 13 September and again the 92nd Bomb Group suffered severely. Four B-17s in the 327th Squadron were lost, including the lead plane, which received a direct flak hit ten miles east of the target and exploded.

In September *Market Garden*, one of the biggest operations of the war, went ahead using American and British airborne divisions to take the Eindhoven, Nijmegen and Arnhem bridges on the Rhine, with support provided by the Allied air forces. The operation has been described in an official report as 'by far the biggest and most ambitious airborne operation ever carried out by any nation or nations.' The aim was to cut the German-occupied Netherlands almost in half and to prepare the way for the invasion of Germany that would bypass the northern flank of Germany's Westwall fortifications (The Siegfried line).[20]

Market Garden was fraught with planning and logistical problems; not least a lack of transport aircraft (which necessitated the dropping of airborne troops over several days instead of *en masse* on one day), and bad weather that made regular air reconnaissance difficult and at times impossible. On 17 September, 1,113 medium and heavy bombers escorted by 330 fighter aircraft carried out bombing attacks to eliminate the opposition before the airborne forces of *Market Garden* went in later that day.[21] On 18 September, when the Germans counter-attacked and forestalled an American attempt to capture the bridge at Nijmegen, 252 Liberators, each loaded with about 6,000lb of perishables and fuel supplies, set off to drop their loads over LZ.N, *Klein Amerika* (Little America), at Knapheide, near Groesbeek.[22] Some Liberators and C-47s got in each other's way over the sea and were forced to abort, while others experienced navigational difficulties. The remaining Liberators dropped to 400ft over the drop zone. Just over 100 B-24 Liberators dropped supplies and ammunition to the American Airborne forces at Grosbeek in the Nijmegen–Eindhoven area. 'Dusty' Worthen, bombardier in Joe Rosacker's crew in the 93rd Bomb Group recalls:

> The view along the route to the drop zone was incredible. Crashed C-47s, burned outlines of crashed gliders, gliders nosed up or on their back – a general mess. Our flight was over farming area. We could nearly see the flying feathers of the fluttering chickens; the cows were in full gallop – right through fences and bushes. The Dutch farmers were waving happily. It was certainly a different sight than we would see at our usual 22,000ft altitude. As we neared the target the small-arms fire became intense. We were hit several times. One slug stopped in the backpack parachute of our tail gunner.[23]

Meanwhile, the 14th Wing dropped their supplies to the 101st American Airborne at Best. Ted Parker, a waist gunner in the 491st Bomb Group recalls:

> At the target I opened the hatch in the floor and had to work quickly because we would be passing the dropping zone fast and at low altitude. In my haste my leg became entangled in the parachute straps attached to the ammunition track and I was pulled out of the hole when the last bundle went out. I just managed to cling to the track, but my legs were dangling out of the hatch. The Quartermaster [who had 'frozen' since take-off] ignored my calls for help. Finally the tail gunner, David Slade, heard me and came to my assistance.[24]

Two groups of P-47s had failed to nullify the almost constant small-arms fire and the 2nd Bomb Division lost sixteen Liberators and seventy more were damaged, while twenty-one fighters were shot down.[25] The Allied and German air forces were grounded by bad weather on the 20th, and on 21 September only ninety P-47s of the 56th and 353rd Fighter Groups were able to provide escort and patrol support for the airborne forces.[26]

Little had been seen of the *Sturmgruppen* since their successful attack on the 493rd Bomb Group on the mission to Magdeburg on 12 September, but all that was about to change on 27 September when it was the Liberators of the 2nd Bomb Division that met with tragic results. While the B-17s headed for oil targets and engineering centres at Cologne, Ludwigshafen and Mainz, 315 B-24s went to the Henschel engine and vehicle assembly plants at Kassel in central Germany. For the 445th Bomb Group it was a mission which would live forever as one of the most tragic and probably the most disastrous raid for a single group in the history of American air warfare. The 445th lost twenty-five bombers shot down and five more crashed in France and England. Only five made it back to England. It proved the highest group loss in Eighth Air Force history. There were 236 empty seats in the mess halls at Tibenham that evening. Altogether, the 445th lost 117 men killed, and 45 officers and 36 enlisted men had been made prisoners of war, some of them after they had been ordered by the Germans to collect the burnt and charred remains of their colleagues from the crashed aircraft.[27]

Lieutenant Stanley E Krivik, once a New Jersey football star and the only man in the 702nd Squadron who returned, crashed in Norfolk trying to put down at Snetterton Heath or Old Buckenham. He told how the Group had been separated from the main bomber stream and had gone too far into Germany. The fighter escort had to stay with the rest of the Wing, which was flying the briefed course. He told how suddenly, out of nowhere, more than a hundred German fighters tore through the formation from behind, blazing away with their cannon. He saw one B-24 after another spin down out of his squadron, some on fire and some wildly out of control. Twenty-millimetre shells had wounded three of his gunners, shattered one of his engines and damaged two more. Over England he lost one of the damaged engines; over Tibenham he saw another crippled plane on the runway he had intended to use and he turned away to head for another airfield. He told of losing a third engine and of the crash. But Krivik did not tell what he did after the crash. He did not mention that after being thrown through the plexiglas pilot's canopy and lying stunned on the ground in front of the B-24, he had picked himself up and crawled back into the burning, exploding wreckage, to pull three of his crewmembers out. The co-pilot was unconscious and strapped into his seat; never mind, Krivik pulled him out, seat and all. He hauled out the radio operator, who was pinned under his own radio equipment on the flight deck. Exploding machine gun bullets did not keep Krivik from tugging at the crinkled metal to free the engineer. Krivik did not tell about all this, but his radio operator and his engineer did. And Krivik was awarded the Soldier's Medal.

But he knew that all the medals in the War Department could not replace his navigator, who was killed in the crash. He knew that all the pompous citations invented by Division Headquarters could not bring back Reginald Miner or Myron Donald or Donald Brent, or Carl Sollien.[28] Miner's co-pilot Virgil Chima, would not be back to keep his date with that little blonde telephonist at the Norwich exchange; Sollien would not be sitting at the piano that night, his fingers wandering through *Begin the Beguine* with strange grace and feeling. Jerry Weinstein would not be back to write his wife that she was prettier than any girl he had seen in England; he would not be peering over the edge of the bar, shouting for a beer at the top of his lungs because the bartender could hardly see him.[29]

Notes

1. Two months earlier, returning from the mission to Politz on 29 May, Lieutenant Conrad 'Connie' Menzel successfully crash-landed *Pregnant Peg* in a field near Shipdham. The left landing gear collapsed and the aircraft was

extensively damaged. The temporary installation of a telegraph pole in the bomb bay enabled the Liberator to be flown out of the field on 10 June by a recovery crew to the 3rd SAD at Watton-Griston for repairs.

2. 'Between 6 July and 9 August we'd logged 167.55 hours.'
3. 'After our mission of 9 August, *Skinny* was sent to the hangar to be used for parts – but a changed decision saw her repaired for combat. She flew her 109th mission in December 1944 to January 1945. It was then decided to send her out one more time to make it an even 110 and on that mission three of her engines failed and the pilot put her down somewhere in Belgium. I don't know whether those miracle men of the ground crew were ever able to get *Skinny* airborne again. I do know I'll always have a warm spot in my heart for her and my wonderful crew.'
4. Leon Croulebois did not see Sergeant Robert F Williams leave the ship. Flak had killed him instantly and he plunged from his upper turret into the flaming bomb bay. He did not see Lieutenant Gordon 'Bud' F Davis, the navigator. His body was shredded by the first flak hit. Lifeless, it rode in *Flush* to the ground. The aircraft crashed at Bois de Clamart, a Paris suburb. He did see Allison leave the ship, shortly after jettisoning the tail gunner's escape hatch. Leon watched as ground fire danced his body around on the shroud lines of his 'chute, leaving him hanging nearly lifeless. Allison died minutes after reaching the ground. Leon watched as Aske hurtled out the waist door. The ship was now low. The same ground fire tore through his body. He died hanging in his parachute. A tricky wind caught ball turret gunner Norman Fernaays as he left the ship. It raced him toward Meudon where, still at speed, he bounced off the tile roof of Madame Braconnier's home, landing heavily in the garden of the home next door. He lived, was sheltered by Madame Braconnier and was the first to return to military service soon after Paris was liberated. Chick Barber and Chuck Nekvasil crashed down in their 'chutes near the Orphelinat *Lazaret* (hospital). The SS captured Nekvasil and Chick was taken only minutes later. Consorto eluded capture for 24 hours but was captured and he and Magargee were taken to Germany. Barber was marched to a German barracks. Nekvasil, his pelvis and his coccyx fractured in the impact of his parachute landing, and shoeless (the force of his 'chute opening had snapped his flying boots off, was marched to the *Lazaret*. Late in the afternoon he was taken on a stretcher to an ambulance, which picked up Barber and took them on a long ride through Paris to the Beaujon hospital at Clichy. After a week and-a-half of minimal care both men made a night escape, with the aid of the FFI, and finally linked up with the French 2nd Armoured Division.
5. R D Russell's crew completed their 35 missions on 28 September 1944. The day after, their B-24J, *King Kong* was lost over Kassel.
6. B-24 42-95150 *Passion Pit* flown by Lieutenant John L Millikin, who evaded. All of his crew survived and they were taken prisoner. It was their 30th and last mission of their tour of combat.
7. In 42-52590. Ralph Elliott made 1st Lieutenant on 9 September, with a raise in pay... almost $400. He made captain on 25 March 1945.
8. The leader's aircraft was B-24H-15-FO, 42-94745 *The Bold Sea Rover* flown by Lieutenant James L Glaze with Major R J Sirks in the right hand seat. There were no survivors. Eight men aboard 41-29473 *Bolicat* including the pilot,

Lieutenant George H Washington, were KIA. John Doyle, the nose gunner, was severely wounded and was helped by Norman C Grant the navigator. A 'chute was put on Doyle just as a second explosion rocked the B-24. He was to follow Grant out the nose wheel door opening and the navigator presumed that he did, but after opening his 'chute and looking around Grant could not see any other 'chutes. Five of the crew were found in the wreckage, two were never found and Doyle's body was discovered some distance from the crash. Grant was captured. See *Helton's Hellcats: A Pictorial History of the 493rd Bomb Group* by Martin W Bowman and Truett Lee Woodall Jnr. (Turner, 1998)

9. 'Aboard all lead planes the first two bombs held by the bomb bay shackles were smoke bombs. The purpose of this was to mark the bomb path as they left our plane. They were known as "Skymarkers" or "Smoke Streamers". When they were released, they started immediately to emit a very dense pure white smoke. The other bombardiers in the squadron would release their bombs on this signal.'
10. 'Flak had become our number one concern. I later found out that during the month the Eighth Air Force lost 131 aircraft to anti-aircraft fire compared with only 39 shot down by fighters. On 10 September 1944, between my 29th and 30th missions, orders were cut for our crew to take official combat leave. The enlisted men were ordered to Pangbourne rest home in Berkshire. The four officers were to proceed to Roke Manor near Ramsey, Hants AAF Station No. 503. These were official Eighth Air Force Rest Homes established to let the combat personnel wind down. All of our crew traveled together to London. There we separated for the respective rest homes.'
11. On 20 August the 20th Wing Liberators were converted for 'trucking' fuel and supplies to the Allied ground forces in France. On 25 August Paris was liberated.
12. A radio for the life raft. It was so named because the distinctive curved yellow hand-crank generator, which provided power for the distress radio signal, was shaped like a Gibson Girl's waspish waist. (The 'hour-glass' figure was attributed to the personification of the feminine ideal in the satirical pen and ink illustrated stories created by Charles Dana Gibson, during more than 15 years spanning the late 19th and early 20th century.) This unit with accessories was for use in case of forced landings on water. It was contained in a yellow waterproof bag, which had buoyant qualities. Originally carried on the flight deck, to be either released on a small tethered parachute just before impacting the water, or thrown out by a crewmember after ditching, the pack was soon repositioned in the dinghy escape hatch and made accessible from outside the aircraft. The set automatically transmitted a coded signal. The aerial wire was carried aloft by either a fold up/down metal frame box kite or balloon inflated by a hydrogen generator.
13. Twenty-five B-17s and B-24s were lost during raids on oil and industrial targets on 24 August 1944.
14. B-17 43-37980 in the 839th Bomb Squadron flown by Lieutenant Joseph A Duncan. 9 KIA, 2 PoW.
15. *Silvered Wings High in the Blue Heavens*, Julian Evan Hart, (Treasure Hunting, November 2000).
16. Tays made the decision to drop out of formation and make it home alone. They landed 30 minutes behind the rest of the group.

17. Following this mission Stanley's crew had a break of almost a month as they were designated a lead crew and they took appropriate training. It meant that they now had only 30 missions to fly instead of 35.
18. On 12 September the 458th Bomb Group alone delivered just over 13,000 gallons of fuel to units in France.
19. See *Century Bombers: The Story of the Bloody Hundredth* by Richard Le Strange. 100th Bomb Group Memorial Museum, 1989.
20. The Allied plan was to capture bridges on the Rhine in Holland at Veghel, Grave, Nijmegen and Arnhem, using Britain's 1st and the American 82nd and 101st Airborne Divisions, cut off the Germany Army in the Belgian sector, and save the bridges and the port of Antwerp for the American army units and British XXX Corps advancing north from the Dutch border.
21. The first airlift alone involved 360 British and 1,174 American transport aircraft and 491 gliders, accompanied by 910 fighter escorts. During the course of the operation 20,190 parachutists, 13,781 glider-borne troops, 5,230 tons of equipment and stores, 1,927 vehicles and 568 pieces of artillery were landed behind the German lines.
22. The day before, some of the Liberators had flown practice trucking missions over Norfolk, and on the 18th six specially modified B-24s in the 458th Bomb Group delivered over 9,000 gallons of fuel to General Patton's forces in France.
23. The First Allied Airborne Army recovered 80% of all supplies dropped by the 20th Wing at Groesbeek.
24. The 14th Wing Liberators flew over a small town and came under small-arms fire from some Germans who could quite easily be seen in the streets. One bullet, well spent by the time it reached the B-24, hit Ted Parker in the cheek. He watched helplessly as the lead aircraft, flown by Captain Jim Hunter and carrying Captain Anthony Mitchell, the air commander, was shot down. 'She took one bounce and struck some haystacks, exploding in a large orange flame,' he says. 'Our altitude was about a hundred feet at the time. The tail gunner was the only survivor. Some Dutch monks hid him until liberated.' The 491st lost four B-24s on the mission.
25. On 19 September, the 458th despatched 24 Liberators to France, carrying 38,016 gallons of fuel for the troops. Colonel Albert J Shower's 467th Bomb Group was also involved in the 'trucking' operations. He recalls: 'From 19 September until 3 October the 96th Wing flew no combat missions, but established a forward base at the airfield at Clastres, near St. Quentin. We ferried gasoline for Patton's tanks and motorized units.'

    During its 14 days of 'trucking' the 467th delivered 646,070 gallons of 80-octane fuel to the Allied armies. In 13 days of 'trucking' missions the 458th also delivered 727,160 gallons of fuel to the tank units.
26. Of over 10,200 British airborne troops landed in the Arnhem area, 1,440 were killed or died of their wounds. 3,000 were wounded and taken prisoner. Some 400 medical personnel and chaplains remained behind with the wounded and about 2,500 uninjured troops also became PoWs. There were also 225 prisoners from the 4th Battalion, the Dorsetshire Regiment. About 450 Dutch civilians were killed. The operation also cost 160 RAF and Dominions aircrew, 27 USAAF aircrew. 79 Royal Army Service Corps despatchers were killed and 127 taken prisoner. A total of 55 Albemarle, Stirling, Halifax and

Dakota aircraft from Nos. 38 and 46 Groups failed to return, with a further 320 damaged by flak and seven by fighters. 105 Allied fighter aircraft were lost.

27. At 2nd Bomb Division HQ, a plan to bring in 28 crews from other groups was considered but by nightfall it had been shelved and the decision taken that all new replacement crews coming into the division would be diverted to the 445th. Ten crews were scraped together for the mission the following day, ironically to Kassel again. *Patty Girl*, flown by another crew, was the only Liberator from the previous day's mission to fly. All 10 crews returned safely to Tibenham on this occasion.
28. Lieutenant Reginald R Miner was the pilot of 42-50961, which crashed at Hersfeld, Germany with two of his crew KIA. Ten were taken prisoner. Lieutenant Myron H Donald was pilot of 42-51287, which crashed at Nesselrowden, Germany with the loss of five men KIA and four taken prisoner. Lieutenant Donald E Brent was the pilot of B-24 42-50324 *Eileen*, which crashed at Ulfen, Germany with the loss of six crew KIA and three taken prisoner. Lieutenant Carl J Sollien piloted *Fort Worth Maid*, which also crashed at Hersfeld, with the loss of five men KIA and five who survived to be taken prisoner.
29. Ira P Weinstein, September 1944, reprinted in the *2nd Air Division Journal*, Winter 1987–88. Ira Weinstein was the bombardier on Myron H Donald's crew in the 702nd Bomb Squadron, which was shot down. Weinstein bailed out and was captured by the Germans, who made him visit the crash site. He removed three bodies from his Liberator and laid them out in woods nearby. It was his belief that Myron Donald had baled out and was then beaten to death by civilians. His chute had been cut off him and he was stripped of all his flying apparel. His face and body were in a badly mauled condition as though he had been clubbed or beaten. One of the civilians nearby said, 'That is what happens to Americans who bomb our cities.'

CHAPTER 8

Blood and Oil

Nearing the target I saw this 'boiling mass' of flak. We started to make a 360° turn and I thought, 'Thank God we don't have to fly through it.' However, I was soon to discover that another group had cut us off and we were only waiting our turn. God, it was awful. I could see planes falling from all over the sky. When the first flak burst was at our altitude I knew we had just 'bought the farm.' It was a hell of a ride through that stuff. Our group just simply dissolved.

Staff Sergeant Adolph J Smetana,
tail gunner, 351st Bomb Group

John W McClane was feeling a little foolish. Although he had flown his thirtieth and last official mission of his tour on 26 September he had decided to volunteer to fly a thirty-first so that he could finish up with the rest of his crew who were on their thirtieth. McClane still felt that it was his duty to stick by Peritti and the crew. They had been through so much together in training, flying the South Atlantic and in combat that he could not turn his back on them. As a lead crew, they could not fly without a lead navigator. They let him know that they did not relish flying with an unknown navigator. Neither the crew nor the CO put pressure on him. It was his own personal decision; well knowing it could cost him his life. He did not regret the decision but before the day was out he had serious doubts concerning the wisdom of his rashness.

They were to be part of approximately 300 aircraft assigned to bomb Hamm, carrying well over 600 tons of high explosives. At first they were scheduled to go to Stuttgart, but it was decided that the rail transport through Hamm was the more urgent target. The importance of Hamm as a major rail route for the Germans to supply their Western Front was so important to the strategic offensive that his 44th Bomb Group was sent there four times during the war. It so happened that his crew went three of the four times, the first on their first mission of 22 April. They returned on his thirtieth mission, 26 September, and the Group went again on 30 September but McClane's crew did not fly that day, and now on 2 October they were once more off to Hamm. Again they were the lead in the same B-24J PFF ship that they flew on 26 September. They were flying very little now between missions but they did take this plane up once on 30 September for one and a half-hours of practice.

The Eighth Air Force dispatched about 1,200 heavies to various targets in Germany. The 44th Bomb Group launched twenty-five aircraft and we were to lead the 14th Combat Wing, which led the whole 2nd Division. Again, McClane and his *H_2X Mickey* radar navigator were to be put to the test.

> Of the two positions, I had much the better job. I was the senior lead navigator working at my desk with full visibility out of the plane. The radar navigator sat in front of his Cathode ray tube in semi-darkness plotting our course by observing a very fuzzy gross reproduction of the ground below. But don't under estimate the value of his work. At times, we could see nothing on the ground in the target area. He then worked with our bombardier to determine when the bombs were to be dropped. When we were finally after two tries ready to drop the bombs, Warga was able to get a fair visual sighting but the H_2X equipment was a great aid to him. Our strike photo showed a 5/10th cloud cover but some squadrons reported a 10/10th. I clearly saw through the clouds where our bombs landed.
>
> But I'm getting ahead of my story. This, my last combat mission, was an almost exact repeat of our mission to the very same target just six days before. Once more we were on the bomb run with our bomb bay doors open when a group of planes crowded us to the point where we had to fly through the tremendous flak barrage without dropping our bombs. Boy! Was I ever mad and scared? As on the previous mission, I once more had to plot our course back to the IP so we could make a second run over the target. All the way in to where we released our bombs and out the other side of the anti-aircraft fire, I kept praying to God to let us make it this one last time. We had survived all the flak the Germans could throw at us in thirty-one missions while sustaining hundreds and hundreds of holes. The Luftwaffe fighters came close several times but they failed also to shoot us down. After an easy flight back to base, we rolled to a stop after 6 hours and 30 minutes of our final combat mission. It was none too soon because in three days, the Nazis threw the first of their Me 163 rocket fighters against our bomber force. After landing, the whole crew gathered around the plane congratulating and slapping each other on the back. This was a happy day for us. But we all knew it was only by God's Will that we made it through without an injury among us. There is no way I can express in words

> the relief we felt. The strain of combat had taken its toll and it would be a full year before most of us would recover from this nightmare.[1]

For others October marked the start of their combat career. On 3 October Lieutenant Bernie L Iwanciow's crew in the 860th Bomb Squadron, 493rd Bomb Group flew their first mission, to Nürnburg, one of the longest the group had flown. Lieutenant John O 'Rams' Ramsey, navigator, recalled:

> The flak seemed to be to our right at the target. We had just taken off our flak vests at the Franco–German border, when a barge on the river between Metz and Nancy fired a four-gun battery at us. Our ship was the only one hit. A piece of flak came through the plexiglas nose, missed Chuck [Charles H Jeske, bombardier] and either glass or flak cut my pencil off in my hand.

The Thursday 5 October mission to Münster is described by Jule Berndt, navigator in Lieutenant Rolland B Peacock Jnr's crew in *Magnificent Obsession* in the 850th Squadron, 490th Bomb Group. It was their third mission:

> This was one of the most memorable of all our experiences. At briefing we were told the target was to be an airfield located on the outskirts of Münster. Our bomb load consisted of five 500lb GP bombs and two 500lb bomb clusters of incendiaries. Our position in the squadron was three in the lead, a truly honorable position for a crew with only two missions behind them. The trip over was made without incident, reinforcing the growing feeling that we were now becoming well accustomed to the tasks and responsibilities our positions called for. As we approached the target the clear skies told us that the raid would be under visual conditions, our first experience of this type of bombing.
>
> Everything went according to plan as we turned on the bombing run from the IP but just a minute before it was time to release the bombs we ran into the most accurate flak we had ever experienced. Our squadron, in particular, was in the area of heaviest flak and it was quite evident that the German gunners were tracking us, for the flak was bursting right off the noses of the planes. Up at the front of our ship a piece of flak burst through the bottom of the plexiglas nose and flung glass fragments all around. By the noises we could hear above the roar of the engines, we knew that our plane was taking hits. Just at the moment the bombardier announced bombs away, another flak burst hurled a second fragment through the bottom of the nose and broken glass struck the bombardier above the eye. Almost immediately a large piece of flak hit the glass port

directly in front of the ball turret gunner, showering him with shattered glass. (After we had landed, one of the other crews told us that they had seen the shell burst directly below us and very close to the plane.)

I took a look at the bombardier and could find only a small scratch on his face. In the meantime the waist gunner had taken the ball turret operator from the ball and had put him onto oxygen in the radio room. When I got back to the radio room I found that the injured man had received lacerations about his eyes and it looked as though he had also particles of glass in the eyes themselves. It was impossible to make a proper examination because by that time the swelling had entirely closed both eyes. We placed him on a sleeping bed, which is standard equipment for planes and covered him with more blankets. I then applied boric acid ointment to his eyes and surrounding areas and placed compresses over them. The waist gunner then stayed on watch over him on the way back.

When I returned to my station I found that the oxygen on his system was almost down to zero, so I called the pilot, who is on the same system, to verify the reading. The pilot's gauge showed the same and later we found that part of our system had been pierced by flak. Fortunately the oxygen system in a plane is arranged in sections so that the failure of one supply will not leave the entire ship without oxygen. The only other damage we were aware of was a broken hydraulic line in our left wing.

To get back to the field and receive medical attention for our wounded gunner as quickly as possible, we broke away from the rest of the Group at the Dutch coast and came back alone. By increasing our air speed we beat the formation back by some time. As soon as we had taxied from the runway the wounded man was removed from the plane and taken to the hospital where about 400 fragments of glass were removed from his eyes and face. The fact that he did retain his sight is testimony to the remarkable skill of our army medics. Back on the ground we examined the plane and found many other holes in it. One worth mentioning was in the horizontal stabilizer of the tail; it was almost six inches in diameter. If it had to hit, we were glad a flak fragment of that size had selected the least dangerous spot. We were more than grateful when our CO stood us down the next day to collect our ragged nerves.

William A Johnson, a pilot of a replacement crew in the 493rd Bomb Group, which had arrived at Debach in September, also flew the 5 October mission. He filled in as co-pilot aboard a Fortress piloted by 1st Lieutenant Arthur A Bisaro for the mission to an airfield near Münster. Johnson recalls:

> We took off just before dawn and as we climbed to our assembly altitude, we flew straight into sunlight. It was a beautiful day and finally, I was going to be part of the war! The climb and the assembly were routine and I soon found out that I needn't have worried about trying to remember a co-pilot's duties. Everything worked out well because I merely did whatever became necessary on my side of the cockpit. I had the responsibility to monitor 3rd Division radio frequency so I could relay any Division messages to the pilot. As we left the coast of England, we continued to climb until we reached our assigned bombing altitude, then we leveled off. As we turned to the southeast, we could see the coast of Holland and the Zuider Zee. We could also see many other groups of planes both ahead and behind us. All were headed east toward Germany. Our 'Little Friends', the fighters, flying as our escorts were dodging in and out and crossing and re-crossing our path, but they also matched our progress to the east. We flew all the way to the target without seeing any flak bursts. I was quite disappointed at this, because I wanted to be able to tell my crew back in England what it felt like to be shot at. We dropped our bombs when the rest of our Group did. Then off to our right wing I spied about eight or nine flak bursts. I was about to ask the pilot if that was all there was to it, when I felt a jarring jolt to the plane. Looking in the direction the jolt seemed to come from, I saw that an 88mm shell had gone completely through our No. 1 engine without exploding. Dense black smoke came from the nacelle. I helped the pilot feather the No. 1 engine and trim the plane for three-engined flight. By this time we had dropped out of our formation and had so reduced speed that the flak battery was tracking us. Again an unexploded shell that had its fuse set for a higher altitude hit us. This time the shell went completely through our right wing between the No. 3 and No. 4 engines. The No. 4 engine went dead and the No. 3 engine began to smoke fiercely. I feathered the No. 4 propeller. The hole in the wing allowed a steady stream of 100-octane gasoline to spew out like the stream from a fire hose. By this time, I was sure that we were doomed.[2]

Nick G Plackis, a bombardier in the 390th Bomb Group, flew his twenty-second mission on 5 October to Münster:

> Just after 'Bombs away' I had to free two jammed bombs in the bomb bay. Our load was six 1,000lb bombs, three on each side of the compartment. The three in the right bay salvoed as programed. Of the three on the left, the bottom one went down fine. But the middle shackle malfunctioned and did not release its bomb, so when the upper bomb came off its shackle, it landed with a shuddering clunk, felt throughout our Fortress, as it smashed into the center

> hung-up bomb, preventing the upper bomb from falling free. When the skipper, Phil Sheridan, sent me back to assess the situation, I realized what I was facing was not going to be a picnic. I saw that when the upper bomb released from its shackle, it also pulled out the wire retainers sometimes called 'pins' that go into the front and rear bomb fuses. When these pins are pulled out, it frees the small propeller spinners on the fuses to rotate a certain number of turns in the windstream, supposedly on its way down to the target. After which a spring releases the spinner, activating a plunger to pop out, arming the bomb, so if the plunger is touched – BOOM. I knew I had to do something fast when I saw that spinner on the front of that 1,000 pounder turning on its fuse in the windstream of the open bomb bay at 27,300ft altitude. The space between the front of the jammed bombs and the forward bomb bay bulkhead was too narrow for me to squeeze into while wearing my chest-pack 'chute, or carrying an oxygen walk around bottle. So, I had to squeeze down into the compartment and straddle the open bomb bay without those luxuries, while trying to release the jam. Just seconds prior to freeing the lower bomb, the spinner on the upper bomb popped off and I caught it in my hand as the plunger popped out, arming it. I had no choice now, since my only way out, was to desperately release the bombs, otherwise if I tried to climb out, either my shoulder, chest or back would touch and activate the fuse plunger, making us history. So, you can be sure I was quite relieved when both bombs gently left the compartment. Lucky too, that I was holding on when the bombs dropped out since I was not prepared for the amount of suction they created. As groggy as I was from lack of oxygen, I scrambled up to the catwalk, assisted by our radioman Sid Levine, who shoved his oxygen mask onto my face saving my life, I guess this event could qualify for 'ABOVE AND BEYOND THE CALL OF NORMAL DUTY'.

On 6 October, when the Eighth went to Berlin, at the IP near Nauen the 3rd Division formation was forced to lose altitude to prevent flying through thick cloud. Unknown to the B-17 crews, in this layer of cloud lurked a strong force of enemy fighters. Using the cloud cover to excellent advantage, the German fighters were vectored by ground controllers right into the 385th Bomb Group formation, flying as the high group of the last combat wing. The surprise was total. To make matters worse, the 549th Bomb Squadron was in the process of turning on to the target and had become separated from the rest of the group. Most of the eleven B-17s shot down were from this squadron. Only the arrival of the P-51 escort prevented further carnage.

Despite mounting losses there was increasing evidence that the bombing offensive, against oil targets in particular was reaping rewards. During

August 1944 German oil production had fallen to a paltry 16,000 tons compared with 195,000 tons in May that year. The Luftwaffe was therefore forced to live off stocks accumulated during the winter and spring and began to feel the bite as the fuel crisis grew.[3] Doolittle continued to apply pressure on the German oil-manufacturing industry, and on 7 October 1,300 B-17s and B-24s in four forces bombed five synthetic-oil refineries in Czechoslovakia and central and northeastern Germany. Opposition was heavy and fifty-two bombers and fifteen fighters were lost. Nineteen escorting fighter groups claimed twenty-two aerial victories. Next day, 8 October, there was no mission for the B-17 and B-24 crews but on the 9th over 1,000 heavies struck at two marshalling yards and an engine plant at Mainz, and bombed Koblenz, Gustavsburg, Schweinfurt and two targets of opportunity in western Germany. Nineteen fighter groups including two in the Ninth Air Force provided support. No missions were flown on 10 October. On the 11th, 130 B-17s, supported by three P-47 groups, bombed Wesseling synthetic-oil plant and the marshalling yards at Koblenz. Next day over 500 heavies attacked marshalling yards at Osnabrück and aircraft industry targets at Bremen and targets of opportunity, including Diepholz airfield. Eleven fighter groups escorted the bombers and claimed eighteen enemy fighters shot down. Two days later, on 14 October, 1,100 B-17s and B-24s bombed marshalling yards and targets in the Cologne area.

Lieutenant Wallace Johnson in the 490th recalls the mission of Tuesday 17 October:

> I was flying our B-17 *Big Poison* on a mission to the marshaling yards at Cologne when we took an almost direct flak hit that severed all the oil lines on No. 2 engine, including the one to the feathering pump. Consequently all attempts to feather that engine were futile; this caused extreme over-speeding of the prop and with no oil to the engine it soon seized, causing the crankshaft to shear. This left me with one prop running wild (windmilling), causing a huge amount of drag which I could not overcome, even with the other three engines at full power. As we dropped out of formation we were picked up and escorted by two little friends, P-51s. As pilot-in-command it was up to me at this point to make the decision to try and make the Channel crossing back home to Eye or attempt a landing on the Continent. I reasoned that there was a high risk of the runaway prop breaking away from its mount and slicing through the nose of the aircraft, with dire consequences. I also knew that there was a possibility I would have to ditch the plane in the Channel. Either way, concern for the safety of my crew made me decide to land at Brussels. Maintenance crews came out to meet us and their inspection revealed that the prop was ready to fall off with the touch of a finger. I was glad that I had made the right decision.

On Sunday 22 October more than 1,000 heavies supported by fifteen fighter groups attacked two military vehicle plants at Brunswick and Hanover and two marshalling yards at Hamm and at Münster. Sergeant Francis W 'Frank' McKinley, a gunner in the 851st Squadron, 490th Bomb Group at Eye, Suffolk recalls:

> After many hours of ground school and flying time to familiarize us with the airfield and the surrounding area we were notified that on the next day we would be flying our first combat mission. We got our wake up call at 02.30 hours and immediately the apprehension set in. After a breakfast of bacon and eggs came the very thorough briefing and we learnt that our target was to be the marshaling yards at Münster. We then went out to the aircraft, carried out the various routine checks and waited for take-off time. Eventually we got a green light from the tower and in the darkness roared down the runway, blue flames shooting out of the turbos, to climb out. We broke out of the solid cloud cover at 10,000ft and the pilot gave the order to go on oxygen. There was a bright moon illuminating the silvery clouds below us as we looked for the red and yellow flares fired by the 851st lead ship to aid us in assembling into squadron formation. By the time the sun had risen the 490th was fully assembled and had entered the bomber stream at the precise time. Our crew, crew 100, was at last on its way to Germany for its first combat experience.
>
> We climbed slowly to our assigned altitude of 25,000ft and flew east into the sun towards Germany. There was solid cloud cover extending in all directions as far as the eye could see. The navigator informed us that we were crossing the Channel and the pilot ordered us to test fire our guns. By this time our fighter escort had joined us and they looked very impressive out there. When we reached the point of entering enemy territory the pilot ordered us to put on our flak helmets and flak vests; he also made one of the frequent oxygen checks, each of us reporting in turn on the intercom. We saw the group ahead of us dropping their bombs. The flak was light and there were no bandits in the target area. The order 'Rainy Day' came in from the lead ship and the radio operator started to dump the metallic *chaff* that served to confuse the German radar-guided guns. By this time our bomb doors were open and we dropped our bombs on the signal of the lead plane, which was bombing by radar due to complete cloud cover. There was some moderate flak but it was inaccurate and no enemy fighters showed up; nevertheless we still kept searching for them just in case – we didn't want to be caught out as we made a sharp break away from the target and headed for home. As we touched down back at Eye everyone had that warm,

relaxed feeling that follows what is called a 'milk run' – all planes back unharmed and nobody injured.

On 22 October Lieutenant Kenneth H French, bombardier in Lieutenant Curtis R McKinney's crew in the 490th Bomb Group flew his twenty-second mission:

> Today we had a fairly easy mission to Münster. We briefed at 07.00 hours and took off at 10.11 hours in a ground fog with 1,000-yard visibility. We climbed to 18,000ft where we joined in formation with our squadron and then took a course across the North Sea. Our fighter support was good; they left us as we were past the fighter danger zone and continued on with the boys who were going to Hanover and Brunswick. There were no enemy fighters seen or reported. After a flak-free run over Holland we reached the target area at about 14.45 hours and as we flew past Osnabrück the flak really started. They were sending up a good box barrage and plenty of rockets but thank God we didn't get mixed up in it. We had a box barrage directly in front of us on the target (we had been briefed for seventy guns) but we turned off to the left to make the run. They sent up more flak but it was low and to the rear of us and we suffered no damage. About twelve rockets came up, right at our altitude and fairly accurate. I saw one explode at Osnabrück and it looked like a flash of lightning.

On 24 October, 415 P-47s and P-51s of the Eighth Air Force carried out fighter-bomber raids in the Hanover–Kassel area. Nine aircraft were lost. Next day, Wednesday 25 October, nearly 1,200 heavies in five forces supported by eleven fighter groups attacked three oil refineries and several other targets. It was Lieutenant Kenneth H French's twenty-third mission and he took off at 08.53 hours for Hamburg, flying lead in the third element of the low squadron:

> We formed at 15,000ft with no trouble and left on time for a change, climbing to bombing altitude as we followed our course over the North Sea. Our fighter escort today was fair: we had four groups of P-51s pick us up at the German coast. Everything had gone well up to this point. We saw flak off Heligoland Island ahead of us just before we turned but no more until we were over our target at Hamburg. We were briefed for 250 anti-aircraft guns on the target and believe me they were all working. They also had fifteen rocket guns in good working order. We went in on our bombing run at 25,700ft. We bombed by PFF through 10/10th cloud cover. Those gunners certainly knew what they were doing: they used tracking and a barrage type flak and were quite accurate despite of all the

> *chaff* we threw out. Fortunately for us, most of it was just off to our right. We were carrying twenty 250lb GPs and spaced them over the target at 100ft intervals. Our ground speed was about 204mph and the temperature at flight altitude was about –28° C. The target was an oil storage depot and refinery just off a tributary of the Elbe 2½ miles south of the city of Hamburg and we think we hit it quite well because we saw four different columns of smoke come up through the undercast and spread out. We certainly hit something. Time of mission was 6 hours 40 minutes. We had no battle damage to our planes and all returned safely to base. But one aircraft from the 493rd Group was seen to go down over the target in a slow spin.

Next day, 26 October, Lieutenant Kenneth H French flew his twenty-fourth mission when over 1,100 heavies attacked a synthetic-oil plant at Bottrop and several other targets, supported by fourteen fighter groups:

> Today's mission got me my third Oak Leaf Cluster and the target was Hanover. After a delay due to bad weather we took off by instruments at 10.53 hours in very poor visibility. Cloud coverage over the base was 10/10 and we had to climb to 8,000ft before we got through the overcast. We were flying lead in the third element of the high squadron and formed at 16,000ft before climbing on course. Our formation today was very poor – we were all over the sky and we saw two planes from another Group collide while forming; pieces of both went down smoking and burning. Just as it had been at home, cloud cover at the target was 10/10th. There had been a few breaks on the way but not many. We picked up our fighter escort of four groups of P-51s and two groups of P-47s just after we passed over the Zuider Zee but fortunately there were no enemy fighters seen or reported in the area. We had been briefed for 140 guns on the target but the flak was only moderate and inaccurate. They used a barrage and tracking method and also had about six rocket guns in action. We bombed ordnance depots, assembly plants and also tool factories. We carried five M17s and five 500lb GP bombs. Our gas load was 2,500 gallons and our ground speed was 215mph; the intervolometer setting was 140ft. We bombed by PFF from an altitude of 26,300ft (temperature –36° C) and the results of bombing were unobserved. We had some flak just as we left the German border but it didn't last very long. The rockets on the target could be seen at least 60 miles away. We had no battle damage today and all the aircraft from our Group returned safely. Time of mission was 7 hours.

On Saturday 28 October over 350 B-17s escorted by four fighter groups bombed the marshalling yards at Hamm and Münster. Lieutenant Kenneth H French went to Hamm once more:

> Using runway 21 we took off at 08.30 hours, using instruments, and climbed to 8,000ft through overcast. We joined the formation at 23,000ft and crossed the English coast nine minutes late. Only five Groups of the 3rd Division flew today; all the others were grounded. The weather was very bad and it almost caused a lot of accidents. We had dense and persistent contrails all the time – they were so thick over the target that we could hardly see each other on the way out and we strayed into flak near Dummer Lake. The flak over the target was a real problem. There were about forty-five flak guns and six rocket guns on the target and they certainly weren't sleeping today. We had a couple of bursts just underneath us that lifted the plane right up. It was too close for comfort but luckily we didn't receive any damage at all. We also got over a flak area at Zwolle that wasn't supposed to be there, both going out and coming back. Our aircraft escaped but some of our planes suffered minor damage. We were carrying twenty 250lb GP bombs with fuse settings of 1/10 and 1/40 and dropped them in train from 25,300ft at 100ft spacing. Our ground speed was about 165mph and the temperature recorded at our highest altitude was –44°C. Bombing was by PFF and the results were unobserved. No enemy planes were seen but Me 410s and Ju 88s were reported in the area. Time of mission was about 5 hours 45 minutes. Though everybody got through OK in the end, the bad weather and the flak made this a most uncomfortable mission and I never want to fly another like it again.

Two days later, on Monday 30 October, over 600 heavies escorted by fifteen fighter groups attacked oil refineries near Hamburg and eleven other targets including the marshalling yards at Hamm and Münster again. Lieutenant Kenneth H French, who was flying his twenty-sixth mission, went to Merseburg:

> We took off at 08.15 hours with a full gas load, On our last four missions we had needed to use instruments to fly through the overcast but today it was clear for our SOP climb. We assembled at 16,000ft, left the English coast at 10.30 hours and were joined by our P-47 and P-51 escorts. We were carrying ten 500lb GP bombs with 1/10 and 1/40 fuses but had to bring them all back with us because we only got as far as 060°40′ E before turning back due to bad weather. There were clouds running up to 32,000ft and that was too high for our bombing. We encountered no flak, nor enemy fighters, though fighters were said to be in the area. We did however see four V-2 rockets going straight up to 40,000ft. Time of mission was 5hr 15 minutes. How I wish that all the missions could be as easy as this one.

By the autumn of 1944 oil targets had assumed top priority. The synthetic-oil refineries at Merseburg in Leuna were attacked on at least eighteen occasions in 1944.[4] Bad weather throughout November slowed down the Allies' advance all along the western front and severely hampered missions. When they were flown they were usually against oil targets.

On 2 November two forces of B-17s, 683 planes in all, attacked the vast *I.G. Farbenindustrie*'s synthetic-oil refinery at Leuna, three miles south of Merseburg, estimated to be producing 10 per cent of all Germany's synthetic oil and a third of all the enemy's ammonia and other chemicals. At briefing crews were warned that German fuel and replacement pilots were in such short supply that Hermann Goering, the Luftwaffe chief, was massing his forces to strike a telling blow on a single mission. All they needed was an opportunity. Norman K Andrew, navigator in Jack Stanley's crew in the 487th Bomb Group at Lavenham, flew his tenth mission, their first as a lead crew. Andrew wrote:

> After landing the boys said Big B was a milk run compared to Leipzig, an area which had 450 guns. Our escort was 850 P-51s and P-38s. They tangled with the Luftwaffe at the IP. What a day! Planes shot up – planes aborting – planes all over the deck coming home.

Henry B Skeen, pilot of *Milk Run*, was flying his first mission with an experienced crew and saw his leader's plane beside them blow up.

> An absolutely terrifying trip. Whitlock's left wing was on fire as well as the section from the radio compartment to the tail. The left elevator had been shot away and the aircraft dropped off to the left, under control. After losing altitude slowly for almost a minute, it went into a steep dive and passed through the undercast out of sight. No 'chutes were seen.

In all, forty-one bombers and twenty-eight fighters were lost.[5]

On 4 November more than 1,000 heavies operating in six forces attacked synthetic-oil plants, oil refineries and benzol plant at Bottrop, Gelsenkirchen, Hamburg, Harburg, Misburg and Neunkirchen. Seventeen fighter groups including a Ninth Air Force group provided support. Next day, Sunday 5 November 1944, more than 1,200 heavies attacked marshalling yards at Frankfurt/Main, Ludwigshafen, Karlsruhe, Hanau and Kaiserlautern and the synthetic-oil plant at Ludwigshafen and rail facilities at Landau, escorted by fifteen fighter groups. Despite the escort, thirty-seven heavies and fighters failed to return. Two of the B-17s that went missing were from the 490th Bomb Group. One was an 849th Squadron B-17G flown by 1st Lieutenant Robert L Jackson. His tail turret gunner, Sergeant Francis A Malachowski was at twenty-three the oldest man on the crew, and was thus nicknamed 'Pops', recalls:

> On this mission, our fifteenth, the primary target was to have been Metz but when we got there it was covered in with 10/10 cloud so we flew on to our secondary target at Ludwigshafen. Over the target flak was intense and seconds after bombs-away we received two direct hits, one near the waist and the other near the right wing. Our ship immediately fell out of formation and apparently collided with Lieutenant [Clarence E] Bridwell's ship [*Penns-Belle*] below us in the [848th] low squadron. As I was to find out later, the sole survivor from the plane we hit was Paul Finot, tail gunner, who survived because the tail section was separated from the rest of the aircraft, enabling him to bale out.
>
> On the bomb run over the target the flak burst near the waist section mostly riddled my flak vest and not me, tearing it off my right shoulder and severing a 'chute riser so that only *one* was left to hook up to my 'chute pack. I was hit though by one fragment that lodged near the bridge of my nose and right eye and a few bits that pierced my helmet and lodged in my head. The impact pinned me against my guns for what seemed like an eternity. Bleeding profusely I finally managed to crawl toward the tail escape hatch and tried to kick it open. The release gear was jammed, so I semi-consciously crawled toward the waist hatch but found only blue sky. The tail was severed and I was coming down alone. It was almost a vertical dive and to this day I have no memory of getting out or pulling the ripcord.

Sergeant Francis W 'Frank' McKinley, a gunner in Lieutenant G D Lyon's crew in the 490th Group, who had flown their first mission two weeks earlier, adds:

> It is a very sobering sight to see your comrades shot out of the sky and no parachutes sighted coming down. We were all saddened on the way back, thinking about the loss of the two crews – eighteen men who will not be with us in the mess hall tonight. At times like that you start to calculate the odds against completing your own thirty-five missions.

Staff Sergeant Richard Skinner in Captain Earl H Johnson's crew in the 861st Squadron, 493rd Bomb Group was flying on the crew's twenty-fourth mission on 5 November. Since their first mission, to Lisieux on *D-Day*, Skinner had flown fifteen missions in a B-24 called *The Witch* before transferring to a B-17 when the Group re-equipped with Fortresses. Skinner recalled:

> Captain Johnson's crew and my Squadron mates were some of the finest men I have ever known. We were now a lead crew. We had

> two extra men with us, a group bombardier and a group photographer to take pictures of the bomb strikes. I had become more frightened with each mission and I was grateful every night that we made it home to a clean bed and excellent meals. The bed and food were the two main reasons I did not want to be a member of the ground forces. On 5 November our plane was hit by anti-aircraft fire just after bombs away over a chemical plant at Ludwigshafen. Over the target the anti-aircraft fire was very heavy and we had just released the bombs when we got hit and lost our No. 2 engine. We were flying at 27,000ft. We started dropping in altitude fast. We took another hit of anti-aircraft fire and within one minute, maybe less than that, Captain Johnson gave the dreaded order to bale out. I was flying in the waist and I removed my oxygen mask to go to the escape door and pull the handle. It was supposed to salvo and fall off. It wouldn't and I couldn't be expending energy fast with no oxygen, but when your life is at stake you don't think and I was pushing and pulling it trying to get it to fall off. I passed out from lack of oxygen and woke up floating down with my parachute open. I knew the plane had blown up because there were pieces of aluminum floating around me like leaves. I was bleeding from the ears and nose, my hands and face were burned, my right shoulder was injured and I no longer had any boots on my feet. I had no idea how my parachute opened. I landed in a plowed field in broad daylight. It was windy, wet and cold. I could not get out of my parachute.[6]

Despite the mauling of 5 November the Eighth was out again on the next day when over 1,000 heavies in six forces attacked oil and chemical installations, a canal aqueduct and aircraft repair plant as well as three marshalling yards and several targets of opportunity in north and north west Germany. Sixteen fighter groups provided support and later strafed ground targets in northwest Germany and Holland. Wayne 'Tex' Frye, navigator in Jack O'Neil's crew in *The Witch* in the 91st Bomb Group went to the oil refinery at Harburg, on the south edge of Hamburg:

> This was really a rough one. The flak had me scared plenty. It was awful close, intense and accurate. Major Taylor's ship, our lead ship, had a direct burst in the waist. We were flying right behind them. A piece of the plane came back and stuck in our No. 2 engine cowling. The ship buckled as it hit, but they kept going. They got the ship back to England but I'll never know how that ship flew. They couldn't get the bomb bay doors closed and that didn't help them any. The waist gunner and the radio-operator were killed and the radar operator was hit in the leg and later lost it. These targets all are

> rough now. We had 134 holes in *The Witch* today. She was getting quite 'patchy'.

The Eighth was stood down on 7 November and then next day over 2,650 heavies attacked the synthetic-oil plants at Merseburg-Leuna again as well as the marshalling yard at Rheine and five targets of opportunity. Bad weather forced the recall of 350 other heavies. Eighteen fighter groups provided support and later strafed ground targets. Twenty-three fighters failed to return. On Thursday 9 November the heavies returned to tactical missions in support of General George Patton's Third Army halted at the fortress city of Metz. The bombers were called in to bomb German lines of communication at Saarbrücken and also enemy gun emplacements to the east and south of Metz to enable the advance through Belgium to continue. The mission was deemed top priority and at bases throughout East Anglia Fortresses taxied out in the mist and bad visibility. The conditions were instrumental in the loss of eight bombers during take-offs and landings and further disasters befell some groups as the mission progressed. It was the twenty-seventh mission for Lieutenant Kenneth H French, bombardier in Lieutenant Curtis R McKinney's crew in the 490th Bomb Group:

> We took off this morning before dawn at 07.30 hours, about an hour late. Two aircraft went off the end of the runway and though they weren't seriously damaged they did put that runway out of action and we had to change to the other one. We climbed up to bombing altitude, which was 18,000ft. We only just managed to get into formation as the Group was leaving for Division assembly. Our primary target was to have been in support of our troops but we couldn't bomb there because of the overcast. We diverted to our secondary target, the marshaling yards at the north end of Saarbrücken, where we had been briefed for 175 guns. We did see a lot of flak and rockets but had none close to us at all. We carried six 1,000lb GPs and the method of release was salvo for the primary and 150ft spacing for the secondary. This mission was all messed up – a 10/10 undercast at the target didn't help – and the official estimate of the bombing was 'missed the target.' I believe they hit a long way short. Air support was good and no enemy aircraft were sighted or reported. We got back just in time as bad weather, a mixture of snow and rain, closed in within fifteen minutes of landing. Time of mission was 6 hours.

While on the bomb run over Saarbrücken, the 452nd Bomb Group encountered an extremely accurate and intense flak barrage. *Lady Janet*, flown by 1st Lieutenant Donald J Gott and 2nd Lieutenant William E Metzger, had three engines badly damaged and the No. 1 engine set on fire. It began windmilling and the No. 2 engine was failing rapidly. No. 4 showered flames back towards the tail assembly. Flares were ignited in the cockpit and the flames were fuelled by hydraulic fluid leaking from severed cables. The engineer was wounded in the leg and a shell fragment had severed the radio operator's arm below his elbow. Metzger left his seat and stumbled back to the radio room to apply a tourniquet to stop the bleeding. However, the radio operator was so weak from pain that he fell unconscious. The bombs were still aboard and Gott was faced with the prospect of the aircraft exploding at any moment. He therefore decided to fly the stricken Fortress to Allied territory a few miles distant and attempt a crash landing. The bombs were salvoed over enemy territory and all excess equipment was thrown overboard. Metzger unselfishly gave his parachute to one of the gunners after his had been damaged in the fire. As *Lady Janet* neared friendly territory, Metzger went to the rear of the Fortress and told everyone to bale out. Staff Sergeant Herman B Krimminger, tail gunner, had died when his parachute had opened accidentally and snagged the blazing B-17's tailplane when he was pulled outside the bomber. Metzger then went back to his seat and the two pilots prepared for a crash landing with only one engine still functioning and the other three on fire. An open field was spotted and Gott brought *Lady Janet* in. At about 100ft the fire took hold of the fuel tanks and the bomber exploded, instantly killing Gott, Metzger and Technical Sergeant Robert A Dunlap, the radio operator. Both pilots were awarded posthumous Medals of Honor.

Over forty heavies and fighters were lost on 9 November when over 1,100 heavies in conjunction with Ninth Air Force aircraft hit targets in the Metz and Thionville area as US Third Army forces launched a full-scale attack on Metz. It was Norman K Andrew's eleventh mission. He wrote:

> Up at 02.00 for 03.00 pre-briefing. Target: a honey right behind the lines. Some forts holding up General Patton. We were group deputy lead. For a while I thought we were going to lead. The primary was visual – secondary PFF. We couldn't see the primary until we were right over it – so we hit the secondary, the marshaling yards at Saarbrücken. We had flak in the high and low squadrons – one ship in the low caught on fire and blew up. Three 'chutes seen – two were on fire.[7] Next day [when more than 600 B-17s and B-24s attacked airfields, marshalling yards and a chemical plant, supported by fourteen fighter groups] the CQ woke Bob and Chuck at 03.50 for target study. Then he woke Jack and me at 03.55 for 04.30 pre-briefing. Target: marshaling yard just south of Koblenz, Germany (Oberlaunstein). We flew deputy group lead until just before the IP. We then took over the lead for a *Micro-H* bomb run.[8] I called Whittnell just before the IP to see if he had it. He said yes, then, as

> we turned we slid into the Trier flak area. No damage. I got a *Gee* fix from the Ruhr chain at Bombs Away. We were right on course and 3½ miles from the target. Load eleven 500-lb GPs.

On 11 November more than 400 heavies supported by eleven fighter groups attacked Oberlaunstein, Koblenz and Rheine marshalling yards, an oil plant at Schloven-Buer and a synthetic-oil plant at Bottrop. Navigator Lieutenant Lawrence W Rasmussen flew his eighth mission in the 493rd Bomb Group:

> Today we were clay pigeons. We were one of the six *chaff* ships, which carried special *chaff* bombs, which were to explode five seconds after dropping. We went over Koblenz, our PFF target (marshaling yards) supposedly to aid the rest of the group. We went over, getting inaccurate flak 29,300ft at −45° C. However, Parker got a motor shot out. We saw a Me 163 on our way back – the jet plane attacked Parker, getting another of his engines and rumor says killed his waist gunner. Parker landed at Brussels. We got back OK, got special interrogation and I had the pleasure of telling Colonel Gerhard his *chaff* bomb concoction was of no avail. Two holes picked up over target. The group was late and didn't even go over target so mission was just flak practise for Jerry.

No missions were flown until Thursday 16 November when the Eighth returned to Western Europe to provide support for the advancing British and US armies.[9] The mission was very carefully planned to avoid bombing friendly troops near the targets just east of Aachen. After the 'softening-up' bombardment by the heavies, the ground troops would advance on the enemy strongholds. The Allied artillery would fire red smoke shells every 500 yards along the front and barrage balloons were also placed along the edge of the area. Other devices, such as radio signals on the SCS-51 sets normally used for instrument landings over England, were implemented. The use of the radio was especially worthwhile when 8/10th cloud covered the front lines and helped ensure accurate bombing. General Doolittle congratulated all groups, saying:

> The Eighth Air Force performed one of its most outstanding operations. The force took off under extremely adverse base weather conditions and successfully attacked targets on the immediate front of our ground troops almost exclusively by instrument technique with very good results. Ground commanders were highly pleased and report all bombs on or near the targets. Only one bomb fell wide but did no damage, with no injuries to friendly troops. It was a difficult task well done and I commend you for the capable and efficient manner in which it was conducted.

On Tuesday 21 November the Eighth returned to Merseburg for the first of three more raids on the refineries in a week. Merseburg had become synonymous with flak and crews hated all missions to the city. Lieutenant Kenneth H French flew his twenty-eighth mission:

> Our briefed target was a synthetic-oil refinery at Lutzkendorf, about 8 miles from Merseburg. We took off at 08.10 hours and climbed in good weather to our assembly altitude of 17,000ft. Our aircraft had a fairly good position in the formation as we were flying deputy lead in the lead squadron. Bad weather had been forecast in front of us and even though we had climbed to 28,500ft to try to get over it we still ran into it when we reached about 8°E. The 1st Division also went to the same target today. They went in first at a bombing altitude believed to have been 21,000ft or less. Fighters hit them between the clouds and we were told that about twenty bombers were shot down. Our escort of P-51s took out sixty enemy fighters. Nearing the target, we received a call that there were fighters in the area but none attacked us. As we were approaching the IP we ran into more bad weather and were forced to turn around. The intention then was to attack our secondary target at Osnabrück but the PFF ship lost it so we diverted again to bomb factories at Lingen. In trying to find this target we flew over a lot of flak areas and our aircraft was holed in seven places. We took two hits in the right wing and one in the left, one in the plexiglas nose just above my head, one just in front of the co-pilot, one in the horizontal stabilizer, another in the fuselage, just missing the ball turret. And a final one in the pilot's oxygen bottle. Our ship suffered more damage on this one mission than it had in all the previous ones put together. There was no flak on the target, though.
>
> We carried twelve 500lb GPs with 1/10 and 1/40 fuses and dropped them from 28,000ft at an intervolometer setting of 150ft with the same ground speed. The bomb bay doors had to be manually cranked shut when the retracting motor froze up. The results of the bombing were later assessed as 'good to very good'. Weather over the Eye field was still clear when we landed. Time of mission was 6hr 20 min.[10]

Late in the morning of Sunday 26 November, over 1,000 Fortresses and Liberators escorted by fifteen fighter groups, headed for the hydrogenation synthetic-oil plant at Misburg near Hanover, a target partially destroyed three weeks before. Timing began to go awry and the 1st Bomb Division formation was spread over 40 miles instead of 20 as briefed and the three escorting groups could not hope to protect all the B-17s. Fifty Fw 190s of III./JG 1 attacked the tightly packed boxes of bombers on a wide front between Uelzen and Perleberg. Three escorting groups of P-51s battled with the enemy for about 20 minutes. No less than sixteen Liberators in the 491st were blasted out of the sky, in the space of just 15 minutes. Further bomber losses were prevented by the timely arrival over the Minden Canal of eight P-51 Weather Scouts, which held the Fw 190s at bay until reinforcements could arrive to save the dozen remaining B-24s.

Command acted quickly to replace the 491st Bomb Group losses. The control Tower log entries for 26 November said, 'Sixteen replacement B-24s arrived from Stansted, Shades of Dawn Patrol.'

Norman K Andrew had flown his thirteenth mission in the 487th Bomb Group on 26 November to the marshalling yard at Hamm where he had 'never seen so many planes in his life'. On the 27th he was 'really surprised' to be awakened at 04.45 for 05.30 pre-briefing. He wrote:

> It was a *Micro-H* run on the marshaling yard at Bingen on the Rhine. Looked like a milk run but there was quite a bit of battle damage from flak. Kramer was leading the group. They had their bombsight, electrical system and oxygen shot out. Aborted at the target. We led home, but only got credit for a squadron lead. I was sure glad to get the lead – we were really skirting three flak areas. We are due to lead the low tomorrow if it's PFF. Saw two V-2s taking off for London – they were still within 10° of vertical when they passed out of sight at least 55 to 60,000ft. Travelling from 500 to 800mph.

On Thursday 30 November about 1,200 heavies set out to bomb four synthetic-oil refineries in Germany. The leading 1st Division force were given the synthetic plant at Zeitz, the 3rd Division, Merseburg, 20 miles to the north, and the Liberators, Lutzkendorf. Wayne 'Tex' Frye, navigator in Jack O'Neil's crew in the 91st Bomb Group, which went to Zeitz, recalls:

> We were in range of the Merseburg guns. Flying time 8 hours. Time on oxygen, 4 hours. Temperature, –35°. Bomb load – twenty 250lb GP delayed action bombs. Flak was intense and accurate. We lost an engine but Jack flew better formation with just three engines than most pilots could with all four. Jack had a wonderful reputation for flying tight formation. There were lots of planes lost. I saw bombers go down all over the sky. We had a visual run on the target but did not hit it. I saw a P-5l hit by flak and go down on fire. We lost three ships. The Germans shot down fifty-six bombers today with flak.[11]

1st Lieutenant Bob Voss, pilot of *The Dorothy V* in the 94th Bomb Group, which was assigned Lutzkendorf, recalls:

> Oil targets were the absolute roughest. When the routes to targets would be uncovered at the early morning briefings and those red ribbons extended to Leipzig, Merseburg and Lutzkendorf an immediate feeling of dread was evident throughout the room. Those were always the targets with the most defensive guns and the most probability of German fighters. I know that those who ended their combat days while attacking marshaling yards, missile sites, airfields and aircraft manufacturing plants and whatever other type targets might offer opinions somewhat different but in my mind the oil targets were those where there was no doubt of intense opposition.
>
> This was certainly one of my roughest missions. The flak was horrendous and its effect on the bomber force was devastating. It's been a long time since that day but the memory of airplanes falling, exploding in mid-air, spinning down out of control some of their crews escaping by parachute will probably remain always. On the bomb run itself with the formations holding altitude, position and direction was the time of the great losses being inflicted. One could look in any direction and see the big planes going down. While on the bomb run our own aircraft took a hit, which became most obvious as we left the target. The engine instruments for Nos. 1 and 2 engines were indicating loss of oil pressure, erratic temperatures and manifold pressures with smoke trailing from the left engines. We were obviously losing power but it was impossible to identify the specific problem due to the instrument indications and we were a long way from home to think about making it on two engines.

Both divisions had flown the route as briefed as far as Osnabrück but the leading 1st Bomb Division formation flew on instead of turning for Zeitz. The 3rd Division wings were 5 to 15 miles south of the briefed route. The error placed the Division within range of ninety flak batteries at Zeitz and the Fortresses were subjected to an intense and accurate barrage. A strong head wind reduced their speed and aided the German defences.

Russell A Grantham, 836th Squadron Operations Officer in the 487th Bomb Group adds:

> As we approached the IP, I noted the Group ahead of us had overshot the IP and in order to insure that we did not collide over the target, I held our turn for 30 seconds or so. The result was that our group approached the target right of the course of the other groups; therefore, we partially missed the 'box'. Our low squadron, which flew to the left and lower did however, have to go through the 'box' and sustained damage. Our group lost four planes out of the low

> squadron. I saw the No. 13 plane in the low squadron fall a few thousand feet and explode with no 'chutes sighted.

The main oil production plants at Bohlen, Leuna, Lützkendorf and Zeitz were severely damaged. The Eighth Air Force lost twenty-nine heavy bombers, the majority shot down by flak. Thirteen of the losses were from the 3rd Air Division. Others like *The Dorothy V* in the 94th Bomb Group made it back on a wing and a prayer, as Bob Voss recalls:

> I had elected to monitor the engines more by visual means of the engines and smoke rather than the instruments. I did shortly feather No. 1 as the smoke increased but came to suspect that we had taken a hit somewhere in the instrument panel as well as the port engines, which proved the case after we made it back to base. Battle-damaged aircraft like ours were among the aircraft landing first and as a result we witnessed the disaster of the two B-17s colliding on final approach.[12]

By the end of November more than forty-three refineries, processing both crude and synthetic oil, had been destroyed. December brought the worst winter weather in England for fifty-four years. Water froze in the pipes and a thin film of ice coated the runways at bases throughout eastern England. The temperature dropped to as low as minus 18°C but the worst feature of the weather was the lack of visibility during missions. The first Eighth Air Force mission of the month went ahead on 2 December when about 275 heavies attacked marshalling yards in Germany but over 150 bombers aborted because of heavy clouds. Eight fighter groups supported the missions and encountered over 100 enemy fighters, claiming 17 destroyed. Three more fighter groups flew sweeps over Cologne–Kassel–Mannheim–Frankfurt/Main area and claimed fifteen enemy machines destroyed. Eight Liberators were lost on the mission to Bingen. No missions were flown from England until 4 December, when over 1,100 bombers bombed marshalling yards in Germany again. Most of the bombers and fighters that failed to return landed safely on the Continent. Next day more than 500 bombers attacked munitions and tank works at Berlin, the marshalling yard at Münster and ten targets of opportunity. Fifteen escorting fighter groups met an estimated 285–300 fighters and claimed 90 destroyed. Lieutenant Charles J Waggoner, pilot of a B-17 in the 729th Bomb Squadron, 452nd Bomb Group, formation struggled back towards England on one engine but over Lohnerfeld the Fortress[13] was shot down by Major Karl Borris of 1./JG 26.

Next day over 650 bombers supported by fighters flying over 750 sorties attacked the synthetic oil plant at Merseburg/Leuna and several other targets in Germany, among which were the Bielefeld marshalling yards and the Minden aqueduct.

Notes

1. John McClane returned to the USA and trained as a pilot but the war ended before he could be posted overseas.
2. A short while thereafter, over Holland, Bisaro's crew baled out. All the crew survived, two to be taken PoW, the other seven, including Johnson, returning to duty.
3. During September 1944 German oil production plummeted to only 7,000 tons and draconian measures were called for. Reich-minister Albert Speer was given 7,000 engineers from the army and an unlimited number of slave labourers to reconstruct the synthetic-oil plants. Hundreds of additional flak guns were erected around the *Hydriesfestungen*, as the plants became known, and workers, who now came under the direct supervision of the SS, built deep shelters in which to take cover during air raids. Plants quickly demonstrated a remarkable ability to regain full production and between bombing raids were able to produce 19,000 tons during October (39,000 tons in November). By this time the Luftwaffe had only 360 fighters and pilots available for combat duty in *I./Jagdkorps*, 90 of which were in action against the US air forces. On 7 October 52 bombers and 15 fighters were destroyed for the loss of 20 German pilots KIA and 4 injured.
4. On the final raid, on 30 November, 29 American bombers and 40 fighters were shot down. Between 8 October–2 November 1944, the Luftwaffe, in an effort to regroup and to conserve forces for Adolf Galland's proposed *Grosse Schlag*, largely avoided combat with the bomber formations. Only on 2 November, fighter forces were again hurled *en masse* against the Eighth Air Force attacking oil plants in central Germany, notably Leuna. However, of the 490 fighters in action that day, 120 were shot down, 780 pilots surviving. 40 bombers FTR, 30 of which were destroyed by Fw 190s of *Sturm Gruppen* IV./JG 3 and II./JG 4, who lost 30 of their 61 aircraft dispatched – almost a 50% loss rate. While raids on oil centres did not noticeably diminish the Luftwaffe's fighter capacity, it seriously hampered He 177 bombing operations in the east, so although Doolittle's oil raids were not directly aiding the Eighth, they were helping to shorten the war. Ironically, the only units not greatly affected by the oil campaign were the Me 262 *Jagdverbande*, which used the low-grade petrol still in abundance. During September Hitler had reconsidered the Me 262's role as a fighter rather than the fighter-bomber he had once envisaged. 40 were immediately formed into a fighter unit, commanded by the Austrian fighter ace, Major Walter Nowotny. Kommando Nowotny, as it was known, became operational in October 1944 and, during the first month of operations, shot down an estimated 22 American bombers.
5. The 91st lost 12 Fortresses. It was for his actions this day that 2nd Lieutenant Robert E Femoyer, a navigator in the 447th Bomb Group, was posthumously awarded the Medal of Honor. Femoyer's B-17 was rocked by three flak bursts, which showered the aircraft with shrapnel. Femoyer was hit in the back and the side of his body but refused all aid despite his terrible wounds so that he might navigate the Fortress back to Rattlesden. He was propped up in his seat to enable him to read his charts and the crew did what they could for him. It was not until they reached the North Sea that Femoyer agreed to an injection of morphia. He died shortly after the aircraft landed.

6. Six were KIA and five PoW. 'Lieutenant James "Jim" Muise, navigator, landed just prior to me unhurt except he was also bleeding from the nose and ears because of the explosion and ran over and spilled the air out of my 'chute and got me unbuckled from it. Sergeant Alfred Atkins, tail gunner managed to jump out of the plane but the rest were blown out. Five of the 11-man crew survived the explosion but all landed far apart with the exception of Muise and me. The last I saw of my three crewmembers was when I was put in jail that night in a small town called Hemsbach.'
7. B-17 44-6290 in the 836th Bomb Squadron, flown by 2nd Lieutenant Joseph I Herring. 2 KIA, 7 PoW.
8. A beacon combination with *H_2X*.
9. It was the largest air and ground co-operative effort to date when over 4,000 Allied aircraft dropped more than 10,000 tons of bombs on enemy targets.
10. The Eighth lost four B-24s and 15 fighters on the Hamburg raid.
11. 'Bill Meyer inherited *The Witch* from us and early in January 1945 they caught a direct burst and exploded in the air with no survivors. *The Witch* must have done close to 80 missions when it went down.'
12. Lieutenant Owen W Winters (who shared the same hut as Voss) and the entire crew of 42-97985, except for the tail gunner, who was seriously hurt, were killed. The crew of 44-8177 crash-landed and were uninjured.
13. Only one man in the 9-man crew survived to be taken prisoner of war.

Chapter 9

Days of Reckoning

We arrived at Molesworth but had several weeks of waiting to be called into action. We were members of Lieutenant Denison's crew. On our first day at the barracks someone's first remark was, 'When did the men in this empty barracks go home?' A voice called out, 'They didn't go home; they're visiting Germany as guests of the Germans, or else they're dead. You rookies look around and pick out a bed.' It was a very quiet time after that. None of us ever knew if the 'old timers' were pulling our leg and we didn't ask. Six of our crew finished thirty-five missions in fifty-seven days, ending on 25 April 1945. Chuck Haynes our co-pilot was hit by flak over Berlin and lost his foot from flak damage. Three trips to Berlin were plenty for all of us. We always had lots of 'black' flak. The third man to drop from our crew got drunk and tried to break into the Red Cross barracks.

Walter 'Don' O'Hearn, tail gunner, El Screamo,
427th Squadron, 303rd Bomb Group

The run to Minden where a canal crosses a river was one that Robert H Tays, the Texan Liberator pilot in the 392nd Bomb Group, wanted to see. During his teenage years in rural New Braunfels, where those without electricity used crystal sets for radio and slow mail for newspapers, teenage thoughts included Model T's, Model A's, girls, school, drive-ins, getting a job and surviving in a dollar-a-day economy. In a world where there was little or no money, he constantly sought new entertainment that might be cost free. The Comal River and the rapids and all the 'beautiful activities at Camp Warneke' did this 'exceedingly well'. The Rapids provided a continuing challenge to good swimmers and entertained the steady stream of tourists to that vacation Mecca. They were always on his mind. They were probably in his thoughts, as he set out across the North Sea for Minden where the bridge carrying the water in the canal was to be destroyed, thereby draining the canal, making it useless and at the same time flooding the river below. The Liberators hit the aqueduct but the formation turned off target in a direction so that

Tays could not see. 'Mission accomplished,' he wrote, 'That's always the important thing.'

But by this stage in the war, coming home exhausted after every mission, war and death and destruction just did not seem to make sense to him anymore. One evening instead of singing and whooping it up at the bar, as was his custom, he chose a table off in the corner to be by himself. His friend, Father McDonough, came over with a drink having noticed the change in the young pilot. Tays told him his problem and asked for help. At Wendling no matter what the mission, the time or the weather, Father McDonough and Reverend Clark, the other chaplain on the base, were always at the take-off end of the runway for take-offs or returning missions. They seemed to be everywhere for both officers and enlisted alike. Both were easy to talk to and both liked to party, Clark playing the piano and McDonough leading the singing. Both would take time and patience to listen to men's problems privately and offer solutions.

Father McDonough was silent for some time, contemplating the drinks and the Texan's problem. Then he looked him square in the eye and said, 'Tays, all of the major religions in the world have as their primary mission to teach man to live in peace and harmony with his fellow man. When I do not do my job as a man of the cloth then you will have to do your job as a soldier.'

It was not the first time that Tays had sought 'patience and wonderful guidance' from an elder. Upon graduation from high school young Tays had gone to work for Mr Paul Bielstein at his service station for a year on a wage of $5.00 a week with every other Sunday off. Mr Bielstein was a veteran of the First World War and would from time to time comment on world conditions and try to make him aware of what the consequences might be. Tays would always be indebted to Mr and Mrs Bielstein for introducing him to meeting the buying public and providing endless meaningful and worthy experiences never taught in school.

Father McDonough's wisdom shocked Tays into reality and it held him on a meaningful course from that day forward.[1]

After a two-day stand down, missions resumed on 9 December when almost 400 B-17s bombed two airfields and a marshalling yard in the Stuttgart area while seven fighter groups escorted the bombers and strafed transportation targets. Next day, over 450 bombers supported by ten fighter groups attacked the marshalling yards at Bingen and Koblenz-Lutzel and several targets of opportunity. Two other fighter groups swept the area east of the target. There was no let up on 11 December when over 1,400 heavies attacked marshalling yards at Frankfurt–Main, Hanau and Giessen, and road and rail bridges at Mannheim and Maximilliansau.

Lieutenant Ken 'Deacon' Jones, a pilot in the 567th Bomb Squadron, 389th Bomb Group had begun flying missions from Hethel in November. Growing up in Janesville, a little Wisconsin sugar beet town with 23,000 population, the hub for surrounding farm communities, his main interest was raising and racing homing pigeons. As a good Methodist boy, he did not smoke or chew or go with girls that do. His contact with girls was the monthly meetings of the Epworth League. Some times they would go roller-skating and hold hands. Then everything changed. The Japanese bombed Pearl Harbor on 7 December 1941 while he was a senior in high school. Two of his cousins were on the USS *Arizona* – one died and one survived. In May 1942, US troops on Bataan surrendered to the Japanese. Before his class of 1942 graduated, ninety-three Janesville members of the 32nd Tank Battalion took part in the Bataan Death March. The class of '42 was anxious to help their older brothers in the war and Jones wanted to be an airplane driver. He successfully passed the aviation cadet exam and was sworn in on 29 November 1942. He would not be called to duty for six months. But the President sent greetings after one month. Instructions were to report to a Chicago reception centre on 30 January 1943. Kenny Jones, civilian/soldier was soon to become Aviation Cadet Jones on the stairway to the stars. This was heady stuff:

> There was a large crowd of enlistees and draftees at the north-western train depot. All were taking the same train to their destiny. My parents, brother and sisters were there to say 'So long' on January 30th. Mom kissed me and cried. Dad shook my hand. In the back of his head he was thinking 'this 18-year-old son was all that stood between him and that mad man Adolph Hitler.' The first letter I received in service from my sister had some inferences that God was watching over me at the train depot. The conductor called 'All Aboard' so I edged forward to get on the train. I had a lump in my throat and a tear in my eye. A female voice called out, 'Ken, wait a minute.' Out of the crowd came this beautiful, long stemmed American Beauty. She took hold of me and planted a big wet kiss right in my mouth. Glamorous Helen Kathleen pressed me close in a bear hug. I could smell her perfumed hair. She was crying and she whispered in my ear, 'Come home safe, Ken.' What a send-off! With Glen Miller's band playing *Moonlight Serenade* in my head, I sat down on the train. A guy in the next seat started talking to me. I didn't hear his words as I was sorting out my feelings. He probably felt I just fell off the turnip truck. It was sad to leave home for the first time. I was still enjoying the thrill of Helen's lips on mine. Now a kiss is not a contract. But it is close to a promise. I spent the next year and one half thinking and dreaming about Helen waiting for me in turnip country.

> In the US Army Air Force, Tactical Officers with sharp teeth screamed, 'Are you on the ball, Mister? Are you an eager beaver?' After fifteen months of anxiety and exhausting training, we graduated from Advanced Flying School with the class of 44D in April 1944. We got our first seven-day leave. I was homesick. I wanted to show Helen the new silver wings and gold bars. Helen was the only young lady who ever waved good-bye to me with a wet hanky.[2]

On 11 December 'Deacon' Jones' crew were among those at Hethel who were awakened for a raid on the railway bridge at Karlsruhe, Germany. Jones recalls the ritual:

> Most combat crewmembers became superstitious. Each man performed a ritual to bring him home safe. You were 'alerted' the afternoon before a mission that you are scheduled for a flight to Germany the next morning. The notice was posted on the bulletin board at your squadron headquarters. The 'word' spread fast on the moccasin telegraph among crewmembers. That same evening things were quiet in the living quarters, called either a 'Penthouse' or a 'Goat Barn'. Some compared the atmosphere to a Civil War song: 'Just Before the Battle Mother, I'm Thinking Most of You.' There was no clowning around. In this subdued climate one Yank said it was like Death Row with the prisoner waiting for his name to be called. Nobody could sleep.
>
> The thing that I remember most is that I was totally exhausted all the time. The intense sleep deprivation took its toll on you mentally and physically. My favorite pastime was 'sack time'. I would dream of going home and sleeping for a month on a real mattress.
>
> Each man had his own ritual, which he performed the night before going to the Fatherland. If part of the ritual was omitted or a symbol was missing, bad luck would come to a crewman. Some lucky charms were clothing such as a pair of sox or a scarf. These charms ware never washed because soap and water removed the luck contained therein. My ritual was to write a letter home and to put a hunting knife in one of my shoes. A clip of ammo was slapped in the .45 caliber pistol and it was placed in a jacket pocket. Then I read a couple of pages from a Daily Devotions booklet. The last step was to go to bed, to roll and toss until the batman shone his light in my face at 3.00 am. A January directive ordered crews to turn in their pistols. Our crew was a holdout. An irate Major gave our crew until 11.00 hours to comply or be court-martialled. The Big Brass bean counters broke the magic of our ritual. We felt naked and no general officer would hold our hand on the way down if we had to bail out over the Third Reich.

There are no atheists in combat. Each bomb run began with, 'Our Father Who Art in Heaven.' The tour and the ordeal were thirty-five missions for wingmen and thirty for lead crews. On the bomb run at Karlsruhe, between layers of dense clouds, we were flying a tight formation in the high right element of the High Right Squadron. A straggler from another combat wing joined our squadron in the slot, slightly low and to our left on the bomb run. There was an ugly box barrage over the target. We assumed later that the tracking flak was locked on the straggler leading them to our squadron, as we had been dumping *chaff*. The straggler took a direct hit with the first four gun salvo and he disappeared in a big orange ball of flame. Our B-24 was rocked by the explosion of gas and bombs and we were showered with bits of debris. The next four gun bursts straddled our bomber, starting low on the left and stepped up, the fourth burst was just overhead and to the right. This occurred precisely at bombs away. We instantly lost both No. 1 and No. 2 engines but gained 200 fresh air vents in our shiny, new bomber. There was one large hole in the left main tank where an 88mm shell went straight through the wing. The exploding 88s caused the left wing to rise up and throw us to the right. The wing came down and we couldn't control the airplane with full rudder and aileron. We skidded toward other bombers in the squadron.

I reversed controls. We went over on our back and I pulled off the power. We did a split-S out of the formation and disappeared into the clouds in an uncontrollable spin from 23,000ft. We lost over 10,000ft and both pilots had both feet on the opposite rudder. After an eternity, the rotation stopped and we were diving at over 350 mph. It took another eternity and super human strength of both pilots to pull out of the dive. This was accomplished on instruments using needle, ball and airspeed because the gyros had tumbled on the other flight instruments. I don't remember how low we were when we pulled out of the dive. We were in the soup and I vaguely recall smelling the odor of *Veeners undt sauerkraut* some *hausfrau* was cooking for the *Herrenvolk*.

There were no injuries but our navigator, Wiley 'Pat' Patterson, had his throat mike shaved from his throat by a piece of flak. In a panic after the spin, Patterson said, 'To hell with all this glory,' and he sat down to bail out of the nose wheel door opening. Bombardier Joe Grady grabbed Patterson by the collar and yelled that the pilot said, 'Stay with the ship' because we're still over Germany. And, more importantly, Patterson in his haste had neglected to snap on his parachute. Patterson lost one of his flying boots in the frigid slipstream and froze his foot. Grady took off one of his heated gloves and put Patterson's foot in the heated glove to thaw out the frozen foot. No. 2 prop was windmilling and couldn't be feathered. No. 1

had the turbo shot off but we were able to restart No. 1 engine. No. 1 then had a runaway prop and eventually the toggle switch worked just once to control the runaway prop and high cylinder-head temperature. Due to extreme inclement weather we could not make a forced landing anywhere on the continent, including occupied territory. We came all the way home on 2½ engines, on instruments. God Bless the mighty B-24, the Queen of the skies.[3]

The togetherness of military life was suffocating at times. You slept in a crowd, ate meals elbow to elbow, trained in a group, shaved and showered together. There were no hidden secrets or birthmarks. No chance to look back or ahead. There was only a yearning for a few moments of solitude. A 48-hour pass to Norwich. Sign in at the Red Cross and for a pittance of a shilling, you got a folding cot with clean sheets, a lingering hot bath before noon and you could shave with warm water. Slap on a little Lilac Vegital shaving lotion, then plot a course to 'arry's Pub, the 'Walnut Tree Shades'. 'Having a go' at a pint of 'alf and 'alf. Running into Bob Wexler from my home town made this day memorable.

A group of obsoletes and a Queen at the afternoon Red Cross dance. I made a bomb run on the Queen – a target of opportunity. She stared at the burn mark on my face. She agreed to dance but she was waiting for a Major. Outranked again! Made her smile while she shared a tender moment with a lonely Junior Birdman. It was not like dancing with a member of the aircrew. Her clothes didn't smell like they were cleaned in 100 octane. Leaving a slightly bruised male ego behind, I went to eat. With falling darkness, I made a solo flight to 'Charing Cross' pub on the outskirts of town. It had an outdoor shindilly. On a course correction, an Englishman told me I'd have to bear left or I'd overshoot the landing. 'Charing Cross' was one of the main hangouts for B-17 and B-24 crews. An evening of false gaiety, wassail and singing old songs at the piano: 'Send me twice a day to the coast of Calais but don't send me over the Ruhr.' Coming all to soon was the ceremony of placing the towel over the ceramic pump handle and announcing 'The monkey is on the tap' and 'Time gentlemen' at the 10 pm closing. Time was precious. We drank a lot – and fast. New friends flew a loose formation through an alcoholic haze and the blackout. We sang the Wiffenpoof Song: 'We are poor little lambs who have lost their way.' Upstairs at the Red Cross, we tip toed into the large dormitory. After several tries, I found my cot, and slept all night for the first time in weeks.

Waking early, I had the luxury of another bath. Going downstairs, I followed my nose to a Red Cross gal making coffee and doughnuts. In the Rec room, I started writing a letter home using a Parker Pen that didn't leak in my breast pocket at altitude. Outside the window, snow covered the ground. The sun was shining after weeks of fog

> and overcast, church bells were chiming. It was Sunday. The distant sound of big Pratt and Whitney engines was a reminder that this was just another working day. I walked to the window. The graceful Liberators were circling Buncher 6 at 8,000 feet. The elements became squadrons, then a group and then a combat wing box. Soon the Libs were strung out on the division assembly line with Forts and one thousand ships were climbing for altitude and heading easterly. It was an awe-inspiring sight while standing in the homeland (sic) of the late RAF pilot, John Gillespie Magee, author of *High Flight*. With the sun warming my face, I had pangs of guilt but not a death wish. My mental outlook was conditioned to the sky – the wild blue yonder. I felt drawn as a kindred spirit to those anxious comrades bound for Germany – bursting flak and swift fighters. Wings aloft – the sun reflecting off shiny metal. Praying for them out loud, I said, 'God go with you.' I just knew they would all come back and if they didn't, somehow it would be all right.
>
> A motherly, English, Red Cross lady suggested the young 'Leftenant' might find forgiveness for his sinful ways by going to the house of the Lord and a church service at the Norwich Cathedral. I did. The Glory of East Anglia dating from 1096. A huge edifice; high vaulting canopies, hundreds of statuary and fantastic medieval art. Leaving the church after a tour, I explored the ancient graveyard. Nurse Edith Cavell is buried there. I walked around Norwich on a mild winter day. Walking seemed to ease the tension in me. The bombing mission would be returning in late afternoon. Cutting the pass short, I went to the Haymarket and caught an early ride back to the base to help sweat the big birds home.[4]

On 12 December almost 1,200 heavies raided more marshalling yards and the Merseburg–Leuna synthetic-oil plant among other targets. Next day over 200 B-17s were recalled *en route* to their targets in Germany when the weather grounded the fighter escort. No missions were flown on the 14th, but on 15 December almost 650 heavies escorted by eleven fighter groups bombed the marshalling yards at Hanover and Kassel and the tank factory in the town. On 16 December, when over 100 B-17s supported by three fighter groups bombed Stuttgart marshalling yard and other targets, Field Marshal Karl von Rundstedt and his panzer formations, using appalling weather conditions to their advantage, attacked American positions in the forests of the Ardennes on the French–Belgian border. They soon opened up a salient or 'bulge' in the Allied lines supported by an estimated 1,400 fighters in twelve *Geschwader*. The Allied air forces were grounded by fog and it was not until the 23rd that the fog lifted sufficiently to allow 400 B-17s and B-24s to be despatched to strike communication lines behind the Ardennes area and offer some hope to the hard-pressed infantry divisions in 'The Bulge'.[5]

Doolittle wanted to throw as much weight as he could against the German airfields to prevent any missions being flown by the Luftwaffe in support of the German land forces in the Ardennes. On Christmas Eve 1944 the Field Order at all bases called for a maximum effort, which most groups achieved by putting up all available aircraft, including war-wearies and even assembly ships. At Rackheath a record sixty-one Liberators, including *Pete The POM Inspector* (the group's unarmed assembly ship), were airborne in only thirty minutes. Lieutenant Charles McMahon, a 'Happy Warrior' pilot now on the Group Operations staff, who had decided to risk one last mission, flew *Pete*. He came through safely though his aircraft was armed only with carbines in the waist positions. Controllers had to work overtime at some 3rd Bomb Division bases that were still congested with 1st Division Fortresses. Many had landed there after the mission of 23 December when their home bases had been 'socked in'. Visibility was still poor and led to many accidents during take-off. At Podington, for instance, Lieutenant Robert K Seeber's Fortress crashed into a wood about 200 yards to the left of the runway. The wood had not been visible during take-off because of the thick fog. About two minutes later Seeber's B-17 exploded, killing six of the crew. At Glatton the 457th managed to get six aircraft off in reduced visibility but the seventh crashed at the end of the runway and operations were brought to a halt for a time. Despite these setbacks the Eighth was able to mount its largest single attack in history, with 2,034 heavies participating. In addition, 500 RAF and Ninth Air Force bombers participated in this, the greatest single aerial armada the world has ever seen. The 1st Division would be involved in a direct tactical assault on airfields in the Frankfurt area and on lines of communication immediately behind the German 'Bulge'. Crews were told that their route was planned on purpose to go over the ground troops' positions for morale purposes.

Brigadier General Fred Castle, former CO of the 94th Bomb Group and now commander of the 4th Wing, drove to Lavenham airfield and elected to fly in the 487th formation to lead the 3rd Bomb Division on what was his thirtieth mission. In his pocket was a thirty-day leave order. Soon, Castle was in the air, flying with Lieutenant Robert W Harriman and crew in *Treble Four*.[6] All went well until 23,000ft over Belgium, about 35 miles from Liège, his right outboard engine burst into flame and the propeller had to be feathered. The deputy lead ship took over and Castle dropped down to 20,000ft. At this height *Treble Four* began vibrating badly and he was forced to take it down another 3,000ft before levelling out. The Fortress was now down to 180mph indicated air speed and being pursued by seven Bf 109s of IV./JG 3. They attacked and wounded the tail gunner and left the radar navigator nursing bad wounds in his neck and shoulders. Castle could not carry out any evasive manouevres with the full bomb load still aboard and he could not jettison them for fear of hitting Allied troops on the ground. Successive attacks by the fighters put another two engines out of action and the B-17 lost altitude. To reduce airspeed the wheels of the Fortress were lowered and the crew ordered to bale out with the terse intercom message, 'This is it boys.' Castle managed to level out, long enough for six of the crew to bale out but at 12,000ft the bomber was hit in the right wing fuel tank and oxygen systems, which set the aircraft on fire, sending the B-17 into a plunging final spiral to the ground. Castle attempted to land the flaming bomber in an open field close to the Allied lines but nearing the ground *Treble Four* went into a spin and exploded on impact.[7]

Navigator 1st Lieutenant Lawrence W 'Ras' Rasmussen flew his twelfth mission in the 493rd Bomb Group on this, 'the maximum effort of all maximum efforts'. He noted that:

> With the German push shielded by three days of fog – a CAVU day called for this. Our bomber stream left Felixstowe after tooling around England all morning – went south of Liège, caught quite accurate flak over the lines – one burst enveloped the ship – caught flak all the way to the IP east of the target. We dropped twelve 500lb Navy incendiary explosive bombs on an airfield southwest of Darmstadt – hangars and installations on north side of field – CAVU all the way, I saw the bombs hit the target through my B-3 drift-master – what a sight! Returned through corridor south of St. Coar. It took us more than 9 hours – took off in dark and landed in dark – never seen so many airplanes in all my life – everything from heavies, mediums, lights and pursuits – gunners claimed they saw a P-51 shoot up a jet and another Me 109. Rest of group went to Frankfurt. We were complimented on the good work. This is Christmas Eve – very tired so hitting the sack.[8]

Overall, the Christmas Eve raids were effective and severely hampered von Rundstedt's lines of communication. The cost in aircraft, though, was high. Many crashed during their return over England as drizzle and overcast played havoc with landing patterns. Tired crews put down where they could. Any who felt like joining in the festive spirit on the bases were disappointed because another strike was ordered for Boxing Day, 26 December. Ground crews worked right around the clock but it was all in vain. The weather and the widely dispersed groups resulted in only 150 aircraft being dispatched. The following day the wintry conditions were responsible for a succession of crashes during early morning take-offs. Max Stout, a co-pilot in the 453rd Bomb Group at Old Buckenham, recalls:

> We were to be the first plane off. It was an instrument take-off. We were late to taxi and when we arrived, a new crew was lined up to take off. Being a new crew in the 733rd I suppose they were eager

> to show their mettle. The order of take-off wasn't all that important. Lieutenant Brown hurtled down the salt strewn, slippery runway. The B-24 refused to rise more than a few feet and crashed near the edge of the field. Three gunners scrambled clear before the bomb load exploded in three terrific explosions. The mission was scrubbed with no more planes taking off.

Eighth Air Force HQ was only too aware of the problems confronting the bomber groups but despite the dangerous conditions, the mission of 29 December had to go ahead. On 30 December more than 1,000 heavies again bombed lines of communication and on the 31st the 1st Bomb Division kept up the attacks while 3rd Division crews returned to oil production centres. Crews in the 4th and 13th Wings were assigned Hamburg, which was the scene of another disaster for the 'Bloody Hundredth', which lost twelve B-17s to JG 300 and to flak over the target; half the total borne by the entire 3rd Division.

The USSTAF was clearly winning the battle of attrition in the war against the Luftwaffe, as trained fighter pilots at this stage of the war were impossible to replace.[9] January 1945 marked the Eighth's third year of operations and it seemed as if the end of the war was in sight. On 1 January the 1st Air Division (this day the prefix 'Bomb' was officially changed to 'Air') encountered enemy fighters in some strength during raids on the tank factory at Kassel, an oil refinery at Magdeburg and marshalling yards at Dillenburg. The Magdeburg force came under heavy fighter attack while the Kassel force was badly hit by flak. The Luftwaffe however, was still far from defeated. The *Jagdverband* had made a few concerted attempts at turning back the bombers late in 1944 but on each occasion they had been beaten off with heavy losses inflicted by escorting P-51 Mustangs and P-47 Thunderbolts. On 2 November the Mustangs routed their German attackers and the 352nd Fighter Group established a record thirty-eight kills on that occasion. Despite losses on this scale the Luftwaffe could still be relied upon to make a major effort against the heavies, and *Unternehmen Bodenplatte*, a desperate gamble to diminish the overwhelming Allied air superiority, was mounted at about 09.00 hours on New Year's Day 1945. The aim was to deliver a single, decisive, blow against RAF and American aircraft on the ground in Holland, Belgium and Northern France using 875 single-engined fighter aircraft, primarily in support of von Rundstedt's Ardennes offensive. The outcome though was far different. Though total Allied aircraft losses during *Bodenplatte* amounted to 424 destroyed or heavily damaged the Luftwaffe losses were catastrophic.[10]

The big gamble had turned into a disastrous defeat. The Wehrmacht advance in the Ardennes came to a halt and ultimately petered out. In the east the Red Army prepared for the great winter offensive, which would see the capture of Warsaw and Krakow and take the Soviets across the German border. Germany had no reserves left. Hitler's last chance now lay in his so-called 'wonder weapons': the V-1 and V-2.

On 2 January 1945 the Eighth once again pounded lines of communication, and raids of this nature continued for several days until the position in the Ardennes gradually swung in the Allies' favour. There was no respite but for once the general 'bitching' on the bases ceased when it was learned that General Ben Lear had been newly appointed to the ETO. Ground crews went about their daily chores with a new greeting, 'Whattya hear from Lear?' connecting the appointment with an announcement that ground personnel would be drawn from the bomb groups as replacement infantry for invalided men who fought in 'the Bulge'. This added to the administrative problems on the bases while the 'ground pounders' began to realize that life in a bomb group was not so bad after all.

On 3 January Norman Andrew in the 487th Bomb Group flew his nineteenth mission of his tour when almost 1,100 heavies escorted by eleven fighter groups bombed targets in western Germany. Eleven of the objectives were marshalling yards and the 487th went to Aschaffenburg. Andrew wrote:

> What a long day! Up at 03.00. PFF. Our new CO, Colonel [William K] Martin [who had taken command on 28 December] rode with us. We led the low. And finally, I really got some help from Lieutenant Wilkinson, pilotage navigator. It was solid 10/10th all the way so he ran the *Gee* box. I plotted the fixes and had time to really navigate. I also gave 'Whit' a workout on his *Mickey* set when we ran out of range of the Rheims Chain. It was a long drawn-out mission – but an easy one. Entered France at Calais and skirted the Belgium–France border to the Rhine just north of Saarburg. Turned north to the target just 23 miles SE of Frankfurt. The only flak we had was four bursts from Stuttgart and that was about a mile off our right wing. The lead didn't drop on the primary but hit the secondary – marshaling yards at Pforzheim, Germany. They almost ran us into the Heidelberg flak. I took the low way to the left and rejoined them after they bombed. Milk run – only eleven, maybe ten to go. The Colonel told us it was nice navigating and the pilotage navigator (27 missions) told Jack that I was the best he had ever ridden with. Bashful, aren't I?

On 5 January the severe wintry weather over England was responsible for several fatal accidents during take-off for a mission to Frankfurt. Snow flurries swirled around the runways and at Mendlesham a 34th Bomb Group Fortress came to grief while attempting to depart. The conditions were also responsible for a mid-air collision in the vicinity of Thorpe Abbotts. A period of fine weather, beginning on 6 January, when more than 750 heavy bombers attacked marshalling yards and bridges and targets of opportunity, enabled the heavies to fly missions in support of the ground troops once more. Missions were flown to tactical targets when the weather permitted, and when it turned bad the Eighth mounted shallow penetration raids to *Noball* targets in France. On Sunday 14 January the Eighth Air Force despatched over 650 bombers supported by fifteen fighter groups to mainly oil and other targets in central and northwestern Germany. A smaller force of 187 Fortresses in the 1st Division, escorted by forty-two Mustangs and preceded by a sweep of the area by sixty-two Thunderbolts, attacked the Rhine bridges at Cologne. The 467th Bomb Group went to the Hallendorf steelworks west of Berlin.

For *Witchcraft*, one of the most famous of all Liberators, it was her 100th mission, all without once turning back. A newspaper reporter flew in *Witchcraft* to cover the unique event. The Liberator went on to fly thirty more missions and no crewmembers were killed or wounded and the aircraft never returned to Rackheath without first bombing its target. By the same token *Lassie Come Home*, a Liberator in the 458th Bomb Group at nearby Horsham St. Faith, was an unlucky ship. It returned from the 14 January mission to the Hermann Goering Works at Halle with one engine stopped and its landing gear down. The pilot, who was on only his third mission, banked into his dead engine. He lost a second engine and crashed upside down on a housing estate near the base, killing the crew and two children who had been playing in a garden.

On 16 January over 550 heavies supported by thirteen fighter groups bombed two synthetic-oil plants, two aircraft engine plants and other targets in central Germany. At Lavenham lead navigator Norman K Andrew prepared to fly his twenty-second mission. He wrote:

> The CQ came in at 03.00 but I was awake. Target: Dessau, Germany. Off the ground 09.05. What a Cook's Tour it was. In over Holland and the Zuider Zee – north of Hanover and Magdeburg. Target: East of Leipzig – Schweinfurt. Over the Rhine River at Strasbourg. At this point we had our only flak – it was one gun (?) at the front lines. The bomber stream was about 5 miles wide and he had so many targets he couldn't make up his mind. Finally hit a ship, wounded two men. Returned to base – but was diverted to a RAF field at Finningley 120 miles north. We started running out of gas at Peterborough so we came down. Landed at Glatton. Travelled over 1,400 miles over five countries.

On 17 January more than 650 heavies supported by eight fighter groups flying close escort and three more flying area sweeps bombed three oil refineries and other targets in northwestern Germany. Next day only 100 B-17s supported by three fighter groups flew bomber sorties, attacking the marshalling yards at Kaiserlautern. After the bombing most of the Fortresses were diverted to bases on the continent because of heavy clouds. Norman K Andrew flew his twenty-third mission:

> Was I surprised this morning! The CQ woke me at 02.45 for target study. I had him check his list three times to be sure he was right. Target: Kaiserlautern, Germany. There were three groups of us in the 4th Wing going. They scrubbed the 1st, 2nd and all of the 3rd Divisions but us. At briefing they told us we would probably be diverted. At the target we (the low) and the high dropped first run. It was supposed to be cat and mouse – but the cat beacon did not have the code sheet delay. We dropped PFF and I had a *Gee* fix just 2½ miles short of the marshaling yards. The Air Leader with us wanted to circle the RP while the lead squadron made a second run. Bandits had been reported in the area and there was no flak at the target – so I said, Hell no – make a 2nd run with the high and lead. Then he told me the high had dropped so we went back over France and waited for them. On the way back we were diverted to Laon Couvron airfield, France. The soup was from 11,000 down to the ground. We made individual letdowns. What a nightmare! Couvron was full so we landed at Laon Athies A/F. The ground pounders were betting even money that at least one B-17 would crash – but no one did.

Because of the weather the Liberators were prevented from flying a mission but at Wendling the 392nd Bomb Group CO, Colonel Lorin L Johnson, ordered a practice mission, which, opined Quintin R Wedgeworth, a navigator in the 578th Bomb Squadron, 'was in complete disregard for the weather.' He added, 'Lieutenant [J C] Decker and crew, from the 577th, disappeared during the snowstorm and were never heard from again. More victims of the North Sea, no doubt!'[11]

By 3 February 1945 Marshal Zhukov's Red Army was only 35 miles from Berlin and the capital was jammed with refugees fleeing from the advancing Russians. This day's strike against railroad stations and freight yards was designed to cause the German authorities as much havoc as possible. Major Robert 'Rosie' Rosenthal, flying his fifty-second mission, led the 100th Bomb Group and the 3rd Division, General Earle E Partridge having approved the selection of a squadron commander to lead the division.[12] The Eighth lost twenty-one bombers over the capital and another six crash-landed inside the Russian lines. The B-17 flown by Major Rosenthal, flying with Captain John Ernst, was hit in the No. 1 gas tank and the bomb bay a few seconds before bombs away and the crew baled out after the bombs were dropped.[13] Of the bombers that returned, ninety-three had suffered varying forms of major flak damage. Among the losses had been *Birmingham Jewel* in the 379th Bomb Group, which had set an Eighth Air Force record of 128 missions.

Further disruption of German defences in the face of the Russian advance occurred on 6 February, when 1,300 heavies, escorted by fifteen groups of P-51 Mustangs, bombed Chemnitz and Magdeburg and the Eighth resumed its oil offensive with raids on synthetic-oil refineries at Lutzkendorf and Merseburg. Bad weather forced all except one 1st Air Division Fortress to return to England while over the North Sea. Altogether, twenty-two bombers were lost in crash landings in England. The sole B-17 continued to Essen and dumped its load before returning home alone without meeting any opposition. Such an occurrence would have been unthinkable a few months before but now the Luftwaffe had been all but swept from the skies. On 9 February 1,200 heavies operating in six forces attacked Rothensee and Lutzkendorf synthetic-oil plants and other targets supported by fifteen fighter groups, six of which later strafed rail and road targets. On 10 February the heavies returned to the ever-diminishing Reich, now seriously threatened by the Russian armies converging from the east. Some 150 B-17s bombed the Dulmen oil depot at the town of Lingen and the E-boat pens at Ijmuiden in Holland, where the first raid using 'Disney' bombs went ahead. The 4,500lb bomb invented by Captain Edward Terrell of the Royal Navy was powered by a rocket motor in the tail and was designed to pierce 20ft of concrete before exploding. Their weight prevented carriage in the bomb bay of a B-17 so the nine B-17s in the 92nd Bomb Group, which were dispatched to Ijmuiden, carried two 'Disneys' under each wing. Colonel James W Wilson, the CO, led the raid and strike photos were later to reveal a direct hit at the north end of the pens. Part of the E-boat shelters had also been hit where a final portion of the roof had not yet been laid, destroying a large section of the structure over three pens and damaging the north wall.[14]

Operation *Thunderclap* should have begun on 13 February with a raid by the Eighth Air Force on the old city of Dresden in eastern Germany but the weather prevented the strike going ahead. However, that night RAF Bomber Command carried out a two-fold attack on the city. So great were the conflagrations caused by the firestorms created in the first attack that crews in the second attack reported the glow was visible 200 miles from the target. In a follow up raid, shortly after 12 noon on 14 February, the Eighth Air Force despatched nearly 1,300 bombers to attack marshalling yards at Dresden and other targets. From this total, 450 B-17s were sent to Dresden. Flying his first mission this day was William C Stewart, a ball turret gunner in the 92nd Bomb Group at Podington who had never heard of this German city before.[15] On 14 February almost 1,300 heavy bombers attacked marshalling yards at Dresden, Chemnitz, Magdeburg and Hof as well as other targets at Wesel, Dulmen, two airfields and ten town areas. Sixteen fighter groups escorted the bombers or flew area sweeps strafing ground targets. The Mustangs also engaged seventy-five enemy fighters and claimed twenty destroyed. On the 15th over 1,000 heavies bombed the Magdeburg synthetic-oil plant and marshalling yards at Dresden, Cottbus and Rheine and several targets of opportunity. Nine fighter groups flew escort for the bombers and they later broke away and strafed transportation targets. Next day almost 1,000 B-17s and B-24s hit benzol plants at Dortmund[16] and Gelsenkirchen and oil refineries at Dortmund and Saltzbergen as well as marshalling yards at Osnabrück, Hamm and Rheine. Wesel railroad bridge was also attacked, as were several secondaries and targets of opportunity. On 21 February more than 1,200 heavies attacked military installations and communications targets at Nürnburg and thirteen other targets of opportunity in the area, supported by ten fighter groups which later strafed ground targets including Hitler's retreat at Berchetsgaden for the first time.

On 22 February, George Washington's birthday, *Clarion*, the systematic destruction of the German communications network, was launched. More than 6,000 Allied aircraft from seven different commands struck at transportation targets throughout western Germany and northern Holland. All targets were selected with the object of preventing troops being transported to the Russian front, now only a few miles from Berlin. It was all part of the strategy worked out at Yalta by the 'Big Three' earlier that same month. The strike was planned by Major General Orvil Anderson, Eighth Air Force Chief of Operations, who said, 'We could lose 300 planes today, but we won't.' Despite the low altitudes flown, five bombers only were lost.[17] *Clarion* ripped the heart out of a crumbling *Reich* and the following two months would witness its bitter conclusion. On 23 February only four heavies failed to return from the 1,274 dispatched. The flak batteries were being deprived of ammunition and gunners had to conserve their meagre reserves. Next day 1,050 heavies attacked four oil refineries, three marshalling yards, shipyards and two rail bridges as well as an industrial area and a city area – all in Germany. Norman K Andrew flew his twenty-ninth and penultimate mission in the 487th Bomb Group on 24 February. The next day, 25 February, when the Eighth put up 1,141 heavies and eleven fighter groups flew close escort, was for him 'Graduation Day!'

> I was almost ashamed to finish up on this one. Except that our primary was visual only. Munich – PFF and the weather was briefed to be 6/10th plus. Also we were given a diversion base in France. What a trip! I rode the bomb aimer's seat. Clouds were 9/10th to Strasbourg. Then 3/10 to 5/10. Had some light accurate front line flak. Twelve o'clock close in at Riegel. Had clouds over the bomb run but about 15 miles out I picked up the target, an underground oil depot on the south banks of the Danube just west of Neuburg. On the way in we wandered off course and nipped Switzerland and

> Austria. Finally Rusty saw the target. All three squadrons put their bombs right on the MPI. Results – good to excellent. I really had an easy day today.

On 26 February 1,102 B-17s and B-24s, supported by fifteen fighter groups, hit three rail stations in Berlin. Even the normally notorious flak defences in Berlin could shoot down only three bombers over Big B. On 28 February 1,104 bombers escorted by 737 fighters, attacked transportation targets in Germany.

By March 1945 the systematic destruction of German oil production plants, airfields and communications centres had virtually driven the Luftwaffe from German skies and the Third Reich was on the brink of defeat. Despite fuel and pilot shortages Me 262 jet fighters could still be expected to put in rare attacks and during March almost all enemy fighter interceptions of American heavy bombers were made by Me 262s of JG 7 *Hindenburg*, by Adolph Galland's *Jagdverband* 44, by EJG 2, led by Oberleutnant Bär and by I.KG(F) 54. However, the German jets and rockets had arrived too late and in too few numbers to prevent the inevitable. On 2 March, 1,159 heavies were despatched to bomb synthetic-oil plants at Bohlen, Ruhland and Magdeburg, two oil refineries at Rositz and Schonebeck and marshalling yards at Chemnitz, Dresden and Magdeburg. Fifteen fighter groups flew 675 effective supporting sorties and parts of these also strafed airfields. Me 262s attacked near Dresden. The Luftwaffe seemed to have found a temporary new lease of life for that night thirty Ju 88s attacked airfields in Norfolk and Suffolk.[18]

On 4 March the B-17s and B-24s headed singly to assembly points over France, adopting a new technique aimed at conserving fuel. The Fortresses formed up at Troyes, while the Liberator groups assembled near Nancy.

The 466th Bomb Group, led by Lieutenant Colonel John Jacobowitz, with Colonel Ligon flying deputy commander in the No. 2 aircraft, led the 96th Wing to its target at Kitzingen after assembly, but thick cloud persisted over the continent and the bomb run was scrubbed. The secondary target at Aschaffenburg was also clouded over, so the call went out to switch to the marshalling yards at Stuttgart, about 80 miles from the Swiss border. Using H_2X, the 466th started a northerly bomb run on the target, but visibility was so poor that crews had difficulty seeing their wingmen. Suddenly, out of the murk roared a group of B-17s, also lost, sending the Liberators scattering wildly in an effort to avert a mid-air collision. The mission was abandoned when twenty B-24s became separated. The remaining eight B-24s, which had retained some semblance of formation, formed up on the lead aircraft and turned for home. In the lead was an H_2X ship, which spotted a town through a hole in the clouds. The lead crew navigator identified it as Frieburg, a town lying a few miles from the Rhine and southwest of Stuttgart. Some navigators suspected that the town might be Basle in Switzerland, which was about 25 miles further south. Frieburg was a target of opportunity and a bomb run was ordered. Several minutes after the bomb run word came through that Basle had been bombed. The order went out for the formation to return to Attlebridge and crews, unaware that they had dropped their bombs on Swiss territory, were to remain in their aircraft until the base vehicles picked them up. News filtered through that the 392nd had also violated neutral territory.

At the turning point south of Stuttgart the 14th Wing received a recall message. The 44th started their turn home and the 392nd followed, although it soon lost the 44th from sight. The 392nd lead squadron, led by Colonel Myron Keilman, made a radar-bombing run on Pforzheim but there was no sign of the second squadron. The 392nd lead squadron returned to England at 13.20. Keilman wrote:

> Shortly after landing, our second squadron returned without apparent difficulty. At their debriefing, the lead crew explained how they got on the outside of the turn and lost us in the cirrus clouds and heavy contrails; that upon breaking out of the clouds they came upon what they believed to be Frieburg and bombed it as a target of opportunity. The debriefing was hardly finished when Colonel Lorin Johnson, the CO, was called to the telephone and a long conflab took place. Zurich, Switzerland, had been bombed.[19]

On 15 March, 1,353 bombers escorted by 833 fighters hit the German Army HQ at Zossen near Berlin and a marshalling yard at Orienburg. Although German jets continued to pose a very real threat, losses from collisions and accidents were often higher than those caused by fighter attacks. On 17 March when 1,328 B-17s and B-24s, escorted by 820 fighters, bombed targets in west and north-central Germany, the 490th Bomb Group was returning from a raid on Bittefeld when they encountered cirrus clouds which forced them to fly on instruments for thirty minutes. The Fortresses moved into tighter formation. Suddenly, a squadron in the 385th Bomb Group cut through the clouds into the 490th formation, causing one of the 490th ships, flown by Lieutenant Arthur Stern, to veer upwards. In no time at all it collided with another 490th B-17, flown by Lieutenant Robert H Tennenberg. The radio room in the lower Fortress took the full force of the collision and the aircraft broke in two. All nine of Stern's crew were killed. In Tennenberg's Fortress, Chester A Deptula, the navigator, dragged the stunned nose gunner, John Gann, from the shattered nose to the radio operator's compartment. Despite a smashed engine, another partly disabled, a wing tip bent, the front of the nose knocked off and the pilot's front view window broken, Tennenberg kept his B-17 airborne and managed to reach Belgium where he made a successful crash-landing. The crewmen stepped out unhurt and surveyed the damage. Among the wreckage was the mutilated torso of a man later identified as the radio operator from the Fortress that had collided with them. He had been forced through the shattered plexiglas nose of Tennenberg's aircraft on impact.

On 18 March a record 1,327 bombers supported by fourteen P-51 groups who flew 645 effective sorties went to Berlin and 1,251 of the B-17s and B-24s got their bombs away over two rail centres and two tank and armament plants in 'Big B'.[20] On 19 March, 1,223 heavy bombers hit marshalling yards at Fulda and Plauen and other targets at Jena and Zwickau as well as airfields and jet aircraft plants. On 21 March preparatory air operations for the forthcoming (23 March) crossing of the lower Rhine by Allied ground forces began. In morning raids 1,254 bombers, in conjunction with aircraft of the RAF and Ninth Air Force attacking other targets, bombed ten airfields in NW Germany, a tank factory at Plauen and a marshalling yard at Reichenbach.[21] In the afternoon ninety B-24s bombed Mülheim an der Ruhr airfield. US fighters flew almost 750 effective sorties in support of the two operations. Philip G Day flew his thirty-fifth and final mission when the 467th Bomb Group made a visual bombing of an airfield near Osnabrück. Day wrote:

> No flak or fighters. Excellent results. After passing over the target we started a left assembly turn and out of the cloudbank to our right, at our altitude and on collision course, popped a group of B-17s. There was grand confusion, a melee of aircraft and a bunch of fright, but all missed and both groups reformed. And so to Rackheath where I greased the B-24 in for the last time, then to debriefing, to critique and to get drunk. The great adventure was finished.

Included in the day's operations was a lone B-17, which was despatched to Oberusel to drop two tons as a *Micro-H* Mk II test. Leutnant Fritz R G Müller of III./JG 7 flying a Me 262 claimed the lone B-17.[22] However, this B-17 does not appear in any loss listings. Müller recalled:

> I took off with a section against a major attack in the area of Leipzig–Dresden. Our radio communications suffered particularly heavy interference on this day. At 7,500 meters I came upon a Boeing flying on an easterly course south of Dresden, separated by about 10 kilometres from the rest of the formation at the same height and escorted by four Mustangs flying above and behind. I assumed that this aircraft had some special duty and decided to attack it. The radio interference was now so heavy that no communication was possible. I passed close below the Mustangs and although they followed my section trailing black smoke (full throttle); my airspeed indicator showed that I no longer had to bother myself about them. The Boeing was now ahead of me in a gentle turn to port and I was

> approaching it at an angle of about 10° from port and about 5° from above. At a range of about 1,000 metres the rear gunner opened continuous fire. What now happened took only seconds. At about 300 metres my wingman and I gave a short burst with a little deflection. We observed about a dozen hits in the fuselage and between the engines of the Boeing – and then we had passed above it. Flying a wide turn (with the Mustangs behind us, trailing black smoke and getting ever smaller) we observed the end of the bomber. It spun for 2,000 metres, several large parts broke away from the fuselage and wings and then it literally burst asunder. All of a sudden the radio interference had ceased. We had received no hits; set course for home and the Mustangs eased the strain on their engines as they realized the pointlessness of any further chase.
>
> The effects of damage to the outer skinning at high speed were enormous. A dislodged, hand-sized piece of plywood from the undercarriage cover lost at 300 metres height and at a speed of 900 kph made the Me 262 suddenly so nose heavy that I was only, and using all my strength, able to pull out just before striking the ground. A strong rushing and rumbling noise made the background music. A harmless hit near the wingtip made a small hole in the slat and a flower-like hole at the exit. The effect: instant turning of the machine around the lateral and longitudinal axis and it seemed that the fuselage would break apart. Again hard work on the control column and rudder pedals. Only after a considerable reduction of speed and trimming out did the machine again become reasonably controllable.[23]

On 22 March, 1,301 B-17s and B-24s bombed targets east of Frankfurt and ten military encampments in the Ruhr in preparation for the forthcoming Allied amphibious crossing of the lower Rhine. The Eighth bombed the Bottrop military barracks and hutted areas directly behind the German lines while 136 B-17s of the Fifteenth Air Force attacked Ruhland again and caused extensive damage to the plant. Twenty-seven Me 262s attacked the bomber formations and claimed thirteen B-17s shot down but only one Fortress was actually lost.[24] Nine fighter groups strafed airfields and P-51s claimed two of the jets destroyed.[25] Next day 1,244 heavies bombed rail targets as part of the rail interdiction program to isolate the Ruhr and cut off coal shipping. Since the loss of the Saar basin the Ruhr was the only remaining source of supply for the German war machine. On 23/24 March, under a 66-mile long smoke screen and aided by 1,749 bombers of the Eighth Air Force, Field Marshal Bernard Montgomery's 21st Army Group crossed the Rhine in the north, while further south simultaneous crossings were made by General Patton's Third Army. Groups flew two missions on 24 March, hitting jet aircraft bases in Holland and Germany, while 240 B-24s, each loaded with 600 tons of medical supplies, food and weapons, followed in the wake of transports and gliders ferrying troops of the First Allied Airborne Army. The 446th, with Lieutenant Colonel William A Schmidt, Bungay's Air Executive flying as 20th Wing Commander, led the 93rd and 448th with twenty-seven aircraft. Flying as low as 50ft, the Liberators droned over the dropping zone at Wesel at 145mph using 10–15° of flap to aid accuracy in the drop. Grey–white smoke shrouded the battlefields and engulfed the city of Wesel. Smoke canisters, which had blacked out over 60 miles of the front for more than two days were still burning. The Liberators passed Wesel a mile to the south and continued to the dropping zone, which was strewn with wrecked and abandoned gliders, smoldering haystacks and dead livestock.[26]

One of the B-24s despatched from Shipdham was *Southern Comfort III*. In mythology the phoenix is 'a bird which can only be reborn by dying in flames.' So it was with *Southern Comfort*, which was lost over Foggia in August 1943. The ground crew had returned to England and were assigned to a fresh combat crew skippered by Lieutenant Waters. Their brand new B-24 was promptly named *Southern Comfort III*. Their luck held through twenty-five missions, the crew returning to the States to participate in a Bond-raising tour. Lieutenant Chandler and his crew, on their fourth operation, flew the 'phoenix' on the supply mission. When the 44th arrived at the dropping zone a fierce battle was raging. The gunners of *Southern Comfort* strafed the German gun emplacements as Allied troops waded across the river with their guns above their heads. The B-24s had to drop their supplies on the opposite bank. *Southern Comfort III* was less than 100ft above the ground, when hit by German small arms fire, it lost an engine. The aircraft rolled over and her belly struck the ground. She raised a cloud of dust, bounced into the air again to about 50ft and then exploded. All the crew except the two waist gunners were killed. Sergeant Vance returned to Shipdham about three weeks later with both arms in plaster. He had been liberated when the British overran the German field hospital where he was being held captive.

Approximately 6,000 aircraft, including Liberators, gliders, transports and fighters, took part in the Wesel operation. Spasmodic and highly accurate small arms fire and 20mm cannon fire brought down fourteen Liberators, and 103 B-24s returned with battle damage. Five of the twenty officers at 20th Wing Headquarters, including General Ted Timberlake, who flew in an escort aircraft, flew on the mission. Despite intense ground fire the Wing hedgehopped to friendly territory and re-formed in the Brussels area for the return flight to England. Some 104 B-24s returned to their bases with some degree of damage.[27]

On 26 March 2nd Lieutenant William W Varnedoe Jnr, navigator in Lieutenant George H Crow Jnr's crew in the 385th Bomb Group flew his fourteenth mission:

> After the success of operation *VARSITY–PLUNDER*, (the isolation of the Ruhr and the Rhine area) targets were dwindling. On this day the 385th returned to a target of the day before to hit a tank factory at Plauen, which put this works out of operation. Our ship was *Possible Straight*. We had in mind to paint some cards with ace, deuce, tray showing and two face down with a sexy female on back of the down cards, but it never got done. George Crow was promoted to 1st Lieutenant since our last mission. Although the mission itself went smoothly and successfully, the trip home got kind of hairy. Once out of Germany and over France we began to let down to stay under an ever lowering ceiling of clouds. A message came through giving us a whole new course with many new headings. Crow wanted to know how long the new course would take, so I began to plot and calculate all the new legs and their times. When done, George said that it would take too long and we'd better go straight home. I looked at the compass to see which leg we were on. We were on none of either the new or the old courses! Just at that moment, the clouds had us forced so low the formation completely split up and we were on our own. I had no idea where we had been going while I was doing all that figuring, so I tried to match us to something on the map. But we were too low. Everything just whizzed by. We were too low to see a pattern. In fact, we were really on the deck. Both Ira and I remember George lifting a wing to clear a church steeple! Well, no problem, I'd just head us to East Anglia and *G-Box* it home from there – except and this was a big except, we didn't want to pass over Dunkirk, which was still in German hands. As low as we were, they couldn't miss us. But we avoided it and were soon over the English Channel. I did a 45° turn right, 90° turn left then another 45° right. This little dogleg let the English radar operators know we were not another German Buzz bomb to be shot down as soon as we got near the English coast. As we performed this manouevre we then discovered that there were three or four other red checkered tails following. I guess they were lost and thought we knew where we were going! Once over the Channel, sure enough, as I thought, *G* came in and the rest of the trip to Great Ashfield was uneventful.

The mission to submarine pens at Hamburg on 30 March was the twenty-seventh trip for 1st Lieutenant Donald J Schmitt in the 493rd Bomb Group at Little Walden. It was one mission he wished he could have missed:

> We had a perfect day but it was also perfect for the Hun. It was uneventful until we hit the target and then things really happened. There were quite a few breaks in the clouds but not enough to allow a visual run. The flak was really rough. It was the most accurate flak

I have been through so far. It reminded me of the flak in '*30 Seconds Over Tokyo*'.[28] After the target, the Low Squadron leader made a turn right into another group. It was either breaking up the formation or cracking up a bunch of 17s, so everybody took off for themselves. We finally got back into formation after much difficulty. Weather on return was very bad. Very bad crack-up at field upon return.[29]

Bomber crews were now hard pressed to find worthwhile targets and the planners switched attacks from inland targets to coastal areas. 2nd Lieutenant William W Varnedoe Jnr, navigator in 1st Lieutenant George H Crow Jnr's crew in the 385th Bomb Group recalls:

On 4 April, my seventeenth, we went back to Kiel again to mop up, I suppose. We flew in *Gypsy Princess* in the High Squadron. The flak, while still fairly heavy, was less accurate and there was no repeat of that 'Big Bang'. However, the 385th did lose two crews. On the return over the North Sea, Crimmins and Ritchie collided and both went down. They were Leads of the Low Flight of the Lead Squadron. Ira remembers that one of them was in a flat spin but the Group moved on out of sight before he hit the water; there were no 'chutes sighted. I gave Bill Kozosky, our radio operator, the location and he gave it to Air-Sea Rescue, but nothing was ever heard from them. A person could only survive a few minutes in the icy North Sea and this area was far from home.

On 5 April the Eighth Air Force's superiority was such that the B-17s assembled over France before flying to targets in the Nürnburg area. 1st Lieutenant Donald J Schmitt, pilot of *Son Of A Blitz* in the 493rd Bomb Group flew his thirtieth mission when he went to the jet airfield at Unterschlauersbach near the city:

We were briefed for bad weather but I never knew it could get as bad as it was today. We entered the soup after we took off and didn't get out of it till 20,000. We assembled over the Continent. We had to raise our assembly altitude to 26,000 because of high clouds and dense persistent contrails we left. We found our Squadron leader without much trouble and the more we flew around, the worse the contrails became. When assembly time was up, we had only a few ships in formation. We flew all the way to the IP in contrails. At IP we let down to 23,500 and found an opening. We bombed the field visually with good results. The lead and high Squadron bombed Nuremberg itself and really laid their bombs in the heart of the city. They were ahead of us so I got a very good view. Fires and smoke covered the whole city. By bombing the airfield, we missed all the flak, which was over the town of Nuremberg itself. It was intense

> and accurate. After bombs away, we started to let down to 1,000ft because of clouds. We crossed the Rhine at this altitude and really saw the sights. Near Brussels we had to let down to about 500ft because of a low front. The weather was pretty bad with quite a bit of rain. We crossed the Channel at about 100 to 200ft above the water. It was a very tiring mission but very interesting. Only five more to go and then I go Home To My Dear Wife and Son.

Schmitt flew his thirty-first mission when the 493rd Bomb Group went to Gustrow ordnance plant:

> Well, here is one for the books. Another exciting mission. Take-off and assembly were normal. We climbed to bombing altitude, which was 15,000. Everything went smooth until we came near Hanover and then things really happened. The thing we dreaded most hit us. That's right – we were hit by fighters. We were flying in the high squadron and for some unknown reason we were their target. They succeeded in making several attacks on us. They knocked out one ship. Our Squadron accounted for two Me 109s. One of them went down right over our nose. Our upper gunner had a hand in shooting him down. Another came up from underneath chased by three P-51s. He pulled up but that was where he made his mistake, because all three of the 51s let go and down went the Hun. Another Me 109 damaged tried to ram one of our ships. He didn't succeed, but did take part of the horizontal stabilizer off. The ship returned safely. We were under fighter attack for about 1½ hour and it sure was no picnic. They finally let us alone at the IP and we went on to the target. We made a visual run and laid our bombs right on the MPI. Great fires and large columns of smoke rose from the whole area. The bombing results were excellent. The return trip was over the same route as we had come in on, but without the fighters. I guess they had enough the first time. The formation flying today was really excellent. The ships were locked wingtip to wingtip. Our group accounted for two kills and four possibilities. We are getting close to the end of our time, but things are starting to get rough.

On 7 April a determined onslaught by *Rammjäger* and Me 262 pilots did not stop 1,261 heavies dropping almost 3,500 tons of bombs on sixteen targets in Germany, and on 8 April, the Eighth put up nine groups in the 1st Division together with six groups of Mustangs. The 2nd Air Division put up nine B-24 groups with four groups of escorting fighters, and the 3rd Air Division put up fourteen groups of B-17s with four groups of Mustangs. In all, more than 1,150 B-17s and B-24s were to bomb targets in the Leipzig, Nuremberg and Chemnitz areas. On 9 April about 1,200 bombers supported by fifteen fighter groups hit ten jet airfields and other targets in south-central Germany. 1st Lieutenant Donald J Schmitt in the 863rd Bomb Squadron, 493rd Bomb Group flew his thirty-second mission when the Group added its bombs to the airfield at Munich. He wrote in his diary:

> Let me tell you, combat is still rough. This should have been a Milk Run and for us (Lead Squadron) it was, but for others it was rough. The weather was just fair. Up until target time it was perfect, but clouds over target forced us to bomb from 22,000 instead of 25,000. We had a visual run and really laid our bombs on the MPI. Just before bombs away, a ship in the Group ahead of us blew up from a flak hit and after bombs away a ship out of our high squadron blew up.[30] The trip home was uneventful. Visibility back at the base was excellent.[31]

2nd Lieutenant William W Varnedoe Jnr, navigator in 1st Lieutenant George H Crow Jnr's crew in the 385th Bomb Group, wrote:

> 10 April. My No. 22. Another airfield was the target, this time at Nurippin. We bombed visually in *Sleepytime Gal*. There was no flak at Nurippin, but there was some light but accurate flak at Wittenberg on the way back. A piece of flak struck my headset control box and bent it all out of shape so I couldn't change the settings, however, I had it set on intercom and it still worked there. This flak was not marked on our flak maps so we supposed it was railroad flak moved in overnight. In fact, the Group was letting down to get off oxygen, this area being briefed as free of flak zones. Yet, we could see the other groups, up ahead, getting heavy flak. We wondered why our fearless leader didn't stay higher a little longer, rather than take us through it at that low altitude. On this one, *Rum Dum* dropped out of formation. Howard A Muchow had a 'pick up' crew and was flying *Rum Dum* on this mission. No. 378 had already completed 105 missions without an abort and the CO as well as the ground crew, were out to capture the all time record for the Group. They knew the flak would be as thick as pea soup over and around the Berlin area and they knew the German fighters would be making their determined stand against their reaching the target. Germany might be coming to its knees but the war was still very real. These thoughts seemed jumbled as we climbed for altitude over the Channel. And how right they seemed going into the target, with the black and gray puffs of flak raining against our old girl. It was like someone throwing gravel, only this metallic gravel was blasting through the airplane. The thought passed through my mind that the gals down below were doing a good job today. Immediately after 'Bombs away', the No. 1 engine took a direct hit and then No. 3 was hit. As

> we feathered No. 3, I saw that No. 1 was on fire and we feathered it. We started losing altitude and falling out of formation, when over the airways we heard bandits being called out by another squadron.
>
> A frantic call was sent out on the fighter channel for help and protection from our little friends. And there they came – three beautiful P-51s to help us down and stay with us – one high, one low, with the third dropping his flaps and gear to come alongside and give us the thumbs up and 'V' sign. Then he saw the fire in No. 1 engine and up came his flaps and gear and he moved away out. I gave the order to bale out, but the crew wanted to stay with 378 and ride it down, hopefully to friendly territory. Who wanted to check out, first hand, the stories of captured airmen?
>
> We were losing altitude rapidly, when suddenly ahead I saw an open field and thought I would try my luck. It was downwind and I recall thinking we could not make it. If only we could hang on a little longer and swing the old girl around and set it down. It was like a dream. We were on the ground and rolling, when suddenly we saw troops coming out of the woods toward us. Were they Germans? No, thank God, they were English ... and they were just arriving to take over the open field for front line fighter support! We had made it and no one was hurt. Only Heaven knows why. Upon our return to Great Ashfield, the FIRST question asked was, 'Can *Rum Dum* fly?' The SECOND question was, 'How's the crew?' But I will always remember the old girl and how she got us back into friendly territory. (Poor old *Rum Dum* never made it back to Great Ashfield, although it did get flown to France, then later crash landed in England, only to be salvaged.)[32]

As a result of the bombing of the jet airfields the Me 262 units were forced to withdraw to the Prague area. However, other hazards sometimes caused casualties in the B-17 groups, as on 13 April when the 398th Bomb Group from Nuthampstead flew its 188th mission of the war, to Neumünster. Over the target a leading aircraft salvoed his RDX bombs in error. Two of them touched about 400ft below, exploded and brought down six Fortresses in the 601st Bomb Squadron, five of which had to be abandoned on the Continent. RDX bombs were fitted with close proximity fuses and were most unstable at all times unless handled with great care. Bombing results were later described as 'excellent,' but at a high price indeed.

Walter Don' O'Hearn, tail gunner in *El Screamo* in the 427th Bomb Squadron, 303rd Bomb Group recalls:

> Our twenty-sixth mission was the most frightening of all. It was to Oranienburg, Germany, almost within sight of Berlin, 40 miles to the south on 13 April. Six to eight Me 262 jet fighters hit our group.

> *Henn's Revenge* in the 555th Squadron flown by 2nd Lieutenant Robert I Murray was shot down in this air battle. Eight men were killed and the flight engineer got out of the aircraft. During this time, a Me 262 dove past me so fast I couldn't turn my two .50 machine guns on him. This 262 dropped down about 5,000 to 6,000ft in a wide turn and then came up directly behind our B-17. We were flying 'tail end Charlie' so I had this aircraft all to myself. I made the very most of this situation; I started firing at him from a long distance and never let up but kept hitting his right engine. I continued to score hits on the engine until he was about 120ft from me. At that time the engine and wing tip blew off. The 262's momentum carried it to within 55 to 45ft from me. We were both looking at each other. Just as suddenly he began his fall from about 25,000ft, approximately 43–63 miles from Oranienburg, Germany. The 303rd Bomb Group interrogation officer really had no interest in a buck Sergeant's report on a 262, which may have been the last Me 262 shot down by an enlisted man in World War II. Lieutenant Denison put me in for a DFC but it was not even considered. The flak was what really startled a B-17 tail gunner to get jumpy. They called us 'flak happy' and that we were.

On 14 April, 1,161 B-17s and Liberators carried out a specialist task. Their target was a pocket of German resistance (some estimates put the force at 122,000 men) manning twenty-two gun batteries along the Gironde estuary at Point de Grave in the Royan area, which was denying the Allies the use of the port of Bordeaux. The bombers were called upon to help dislodge them after all appeals to surrender had proved in vain. Conditions were perfect and crews at briefing believed it would be a 'milk run' as the defences were negligible and the flak was unlikely to reach the high-flying bombers. However, almost from take-off things began to go wrong. At Horsham St. Faith *Hookem Cow* and another B-24 in 754th Squadron crashed shortly after take-off within minutes of each other. Altogether 1,161 heavies hit twenty-two defensive installations along the Gironde estuary. The 467th successfully dropped all their 2,000lb bombs within 1,000ft of the MPI; half the bombs falling within 500ft. This was a bombing pattern unsurpassed in Eighth Air Force history. The 389th Bomb Group lost two Liberators when 3rd Air Division B-17s, making a second run over the target released their fragmentation bombs through the 'Sky Scorpions' formation. Two more crash-landed in France and a fifth limped back to England.

The next day nearly 850 2nd and 3rd Air Division aircraft returned to the area and for the first time carried napalm: 460,000 gallons of it. The 1st Air Division carried 1,000lb and 2,000lb GP bombs, while three fighter groups snuffed out any gun emplacements which opened fire on the bombers. Mosquitoes were also called in to sow a cloud of *chaff* to snow radar screens, which might be used to direct the radar-controlled flak guns. These precautions were the only protection the bombers had to prevent their lethal cargoes being exploded by German gun batteries. The bombers released their 75–85 gallon liquid-fire tanks, along with conventional incendiaries, on the east bank of the Gironde estuary. Captain Ralph Elliott, flying his twenty-fifth mission in the 467th Bomb Group, flew group lead with Major Seiler as command pilot for the raid. Elliott recalled:

> Each napalm tank was about 8ft long and one and a half feet in diameter and when it exploded it covered an area of 60 square yards, taking the oxygen out of the air and destroying everything there. What a show it was. At 15,000ft the smoke was so thick we couldn't see our wingmen. A few puffs of flak about 100 yards out. Just before bombs away, No. 1 engine started to smoke and oil pressure began to fluctuate. When the engine began to shake, I feathered it. I increased power on the other three engines to maintain our usual 160mph on the bomb run and held the formation together so Archie bombed with no difficulty. We weren't worried about bombing accuracy – just hitting the general area. The napalm containers had no ballistic characteristics whatsoever. They were made of heavy cardboard and at altitude some of the detonators popped out like loose corks, so the bomb bay smelled of raw gasoline most of the way to the target. We all sort of held our breath and hoped no wayward spark would set the whole thing off. For once I didn't have to mention NO SMOKING to the crew. I held the lead till the rally and then left to come home on our own. We headed toward the main emergency field at Merville at 800ft and for 300 miles and 2 hours had a birds-eye view of all France. Landed OK and left our ship for an engine change.[33]

On 16 April Orders of the Day No. 2 from General Spaatz ended the strategic mission of the Eighth Air Force, and only some tactical missions remained.[34] Men such as 1st Lieutenant Donald J Schmitt in the 493rd Bomb Group who were coming to the end of their tours were sweating out each and every mission, any one of which could be their last. The *Son Of A Blitz* pilot had flown his thirty-third mission, to Royan, on the 14th, when his navigator had finished up. Schmitt noted in his diary. 'I'm really starting to sweat now.' His thirty-fourth mission had followed on 15 April, which again was to Royan. He recorded that both missions were 'Milk Runs in a run' and he was 'sure am glad'. The day after was the day he had anxiously been waiting for and he 'sure hoped to fly'. He did. His thirty-fifth mission on 16 April was to Rochefort, France, where a German pocket was holding out. Schmitt need not have worried. It was an 'easy' mission. He was so happy he could not even write anything on the mission except 'Visual bombing. Good results.'

On 17 April more than 950 B-17s and B-24s attacked eight railway centres, junctions, stations and marshalling yards and an oil depot in east Germany and western Czechoslovakia. Eighteen US fighter groups flew support, encountering about fifty fighters, mostly jets, and claimed thirteen destroyed, including four jets. The American fighters strafed numerous airfields and claimed over 250 aircraft destroyed on the ground. Eight B-17s and 17 fighters were shot down, including six B-17s by Me 262s of JG 7. One of the victims was *Towering Titan* in the 305th Bomb Group, flown by Lieutenant Brainard H Harris, which appeared to be rammed by a Me 262. The collision tore off a wing panel from the left wing of the B-17G, the jet exploded and *Towering Titan* went into a gradual dive, disappearing through the clouds. One parachute was seen.[35]

The German corridor was shrinking rapidly and the American and Russian bomb lines now crossed at several points on briefing maps. During the week 18 to 25 April, missions were briefed and scrubbed almost simultaneously. General Patton's advance was so rapid that at least on one occasion crews were lining up for take-off when a message was received to say that Patton's forces had captured the target the B-17s were to bomb! The last major air battles between fighter groups of the Eighth Air Force and the Luftwaffe took place on 18 April when 1,211 heavies escorted by more than 1,200 fighters were sent to attack Berlin. Forty Me 262s of *Jagdgeschwader* 7 shot down twenty-five bombers with rockets. It was the final challenge by a dying enemy. The Luftwaffe was finished, destroyed in the air and starved of fuel on the ground.[36]

Notes

1. Adapted from *Country Boy–Combat Bomber Pilot* by R H Tays (Privately Published, 1990).
2. 'When I finally went home I had the window open as the train slowed down for Janesville. My head was out the window scanning the train platform. Helen was nowhere to be seen. Just because we didn't exchange letters didn't mean there wasn't a hot fire burning somewhere. She probably wanted to keep our romance a secret. How soon they forget! She married her high school sweetheart during the war. The face that launched a thousand dreams my Helen of Troy. The last time I saw Helen Kathleen was in a Walgren drug store after the war. She saw me first and came over – this vision of loveliness. She was an easy person to talk to. I revealed to Helen how she sustained my morale while I was in service. She blushed, then gave me a hug, and whispered, "Oh, Ken." That silky voice, softly whispering my name. It was 1943 again! I never got to sit under the apple tree with sweet Helen. But we came close once. Glen Miller's band was playing *You Came To Me From Out of Nowhere* as I walked out of the store.'

3. Ken 'Deacon' Jones' letter to *Briefing* magazine, winter 2002.
4. Adapted from the 389th Bomb Group Newsletter, spring 1994.
5. The 1st Bomb Division's attack on the marshalling yards at Ehrang, Germany, earned a commendation from Brigadier General Howard M Turner: 'I wish to extend to you and all officers and men of the bombardment groups which participated in the mission of 23rd December 1944 my congratulations for the excellent manner in which the mission was executed. Operating in extremely adverse weather conditions, these units exhibited a high degree of determination and skill in clearing the Division area, attacking the marshaling yards at Ehrang and landing in weather conditions equally as adverse, without the loss of a single aircraft. Excellent bombing results were obtained. Convey to participating officers and men my appreciation of a job well done....'
6. 44-8444.
7. Brigadier General Castle was posthumously awarded the Medal of Honor; the highest ranking officer in the Eighth Air Force to receive the award. General Henry H Arnold, Chief of the US Air Forces, later dedicated Castle AFB in his honour. His loss was felt greatly by many in the 94th Bomb Group at Bury St. Edmunds where he had taken over a demoralized outfit after relinquishing a staff job and had knocked it back into shape. At the end of the war one of the prisoners held in a PoW camp near his former base at Bury St. Edmunds was, ironically, Field Marshal von Rundstedt.
8. Rasmussen flew 23 missions, his last on 8 April 1945, and three food drop missions.
9. German production of fighter aircraft actually increased through 1944 into 1945. It had peaked in September 1944, when 1,874 Bf 109s and 1,002 Fw 190s were completed. (Though that same month, an average of three German fighters – and two pilots KIA – were lost for every B-17 or B-24 shot down.) The dispersed manufacturing plants were beyond the power of the Eighth Air Force to seriously damage. Therefore, some postwar surveys concluded that the Eighth Air Force bombing offensive was a failure. But the bombing was just good enough that the Luftwaffe fighters had to keep rising to attack, and then the P-51s and P-47s mostly destroyed them.
10. 300 aircraft were lost, 235 pilots were killed and 65 pilots were taken prisoner.
11. B-24 42-95223 *Little Lulu* and the five crew aboard were lost.
12. Accompanied by 900 fighters, 1,200 B-17s and B-24s dropped 2,267 tons of bombs into the *Mitte*, or central district of Berlin, killing an estimated 25,000 inhabitants and destroying 360 industrial firms, heavily damaging another 170. Photo-reconnaissance revealed that an area 1½ miles square, stretching across the southern half of the *Mitte* had been devastated. The German Air Ministry sustained considerable damage, the Chancellery was hard hit and the Potsdamer and Anhalter rail yards were also badly hit.
13. Ten of the crew of 44-8379 reached the ground safely. Rosenthal landed in Soviet territory and he was later reported to be in Moscow. The bombardier was KIA. Ernst caught his leg on a jagged edge of the bomb bay while baling out and he later had the leg amputated. Four other B-17s in the 100th Bomb Group FTR. (See *Century Bombers: The Story of the Bloody Hundredth* by Richard Le Strange, 100th Bomb Group Memorial Museum, 1989).

14. Colonel Anthony Q Mustoe, CO of the 40th Combat Wing, Captain Edward Terrell, Lieutenant Commander John B Murray RN and the First Sea Lord were at Podington when the bombers returned and later examined the strike photos. Both Terrell and Murray had worked closely in the development of the explosive. Although only one hit had been scored, the officers were shown what the 'Disney' bomb was capable of and further trials were ordered. On 4 April the 92nd Bomb Group dropped 'Disney' bombs on U-boat pens at Hamburg However, the Allies' sweeping victories in the Low Countries and the vast distance to suitable targets in Norway, brought the 'Disney' missions almost to an end.
15. 316 B-17s actually attacked Dresden. The Eighth Air Force was to return to the city of Dresden again in March and April 1945 on similar raids but the Allied air forces' top priority remained the oil-producing centres.
16. The Hoesch coking plant at Dortmund was estimated to be producing 1,000 tons of benzol a month.
17. Including two B-17s to a Me 262 jet fighter of III./JG 7 flown by Gefreiter Notter.
18. Six of the attackers were shot down, two of them by RAF Mosquitoes. The attack on Bury St. Edmunds damaged the control tower. Great Ashfield was bombed and strafed and Rattlesden, Lavenham and Sudbury were also attacked. The intruders returned again on the night of 4 March but damage to the bases was insignificant.
19. Stringent interrogations by intelligence officers followed the debacle and some crews had their return to the States blocked because of the six-weeks investigation into the incident. The US Ambassador had only recently attended a memorial service and visited reconstruction projects resulting from the previous bombing of Zurich on 18 September 1944. General Marshall urged Spaatz to visit Switzerland secretly and reparations involving many millions of dollars were made to the Swiss Government. A court martial was held with Colonel James M Stewart appointed president of the court. Jackson W Granholm, a 458th Bomb Group navigator at Horsham St. Faith and defence counsel, recalls, 'I had the unpleasant honour to be the defense counsel for the pilot and navigator of a lead squadron crew who put a beautiful bomb pattern on the railroad yards in Basle. They thought they had bombed Freiburg, Germany and were tried in a general court for culpable negligence in the performance of duty. Because the questions were those of navigation, I was named to the defense board. The court was held at our group base at Horsham St. Faith.... We achieved an acquittal after a week-long court, longest in history of the Eighth Air Force.'

    No further action was taken though at least one lead crew was restricted to base until April 1945.
20. Twelve B-17s and a B-24 were shot down and 16 bombers were forced to land inside Russian territory. Although flak was particularly hazardous on this mission the defensive honours went to 37 Me 262s of the Geschwaderstab and III./JG 7 who claimed 12 B-17s shot down and six *Herausschüsse* (HSS) as well as one fighter for the loss of only two jets. The 'Bloody Hundredth' lost four bombers this day, including one ship which was cleaved in two by Me 262 gunfire. By the end of the month the Eighth was to lose 30 bombers to the German twin-engined jets.

21. The 21 March missions were the start of a massive four-day assault on the Luftwaffe, with 42,000 sorties being made over German airspace.
22. At 09.50 at 7,500m, S of Dresden.
23. Müller was credited with 16 *Abschüsse* whilst serving with III./JG 53 in 1943–44 and six (one RAF Mosquito and five US aircraft) flying the Me 262. On 25 March 1945 he shot down a Liberator in flames at 10.25 at 7,000m, S of Lüneberg. No parachutes were observed. (The left turbine of Müller's 262 was hit by return fire and he force-landed at Stendal, where he rammed into a Ju 88 parked in Hangar No. 5. He managed to douse the fire before it got out of control). On 4 April 1945, he shot down a Liberator at 09.45 at 7,000 meters in the Bremen area. On 9 April 1945 Müller destroyed a Thunderbolt at 8,000m, W of Berlin. On 17 April he shot down a B-17 at 7,000m in the Elbschleife, N of Prague.
24. Captain Robert B Grettum's crew in the 392nd Bomb Group returned to Wendling in their PFF Liberator, firing flares at 2,000ft in celebration of completing their final mission. Somebody fired a flare from a gun that was probably not locked. The flare-gun probably spun round, because the aircraft caught fire. Grettum and seven others perished in the ensuing crash.
25. Oberfeldwebel Lübking with 38 *Abschüsse* and Feldwebel Eichner, both KIA.
26. Eight of the nine 20th Wing squadrons loosed their wicker loads with attached multi-coloured parachutes in the dropping zone. They encountered spasmodic and highly accurate small-arms fire. This and heavy 20mm cannon fire caused the loss of six 20th Wing Liberators – three in the 446th Bomb Group and three in the 448th Bomb Group. 17 of the Bungay Buckeroos' B-24s sustained battle damage, while the 448th's lead ship, carrying Colonel Charles B Westover, the CO, crash-landed in England with two men wounded. The deputy lead crew was forced to bale out over England. 20mm fire pierced the armour plating and struck the control column of one of the 93rd Bomb Group Liberators but the two pilots escaped injury in the subsequent explosion.
27. On 24 March, the Fifteenth Air Force bombed Berlin for the first time when more than 150 B-17s hit the Daimler-Benz tank works in the city. Meanwhile, 271 B-24s finished off the Neuburg jet plant bombed on 21 March. On 27 March, Twelfth Air Force P-47 Thunderbolt fighter-bombers strafed Lechfeld airfield in Bavaria and destroyed large numbers of German jet aircraft.
28. B-17G-85-BO, 43-38311, in the 860th Bomb Squadron, piloted by Lieutenant Lewis B Hoagland, was hit by flak and crashed near Buchholz, Germany. 1 KIA, 9 PoW. B-17G-105-BO, 43-39226, in the 861st BS, piloted by Lieutenant Martin Dwyer Jnr, was also hit by flak and crashed near Pinneberg, Germany. 1 KIA, 9 PoW.
29. The 'very bad crack up' was the B-17 piloted by 2nd Lieutenant Russell A Goodspeed in the 861st Bomb Squadron, whose crew were on their first mission. See *Clash of Eagles* by Martin W Bowman (Pen & Sword 2006).
30. *Boise Bell* in the 860th Bomb Squadron, piloted by Lieutenant John E Silverman was hit by flak and crashed near Munich. 10 KIA.
31. On 10 April German jet aircraft shot down 10 American bombers but 297 German aircraft were destroyed on the ground.

32. On 11 April Varnedoe flew his 23rd mission when he was assigned to 2nd Lieutenant Harold A Lovegreen's crew in 6569: 'By now there were no more oil targets and German factories were no longer a menace. Only tactical bombing on behalf of the onrushing ground forces remained. That is why we again went to a railroad marshaling yard, this time at Ingolstadt. We bombed it visually with no flak at the target. Bombs away with excellent results. A real "milk run." ' On 14 April 1945 Varnedoe flew his 24th mission when he and the rest of the crew were back on *Possible Straight* on the mission to Royan. On 16 April the crew had another pass and they went on what was their last trip to London while in the Army Air Force.
33. One 458th Liberator left the formation after bomb release and headed inland with one engine feathered. A total of 180 heavies, supported by the French ground troops of the 6th Army Group, bombed 16 defensive installations. French forces later captured the port. *The Stars And Stripes* on Monday 26 April announced: 'Heavies Throw Fire To Free Bordeaux; Using a new type of fire bomb for the first time, as well as thousands of high explosives, Eighth Air Force Fortresses and Liberators flew more than 2,450 sorties Saturday and Sunday in a drive to wipe out German pockets of resistance in the Gironde area and free the big French port of Bordeaux.... Many of the 1,300 bombers taking part in yesterday's clear weather assault were loaded with tanks which explode on impact, ignite incendiary material and splash the flaming contents over an area of approximately 60 square yards. Tanks containing more than 460,000 gallons of this liquid were showered on the target areas in the vicinity of Royan on the east side of the Gironde estuary in an assault co-ordinated with movements of French ground forces. In addition to the new fire bomb, more than 6,000 100lb incendiaries were dropped in the same area – there was no enemy opposition – and the bombers were unescorted.'

    Ralph Elliott concludes: 'As a result of the Royan mission the French awarded a batch of *Croix de Guerre* medals to the crews who led the mission. At least, that was the intent, as we knew it at the time. Unfortunately, the French didn't make that designation clear and the medals were awarded in the Eighth Air Force in order of rank (RHIP – Rank Has Its Privileges), so the furthest down the medal got was to 467th CO, Colonel Shower, plus several 2nd Air Division officers – none of whom flew on the mission.'
34. On 16 April over 700 aircraft were destroyed.
35. Post-war enquiries revealed that the parachute was that of Major Georg-Peter 'Schorch' Eder who was the pilot of the Me 262 that rammed *Towering Titan*. There were no survivors aboard the Fortress. Eder's Me 262 had been damaged by gunfire and the pilot, who chivalrously allowed opponents to escape the final lethal burst when they were obviously finished, baled out for the 17th time in the war, having been wounded 14 times in the process! *Towering Titan* was Eder's 78th and final confirmed kill. See *John Burn One-Zero-Five... : The Story of Chelveston Airfield and the 305th Bomb Group in Pictures* by William Donald. (GMS, 2005).
36. The end came on 25 April 1945 when 306 B-17s of the 1st Air Division bombed the Skoda armaments factory at Pilsen in Czechoslovakia, while 282 B-24s, escorted by four fighter groups, bombed four rail complexes surrounding Hitler's mountain retreat at Berchtesgarden.

Index